THE TALLOW CHANDLERS OF LONDON

Volume Four

EBB AND FLOW

Plate I. Charter of 29th July 1677 granted to the Tallow Chandlers Company by Charles II.

(First skin with decorated capital containing Royal portrait)

[Frontispiece]

THE TALLOW CHANDLERS
OF LONDON

Volume Four

EBB AND FLOW

by

RANDALL MONIER-WILLIAMS

1977
KAYE & WARD LTD
IN THE CITY OF LONDON

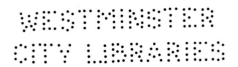

First published by Kaye & Ward Ltd
1977

Copyright © 1977 Randall H. Monier-Williams

WRF/W9C

ISBN 0 7182 1132 4

17802 338·632

All enquiries and requests relevant to
this title should be sent to the publisher,
Kaye & Ward Ltd, 21 New Bond Street,
London EC2M 4NT, and not to the printer.

Printed in Great Britain by
Adlard & Son Ltd
Bartholomew Press
Dorking, Surrey

25. OCT 1977

Contents

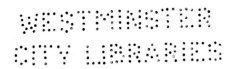

List of Plates

Acknowledgement

I wish to express my thanks to Dr Marc Fitch for his valuable assistance in making available to me his unpublished extracts from the Husting Rolls of wills and title deeds of early tallow chandlers, of which I have made full use in this and previous volumes.

List of Abbreviations

Archd. London	Archdeaconry of London
C.B.	Court Book
Com. London	Commissary Court of London
E.M.C.R.	Early Mayor's Court Rolls, Calendar of, 1298–1301
G.L.	Guildhall Library
Jor.	Journal
L.A.B.	Livery Account Book
L. Bk.A., etc.	Letter Books of the City of London, Calendar of, ed. R. R. Sharpe
O.E.D.	Oxford English Dictionary
P.C.C.	Prerogative Court of Canterbury
Rep.	Repertory
Riley, Memorials	Memorials of London and London Life in the XIIIth, XIVth and XVth centuries, 1278–1419, ed. H. T. Riley (1868)
T.C.C.	Tallow Chandlers Company
T.C.C.R.	Records of the Worshipful Company of Tallow Chandlers, 1897, Part I, edited by M. F. Monier-Williams
Y.A.B.	Yeomanry Account Book

The superior numerals in the text refer to the notes in the Authorities commencing on page 314. The superior lower case letters refer to the footnotes on each page.

Documents and events are dated according to the provisions of the Calendar (New Style) Act, 1751.

The parishes mentioned are some of those existing in 1907.

Figures

Most of the illustrations, as in earlier volumes, consist of nineteenth century engravings.

Early Searches
The Curriers and the Soapmakers
Sauce, Herring and Cheese

I

We have seen how in the spring of 1518 our Company was successful in obtaining, jointly with the Salters, a right of search over *all persons of both companies selling candles and sauces*, on the distinct understanding that the searches were to be conducted by at least one Warden from each fellowship.[a] A milestone in our history was reached six years later with the allowance by the Court of Common Council on Thursday, 28th April 1524[1] of a 'bill' presented by our Wardens[b] conferring upon them for 'as longe as it shalbe seen to my Lorde Maire and thaldremen to be good and beneficiall for the commen weale and profight of this Citie' what amounted to *an unconditional right of search* for tallow and candle in the hands of men of no matter what occupation.[c]

It was the petitioners' contention that the *'greate scercitie of Talugh and Candelles'* within the City and *the excessive price thereof* were due to the fact that these commodities were

solde & delyuered to soo many parsones of duyerse & sondry occupacions that no man hath correccion nor serche of theym.

---

a   Volume III, p. 69.

b   Commentary, p. 230.

c   Commentary, p. 230.

The buyers were said to 'selle, deluyere & convey' their tallow

in somerseason oute of this Citie *when moost plentye* is at their liberties & pleasures/by reason wereof when wynter season commeth there is noo somer store remaynyng within this Citie to serve the habitauntes and other therewith,

for reformation of which abuses our Wardens requested his 'good Lordshippe' and their 'maister-shippes with thassent of the Common Counsell' to authorize them and their successors

wekely & [sic] monethly or otherwise as it shalbe thought vnto theym convenyent to entre vewe and searche in the houses or other places of all & every such parsone or parsones/aswell for byinge *as for conveying of such Talugh*

and to see that only 'good, clene and laufull stuffe be solde within the same Citie'.

The order contained a direction that the Wardens and their successors should 'doo their good and true diligence concernyng the same' and provided for the forfeiture of any tallow '*soo conveyed owte of the Citie accordynge to thauncient actes & ordynnaunces thereof made*'.

The powers conferred upon the Company by the passing of their bill were soon put into operation. A routine report of 'howe myche talough & candell ys yn ther Craft, with ther names And what bochers serves them',[2] was followed at a meeting on 22nd November (1524)[3] by two bills of search made by three of our Wardens, John Hampton, John Hone and Guy Clerke, giving particulars not only of the quantities of tallow and candles within the craft of Tallow Chandlers, *but also in the hands of Salters, Fishmongers and those of 'other occupacions'.*[d] Of these three Wardens, only the name of Guy Clerk is new to us.[e] We do not meet him again and nothing more seems to be known of him.

During the next six years much of the time of the Court was taken up with wrangling with the Butchers about the price of

---

d   *Commentary*, p. 230.

e   Hampton, as we have seen, had previously been a Warden and he became Master in 1537. We first met Hone as a Warden in 1516 and we shall hear more of him (see Volume III, p. 67, *passim*, 76).

tallow, while candle-makers in the main seem to have adopted a more passive attitude. This era begins in May 1525 with two of the Butchers' Wardens refusing to sell their tallow at 9s. 8d. the wey and being committed to the prison of the Compter in the Poultry.[4] Nearly two years later, the price is again set at 9s. 8d.[5] The Butchers protest and are advised to make delivery 'to then-tent that they may fynde this Courte better to theym hereafter.'[6] The case is referred to 'the commyng of my lorde Mayre', and at the next meeting,

considerynge that this wedder hath soo long contynued in greate rayne & moystnes whereby that moche catell ys dede & [there is] grete derthe of bestes/and the price ys high and very excerssiue of catell,

the price of tallow is increased to 12s. the wey, a modest increase of $\frac{1}{4}d.$ on the current price of 1d. the pound for candles seeming to satisfy the Tallow Chandlers.[7] A year later the Butchers' price is again set at 9s. 8d. the wey and candles are again a penny the pound with thirteen pounds for the dozen.[8] The Butchers object. This time their protest is apparently unavailing,[9] but next year their persistence brings a small reward,[10] when in April 1529, the price of tallow is declared to them at 10s. the wey, 'so they haue a grote[f] more'. There is comparative peace until the autumn, when they again demand a better price, which is refused. One of their Wardens declines to accept and is committed to prison, to be followed by four others,[11] but two days in prison prove to be enough.[12] A contingent of butchers promises

for theym & all their Company to delyuer forthwith all suche Talough as they & euery of theym haue in y^{er} handes.

The mayoralty of John Rudstone, who took office in the Autumn of 1528, is notable for the fact that our Wardens were commanded on one occasion at least to check the quantities of tallow in the hands of *butchers*.[13] From an entry dated 22nd April

---

1529 we learn that

> John Hoone and others the Wardens of the Talughchaundelers be sworne to enserche all the houses within this Citie & liberties of the same *as well of Bochers* as of all others for the store of Talugh And therof to make true certificat to this Courte on Tewsday next.

Up to the present our searches have been among candle-makers and other purchasers of tallow. *We are now, it seems, to search our suppliers as well.* No details appear to have come down to us of the result of this search, if indeed it took place, and the next recorded stock-taking appears to be in October 1536 when the Tallow Chandlers certify what tallow they *and others* have in store.[14] These 'others' could have included the butchers, but the evidence points the other way, for in the following April the Butchers themselves bring in 'theyre byll of talloughe', while the tallow chandlers declare their stocks of candles,[15] pursuant to an order of the Court made two days before.[16] On the whole it seems likely that it did not take this powerful guild long to put a stop to what must have been considered gross impertinence on the part of their customers. The supervision of *foreign (un-free) butchers* which, as we shall see, became the settled policy of the City, was an entirely different matter.

In May 1530 the Butchers were at last allowed a more liberal price for their tallow and the price of candles was correspondingly increased. The price of tallow was set at 12s. 6d. the wey and of candles at $1\frac{1}{4}d.$ the pound with thirteen pounds for the dozen. At the same time a grievance of the Tallow Chandlers, of which we have not previously heard, was redressed. Our complaint was that the Butchers had sold us tallow 'myxed with water, guttes,g butter, and other corupte thynges.'[17] A number of the Butchers present at the meeting faithfully promised for themselves and all their company that they would

> wekely euery Monday weigh with the saide Chaundlers And also then delyuer to theym goode and clene Talough withoute eny suche corupte thynges.

---

g Entrails.

We are not told for how long this order for a joint weighing was observed, but in October 1538 (over eight years later) one John Hyggons, 'bocher', when found to have sold 'veray evyll talowe mixted with guttes', as well as being fined, was directed by the Court to *'delyuer so moche good stuffe as he hath delyuered evyll* to the partye that hath receyuyd yll talowe'.[18]

During Thomas Pargetter's mayoralty (1530-1) a certain amount of pressure on our Company to exercise its new power of general search is to be observed. In an entry in the *Repertories* dated 16th February 1531 the clerk observes that

this day yt ys agreed that my lorde Mayr shall sende his Officers to euery of my masters thaldremen or to their deputeis commaundyng theym to se in their Wardes that the Talughchaundlers & all other that sell eny candell *shall seurve the people of Candell* at peny & farthyng the pownde And that such as refusen so to do commytte theym & euery of theym to warde.[h]

The recognizances of our four men who were bound to make search declared that the Court had given them sufficient authority to *'peruse* this Citie & the liberties of the same *& all the houses of theym that sell eny Talugh Candell'*. The condition of their bond was that from thenceforth they should 'do theire beste diligence to se that the Kinges people be serued of candell' at the set price.[19] All four are known to have been prominent members of the Company,[i] namely our Warden, Henry (or Harry) Nortryche, whom we have already met,[j] Richard Blake (who was Master from 1541 to 1544), Thomas 'Skuttyl' (Cuttle), his immediate successor, and Thomas Belle (or Bell), an Assistant of our Court in 1537-8.[k] Norteryche was Governor of the Yeomanry from 1525 to 1528 and was succeeded by Bell, who also served several years. Blake became Governor in 1536 and served for three

---

h   Custody, imprisonment, *O.E.D.*

i   See their names in Group I of the list of members in Appendix F of Volume III, p. 126.

j   Volume III, p. 73, *passim.*

k   See Appendix C.

years.[1] The first named was the owner, according to his 'will of lands', which he made in 1543, of property in Kingston-upon-Thames and elsewhere in Surrey. By his 'will of goods' made at the same time he left 6s. 8d. to the maintenance of the common box of his 'company of tallowchandlers' and 'a silver pot with a cover all chased and all gilt'.[20] He wished to be buried in his parish church of St Michael at Queenhithe and 'willed' that four of his Company 'being honest men and in the livery of the said Company' should bear his body to the church, leaving 'to every

Fig. 1. General costume in the time of Edward VI.

of them for their labour 20d. a piece'. He bequeathed the sum of 26s. 8d. 'towards the sustentation and keeping of the brotherhood of Jesu which is found and kept in the crowdes[m] under the

---

1   These and later names are taken from a list compiled from the Company's records by Mr Story Maskelyne, whose work for the Tallow Chandlers Company has been referred to in earlier volumes. For an account of the organization known as 'the Yeomanry' see Appendix A.

m   The Crypt. O.E.D.

Cathedral Church of St Paul in London', a fraternity otherwise known as 'the Gild of the Holy name of Jesus', with which *the Wax Chandlers Company* was closely linked.[21] Our Company's Clerk, Martyn Gowsse, scrivener, was a witness to both wills.[n] Richard Blake, who died in the following year, willed that his executor should deliver to the Wardens of his Company of Tallow Chandlers 26s. 8d. 'to the entent' that a repast[o] might be had among the Company. To his son John he left his 'gown cloth, his gown furred with fox (as befitting his position as an Assistant of the Court)[p] and his worsted jacket' as well as the 'panne' (presumably a melting pan for tallow) 'over the warehouse'.[22] Thomas Cuttle (or Cuttell), thrice Master of the Company,[q] whose will was proved in the Prerogative Court of Canterbury in January 1560,[23] appears to have been a man of considerable means with 'messuages, lands and tenements' in the parish of St Dunstan in the East. Among his numerous legacies he made a substantial bequest to 'the Master and Wardens of the company or livery of the Tallowchandlers of London' to be employed for the benefit of poor young men of the Yeomanry. Nothing further appears to be known of Thomas Bell, and we do not meet him again.

In the following August (1531), our Company was again directed, through its Wardens, to take an even more active part in controlling the trade.[24] The Wardens were to make a *weekly* search for tallow and also to make a 'bill' of the names of 'all suche bochers & other persons *that conveys talough owt of the liberties*'.[r] For the next six years there appears to have been no serious trouble. Prices remained stable and in fact there seems to have been no significant rise until tallow again became scarce in the 'forties.

---

n Commentary, p. 230.

o Frequently referred to by testators as 'a recreation'.

p See Appendix C.

q 1544–9, 1553–5, and 1558–9.

r Compare our Wardens' own proposal in 1524 for a weekly (or monthly) search and the Court's direction respecting the illegal conveyance of tallow out of the City (p. 10).

In December 1536 the ordinance (or standard edict) of 5th October 1474[s] is cited as *'the lawe for bochers & chaundelers'* still regulating prices 'withyn thys Cytie *& other thynges* concernyng conveyng of Talowgh *without Lycens*, etc.',[25] and just over a year later we witness the seizure of six barrels of tallow[26] declared to be 'forfayt by the lawes and customes of this Cytye', which tallow was

solde to be occupyed without the Cytie & the same solde to them that make no candelles/whiche colorablye & craftelye beinge hydd by the seller was affyrmed to be *butter* and not Talloughe,

contrary to the said 'Acte of Common Councell'.

II

Up to the present we have mentioned neither the Curriers nor the Soap-makers, with both of which crafts our Company, along with the Butchers, is seen, from the early memoranda books of the City, to have been closely associated.[a]

We meet the Curriers first in May 1509, when two butchers are reported by John Bodfield, one of their Wardens, *to have sold tallow to curriers* 'a boue the price sette by the Maire & his brethern'.[27] The currier's job was to dress the substance produced from the skin of animals by tanning, a process which involved shaving the leather with a special knife and then introducing grease into the skin,[28] for which operation, as we learn from this and subsequent entries, he was a buyer of tallow—*whenever he could get it*. The consumption of tallow by curriers is again officially recognized eleven years later in two orders of the Court of Aldermen, the first in June (1518)[29] 'for thavoidyng meltyng of Talugh' by curriers 'out of (within) this Citie',[b] the second, in the following November,[30] when an inquiry was ordered to ascertain *'what Talugh shall serue theym'*. But next year we see them in

---

s   Volume III, pp. 58–9.
a   This early relationship on the part of the Butchers and Tallow Chandlers seems to have escaped the notice of other writers.
b   *Commentary*, p. 230.

difficulties. In an entry dated 31st January, 1519[31] we read that

> wher afore this tyme Bodfeld Butcher solde to diuerse Cur(iours) within this
> City certyn tallough *by reason whereof the Chaundelers of this towne shulde be
> destitute of talough for makyng of Candell*/In consideracion whereof my lorde
> Maire commaunded the said Bodley (sic) to make no deliuery of the said
> talough Now att this Courte iniunccion ys given by the same to the same
> Bodfeld *to sell the same talough to suche candellmakers of this City as this Courte
> shall assigne* & . . . after suche prices as shall be lymyted by this Courte/that ys
> to say xjs.vjd a weygh/ & for the melting[c] of the same as shalbe thought
> reasonable by this Courte/

This decision seems to set the pattern for future dealings *when
stocks were low*. A Warden of the Tallow Chandlers agrees to pay
the Mayor's price. Bodfeld delivers the tallow and two other
curriers are forced to give way. Ten years later we hear of a
salter being reported by our Wardens for buying tallow and selling it '*ageyn to the Coryours*',[32] but on 31st August 1531[33] certain
curriers, as well as soapmakers, are

> sworne to enquer amonges their Companyes howe moch Talough they &
> all their Companye haue bought sythens Christmas last

and to certify the same; and certain butchers are

> sworne (to inquire) howe moche Talough they haue solde to the Coryours &
> Sopemakers & in lyke maner to certyfye, etc,

suggesting that, after a period of scarcity, *stocks had again become
plentiful*. Except for a protest in February 1538[34] by the Curriers,
among others,[d] against the 'regratynge and forstallynge' of tallow,[e] we hear no more for nearly sixteen years, when the entries
in the *Repertories* make us wonder whether after all the Court had
any settled policy. In April 1547 the price of tallow was 'rated and
sett by the Court' at *xvij. s.* (the wey).[35] On 14th June 'the

---

c   *Commentary*, p. 231.

d   *Commentary*, p. 231.

e   Regrate: To buy up (market commodities, esp. victuals) in order to sell again at a
profit in the same or a neighbouring market. Forestall: to intercept (goods, etc.)
before they reach the public markets; to buy (them) up privately with a view to
enhancing the price. *O.E.D.*

Taloughchaundelers byll declaring the cause of *scarcytie of talough* & the remedy *after their fantyse* for the same' is read.[36] We shall have more to say about this bill later and about the penalties imposed on certain candlemakers—including one Thomas Marshall, a salter—for breaking the price of candles at this time. For the present we need only say that over six weeks elapse before the bill is read again, when on 28th July[37] Marshall declares 'upon his othe' that

Wylliam Bradfote talloughchaundeler confessed unto hym that he had bought talough for xx.s. the weye and that John Baynton the grocer sellyth very commenly *a grett quantyte of tallough to the corryors* And he the seyd Marshall dyd nott denye but that he bought Howe (?) the bocher's talough for xx.s the wey this present yere.

Yet only two days later the Court agrees[38] that

My lorde Mayer shall permytt the Coryers to provyde & take *as muche talough within the Cytie for their necessarye use as by his good dyscrecion he shalthynke mete.*

Bradfote (or Bradfotte) was a Warden of the Yeomanry in 1518[39] and appears as a householder in 1537-8.[f] On his death in 1555 he left all his lands and tenements 'with appurtenance lying in the parish of Beckenham, Co. Kent' to his wife, Alice, for life, and after her death to his daughter Johan, who inherited also a further three acres in the same parish.[40] Another daughter inherited his 'two little tenements with two gardens lying by the midst of the town of Bekingham aforesaid'.[g]

From a Court order of 19th May 1552 it appears that the Curriers had recently brought in a bill against the Tallow Chandlers and other candlemakers of the City 'the trothe thereof' the Wardens of the Tallow Chandlers were directed to examine,[41] but we are not told its nature or what report was made.[h] Apart from this entry there is nothing further to relate respecting the Curriers' consumption of tallow until 6th April 1559, by which date a new system of rationing appears to have been introduced.

f   See Volume III, Appendix F. Group II.

g   *Commentary*, p. 231.

h   *Commentary*, p. 231.

The Court then agrees[42] that

the Wardeyns of the Coryors and also the Sopemakers of this Cytie shalbe
warned to be here next Court day for order then to be taken with theym for
suche talloughe as they shall be permytted to have and occupye,

giving the impression that, so far as the Curriers at any rate are
concerned, the policy of the Court has again become one of 'stop
go'.
  In May 1563 it is ordered[43]

that the Tulloughchaundlers & other Candlemakers shall have & receyve of
the Bochers bothe freemen of this Cytie & *of the forreyns also* all their *rough
talough*/and that *they shall then serve the Company of Coriors* of so moche good
clene & hard *molten talough* as they for their occupacion of curryinge of lether
from tyme to tyme shall necessaryly expende.

On 24th July of the following year, in a decree of the Court[44]
made in 'the matter here dependynge in question & varyaunce'
between the company of Tallow Chandlers and the companies
of Curriers *and Cordwainers*, the curriers' entitlement to *molten
tallow* from tallow chandlers is confirmed 'durynge the space of
one hole yere next ensuynge' and the price is fixed at xxxv.s the
wey,[i] in addition to which they are to have

all the *flotts* (kitchen stuff)[j] that shalbe gatheryd & put to sale within the cytie
& the libertyes thereof.

The Tallow Chandlers and other candlemakers are forbidden to

buy receyve use or occupy eny part of the saide flotts in eny kinde or sorte of
candells

during the said period of one year, and the Curriers are forbidden
during that period to

buye or receyve or cause to be bought or receyved to theire owne uses eny
maner of rough tallough . . . uppon payne of forfayture of the same tallough.

Moreover, to ensure supplies, 'ij discrete persons of eyther of the

---

i   *Commentary*, p. 231.

j   *Commentary*, p. 231.

saide companies of the Cordewayners & Curryours' are directed 'by theire dyscreccions' to

devyse & take summe good & convenyent weye and meane not onely for the dyligent & sure collectynge & gatherynge toguether of all the seid flotts but also for the brynginge & holy conveyinge the same to thands of the saide companye of the Curryours.

In the following November (1564) the Curriers' consumption of a reasonable amount of molten tallow according to the last recorded decree seems to be confirmed.[45] But a few months later the picture changes completely with the reappearance of the 'foreign' butchers, who take the centre of the stage in a Court order dated 22nd May 1565. To understand this, and the next succeeding, entry, we must go back very nearly twenty years[46] when the Court directed that there should be 'certeyn apte & convenyent places made & prepared within *Leadenhall* by the oversyght & appoyntment of my lorde mayor' and three Aldermen' for the foreyn bochers that nowe use to stonde in the high strete besyde the Ledenhall,[k] to stonde & kepe their markett.' The new order[47] established

that the severall companyes of the Talloughchaundelers & of the Corryours shall wekely by turne have all suche tallough as shalbe brought to Leadenhall to be solde (that ys to saye) the sayde Talloughchaundelers to have holye one weke & the Curryours lykewyse holye another weke/ & that the wardeyns of the sayde companyes shall appoynte their common officer or somme other sadde person to collect & receyve the sayde talloughe,

and a few months later it is recorded[48] that the Wardens of both companies willingly assent to the proposal, and agree

therewith quietly from hensforthe to content theym selfs/ & *no more to trouble or molest this court therewith.*

We do not know how long these new arrangements lasted. Not only were the operations of foreign butchers confined to Leadenhall Market, but the sellers were compelled to bring with the carcases all the rough tallow and suet.[l] There were repeated

---

k   Commentary, p. 231.

l   Commentary, p. 231.

orders to that effect, of which one of the first examples is to be found in the *Repertories* for the early 'thirties of the century when tallow in particular is mentioned.[49] Again in April 1552[50] it was agreed by the Court that the Lord Mayor should

take order with the forreyn bochers at Leaden Hall that they fromhensfurth do brynge *all their Tallowgh* that cometh of the cattall that they putt there to sale hether to this Cytie/with their fleshe/to be sold at lyke pryse as is gyven to the bochers of this Cytie for their Tallowgh/*orelles that they shall not be suffered to sell anye more fleshe there.*

Ten years later as a result of a bill exhibited by the Tallow Chandlers, the Court agreed that 'the contents of the former acts and ordinances of this Court' mentioned in the same bill should be 'holy and spedely put in vse by the wardeins of the saide company' and that there should be a proclamation made at Leadenhall.[51] The proclamation, which expressly referred to beef and mutton,[m] followed within a few days,[52] and two days later *the wardens of the Tallow Chandlers*, taking with them Richard Foster, one of the Lord Mayor's officers, were ordered 'uppon Saturday next & thre or foure market days after' to 'visit and peruse the fleshe market att Ledenhall and there quietly and discretely searche & learne' whether the 'forens' were acting 'according to the tenor & true meanynge' of the proclamation.[53] Finally on 10th May 1575[54] it was ordered that Thomas Redknyghte, described earlier as 'citizen and tallow chandler',[n] should

wekely from hensforthe every marquett daye duely serche and inquyre whether all and every the bochers commonly resortynge unto Leadenhalle being *forreyns* from the liberties of this Cytye and usynge to brynge fleshe thither to be solde

do observe the conditions laid down in the proclamation 'lately made and provyded', and that

every marquet daye from henseforth there shalbe twoe of thoffycers unto the Lorde Mayor and twoe other offycers unto the Sheryffes of the said Cyttye

---

m   See Volume I, p. 35, indicating that sheep's tallow was considered to be superior to that of cows for candle-making.

n   *Commentary*, p. 232.

namyd and appoynted by the Lorde Mayor of this Cyttye to ayde and assyste the sayd Thomas Redknyghte in thexecutynge and doynge of the premysses ...

It looks very much from the memoranda books of the 'seven-ties[55] as though the Curriers' promised supplies from foreign butchers were either forgotten or neglected. The directions to sell the tallow, except in the earliest order, which actually names 'the *Butchers* of this Citie' as the buyers, are either stated in general terms, or refer generally to sales 'within this cytie'. It seems that the unfortunate currier was thus thrown back on 'kitchen stuff'. On the same day that the Curriers' bill against the Tallow Chandlers was read there had been an order[56] that

the Watdeyns of the taloughchaundelers shuld brynge all suche wyfes and other persons as goo aboute the cytie and bye upp *mens kychenstuffe* before my Lorde Mayer/to the intente that they maye declare to whome they utter the same,

and on 11th January 1574[57] we read that *only the Wardens of the Curriers* are henceforth to have

the noninacion and appoynting of all suche women and other persons as shalbe permytted and suffred to buy collect and gather anye maner of flottes or other kytchen stuff of anye persone or persones withyn this Citie or liberties thereof duringe the pleasure of this courte.

No other person was permitted to acquire 'anye manner of flottes or kytchen stuffe' upon pain of imprisonment or payment of a fine.

Fig. 2. Crown of Queen Elizabeth I.

And now for the soap-makers.

It so happens that our introduction to soap-making, like our first meeting with the Curriers, is in 1509. From a mortgage dated

27th July of that year,[58] we learn of a soap-house 'in the parysshe of Saint Alborowe (Alborgh) within Bysshoppes gate of London, w'in an Aley caulled Saint Elyns Aley'.[o] The borrower was one Henry Malyn, 'Citezein and Talloughchaundiller of London', the implements of whose trade, comprising 'his Sope panne, xij Sope fattes (vats) w[t] xij Tappes of iron, a ladle of Brasse and ij Sope Coulles',[p] were all pledged to the lender, another tallow chandler, one Thomas Hamond,[q] to secure 'the somme of xij li. sterlinges' repayable 'att the Feste of Saint Mighell tharchaungell (29th September)', in the following year, the borrower reserving to himself

two Bowyles (boils) of soppe w[t] his aune stuffe w'in the sayd zere yevyng the sayd Thomas Hamond xiiij days warnyng be tweyn euery Bowyll.

The first entry in the memoranda books of the Corporation to claim our attention is in the following year, when there is an ordinance dated 20th May 1510[59] made by the Mayor (Sir William Capel) and Aldermen, on the petition of a number of freemen of the City, headed by William Grene, whose name we find in our Yeomanry list for the years 1538–9[60] 'occupying the feate of makyng of *blake Sope* within the said Citee and liberties of the same'. The applicants draw attention to

the manyfolde deceytes wronges and vntrue actes commytted doon and vsed within the same Citee and libertees in makyng and vttering of suche blake sope,

and in the first article it is ordered

That yerely within xvj daies after the Fest of Saint George (23rd April) ij honest parsones being fremen of this Citee *hauyng experience and knowledge* in the feate of makyng of blake sope be named and appoynted by the Maire & Aldermen of the saide Citee for the Tyme beyng to haue the ouersight and serche of *euery boyle* of blake sope made within this Citee or Subarbes of the

---

o   Saint Alborgh (Ethelburga) was one of the old parishes taking its name from the Church on the east side of Bishopsgate. *Harben*. Saint Elyns Aley. A name, perhaps, for the common way mentioned by *Harben* on which stood the great Gate of the Priory, called 'Saint Elyns (St Helen's) Gate' leading to Crosbyes Place.

p   Query, coolers.

q   Nothing further seems to be known of either of these two men.

same afore it be putt to sale or closed in barells And also to ouersee & serche almaner of blake sope made in the parties of beyonde the See and brought or conveyed in to this Reame of England.

The second and fourth articles are concerned with the marking of barrels and the weighing of the contents, while the third directs

that fromhensforth no parsone occupying the makyng of blake sope make nor cause to be made any blake sope within the liberties of the said Citee with Trane heryng seme/pompe oyle butter or Nutte oyle/nor with any other grece licour or fatnes *except oonely with oyle called oyle olyve/or Rape oyle.*[r]

Trane oil appears from an eighteenth century Patent to have been prepared from the fat of whales,[s] while 'seme (or saim)' means the grease of animals generally. The meaning of 'pompe (or pump)' oil is obscure. The fifth article forbids the packing of black soap made 'in the parties of beyond the See *in to any other vessels*', upon pain of forfeiture, and further articles govern the presentation of offenders and penalties. The Ordinance is followed immediately by a Proclamation, a copy of which will be found in Appendix F.

From these documents it seems certain that soap-boiling had become an industry in London at least as early as the first decade of the sixteenth century and that the antiquary, John Stow, writing in or about the year 1603, was in error in affirming in effect that it was unknown there prior to 1523 when 'John *Lame*, dwelling in Grassestreet[t] set vp a boyling house'.[u] Strype, in his enlarged 'Fifth Edition' of Stow published in 1720, gives the man's surname as 'Lane', which, if correct, would lead us to believe that he was none other than our third Warden of the year 1518[v], but it seems more likely that Stow was speaking of a John

---

r   A thick brown yellow oil expressed from rape-seed. *O.E.D.*

s   *Commentary*, p. 232.

t   Gras-cherche, now Gracechurch Street, *Harben.*

u   *Commentary*, p. 232.

v   Volume III, p. 70.

Lambe,[w] reported to the Court in 1530 as one of those men making 'soope' and keeping 'soope houses'.[61]

Fig. 3. Stow's monument in the Church of St Andrew Undershaft. (The monument survives, although the function of the church has changed.)

There is indeed evidence that a *soap-makers' company* had actually been formed in London far earlier than has been generally supposed, although the industry itself seems to have remained in the hands of only a few men for many years. In August 1531 there is an incomplete entry in the *Repertory* Book which mentions 'the Wardens of Sope makers',[62] and the record of curriers and *soap makers* (who may be presumed to have been their Wardens)—to which we have already referred—follows two days later.[63]

Positively linking our Company with the soap trade early in the sixteenth century we read, in the will of Robert Sylver,[x] proved in April 1524,[64] of a bequest to the testator's son Anthony,

w   The *O.E.D.* gives *lame* as one of nine alternative forms of *lamb*.

x   Master in 1519–22. See Volume III, pp. 63, 70.

after the death of the boy's mother, of all his right, title, etc.

of and in that house with appurtenances called the '*sopehouse* being in the parish of St. Botolph without Bishopsgate of London the which I and Richard Choppyn do hold by lease . . . of the *Tallowchandlers of London.*[y]

This was the old 'Dolphin', the gift of John Steward, which, as mentioned in Volume III, fortunately escaped the operation of the Chantry Acts. Choppyn[z] was later to take a lease from the Company in his own name of this property, which, at the time of his death in 1536, was 'in the holding' of one Richard Sopemaker, and which Choppyn left by will[65] to his wife Joan. Five years later it was re-let

withe shopp sollers[aa] wythe roomes/fathowses boylyng howses yardes coopers howses wells & garden wythe thappurtenances

to James Quycke (whom we shall meet later in another role) for a term of forty years.[66] On his death in 1543 Quycke left the lease to his wife Johan 'with all implements, vessels and profits thereof' for her life, and on her death to his 'bastard son' Thomas,[67] who appears to have taken the name Belson. Over the years the premises were allowed to get into a serious state of disrepair, as a result of which Thomas Belson was arrested and the lease was forfeited.[bb] In October 1557 they were re-let as a 'soap-house' at an annual rental of £4 with a fine of £36 6s. 8d. for the goodwill,[68] but by 1569 the character of the property had changed. In January of that year 'the houses', as they are called in the minutes, acquired a new tenant in the person of *Roger Tyler*. The lease refers to the property as 'late a soap house', although Tyler appears to have found a use for the tenant's implements left on the site, which were 'prised' at £53.[69] Seven years later we learn that these houses are still 'letten to Roger Tiler',[70] but there seems

---

y   See Volume III, p. 63.

z   Master 1523–5 (Volume III, pp. 33, 63) and later an Alderman; Sheriff of London in 1531. He was also the first Governor of the Yeomanry, of whom we have any record, serving from 1518 to 1525. (See *Commentary*, p. 232.)

aa   Upper stories (see Volume I, p. 58).

bb   T.C.C.R., Appendix G, pp. 293–6.

to be no record of how long he remained our tenant. *Roger Price*, our famous clerk, tells us in his abstract[71] of the 'Perpetuity', so called, confirming the Company in its landed possessions,[72] that at the date of his narrative, which is believed to have been completed about the year 1630,[73] the land is called '*Sope house Alley*[cc] and is in his (Price's) occupation, (Appendix C) and it seems from the accounts[74] that he had held a lease for the past twelve years, for which he paid a 'fine' (or premium) of £200.[dd] We shall hear more of both these men in due course.

Another comparatively early sixteenth century link with the soap trade is seen in the will of Richard Hudson, chandler,[75] who died in 1533, leaving to his 'servant and prentice' his featherbed, all his shirts and *one* barrel of 'grey' soap,[ee] with all earthen pots in his shop, and to 'Master Hale'[ff] *one barrel of soap*. A much later instance occurs early in the next century in a lease dated 4th June 1611 granted to Randall Carter[76] (whom we shall meet later), of

a great messuage or tenement *now used as a soap-house* lying on the Bankside end of an alley and divers tenements therein and of two tenements towards the Thames side and of a garden or garden plot lying behind the same alley all of which are called the Tallow Chandlers Rents'.[gg]

These were the properties, known as 'the Elephant' and 'the Crane', left to the Company by Stephen Littlebaker in 1504.[hh]

In 1530[77] 'the Names of thym that make Soope and kepe soope houses', of which there were six, including John Lambe (p. 25),

---

cc   One of two courts, viz. Horshoe Alley or Yard and Soapers or Sopers Alley, which later (according to Strype) were together to become Sweet Apple Court (*Harben*, p. 565). The former is mentioned in the will of Walter Mafye, citizen and tallow chandler, as one of the properties in which he had an interest on his death in 1587. (See *Commentary*, p. 232.)

dd   *Commentary*, p. 232.

ee   *Commentary*, p. 232.

ff   *Commentary*, p. 232.

gg   No property of that description is mentioned in *Wheatley*, a work which extends to Southwark. The Company at one time owned a number of houses in the Wardrobe which went by the name of 'Chandlers' Rents'. See *Harben*.

hh   *Commentary*, p. 233.

are given in the *Repertory* Book as well as a *salter's* recognyzance binding himself henceforth not to

boyle nor occupye eny talowe in the makyng of eny sope.

This must be one of the earliest entries forbidding the use of tallow in soap, a prohibition to which we become well accustomed as time goes on. Next year we find this substance (not specifically mentioned in the Ordinance of 1510) officially classed, *along with trane oil*, as a prohibited article in a *memorandum*[78]

that no maner sope maker shall boyle eny *talough* butter blubber nor trane oyle.

Nevertheless, the year is hardly out before we find a soapmaker admitting 'uppon his othe that in his last boyling he putte in a barell & more of oyle of trane', while another declares that he 'never knewe but that he myghte boyle oyle of trane, and in his last boylyng he putte in iij or iiij barels of trane'.[79] No wonder that in April 1532 a committee is directed to examine the articles touching the making of soap,[80] that in September there should be published what amounts to a re-issue of the Ordinance, or rather the Proclamation[81] (Appendix F, Part I) and that in July of the following year[82] three salters *and an ironmonger[ii]* should be appointed to view and 'hable'[jj] the soap before it is 'heddyd'.

Having introduced the London soap-makers' Ordinance we turn to the Statute relating to oils, which followed within two years, being dated 4th February 1512,[83] the effect of which was, in theory at least, to give the Tallow Chandlers Company control over the soap trade. It provides that

the Mayre of the Citie of London for the tyme beyng/wyth the Maister and Wardens of the misterie or crafte of Tallough-chaundelers of the same Citie for the tyme beyng/shall fromhensforthe have full power and auctorite to serche *all manner of oyles* brought in to the seid Citie of London to be solde in whos handes so ever they be or shalbe founde And that as often as the case shall requyre.

---

ii   The ironmonger was presumably concerned in hooping the barrels before they were headed (*infra.*).

jj   *Commentary*, p. 233.

It goes on to direct that the Mayor with the Master and Wardens

shall truely serche and oversee that the same Oyles to be putt to sale, *be not myxte nor altered frome their ryght kyndes*/but that they be good and lawfull as they ought to be And that yt shalbe liefull to the seid Mayre wyth the seid Maister and Wardens for the tyme beyng to dampne (destroy) avoyde and utterly to caste awey all suche Oyles as they shall fynde defectyfe or falsely or deceyvablye myxed and altered frome their right kynde as is aforesaid/wyth-oute eny lett or pturbaunce of eny psone or psones what so ever they are or shalbe And 'also the seid Mayrr Maister and Wardens to comyte such psone or psones as shalbe found defectyfe (sic) for usyng of such deceyte or crafte to Warde/and to punnyshe hym or theym therfore by theyr discrecion/accordyng to the lawes and customes wythin the seid Citie or libtie of London used hadde and made . . . for oder misdowers & offenders . . .

Early dealings in oil by tallow chandlers are not unknown,[kk] but there appears to be no surviving record in London of the circumstances under which the powers conferred by this Act were

Fig. 4. Public washing-grounds in 1582 (Harleian collection).

---

kk   *Commentary*, p. 233.

sought or obtained, and indeed there are comparatively few instances of its enforcement. It appears from its recital that the special occasion of the Statute was the use of oil in 'drapyng of wollen clothes', (Fig. 4) and it concludes by conferring on Mayors, etc. of other places, acting alone, the same powers as are conferred thereby on the Mayor of London acting jointly with our Master and Wardens. The first occasion after its inception on which it seems to be mentioned in the memoranda books of the City is over twenty years later, when there is an entry in the *Repertory* Book dated 23rd July 1532 of a meeting of the Court of Aldermen with the marginal note 'Presentacion of Oyles not goode',[84] which commences with a recital that,

where by *an Acte of Parliament in Anno tercio domini Regis nunc* the Mayr of this Citie ... with the Wardeins of the Talughchaundelers for the tyme beyng shall haue the serche of all maner oyles, &c. as by the seyd Act emore playnly apperythe ...

The clerk, thus having discharged his first duty to record his masters' awareness of the existence of the Act, continues as follows:

The Wardens of the Taloughchaundelers now beyng haue presentyd iiij persones havyng Oyles mixte as hereafter ensueth/
    Thomas Walle/Salter/a type of oyle myxed not laufull to be solde
    Cokkes/Grocer/a barell of oyle of xxxiiij galons myxte not to be solde
    John Sampson/Salter/[ll] the iij^d parte of a tonne of oyle myxed not laufull to be solde

That this revival of interest in the Statute should coincide with the re-issue of the soap-makers' ordinance may not have been an accident, yet nothing further seems to happen for nearly three years when, in April 1535,[85] there is a Court order that

the talowghe chaundelers shall have the serche of candell & *oyle/* & to brynge the same to the Chambre.

In October 1538, as we shall see, the Company obtained the approval by the Court of Aldermen of their earliest recorded

---

[ll]   For earlier offences against law and order by this notorious character, see Volume III, pp. 65, 71.

Ordinances containing a provision (article No. 21) for regulating 'bargains' for the purchase and sale of a number of commodities *including 'oyles'*, and also an article (No. 24) authorizing their Wardens to make searches among persons dealing in these commodities who seek to evade the payment of quarterage. In an Inventory made in November 1549 'concerning the Implements remaining at the Tallow Chandlers Hall' we find 'a tester for the oil',[86] and nearly six years later in another Inventory 'a gager for oil' is mentioned.[87] In the accounts for 1559–61 3s. is entered as having been paid 'for making a new *iron* to mark the oil withal',[88] and the accounts for 1564–5 record the payment of 4d. for 'a black box for the *seal* of the oil'.[89] It appears from these entries that we were provided both with a *measure* and *an iron for branding casks,*[mm] but, in the absence of other records, we have no means of telling to what extent these appliances were used. The first evidence of any positive action comes in 1550, when we read[90] that an official of the Court has been

enioyned to cause the wardeins of the Taloughchaundelers to see the Butt of oyle that is supposed to be yll & corrupte & *also to use honest language to the same wardeins* . . .

with what result we are not told. There is an entry in October 1553 in our *Livery (Wardens) Account Book* that 'the *suit* in the Parliament House for the Bill for search for oils shall be at the costs and charges of this House'.[91] The Recorder of London is paid 6s. 8d. for 'penning the supplication exhibited into the Parliament House', the clerk to the Keeper of the House receives 12d. 'for to put his Master in remembrance of our suit.' and 6s. is paid for a copy of the Bill, while 'Thomas Hone, our Clerk', is awarded 13s. 4d. 'for his pains in following the suit . . . and for writing of the Bills three times as by the Assistants it was agreed'.[92] But no Act of Parliament appears to have been passed, and no further record of the Bill has been found. Not until the 'sixties does there seem to be any determined effort to enforce the provisions of the Act of 1512 and then for a period of little over a

---

mm   Burning seal (scots): an iron for branding casks. *O.E.D.*

year. On 3rd September 1560[93] it is agreed, at a meeting of the Court of Aldermen,

that there shalbe an enquest of office[nn] warned agaynst the next court day to trye whither certeyne Oyles lately presentyed by the master and wardeyns of the Taloughchaundelers to be myxt & *naughte* be so in dede or not.

We learn from a subsequent report[94] that these oils were found to be 'defective & myxt', and it is ordered that the Chamberlain shall cause them

to be *buryed in the ground or otherwise destroyed* with sped/according to the forme of the Acte of Parlyament *anno 3 H.8 c. 14* (4th February 1512) thereof made.

On 28th November of the same year (1560) there is an order[95] that

the wardeyns of the Talloughchaundelers shall goo foreward and *styll contynewe* their serche of oyles . . .

and, in January 1562, a further order[96] directing that John Kynge[oo] (then Master), of whom we shall hear more later, with *two servants of the Chamber*, one of them being the Lord Mayor's officer, Foster, (p. 21)

shall cause and set ij pipes of myngled & defective rape oyle lately presented tried & found by verditt of an inquest of office to be naughte & not merchaunttable or meate to be occupied to be brent (burned) uppon Friday next in Fynnesbery feld.[pp]

In less than three years the Court has no compunction in again requiring its memory to be refreshed. In September 1564[97] it is ordered that 'the lawes *heretofore dyvysed and made* ageyn suche as doe putt corrupt oyles to sale shalbe lokydup . . .', and in the Spring of the following year there is a fresh burst of activity. On

---

nn   *Commentary*, p. 233.

oo   He came into office on 6th August 1559 and served for three years.

pp   Finsbury Fields, the open tract north of Moorfields. Popularly the name was given to the fields 'which stretch along the north part of Cripplegate through Moorfields and reach to some part of Shoreditch parish'. (Strype's *Stow*, B. IV, p. 60) to Hoxton, and as far north as Islington Common . . . *Wheatley*. The name survives in Finsbury Circus, etc.

THE ARMS OF THE STUART KINGS
CONTEMPORARY WITH THE
REBUILDING OF THE HALL AFTER
THE GREAT FIRE OF LONDON

THE SITE WAS PURCHASED BY THE
TALLOW CHANDLERS COMPANY
IN THE REIGN OF EDWARD IV
WHOSE ARMS ARE SHOWN IN THE
ORIEL WINDOW IN THE
BANQUETING HALL

Plate II

Facing page 32]

22nd March (1565) after a search, in the course of which 2s. 1d. was spent at 'the Red Lion'[98]—one of many inns of this name— we are informed[99] that the Court has ordered

that so muche of the oyle lately seized by the wardeyns of the Tallough-chaundelers of this cytye and presented by them to this courte as defectyve and myngled as ys founde now by an inquest of offyce to be good and merchaunt-able/ . . . /shalbe forthwith redelyvered to the owners thereof/and that the residue of the said oyle . . . shalbe burnyd or otherwyse destroyed . . .[qq]

We learn of what appears to be the last 'search of oils' to be carried out under the old Act from our accounts for 1566–7, when 2s. was spent on 'the Wardens breakfast'[100], but no record seems to have been made in the Repertory Book.

To return to the soap-makers. When we come to consider the steps taken, after a slow start, to enforce the Ordinance of 1510, we find that theirs is a more convincing story. We left them with the appointment of 'viewers' in July 1533, and meet them again in November 1545, when the use of tallow in soap is again the problem. All the soap-makers of the City are warned to be present at the next meeting of the Court[101] and

the taloughchaundelers have a comaundement to certyfye here the same day/ bothe theyr owne hole store of talough that they have amongst theym/ and also the store that all other that use & occupye makyng of candells here in the Citie have amongst them.

There seems no doubt that tallow was one of the earliest ingre-dients used in making soap. According to Pliny the Elder, soap was anciently made by boiling goat tallow and causticized wood ashes.[102] But in London the civic authorities were bent on pre-serving tallow for candle-making, to the detriment of both cur-riers and soap-makers. Some twelve months after the inquiry of 1545 there comes an order that butchers 'that use to sell theyr tallowe to sopemakers' are henceforth to bring it to Leadenhall and 'nott to sell yt in eny wyse to eny sopemakers upon the perylls that may fall theron'.[103] These butchers were probably 'foreins', whose activities, as we have seen, had earlier that year been con-

---

[qq] Commentary, p. 233.

fined to Leadenhall Market. In the following year 'the Act temp. Capel' (the ordinance of 1510) 'for the true making of soap' was proclaimed,[104] and shortly afterwards information was sought by the Court as to the persons most expert in soap-making.[105] A little later a book 'touching the ordering and making of soap' was ordered to be read,[106] followed by a bill and a warning to persons to appear 'to declare their opinions'.[107] Next year 'certain Artycles concernyng the true makyng of sope' were read. It was agreed *'that the old lawes of this Cytie provyded for the same shalbe putt in due execucion with convenyent spede'*,[108] and soon afterwards persons were appointed to see that the 'Act' (ordinance) was observed.[109]

Prior to March 1558 there seems to have been some relaxation in the rules, for in March all the 'talloughecandlemakers of this Cytye not beynge free of the felowship of the Talloughechaundelers *and also all the sope makers'*, along with the curriers, are required to furnish the Court with the names of all those butchers who have supplied them with tallow and to state the quantities,[110] and in April 1559 (as we have seen) the soap-makers, as well as the curriers were summoned to attend Court to receive an order *'for suche tallough as they shall be permytted to have and occupye'*,[111] but five years later 'the severall companyes of Talloughe Chaundelers, Iremongers (note *ii*) & Bochers & also the Sopemakers' are warned to appear before the Court[112] to hear the *supplication* of our Company[113]

ageynst the Sopemakers of this cytie for their consumynge & spending of greate quantitie of tallough in the boylynge & makynge of their sope to the greate hynderance & preiudyce of the common weale of this citie/of the which sopemakers *some doo also make candle.*

The hearing resulted in a compromise. Those who used and occupied the 'arte or occupacion of sope-makynge within the seid cytie or the liberties thereof' were forbidden to make tallow candles for sale upon pain of forfeiture. Conversely 'noe manner of Talloughchaundeler' or other citizen or person using and occupying 'the crafte or occupacion of a Talloughchaundeler' might thereafter 'boyle or make or cause to be boyled or made

eny manner of sope'. Yet within a few weeks there was an order
that all soapmakers of the City should attend the Court 'for the
matter concernynge their puttynge of so greate a quantytie of
talloughe in their sope, *as yt is allegid they doe*',[114] and a week later
a warning was issued[115] that they should all 'be here the next
courte day for order then to be taken with them *to desyst from
puttynge of eny talloughe into their sope*'. Our 'supplication' having
proved so successful, we acted promptly in seeing that an order
was drawn up with the help of a lawyer at a cost of 21s. We paid
the Lord Mayor's officer 20s. 8d. 'for *warning* the soap boilers
before my Lord' and a further 4s. 6d. 'at the search of the Soap-
boilers at My Lord Mayor's commandment'.[116] The order was
nevertheless modified within a month, when, at the meeting held
on 24th July (p. 19) it was decreed that 'for one hole yere' soap-
makers should not use 'eny maner of *Englyshe tallough* in or aboute
the boylynge of their sope',[117] but, without knowing to what
extent tallow was being imported at this period, we cannot tell
whether the new order made any great difference. There are
infrequent references to *muscovy tallow*, one of which occurs in
the *Repertory* Book in the summer of 1568,[118] which was a time
of scarcity.*rr* There is another entry in our accounts for 1591-3,
from which we learn of a purchase at that time 'for the use of
the Company' of '20 fats . . . weighing altogether net twenty
thousand eight hundred and five pounds at 32s. the hundred: sum
£331.'[119] This tallow appears to have been bought for members
and invoiced to them at the same price. One of the defendants in
the Star Chamber proceedings in 1598 (p. 38) also refers to
'tallowe thatt is brought into England of Muskovie, Denmarke
and Poland and divers other cuntries' and concludes 'thatt there
is sufficient tallowe in England, as well for makeing of candells
as alsoe to use in sope, and for all other necessarie uses within the
realme.'

---

rr Muscovy. The name of the principality of Moscow applied by extension to Russia
generally. O.E.D. Tallow was among the imports from Russia for which the 'Muscovy
Company', founded in 1555, was responsible. *The Reign of Elizabeth, 1558-1603* by
J. B. Black, second edition, 1959, pp. 237, 239. (See *Commentary*, p. 233.)

In any case the distinction between domestic and imported tallow was soon abandoned. In the autumn (of 1564) the ordinance of 1510 was again ordered to be proclaimed on 'ij markett dayes', after which it was to be 'fyrmely observed accordyng to the tenor of the same'.[120] This decree was followed in the autumn of next year by a further order restraining soap-makers from using '*eny tallough* in the boyllynge & makynge of their sope' as a supplement to the Act of Common Council, or Standard Edict, of 1474 'concernynge the Bochers & Talloughchaundelers of this Cytye & other persons of the same cytye havynge tallough to sell.'[121] Later that year (1565)[122] we see Rychard Syberye, tallow chandler, 'presenting' a soap maker for using tallow for soap boiling, for which the offender was fined l*s*., whereof xxx*s* was applied for the use of the Chamber, xxx*s* was paid to Syberye and x*s* was to be to the use of 'my lord mayor's' officer

that dyd *paynfully & dylygently travell aboute the saser of the sayd sope.*

Sybery, who served for some time as an Assistant of the Court, and was a Warden the year before he died,[123] owned a number of 'messuages' and cottages in the parish of St Andrew, Baynard's Castle,*[ss]* which the Company acquired several years before his death in 1596.[124] He left 'the Master, Wardens and Commonaltye of the Tallowchaundlers' the handsome sum of 40*s*. 'for a banquet' on the day of his burial, as well as all his lands at 'The Wardrope',*[tt]* for ever, they paying therefor to one John Dawson £150 'to redeem the foresaid lands and tenements forth of his handes'. They were also to pay to the President and Fellows of St John's College in Oxford the sum of £4 yearly as from a certain date,[125] for which the Company afterwards compounded.*[uu]*

---

ss   St Andrew Castle Baynard. Another name for St Andrew by the Wardrobe, on the east side of St Andrew's (Andrew) Hill, north out of Queen Victoria Street, *Harben.*

tt   The King's Wardrobe. Between Carter Lane north and St Andrew's Church south, Puddle Dock Hill west and Addle Hill east. Shown in Ogilby and Morgan's Map of London, 1677 as a large vacant space. 'The King's Wardrobe was here' . . . Described as a branch of the Exchequer for the receipt and disbursements of monies in the personal expenditure of the sovereign (*Lib. Cust.* Glossary, s.v. 'garderoba') *Harben.*

uu   *Commentary*, p. 233.

In November 1574 the law against using tallow for soap-making appears to have been again either suspended or relaxed, for we read then[126] that 'specyall comawndymente' has been given in open Courte to two of the Lord Mayor's officers

that they shall make dyligente searche in all & every of *the soape makers howses* of this Cytie and lyberties thereof howe moche talloughe nowe remeynethe in their severall custodyes ether in their howses or ware howses

and that those resisting the search shall be committed to ward.

But from the early 'seventies onwards there are many instances of soap-makers being forbidden to use tallow and of the steps taken to enforce the regulations, of which we may mention four, as of special interest. In the winter of 1573 our Thomas Redknight, (p. 21) was empowered to search throughout the City and Liberties for tallow and tallow candles, conveyed or intended to be conveyed out of the City, or sold to 'forreyne or strangers', or *'conveyed or intended to be conveyed to sope boylers to and for the boylinge of sope'*, for which purpose he was 'to cause to be made a small instrument of iron' wherewith he might search 'suche vessells in which at any tyme' he should suspect any such tallow or candles, which offending merchandise, when identified, he was directed to seize.[127] In March 1575 it was asserted in an Act of Common Council[128] that the illegal employment of tallow in soap-making, an operation which was said to be difficult to detect, particularly in summer, was a contributory cause of the dearth of candles, and strict tests were prescribed, accompanied by stringent provisions for protecting the accused against the action of corrupt officers.[vv] Thirteen months later[129] we learn that two Salters

were by this Courte severally comytted to pryson into the Compters of this Cytie, there to remayne durynge the pleysure of this Courte for that they use and occupye the makynge and boylinge of soape within the sayd Cytie and the lyberties thereof/*and doe refuse to be bounde by recognyzaunce* not to boyle any soape in tallowe accordinge as all other soape boylers stande bounde.

Lastly in the spring of 1577 we are told that one Ralph Calveley,

---

vv   See Appendix F, Part II for an abstract of this Act.

a tallow chandler, has been 'comytted to prysone in the Compter in the Powltrye'.*ww* for a like offence.[130]

On 15th April 1577 the Company obtained the Elizabethan Patent *for the search of soap, vinegar, barrelled butter, oil, and hops,* with which Patent we shall be more particularly concerned in a later Chapter.[131] It opens with a recital that her Majesty has been

credibly informed that many unmeete devises have byn and yet are practised by dyvers persons occupinge the trade of makinge sope and vinyger (page 145) within this our realme/by mynglinge of unkindly and hurtfull stuffe in steade of holsome and good thinges/as in makinge of *sope*/to mixe *tallowe* and other impertynent and unswete thinges/not meete nor holsome for the washing of lynnen for the body/and yet is uttered and solde for good and swete sope . . .

and it is declared that, after allowing a short period in which offenders may '*utter and doe away with the said evill and corrupt sope*', *etc.*, the searchers are to 'take, seise and carry away as corrupt and unwholsome all such sope as shall be . . . found and proved . . . to be *myngled with tallowe or other corrupt thinges* . . .' In 1598 there is a recorded instance of action having been taken in the Court of Star Chamber*xx* on 'a Bill of Complaint of the Master, Wardens and Commonalty of the Mystery of Tallow Chandlers' against Thomas Hunt, soap boiler, dwelling in Thames Street and Thomas Bromefield, soap boiler, dwelling in Southwark,[132] in which proceedings their main defence was that soap

was never the worse butt the better for haveing some tallowe therein . . . for without tallowe yt will neither be stiffe nor scoure soe well nor bleach soe white.

The result of the case is not known, the Company's records being silent on the subject, and a search at the Public Record Office having yielded only the depositions.

After the decree in July 1564 (p. 35) *English* tallow is not mentioned specifically until October 1587. In an entry of a Court Meeting[133] attended by 'the greatest number of the sopeboylers

---

ww   On the north side of Poultry, south of Grocer's Hall. A prison-house belonging to one of the Sheriffs—*Harben.*

xx   *Commentary*, p. 233 (See Fig 5).

Fig. 5. The Old Star Chamber, Westminster.

within this Citye and the fredome and liberties of the same and the wardens of the severall companies of the Butchers and the Tallow-Chaundlers' it is recorded that 'straight charge and comaundement' has been given to the said soap-boilers that 'after Satterdaye nexte ensueinge' they do not

at anie time use or occupie anie manner of Englishe talloughe in the boylinge and makinge of sope uppon the paines conteyned in *the acte of Common Counsell* to be inflicted upon them *without favor*.

The command which follows, that butchers and tallow chandlers are to sell their tallow only '*to suche as shall melte and converte the same into candells to be spent within this Cittye*', does not actually specify English tallow, but this is probably intended.

Subsequent entries are scarce, but it seems clear from a report made to the Court of Aldermen in 1620[134] that the use of *English tallow* in soap-making, although a common practice, was not yet accepted. The Committee informs the Court that the soapmakers have agreed that in future there shall be but three sorts of soap made, viz: best, second and third, and that the best bee made meerely with olive oile *and tallough* without the mixture of any other kindes of oile or kitchen stuffe or grease/and the second sort of soape for ordinary use called course soape to bee made of seed oile, nutt oile, fish oile, as whale oyle and the like *without mixture of any tallough or stuffe*/and the last or third sort of soape knowne by the name of Black Soape (page 23) to bee made only of fish oile and of soote[yy] according to the medicinable use and auntient kinde of makeing thereof without other mixture.[zz]

But because 'great quantities of tallough and stuffe have binn of late yeares spent by Soapeboylers in the makeing of soape, which (as they conceive) hath been a meanes to the greate enhaunceinge of the price thereof, *and of candles*', they think fit

that the Soapeboylers bee restrained from the use and expence of *English tallough* as formerly they have been [*accustomed*], *and to make their provision elsewheare as they shall have occasion.*

III

We turn next to the organized searches for *vinegar* for which we were mainly responsible prior to 1577 and, so far as our knowledge extends, to our dealings in *herring*, butter and cheese.

Vinegar, as we know, was an important branch of the chandlers' trade. We have learnt how early in the fourteenth century *searches for sauces* were being conducted by members of our Company,[a] and how, towards the close, it appears to have been the custom for one of our men to accompany the Vintners in their searches for wines, when the viewing party was directed to survey 'vinegar and sauces' kept in the shops and cellars of chandlers.[b] It later became the practice for the Vintners to 'present' wines which they considered unfit to drink to the Tallow Chandlers for them to ascertain whether such wines were suitable *as vinegar for making sauce.* We do not know how long this practice had prevailed. There is a record in the *Journal* early in the fifteenth century that

---

yy   'Soot'. A black carbonaceous substance or deposit consisting of fine particles formed by the combustion of coal, wood, oil, or other fuel. *O.E.D.*

zz   *Commentary*, p. 234.

a   See Volume II, pp. 42, 43. The searchers included Roger de Cloville, a prominent member of one of the parish fraternities (Volume III, pp. 32, 33).

b   Volume II, p. 46.

wines 'not good and fine' are to be thrown away.[135] But inspection had evidently become an established custom by the middle of the next century. There is an entry on 27th November 1543 recording that *'the Wardeyns of the Talough Chaundelers'* have been *'sworne for the serche & survey of suche wynes'*, as were presented at the Court a week earlier,[136] and in the following week they state in their report[137] that these 'eager[e] (or eger) wines', as they are called a little later, are 'so evyll & vnholsome that they are nott mete to be occupyed, or applyed *to eny good vse* butt onely to be cast awey . . .'[d] From an entry in November, 1551[138] it seems that our rejection of these unwholesome wines was not an uncommon occurrence at that time. But in the spring of 1553, on receiving our report,[139] the Court agreed

that *parte thereof* which they (the Wardens) dyd presente not to be holsome for mans bodye shuld be ordryd accordynge to the lawe And that they shuld have *the resydewe thereof* of the owners of the same/att reasonable prices *to make sawce therof.*

In November 1555 we are given (for the first time) the names of the searchers,[140] of whom the first two, namely Richard Dowset (or Dowcett) and Richard Eve (or Ive, as he signs his Will) were members of the Livery in 1537–8.[e] William Dobson (whose name appears in Group III) comes next, followed by Roger Pynfolde and Hugh Beney (Benney). Dowset, Eve and Dobson were all substantial property owners. Dowset, who died in 1562, had 'lands and tenements in the parish of St Mary Magdalene nigh Bermondsey, County Surrey' which he left on his wife's death to the Master and Wardens of the Tallow Chandlers Company, subject to certain charitable trusts in favour of poor men's children of the parish of St Olave in Southwark, and he gave to the Livery of the Company 30s. 'to be delivered them' the day of his burial 'for a recreation to be merry withall'.[141] Eve (a Warden in 1545)[142] had lands and tenements in the parish of St

---

c   O.F. *Aigre*, sharpe, keen, sour. *O.E.D*

d   *Commentary*, p. 234.

e   See Volume III, Appendix F.

Fig. 6. Bermondsey. Old Conventual buildings.

Dunstan in the East and also in Essex. He gave to his colleague Hugh Beney, 'a silk hat of the price of 8s.' Like Dowset and many others, he left a small sum of money 'for a recreation' and he made gifts to the Company's poor box and to the Yeomanry.[143] Dobson (Governor of the Yeomanry from 1554 to 1557), who died, as did Eve in 1558, held property in different parts of London, including a 'capital messuage' in Botolph Lane,[f] which he disposed of by a separate will of lands.[144] Roger Pynfolde, having been Governor of the Yeomanry in 1552–3, soon afterwards incurred a fine 'for certain disobediences by him showed unto the Wardens and Assistants'.[145] Nothing appears to be known of his private life. Hugh Beney was Governor of the Yeomanry in 1559–60 and Master of the Company from 1571 to 1573. He too was in trouble with our Court on one reported occasion. In January 1566, when Upper Warden, he was called upon to answer for 'being here present and *afterwards departing without just cause.'*[146] The outcome is not recorded. Beney is one of our few prominent members of whose private life very

---

f   Named after the church of St Botolph, Billingsgate, on the south side of Thames Street, destroyed in the Great Fire of London and not rebuilt. See *Harben*.

little is known, and no will has been traced. These five men were sworn

to searche and trye whate quantyty and sortes of the eger and defectyve wynes that the vynteners sworne shall fynde and presente not to be perfecte to be drunken may saufely be usyd for vyneger or for eny other good use ...

Following a search by the Vintners in December (1555)[147] the Wardens and others of the 'fealowshippe of Talloughechaundelers' made their presentment[148] declaring

whate parte thereof may saufely be applyed to the makynge of sauce and other good uses/and further declarynge that part of the saide defectyve wynes presentyd by the saide vynteners *were conveyed away oute of and frome the sighte of theym the said talloughechaundelers* ...

In November of the following year there is a long report by our Company[149] giving the names of numerous traders having wines which have been 'presented' by the Vintners as 'not meate to be dronken' together with the places where such wines can be inspected,[g] among which traders we notice a mercer, a salter and several haberdashers as well as a number of vintners and coopers and a few 'merchant-strangers'.[150] The search was a satisfactory one for the Tallow Chandlers, all the wines being reported as '*good for sawse*', except at one Inn, where the searchers found 'none marked with the Vynteners marke'.[h]

That year there were eight searchers,[151] among whom were Dowsett, Dobson and Beney, the others being Henry Ive (or Eve), John Bedyll, Edwarde Gregory, William Prowtyne, and William Crokes (Crookes). Except for John Bedyll, of whom nothing further appears to be known,[i] we have a good deal of varied information regarding these men. Henry Eve (Governor of the Yeomanry in 1558–9), who died in 1560, 'willed' that the Master and the Wardens of his Company should come to his

---

g   The names and addresses of numerous inns, hosteleries and cellars in different parts of the City are mentioned in this entry, and in other sixteenth century entries in the *Repertories*, which do not appear in *Harben*.

h   *Commentary*, p. 234.

i   *Commentary*, p. 234.

burial *with all the rest* of his 'clothing',[j] and he bequeathed 'unto them, for their pains taken, to be spent in a banquet 40*s*'. He had a leasehold house, in which he lived, as well as a 'workhouse' in Fetter Lane, both of which he left to his wife for life.[152] He appears to have been one of two Wardens of our Company who are recorded in the minutes of the Court of Aldermen for 11th July 1538 as having failed without excuse to attend the Court when summoned, for which they were committed to ward.[153] His name does not appear in any group in the list of 1537–8, indicating, perhaps, that his period of office in the Company was short. Edward Gregory, a senior Liveryman in 1537–8,[k] was Master from 1549 to 1551. He was the vendor of two messuages, etc. in Redcross Street,[l] St Giles Cripplegate in 1559,[154] but no will has been traced. In January 1566, being then 'an ancient Assistant' of our Court, he was in disgrace for 'not coming upon lawful summons according to orders *divers times*', for which he was committed 'with the assent of the Wardens and Assistants' *by the Mayor's officer to prison*[155] until he should be 'reformed in himself'.[m] Another Assistant was committed at the same time for his absence, our Court agreeing that such punishment, when merited, should continue to be 'justly executed . . . without any favour or affection'. William Prowtyn, another liveryman, of whom we know very little, died in 1563 having made a will leaving, among other gifts, 'his best cloak' to Hugh Beney, but not disposing of any property interests.[156] The name of William Crookes (or Croke) appears in group III of our members in 1537–8 and in the Yeomanry list for 1538–9.[157] He and his wife Elizabeth appear to have owned (in the 'forties) the property known as the Saracen's (Sarsons) Head,[158] south out of Little Carter Lane in the parish of St Mary Magdalene,[n] as well as other

---

j   His brother Liverymen. See Appendix B.

k   See Volume III, Appendix F, group II.

l   North from No. 1 Fore Street to Barbican. In Cripplegate Ward Without. (See *Commentary*, p. 234.)

m   *Commentary*, p. 234.

n   In the ward of Castle Baynard. First mentioned in 1544. *Harben*.

properties in the City.[159] He is known to have been a Warden in July 1563[160] and an Assistant in March 1565,[161] in neither of which offices can he be said to have had a blameless record. While a Warden he was engaged in a controversy with another Livery-man, when 'unseemly words' were spoken between them in a Tavern and elsewhere, as a result of which they were bound over, each in the sum of £5, not to 'revile, check, slander or otherwise misuse the other of them by word or deed, either privily or openly . . . and so from henceforth to continue *lovers and friends*'.[o] Later, while an Assistant, he was found guilty of not keeping the secrets of the Court, for which he was 'dismissed the assembly' until such time as there should be found an amendment and reformation in his conduct.[162] It was over five years before he was 'restored to his former place and sitting' among the Assistants.[163]

The searchers in December 1557[164] were again Richard Eve, Henry Eve, Roger Pynfolde and William Crookes, accompanied by Richard (probably William) Prowtyne and William (probably Walter) Westmoreland (Governor of the Yeomanry from 1561 to 1564) who was to become Master in 1575. His name appears in the third group of members in the list of 1537-8, but his is a case of another prominent member of our Company of whose private life little is known.

Separate searches by Vintners and Tallow Chandlers continue year after year and there are entries in our books of expenses incurred by our searchers on such occasions.[p] On 20th July 1559, our Wardens are to 'peruse and trye how moche' of the wines presented by the Vintners '*wyll serve to make vyneger*',[165] and a week later they produce their certificate of the 'eger wines' that they consider suitable for that purpose,[166] when the Court declares

that *all the resydue* of the same eger wynes not beinge holsome for man's body shalbe pored out into the cannells in Chepesyde and other markett places of

---

o   *Commentary*, p. 234.

p   *Commentary*, p. 234.

this Cytie accordynge to the auncyent lawes and customes of this Cytie in that behalf.

On 6th February 1560[167] specific instructions are given that the common cryer shall cause all the 'vessells' of the eager wines condemned by the Vintners 'upon their auncyent accustomyd yerely serche' and rejected by our searchers to be

conveyed and brought upon Saterday next into Chepesyde and there/after the old accustomed maner/and in the usyall place/to be layed downe/and the hedds of the sayd vessells then and there to be broken out and the sayd wynes to be pored downe into the cannell/and so to be consumed and dystroyed without damage of any maner person.

In November 1561 our search is conducted by 'John King & *the rest of the wardens*',[168] when the party bring in their presentment,[169] by which

it doth apeare that albeit the saide wynes be not mete to be droncken yet they are swete and will serve very well to make sauce of.

John King (or Kynge), to whom we were introduced as *Master* in January 1562 (p. 32), when he became responsible for dealing with defective oil, was in fact already Master at this time.[q] His name appears in Group II of our list of 1537–8 and in the Yeomanry list for 1538–9, but his is another case of a member of our Company holding a prominent position, for whom no will has been traced, although we know he had a brother, William Kynge, of St Mathew, Friday Street, who made a will in 1560 appointing him his executor and leaving him £10 and a satin doublet.[170]

In the following year (1562) there is (exceptionally) a combined search by Vintners, Tallow Chandlers *and Coopers* of 'certein wynes of a strainger cellered in a longe celler upon Grenberys Key (or Quay)'[r] brought into Court by the Wardens of the Coopers,[171] when the viewing party is instructed to report

whether the same be able and holsome to be dronken, or eles to make sawse of.

---

q   *Commentary*, p. 235.

r   The situation of this Quay is not known. There was, however, a Greenberry (or Barrow) Hill adjoining Primrose Hill on the north side of Regent's Park. *Wheatley*.

In November 1564 our Wardens are 'to taste and try whether the wines presented by the Vintners be sour or not'.[172] Again in December 1568 they are to declare what quantity of old wines is sour'.[173]

In December 1572[174]

Richard Clerke, Thomas Astall and Robt. Atkinson wardens of the company of TallowChaundlers were this [day] *assigned to viewe* the corrupte wynes lately presented to this Courte by the wardens of the company of the vynteners sworne for that purpose & to present to this Courte howe moche of the same wyne shalbe mete for vynegar or *other holsome sauces.*

Clerke (Clarke or Clarck), of St Andrew Undershaft, was Master in 1580–1. He made a nuncupative will[s] during his year as Master, leaving all his goods 'moveable and imoveable' to his wife,[175] but it is not known whether he had any significant property interests. Astall was Governor of the Yeomanry from 1575 to 1577 (after having 'fined' for Warden in 1560)[176] and Master in 1587. We know nothing of his private life or how, in the early 'seventies, he came to be called a 'cosener' by a brother liveryman, for which the latter was fined.[177] He was followed in office as Master by Atkinson, Governor in 1578–9 (after fining for Renter Warden),[178] who was the owner some years before his death in 1590 of 'le Swanne with two necks[t]' in Goldinge lane, St Giles, Criplegate'.[179] This was the name given to several well-known inns in the City, of which the nearest to Golden Lane (leading out of the Barbican) was on the north side of Lad Lane, since swallowed up in what is now called Gresham Street. He made a will,[180] which does not mention this property by name, but does specifically mention his 'customary messuage or tenement *Brew-house,* commonly called the Bell, and the close of land thereto belonging in the parish of St Leonard, Shoreditch' which he left, together with two other houses adjoining, to his wife for life, with reversion to one of his sons, and ordered a valuation of 'his *brewing vessels* and coppers' *remaining in his said dwellinghouse.* He

---

s   Orally declared.

t   The name is a corruption of the name 'Swan with Two Nicks', the mark of the Vintners Company for their 'game of swans' on the Thames. *Harben.*

left £10 to one of his apprentices to be paid within one year next after the end of his term of years on condition that he be 'as good servant' to his wife, as he had been to the testator, and he directed her also to pay the boy his year's wages amounting to £10 8s. after his time of apprenticeship expired, he '*being brewer* and doing his duty'. This seems to be a rare example at the time of a tallow chandler being engaged in brewing, but in 1620 the practice was evidently fairly well established, for we learn of a Court order directing that Chandlers selling beer or ale are to be accounted 'un-licensed victuallers'.[181] The reader will recollect the translation of a brewer to our Company in the 'twenties of the fifteenth century,[u] and there was another such case in 1550.[182]

In November 1577 there is a report of what appears to be the last of the independent searches by Tallow Chandlers before the Elizabethan Patent of that year came into force. On that date an Inquest of office was ordered[183] to inquire

whether all suche *viniger* lately presentyd by the Wardens of the Companye of the tallowe chaundlers to be evell and corrupte, and not holsom for mannes bodye, be defectyve or not. And that such vinigre as by the sayd enqueste shalbe founde evell or corrupte, to be forthwyth broughte to the Guyldhall of this Cytie, there to be by the dyscreacion of Mr. Chamberlyn orderyd and dysposyd, *accordinge unto the auncyente lawes and customes of this Cytie in suche lyke cases used and accustomyd*.

It only remains to say on the subject of vinegar that, among the regrettably numerous sixteenth century members of the Company, being candle-makers, who, as we shall see, were later found guilty of breaking the law, were several of the men whom we have met in this Chapter.

Our knowledge of the Company's dealings in *herring* is scanty. Salters, as the main purveyors of salt, might have been expected to control, with the Fishmongers, the sale of '*red herring*'[v] in

---

u   Volume III, p. 23.

v   *Harang sore* (L. Bk. G, p. 221) A herring having red colour from being cured by smoking. O.E.D. 'Red herrings' were ungutted herrings, hard salted and then hung in kilns for several weeks over smouldering sawdust fires, and were once popular in England, but are now mainly exported to the Mediterranean and the Levant. *Encyclopaedia Britannica*, Edn. of 1968, Vol. 9, p. 360.

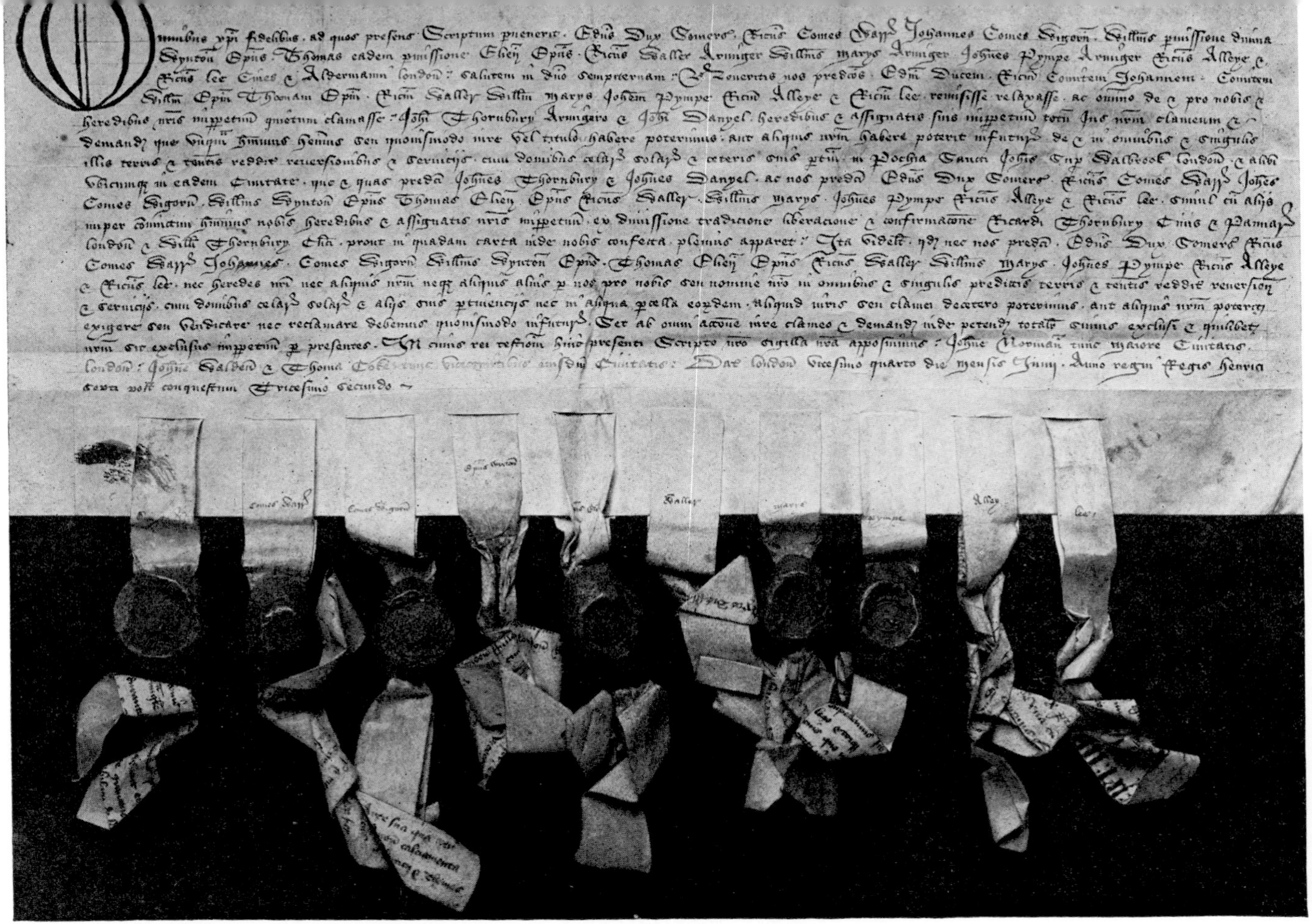

Plate III. Deed of 24th June 1454 in the series relating to the purchase of the Hall site, bearing the seals of Edmund, Duke of Somerset, Richard, Earl of Warwick (the wax dinted with his thumb mark), Thomas, Bishop of Ely, and others.

Facing page 48]

particular, and there is indeed an early fifteenth century record of the former having agreed to sell 'six herings for one penny during Lent and to supply the City sufficiently with herrings until Easter', although enjoined 'not to sell either fresh or red Herrings at their stalls',[184] but to go in their accustomed places only.[185] But, towards the close of the century, we find an entry recording that the Wardens of the Fishmongers, Salters *and Tallow Chandlers* are to make search in their several crafts what store of herrings is among them, both white[w] and red.[186] Early in the next century there is a Court order setting the price of red herring at five for a penny until further notice 'provided the poor people shall have three for half penny'.[187] Frequent orders and proclamations follow fixing the prices, sometimes of white and red herring and sometimes of white or red alone,[x] and there is an early recognizance *binding tallow chandlers* before Easter to sell eight red, and six white, herrings for a penny.[188] *Grocers* and Salters were similarly bound.

In March 1523 we have further positive evidence of a tallow chandler dealing in herring,[189] when Robert Heron, or Herne,

because he hath retayled heryng contrary tothe commaundement & price of my Lorde Mayer & other misdemeaners,

was committed to the prison of Newgate, where he appears to have spent the week-end in reflection, after which, presumably as a condition of his release, he and his wife and servants were bound by recognizance thereafter[190] to

obserue & kepe my lorde Mayers price of Candell *Rede & Whyte Herynges* & of all other thynges & Vitalles that he or they shall sell & the same sell nott aboue the seid price.

In January 1535 there is an entry recording that 'the Talowgh-chaundelers have certyfyed thys courte *what salte store of fysshe*

---

w   *Harang blank* (*L. Bk. G*, p. 221) 'White herring' a (a) fresh herring, (b) herring salted but not smoked. *O.E.D.*

x   *Commentary*, p. 235.

remayn yn theyre handes',[191] an entry which immediately follows a record of certificates by the Fishmongers, Salters and Ironmongers[y] of their respective stores of fish.[192] In the last years of
Philip and Mary (1557–8) there is a Mayoral Proclamation[193]

Fig. 7. Gold sovereign of Queen Mary.

styled 'A Proclamation for Vyctualles', the object of which was
to ensure the sale 'at reasonable rates and pryces', both by citizens
and 'forrens', of various commodities, which included tallow
candles, cheese, butter and herring dealt in by tallow chandlers
and other persons using their 'art or occupacion', those dealing in
herring being compelled to sell no fewer

red hearynges then fyve for 1d/nor any fewer whyte hearynges than fowre for
jd/vpon payne of imprysonment of there bodyes at the dyscrecion of the said
lorde mayer and Aldermen for the tyme beyng.

'Herring' is one of the commodities included in the article in
our Ordinances of 1538 regulating 'bargains', to which we have
referred in relation to oil (p. 31), although not specifically mentioned among the objects to be *searched*, but, apart from the
comparatively few entries which we have cited as linking our
Company with the trade in herring, our activities in the fish
market do not seem to have attracted the notice of the civic
authorities to any marked extent.

As for our dealings in *cheese*, again very little is known. Our
young friend David Tompkins (or Tomkyn)[z] is on record as a

y   There seems no reason for the inclusion of ironmongers, unless it be the hooping
of barrels as suggested in note *ii* (p. 28).

z   Volume III, p. 35.

buyer of 'Grene Chese' from Suffolk in 1521, the price of which
was fixed by the Mayor,[194] but no dealings with cheese by any
other tallow chandler have been traced. There was an ancient guild
of Cheesemongers in the City, whose Ordinances were approved
by the Mayor and Aldermen in 1377. These cheesemongers were
invited to devise and ordain how the price of 'cheese and butter
might be amended'. Their proposed articles, which were adopted,
made provision for 'foreigners' to bring their wares to certain
markets and nowhere else. Others who had made a practice of
bringing wares by water for sale in secret to 'hokesters'[aa] and
forestallers, regrators and 'bersters'[bb] were now to bring their
goods to one of the markets. Cheese from Wales in particular
was not to be housed in 'Fletstrete and in Holbourne' for sale in
secret, and 'hokesters' were not to be allowed to buy up cheese
and butter from 'foreigners' before 'the commonalty' was
served.[195] Nearly two hundred years later, in an Act of Common
Council recorded in the *Journal* in 1570,[196] 'diverse and sondry
persones' in the City and liberties and suburbes of the same

of there gredy and covetuose mynde and for theire owne singular and pryvate
gayne and comoditie/to thentente to enhaunce and raise the prises of cheese
and butter,

are said to have commonly resorted to the country, and there to
have

bought regrated and ingrossed grete quantities of *butter and chese* that shoulde
have bynne brought to the Cytte of London by the makers and gethers therof/
to be solde at reasonable prices/and the same have brought and conveid to the
said Cyttie to the intent to sell the same agayne by retaile and at excessive
prices . . .

Such persons being freemen, or inhabiting or dwelling in the
City, were forbidden to buy butter or cheese in the country for
sale by retail in the City under the penalty of forfeiture. Again

---

aa   Huckster: A retailer of small goods, in a petty shop or booth, or at a stall; a pedlar,
a hawker . . . 1641.BEST Farm Bks. (Surtees) 29 'Wee buy our molten tallowe of the
hucksters and tripe wives'. [cf. 'butter wives'. *infra*] O.E.D.

bb   Hucksters, male or female; more generally called '*birlsters*' or '*burlsters*'. Riley
Memorials p. 406 (footnote). (See note *aa*.)

no Crafts are mentioned as dealers. On the contrary, it is 'the farmers, makers, gatherers and owners' who are to bring these commodities 'at their owne costes and charges' to the City for sale. Prices, as we see, are to be 'reasonable', and there is some evidence of price control.[197] The provisions of the Act were not new. Orders had been given in the 'fifties that persons 'going down into the country to buy butter and cheese' were to be disfranchised.[198] The City seems to have adopted a policy different from that prevailing in the rest of the country. An Act, 3 & 4 Edward VI. c. 21 (AD 1549–50) stipulated that no person might buy butter or cheese to sell again *otherwise than by retail in open shops*,[199] an enactment which was repealed by an Act 21 Jac. I. c. 22 (AD 1623–4) in so far as it extended to Cheesemongers or *Tallow Chandlers* free of the City of London brought up as apprentices trading in butter and cheese,[200] but the reference to our Craft seems to be an isolated one. An Act passed in the reign of William and Mary, 4 Gul. & Mar. c. 6, 7 (AD 1692), to deal with the weighing of butter and cheese and the packing of butter[201] mentions only the cheesemongers.[cc]

Barrelled butter is, nevertheless, among the articles included in the Elizabethan Patent, and it seems from an entry in our minutes in 1559[202] that some of our men were accustomed to deal in this commodity.[dd] In May 1574[203] the Court of Aldermen made an Order

that noe barell butter shalbe hereafter solde in the marketts of this Cyttye, but that suche barellyd and *salte butter* shalbe solde owte of the retaylors shopps as hathe byne accustomyd,

and it is evident from our Wardens and Yeomanry accounts that, towards the close of the century, we were disturbed by the operation of others breaking this law. The accounts for 1586–7 record the payment of 45s. 'layed out about the suit for to have those that sold salt butter *out of* the market.'[204] A little later our Clerk (Francis Kydd) was paid 12d. 'for his painstaking in writing

---

cc   *Commentary*, p. 235.

dd   *Commentary*, p. 235.

of the names of the sellers',[205] and warrants were obtained for
putting out these butter sellers *and others*.[206] It seems that our
Warden, Christopher Nodding, whom we shall meet again,
was actively engaged in this matter.[207] Six or seven years later
a payment was made to the Lord Mayor's officers *'for suppressing
of the Butter Sellers'*[208] after several attendances on his
Lordship.[209]

From the *Yeomenry Account Book*, as well as from the
Wardens' accounts, it is clear that *the Yeomanry* played an important role in this business. At a Court attended by the Governor,
Wardens, etc. of the Yeomanry, held on 18th July 1588,[210] it
was agreed

> that the warrant and Commission in writing obtained by the Wardens of the
> Company of Tallow Chandlers and to this said Company directed under the
> hands of Sir George Bonde, Knt., now Lord Mayor, shall be executed and the
> contents of the same duly performed by the Wardens [of the Yeomanry] that
> now be, viz; Randall Carter,[ee] who is appointed for the Markets at Leadenhall,
> Gracechurch and in the Borough of Southwark, and such of the Assistants and
> other of the Yeomanry as are set down in a Bill to the number of 15 delivered
> to the said Randall Carter/and also by William Yomans one other of the
> Wardens who is appointed for the Markets in Cheapside and in Newgate
> Market and such of the Assistants and other of the Yeomanry as are set down . . .
> That either of the said Wardens shall every market day with the aid of two
> of the Assistants to him appointed diligently go and attend in the markets to
> him assigned *and see to the reformation of the disordered persons* and matters
> contained in the said Warrant . . .

Randall Carter was a Southwark man, who died in 1615 leaving
his 'lease and term of years' in his dwellinghouse and soaphouse
in the liberty of 'the Clink',[ff] which, as we have seen (p. 27) he
rented from the Company, together with the 'goods, household
stuff and implements' therein, to his wife for life and on her death
to his kinsman Thomas Waller,[211] who later obtained a direct

---

ee   Governor 1613-4.

ff   The Bishop of Winchester's liberty or manor known as the Clink consisted of about
70 acres, most of which were included in the park attached to Winchester House, the
Bishop's palace. The liberty extended north to the Thames, west to Christ Church or
Paris Garden, east to St Saviour's Dock, south to the boundary of St George's parish.
The mansion of John de Mowbray was here in 1363, but the locality was known as
the Stews Bank, notwithstanding that it contained houses of distinguished persons.
Wheatley.

lease.[212] Nothing seems to be known of the other Warden named in the Yeomanry records.

We learn from the Yeomanry accounts for 1602–3 that our Clerk, Thomas Hiccock, obtained a copy of an Act of Common Council[213] 'concerning stragglers'*gg*, and about the same time a warrant was procured from the Lord Mayor 'for suppressing of stragglers selling wares about the streets', in which business the Recorder of London, the Town Clerk, certain attornies and 'other officers' were all engaged.[214] In one case two men were caught 'straggling'*hh* about the streets with wares.[215]

In March 1606[216] we find the Yeomanry concerned in following

the cause of the restraint of *Hawkers*[ii] that go up and down the streets to sell wares,

and about two years later we read of a petition to the Court of Aldermen touching the *Butter Sellers*.[217] Hawkers had long attracted the attention of the civic authorities. An early example occurs in 1480 when a Precept was issued against 'foreigners selling in the open streets'.[218] Early in the 'sixties of the next century there was a Proclamation against unlicensed hawkers of flesh, fruit and other victuals,[219] and in certain Wards those who were licensed were bound to have their badges openly hanging upon their breasts.[220] Commencing with the accounts for 1613–14 there are numerous entries in our books recording that the Company has obtained warrants for the apprehension of hawkers.[221] Petitions were brought by other companies against hawkers of various wares,[222] and in our Yeomanry accounts for 1622–3[223] there is a record of £7 18s. 10d. having been received from 'divers persons using the Mystery of Tallow Chandlers (presumably strangers) towards repressing hawkers *not being Free of this Incor-*

---

gg   Straggler: A merchant who intrudes into a market without licence to trade there; an interloper. *O.E.D.*

hh   Straggling: Trading in a market, of which the merchant is not free. *O.E.D.*

ii   Hawker: A man who goes from place to place selling his goods or who cries them in the streets. *O.E.D.* It was the settled policy of the City to discourage such traffic.

poration' (note *gg*). More than thirty years earlier we had been engaged in a 'suit to the Lord Mayor[224] about the *Butter Wives*' (note *aa*, p. 51). Many of the hawkers and stragglers, of whom we read in the first quarter of the century, were no doubt engaged in hawking candles or molten tallow (note *aa*), but it seems fair to assume that others were butter sellers.

One other commodity, namely 'honye', remains to be mentioned, although its inclusion, along with 'oyles, hering and talough', in the article on 'Bargains' in our Ordinances of 1538 cannot satisfactorily be accounted for. Bee-keeping was practised in this country not only for the production of wax, but also for the honey, both honey and wax being collected from the hive. A great deal of beeswax was imported,[225] but honey is specifically mentioned and its sale in England controlled, along with wax, by an Act of 1581.[226] The Wax Chandlers had the exclusive right to deal in wax, and logically they might well be expected to deal also in honey. It seems that, in naming honey in our Ordinances, our forbears may have intended to encroach on one of the preserves of the wax-chandler, but there appears to be no evidence that they actually did so. We believe that only in the matter of *links* and *staff torches* were the two companies ever seriously at variance, and that the dispute did not last long. An account of this troublesome affair will be found in Appendix G.

Tallow and Candle

I

WE have seen the price of tallow in 1530 at 12s. 6d. the wey, and of candles at 1¼d. the pound, with thirteen pounds for the dozen (p. 12). We have yet to consider the subject of the *wick*. We saw from an order of Common Council in 1473 that wicks had then to be made entirely of cotton.[a] We learn from a certificate given to the Court of Aldermen in April 1534 that Mercers, Grocers and Drapers all dealt in wick material. The spun cotton was priced at xd. the pound and the 'wool' (raw cotton) at vid or vijd.[1] On 17th April 1537 we find our Wardens being called upon to certify 'what cotton, talough & candell remayn yn theyre handes & others'.[2] But two days later we get the first intimation that it had become lawful by this time to make wicks *not consisting wholly of cotton*.[3] The Court order, which set the price at 1¼d. the pound 'bare', required the candles to be made 'the one half cotton *and the other half weeke*', and this direction was repeated in April of the following year in the Mayoralty of Sir Richard Gresham.[4] In 1473 it was apparent that 'wick', in the context, meant spun cotton;[b] in the new orders it is evident that it is being given a new and specialized meaning, and what is meant by 'half cotton and *half wick*' becomes clear from the minute of a 'bill' presented by our Company in May 1538 requiring that 'all makers of candells as well Tallough Chaundelers as others' may be bound to

---

a   Volume II, p. 57.

b   Ibid., pp. 57–8.

put in theire small candell one threede^c of cotton *and one of weeke* And so in lyke wyse in other greate candell *as many threedes of the one as of the other.*

The bill, of which there appears to be no other record, is reported as having been read at a meeting of the Court on 14th May.[5] It is presented in the form of a petition

of suche as be not serued of Talloughe for thys year to make candelles of whiche they cannot doe by reason that other of other Companyes occupyinge makynge of candelles engross the same,

a complaint which is reminiscent of that made in our Wardens' bill considered by the Court in 1524 (p. 9). This stipulation that candles should contain an equal number of threads of cotton as of wick appears two days later[6] in a recognizance entered into by our Master, John Hampton, and three of the Wardens, for themselves 'and euerye of theyre Companye',[d] and it occurs again[7] in the following July.[e] Thus, by 1538, the word 'wick' had become descriptive of a kind of thread *inferior to cotton.*

Fig. 8. Gold crown of Henry VIII.

In April 1540 it is reported that the Tallow Chandlers have 'confessyd' that they have 'provyded cotton for theyr candelles' *and that they have promised 'to make candelles with Cotton & weeke as afore hath been provyded.'*[8] The price of tallow had remained constant for the past ten years at 12*s*. 6*d*. the wey and *of candles at* 1¼*d. the pound*, and in November[9] our Wardens

---

c 'Thread' is defined as a fine cord composed of the fibres or filaments of flax, cotton, wool, silk, etc. . . . specifically such a cord composed of two or more 'yarns'. *esp.* of flax, twisted together (Yarn. Originally spun fibre as of cotton, silk, wool, flax . . .). *O.E.D.*

d *Commentary*, p. 235.

e *Commentary*, p. 235.

promise the Court that 'they & theyr Company' will serve the
City 'of good candelles' at that price 'accordyng to their recognysaunce therfor made tempore Mr Gresham, Mayer.'[f] In the
following May 'a derthe of talough candelles' is reported and the
Court agrees that four Butchers, 'and two of the Company of
Taloughchaundelers' named Blake & Cuttle[g] with a grocer and
a salter, in company with two Aldermen, shall consult together
and report.[10] Five days later 'the cawses of the derth of Talough
& the naughtyness of talough candell' are debated, after which
it is agreed that the Butchers and the Tallow Chandlers shall each
bring in 'a boke' giving particulars of all sales and purchases of
tallow.[11] We are not told the result, but on 5th April 1543 our
Company renews its promises to the Court.[12] We read that the
Butchers have undertaken to sell their tallow 'onthyssyde' the
feast of Easter for xijs. vid the wey & not above and that the
Wardens of the Tallow Chandlers

for theym & theyr hole Companye haue vndertaken that they fromhensforth
shall see the seyd Cytye suffycyently seruyd of *good candell* by all the seyd tyme
for jd q^r (1¼d.) the pounde & not aboue/and that they shall make the weke
of all suche Candell both of cotton & *threde*[h] & further use theym selfes in
euery poynt accordyng to the condycion of theyr recognisaunce here taken &
made for the same xvj° Maij A° 30 H8[i]

As we have seen[j] the Butchers had frequently to be reminded
that they must maintain adequate stocks of tallow for candle-
making. In the first week of May 1541 'dyuerse Bochers & other
persons' were accused by our Wardens of 'sellyng & also regrat-
yng of Talow' contrary to the laws of the City[13] and a few days
later the Court decrees[14]

---

f   The recognizance of 16th May 1538. (Supra, note *d*.)

g   The Christian names of these tallow chandlers are omitted, but the men were
     evidently Richard Blake, one of the three Wardens bound by the recognizance of the
     previous year, who was to become Master in 1541, and Thomas Cuttle, who succeeded
     him in 1544 (p. 13).

h   Here we see the word 'wick' being given its natural meaning and the word 'threat'
     (instead of 'wick'), being used for the inferior article.

i   Note *f* (supra).

j   Volume III, pp. 59, 61.

that the bochers shalbe bounden to serue the Citye of Talowe for xij.s. vjd. the wey and not aboue from hensforth/And shall delyuer to the Talough-chaundelers of this Citye *all the same Talowe to make candell therewith* . . .

In April 1542[15] the Butchers' Wardens were commanded that they and all their Company should sell and utter all their tallow 'to the Talough-Chaundelers of this cytye onely *and not to eny foreyn or foreyns vntyll the fest of Ester next coming*',[k] which suggests that stocks were shortly expected to become more plentiful, an impression which was confirmed a year later when there was a baffling departure both from the customary practice of confining supplies to candlemakers and from the usual rule forbidding butchers to make candles except for their own use.[l] At a meeting of the Court in April, 1543[16] the Wardens of the Butchers declared in the presence of the Wardens of the Tallow Chandlers

that they had moche Talough remayninge in their handes & in the handes of their Companye/which the same wardens of the Taloughchaundelers & their Companye & other vsynge the feate & Crafte of making of candell . . . *refusyed to bye* & take of theym att the pryce of xijs vjd the weye

The Court was reminded by the Butchers that 12s. 6d. was the price set by the 'mutuall consentes of the Wardens' of the two companies only three weeks earlier, and they desired thereupon that they

might make candell of their seid Taloughe so nowe remayninge/ & that her-after shall remayne in their handes/ & put the same to sale within this Cytie & the suburbes thereof/*withoute punyshment or offence* of the seid wardeyns of the Taloughchaundelers or of eny lawe acte or ordennaunce . . . to the contrarye . . .

The request was granted '*with free consent of the Wardens of the Tallow Chandlers*' on condition that the complainants

make good stuff & utter the same at the lorde Mayers pryce for the tyme beinge.

A breach of our Company's undertaking that the City should be served with 'good candles' has alas to be recorded within the

---

k   *Commentary*, p. 235.

l   *Commentary*, p. 235.

year. On 11th December[17] our Wardens brought into Court

certeyn candelles whiche they vpon theyr serche have founde *aswell amongest their owne Company* as other that vse to make candelles within this Cytye to be putt to sale/*Whiche be clerely forfeyted for that they be made all of weke without eny cotton & also of very evyll stuffe* contrary to the lawes & ordynaunces of this Cytye . . .

All offenders in other companies were warned to attend the Court '*to be bounden by lyke recognysaunce as the Tallow Chaundelers be*', and we read two days later[18] that seven salters, two cutlers, three leathersellers, a wax chandler, a saddler, a vintner, a tailor, a fishmonger, and a barber, as well as the widow of a soap-maker, all dealing in tallow, have bound themselves to 'make all suche Talowe as shall come to theyr severall handes & possessyon gotten within this Cytie & the libertyes of the same into Candelles *And* [*to*] *make all the same candelles of good stuff & nott of eny maner of flottyce or other naughty stuffe*' And to

put in to euery of theyr small candelles one threde of Cotton *att the least*/And into euery of theyr grett candels asmany thredes of Cotton as they putt of weke.

This seems to be the last time that we hear of wicks, in the accepted sense, being made partly of cotton and partly of inferior thread. A fortnight earlier, that is to say on 29th November (1543),[19] the Wardens of the Tallow Chandlers had been required to secure the attendance before the Mayor and Aldermen 'at the next Court day' of

all theyr Company & all other persons vsyng the occupacion of makyng of Tallough Candelles within this Citye & the libertyes of the same to be putt to sale . . . *for the reformacion of the weke & price of the same for theyr candelles.*

In speaking of the reformation of the wick, it would appear that the subject for discussion among candle-makers was the mixture of inferior thread with cotton, but there seems to be no record of the matter having actually been debated. When the Court meets on 4th December it is to read to the Wardens of the Tallow Chandlers and others[m] 'the Condycion of the recognisaunce' of

---

m   'Dyverse other of the same felowship', as well as two salters, two leathersellers, and a saddler.

16th May 1538 (p. 57) and 'after monycion and charge', to bind them 'truely to observe euery poynt of the seyd condycion'.[20] Again, when calling the offenders together on 13th December (1543), the Aldermen were evidently insisting on the mixture as before![21] But, in April 1548, when candles are next mentioned, the only reference to the wick is that it shall be 'good weke',[22] and when, a year later, we find a reference to *cotton candell*[23] we suspect that there has been a change of policy. We are not surprised, therefore, to learn from two entries in the *Repertory* Book in November 1551 that we are indeed entering a new era during which a clear distinction is drawn between *different kinds of candles*. Moreover, on the 5th, when the price of candles is set at $1\frac{3}{4}d.$ the pound, an exception is made of *watchynge candle*[n] which the Court is content shall be sold 'for ijd. the pound and not above',[24] and, less than a fortnight later, tallow chandlers and other candlemakers are forbidden to 'make eny candell from hensforth of *clene cotton above vi in the li (pound)*', and they may not 'sel any of theym above ijd q^a ($2\frac{1}{4}d.$) the li. upon payne of forfeyture of their Recognysaunce'.[25]

The price of *tallow* had been again set by the Court of Aldermen at 12s. 6d. the wey in the Spring of 1545.[26] There appears, however, to have been a meeting of our own Court very shortly afterwards to settle a private dispute between two of our men when the price for their 'bargain of tallow' was fixed 'by the Master and four Wardens' at 13s. for summer tallow and 13s. 4d. for winter tallow.[27] The purchaser was Gilbert Lawson whose name appears in Group III of the list of 1537–8 and in the yeomanry list of 1538–9. He may have been a Warden of the Yeomanry[o] in July 1538[28] and is seen from our accounts for 1551–3 to have fined for Renter Warden of the Company.[29] He died in 1552 leaving his son Richard and daughter Dorothy 'the third part' of all his goods 'according to the custom of the City of London'. It appears from his will that he had two leasehold

---

[n]   Watching-candle. A candle used at the 'watching' of a shrine or of a corpse . . . O.E.D. (See *Commentary*, p. 236.)

[o]   *Commentary*, p. 236.

houses,[30] in one of which he lived, but neither house has been identified.

In April 1547 the set price of tallow had risen to 17s. the wey with candles (apparently for the first time) at 1¾d. the pound;[31] next year it was 18s.[32] On 30th April 1549[33] it was assessed by the Court at 20s. the wey, with candles again at 1¾d. the pound, our Wardens being directed

> to call a courte at their hall & make answere here the next court daye whyther they & their companye be contentyed so to serve the Citie or not.

Tallow had fallen to 19s. the wey in April 1550,[34] but in March 1552 the price had again been set by the Court at 20s.[35] Then on 3rd November there comes a dramatic change, as we see from the following record,[36] which begins by setting the price of *candles*.

> Item It was this day agreid and orderyd that the Talough Chaundelers and other candle makers of this Cytie and lyberties thereof shall for certeyn consyderacions especyally movynge the Courte/and namely *in respecte of the great pryce of Talough and scarcytie of candle*/be permytted durynge the pleasure of the same courte to sell their *cotton candles* for iid. ob q^q (2¾d.) the pounde & *their other candles made with weke and watchynge candles* for iid. ob. (2½d.) the pounde and not above.

The order continues with a direction that they are to make 'all their seid candles' of good and clene Talough. It repeats the prohibition of the previous year against making any cotton candle above six in the pound and takes care of public demand by requiring suppliers to

> make suche store from henseforward of every of the seid sortes of candle that all the cytezens and inhabitauntes of this Cytie may alweyes be redely servyd of the same for the prices above recyted,

adding (for the customers' protection)

> *withoute takyng of sawse, sope or eny other thynge of any of theym*/but onely at their freewyll and pleasure.

Four years later it became necessary to repeat this last warning in two orders of the Court. The first (dated 15th October 1556) which directed that, when purchasing candles, no person should be compelled 'to take sawse or other thinge withall', was coupled with an order that tallow chandlers *'should denye not* to sell any persone any candell otherwyse then by the hole pound' under pain of imprisonment.[37] The second (dated 24th November 1556) bade them to 'put and hange oute theire candells in theire shoppes to be solde to the pore people and that they do not compell theym to take other thinges withall *as they have usid to do'.*[38]

The Butchers' price fixed by the order of the 3rd November 1552 is to be *'xxvi s. viiid. of curraunte money of Englond'* and they are not to

trye oute the beste and cleneste of their talough in to suet/in fraude and hynderaunce of the seid Talough chaundelers and candlemakers *in suche sorte as they of late have usyd.*

Next year (1553) the price of tallow has fallen to 21*s.* the wey,[39] and, for a time, candles are at 2*d.* the pound without any mention of different sorts.[40] Then, in April 1556, the customary distinction is made between cotton candles (at 2½*d.*) and those without cotton (at 2*d.*), rough tallow being 21*s.* as before.[41] In July it appears from a 'bill' brought in by the Butchers and from the Tallow Chandlers 'bill' in reply[42] that since 'Easter laste paste' the 'talloughchaundelers & other chandlemakers' have

receyved moche more talloughe than they have eyther made candles of or nowe have furthecommynge,

and, from a report made a fortnight later, that the Butchers have convinced the Court that, in again accepting a price of 21*s.*, they were over generous to their buyers. This is seen from an entry dated 12th August, which states that 'for certayne necessary and urgente consideracions and causes' it is agreed that until Michaelmas next 'the Talloughechaundelers and all other talloughe candle makers' shall pay *'xxiijs iiijd. the wey'* for their tallow, while the buyers also are successful in obtaining a higher price for their candles.[43] It is rare for such decisions to find their way into our own records, but our Clerk, Thomas Hone, evidently considered that this was a special occasion. In a minute on the following day in the Wardens' account book we are told that the Master and Wardens reported that the Lord Mayor and Court of Aldermen had given the Butchers *a higher price for tallow.*

He quotes the price of 23s. 4d., and also gives the prices at which candle-makers are now permitted to sell their three sorts of candles, in which respect he improves on the record of the clerk to the Court, who is content to state only the price of candles made 'without cotton', namely 2¼d. the pound.[44] This we note from another entry in the accounts is the price paid at this time by the Company for *'candles to work by'* ![45]

The mention in the Aldermanic record of 'travel and co-operation' between the two companies prepares us for the entry which follows on 12th November (1556)[46] recording the agreement of the Court

that the Wardens of the bochers shall put all suche matters as they inforemyd the Courte of here this day/where with all *they fele themselves grevyd* and the common welthe of this Cytye *annoyed*/in wrytynge and theire best advyses also for the remedy and reformacion of the same And that they then shall have the ayde of this Court therein.

Item Yt was orderyd that the Wardens of the Talloughechaundelers shalbe warnyd to be here the nexte Courte day *for thanswerynge of the matters obiected agaynst theyme by the saide Wardens of the bochers* and namely for the breache of the pryce of theire candle gevyn by this Courte.

The clerk is regrettably reticent on the subject of the Butchers' grievances and all we are told a few days later[47] is that their Wardens are to

devyse and put in wrytynge some good ordenaunces to be observyd and kepte by theyme and theire hole fealowshippe for the reformacion of soche mysorder and enemytye as they/the saide wardens/informyd the Courte of here this day . . . so that the same may be ratyfyed and confirmyd by this Courte/if they shall seame reasonable and proffytable for the common welthe of the Cyty.

It would appear from this entry that the Court has placed the blame on the Butchers for the matters in dispute, but again the clerk is silent. We may wonder what our suppliers would have thought a year or two later had they known of the back-door approach revealed in our Wardens' accounts,[48] from which we learn of the payment by 'Mr Westermerland and Mr Benye'[p] of forty shillings

---

p   Beney was Governor of the Yeomanry about this time, and Westmoreland followed him in 1561

to my Lord Mayor for the behoof of the Company *to the intent that the tallow might come into the Company's hands* (and not elswhere) at which request my Lord Mayor promised to be good unto the Company.*q*

Watching candles, although referred to by our Clerk in his minute of 13th August 1556, are not (as we see) mentioned in either of the Court orders of that year, and we read only of two sorts of candles for the next five or six years.*r* Of these,[49] the more expensive candles, varying in price from $2\frac{1}{4}d.$ to $3d.$ the pound are described sometimes as 'Cotton candles' or 'Candles made with cotton' but more often as 'candles made *holy* with cotton', while the cheaper candles, varying in price from $1\frac{3}{4}d.$ to $2\frac{1}{2}d.$, are described either as 'candles made with weke' or 'with weke *only*'.*s* It seems likely that the appearance in 1551 of watching candles *made of tallow* can be accounted for by the banning of candles from the Church at the Reformation, thus causing the Wax Chandlers to cease production. It may also be the case that

Fig. 9. Edward VI and his Council.

q   *Commentary*, p. 236.

r   *Commentary*, p. 236.

s   *Commentary*, p. 236.

E

their disappearance later from the record for a time is due to *the return of wax candles* through the influence of their Catholic Majesties Philip and Mary.[t] In April 1563 they re-appear and are mentioned in every entry giving the prices of tallow candles for the next twelve years[50] after which they are not heard of again.

II

The fluctuations, some of which we have already noticed in the price of tallow, are a feature of the times. The new setting of the price at 17s. in April 1547 had followed a period of relative stability. The rise may have been partly due to the debasement of the coinage which took place during the years 1542–51.[a] But,

Fig. 10. Process of coining. Sixteenth century.

whatever the cause, it appears to indicate that what has been called 'the price revolution' of the sixteenth century had secured a firm grip on the tallow trade by this date.[b] There were the usual seasonal changes, and the rise to 26s. 8d. in November 1552 was,

---

t   Commentary, p. 236.

a   Commentary, p. 237.

b   Commentary, p. 237.

as we have seen, not maintained. Having been as low as 21s., the price of rough tallow was set by the Court on 16th March 1559 at 24s. *the wey*,[51] that of cotton candles having been raised in the previous October under pressure from our Wardens, to 3d. the pound.[52] At the meeting in March

the wardeyns of the severall felowships of the Bochers and of the Tallough-chaundelers were streightly charged and commaundyd by the hole court to take suche order with all their seyd several felowships that neyther the sayd wardeyns nor none of their seyd fellowships do at any tyme hereafter breake or excede any of the sayd severall prices by takynge of fyne/gods peny[e] or other reward whatsoever/upon payne of dysfraunchesment from the liberties of the seyd Cytie for ever.

But, less than a month later[53] we read that 'the pryce of the waye of rough talough' has again been

set & gevyn by the Court here for the yere insuynge *for diverse gret and urgent causes and consyderacions movynge* the same Court at xxvjs viijd.

Doubtless to the disappointment of our Wardens there was no increase in the price of candles. On the contrary, it was ordered 'that the prices of candell here sett and stallyd *the xvjth day of Marche ult*, shallbe observyd and kept for the seyd tyme', and the Wardens of both companies were admonished that none of their several fellowships

by any maner of subtyle wayes practyce or means do excede or breke any of the seyd severall prices,

again under the penalty of disfranchisement.

A Mayoral Proclamation made in the year 1558 has been referred to in connection with the sale of herring.[d] Its stated purpose was to ensure that *all goods covered by the decree* were sold 'at reasonable rates and pryces'. No Tallow Chandler or other person occupying or using 'the arte or occupacion of Tallough-chaundelers' was permitted to 'vtter or sell or by any manner of

---

c   So-called from being originally devoted to some religions or charitable purpose . . .
     A small sum paid as earnest money on striking a bargain . . . O.E.D.

d   *Commentary*, p. 237.

wayes or meanes cause to be vtteryd or solde' within the City or the liberties thereof

any Cotten Candell above the pryce of ijd. ob (2½d.) the pounde nor any candles made wth weke above ijd the pounde

and suche persons were to

retayle the same candelles made wth weke and not wth cotton *to pore people* by the quartern of a pounde by waighte for an halfe penny if they do requyre so to have the same.

The penalty for disobedience was 'imprysonment of there bodyes at the dyscrecion' of the Lord Mayor and Aldermen. In April 1560[54] there is a Court Order setting the price of tallow at the old price of *26s. 8d. the wey* and of cotton candles at *3d. the pound*, while the price of candles 'made with weake' is maintained at 2½d. 'Streight charge & commaundement' is given 'to every of the wardeyns' of the two fellowships of Butchers and Tallow Chandlers

so that neyther they or any of the same felowships do at any tyme hereafter transgres or excede the sayd severall pryces upon payne conteyned in *the pro-clamacion lately made for pulters (poulterers) and other victulers,*^e

thus recognizing the penalty clause in the decree as valid, not-withstanding the abrupt rise in the price of one of its stated commodities. A drop in the price of tallow to *20s.* and of cotton candles to 2¼d. in April 1561[55] follows for a time the pattern set in the 'sixties by other commodities.[56] But in April 1562 the price of tallow is *23s. 4d.*[57] A year later it is again *26s. 8d.,*[58] and this rising trend is noticed for the next twelve years,[59] the price at one time being as high as 30s.,[60] an event which the Clerk to the Butchers Company thought worthy of record in their accounts.[61] We have seen tallow at around 10s. the wey in the early years of the century^f and at around 20s. in the early 'fifties. Statistics show that during these fifty years or so the prices of commodities in

---

e   That is to say the Mayora lProclamation of 1558.

f   Volume III, pp. 62 to 66.

general rather more than doubled, so that tallow prices in the City at this period were inclined to lag behind. The reverse is, however, the case in the next twenty-five years, for the three-fold rise which was common with most commodities during that period[62] came, as we have seen, a little earlier in the tallow trade.

In November 1574 we see tallow for the first time at 32s.[63] and for the next nine years the price fluctuates between 28s. and 30s. the wey,[64] during which era, commencing in 1577, the entries refer only to 'the best sort of tallow'.[65] After 1583 we look in vain for any setting of the price until the autumn of 1588 when the price of tallow, specified as 'rough and untryed', is 40s. the wey.[66] A few days later[67] the Wardens of the Butchers are 'once agayne charged and inioyned' by the Court

that they take order with all theyre companye that none of them do after Saterdaye nexte presume to sell any talloughe duringe the pleasure of this Courte above the price of xls. the weygh uppon payne for every one offendinge to the contrary *to be sett upon the pillorye* accordinge to the late Acte of Common Councell in that case made and provided.[g]

Fig. 11. The stocks (see footnote g).

In December (1588) we read that the price of 'rough tallough of the best sorte' has been set 'during the pleasure of the Court' at

---

g   Pillory: An instrument of punishment which consisted of a wooden post and frame fixed on a platform raised several feet from the ground, behind which the culprit stood (Volume II, Plate II), his hands being thrust through holes in the frame, as are the feet in the stocks (Figure 11), so as to be held fast and exposed in front of it. *Encyclopaedia Britannica*, Vol. 17 (1968), p. 1079. (See *Commentary*, p. 237.)

35s. 'uppon payne of imprisonment and suche fyne as shalbe imposed'.[68] For the next three years the records are again silent on this subject of prices, and it seems likely that the rapid extension of the built-up area around the square mile of the old City and the growth of suburban production, to which we refer in a later chapter, was impressing the Corporation more and more with the difficulty of maintaining price control. We next hear of the setting of the price of tallow and candles in October 1592, when, for the first time, tallow is quoted *by the stone*.[69] The price of 'tallowe of the best sorte was rated and sett at ijs. the stone', (or 32s. the wey, if the prevailing standard, for cheese[h] is any guide) and the Wardens of the Butchers and 'sundrie others of the sayde Companie lykewise present' were straightly charged that the price of 'anie sort of Tallowe' must be kept *until the Court* 'take order to the contrarie'. The next hint of price control comes five years later, when the Court meets to consider means 'for reformation of the excessive price of tallow and tallow candles',[70] but we are told nothing more.

The price of candles, relatively speaking, had kept pace with the price of tallow. In 1592, when, as we have just seen, tallow was rated at 2s. the stone, the price of cotton candles was set at 4d. the pound and of 'weeke candles' at $\frac{1}{2}d$. less,[71] which signifies a quadrupling of the price since the early days of the century and follows the pattern in other trades.[72] In the first week of September 1620[73] there is another approach to the problem of controlling the sale of tallow and candles, when it is recorded that

this Courte havinge taken into their consideration the greate rates and prices of tallowe and candles at which they are nowe alreadie solde *have resolved to set a price thereof,*

and, after a warning to the Master and Wardens of both the Butchers and Tallow Chandlers, it is reported at a meeting on 14th September that the Court has 'conceived it needfull to sett prices . . . accordinge to former precedents'.[74] While we have no positive evidence, it seems reasonably clear from these two entries

h   *Commentary,* p. 237.

and from the absence of any record of price-setting from the City's memoranda books that during the past twenty-eight years the Court has allowed the prices of tallow and tallow candles to find their own level, a policy which it is now minded to reverse. The price of *English Tallow* is accordingly fixed at 'xxvjs. viijd. the hundred weight, or 53s. 4d. the wey,[i] while 'good cotton candles are not to be sold above iiij¼d. the pounde' and 'good weeke candles at iii¼d. the pounde.' These prices are to be kept 'untill further order . . . uppon paine and perill' to fall on delinquents, for which purpose 'a proclamation is to be drawne by advice of Councell and to be printed'.[j] Four weeks later[75] the Master and Wardens of Butchers and Tallow Chandlers, after being heard by the Court

what they could saye for themselves why they should not performe the proclamation latelie sett forth by the Lord Maior for the prices of tallowe and candles,

were commanded to observe the Proclamation 'upon peyne of severe punishment'. Our answer is not recorded, but the Butchers promised the Court[76] to observe 'the prices of tallow', *if the foreign butchers were compelled to keep the same.*[k] The immediate result of this new attempt to control prices is not known. There seems to have been no report of the order having been enforced or of penalties having been imposed for disobedience, and in fact we hear no more of price control for ten years, when there are three entries which relate to candles, and which prove to be the last. On 28th September 1630[77]

it was thought fitt and soe ordered by this Court that from and after Michaelmas daie next the best cotton candles shalbe sold by the candle makers within this Cittie and Liberties thereof after the rate and price of *fower shillinges and eight pence the dozen of candles,*

and the Master and Wardens of the Company of Tallowchandlers

---

present at the meeting were 'required to see the same price duly observed and kept'. On the 7th October[78] it was

thought fit and soe ordered by this Court, that *the Tallowchandlers* within this Cittie and Liberties thereof, be required to observe from henceforth

the above mentioned price. A little later,[79]

to the end that the price of candles may be abated,

there is a command that the tallow chandlers and candle-makers shall not from henceforth sell any English tallow to *soap-makers*, which, from what we have learnt about soap-making, must have been one of the last of such orders to be issued.

III

As well as the usual Orders of the Court of Aldermen, Acts of Common Council, and frequent Mayoral Proclamations, there were a number of other steps taken in the sixteenth century and later to enforce the regulations for the distribution and sale of tallow and candles.

We have seen how in 1518 and again twenty years later[a] our Master and Wardens were bound by 'recognysance' to observe the usual conditions relating to the supply and sale of candles. Another instance of our officers being under compulsion, as candle-makers, to keep the law occurred in May 1546 in the Mayoralty of Sir Martin Bowes,[b] when a recognizance lately entered into by Thomas Cuttle while Master (p. 13) was quoted as a precedent.[80] Each 'recognizor' occupying 'the feate & crafte of a taloughchaundeler & makyng of talough candels within the Cytie of London & suburbes of the same' was commanded 'nott by eny maner of colour, wayes or meanys' to 'bargayne, sell or utter' (or cause to be uttered and sold)

eny parte or parcell of talough that hereafter & by eny whatsoever wayes or meanys shall come to his hands or possessyon but onely to suche persone or

---

a   See Volume III, p. 70.

b   Lord Mayor 1545–6.

persones as do & shall make candells within the seyd Cytie & suburbes to be put to sale/*or els utter spende set & make all the same talough in to talough candells hym self.*

His purchases were to be confined to eight weys in any one fort-night, presumably to stop him from forestalling tallow, for the breach of which order he could be committed to ward. Candle wicks, as we have seen, were still being made with mixed cotton and inferior thread, of which there must as usual be an equal number, and the candles themselves must be made of 'good & clene talough'. Lastly he was forbidden at any time to

utter or sell eny suche candells att eny higher or greter pryce than shalbe sett & yeven by the lorde mayer of the seid Cytie for the tyme beyng for the same *wythout the especiall lycence of the seyd lorde mayer.*

That a seller should be permitted to break the price on occasion is novel and no reported instance of any such 'licence' having been issued has been found. Cuttle himself had appeared before the Court earlier in the year when one Christofer Dray, a plumber, had 'deposed upon the Evaungelist' that he (Cuttle) had 'sayde & reported before hym that he had gevyn monycion of *derth of talough* to Sir Wylliam Laxton,[c] att Easter last past & if he (Laxton) had folowyd his consayll yt *had nott ben as it is nowe*'[81]. The reason for this outburst is not known, but the record goes on to state that 'the seyd Cuttle by this Court was commytted to warde' and it was agreed 'that he shall sue to the seyd Mr (sic) Laxton for his libertye ageyn'. This is followed by a paragraph referring to a 'sute comensed by Mr Chamberlyn ageynst the Taloughchaundelers', which is to

surcesse upon their honest behaviour in servyng the cytie with candells tyll suche tyme as yt shall seme good to my lorde mayer to take other order therin,

from which it appears that on this occasion it was our Company that found itself on the wrong side of the law, and that Thomas Cuttle was in some way personally involved. We do not know the result of his appeal for clemency.

---

c   Lord Mayor 1544-5.

In addition to the general powers of search conferred upon our Company, which we have noticed more than once, powers were conferred at times upon *individuals*. For instance, early in June 1525 one Stephen Wynke, a tallow chandler,[d] acting at that time as 'oon of thofficers of this Citie' was employed 'in the seasour of Talugh to be conveyed out of this Citie',[82] for which, and other like duties 'yn serchyng for Candell and Talough with other basynes (business) for the welth of this Citie,'[83] he received 26s. 8d. yearly at the hands of the Chamberlain 'with *bothe his liveryes*[e] at the costes of the said Chamberleyn and mete & drynke at the Mayer's'.[f]

We have noticed the command given to the Aldermen in 1531 (p. 13) that they should see to the service of the people with candles at the set price, in breach of which duty offenders might be committed to ward. Another instance of the Court's surveillance occurs fourteen years later when, in March 1545, we were called upon to answer a complaint made to the Lord Mayor that our candles were being sold at an excessive price.[84] Our Wardens were examined as to 'how they do sell theyr candells & whethyr the seyd complaynt were true or nott', to which they replied

that neyther they nor eny of their companye dyd sell above jd.q. (1¼d.) the pounde *but yf eny man dyd in suche wyse offende they were of other felowshipe & nott of thyrs*/desyeryng the Court that they myght be punyshed & promysyng for theyr (the Wardens') hole company not to offende therein.

Again in February 1547 an Alderman was required to 'cause serche to be made in the Custom howse for the names of all suche persones as of late have shipped over eny Talough beyonde the See & for the quantyte thereof',[85] and in our Wardens' accounts for 1549-51 we read of money being paid '*for the officers'* pains *in the search for tallow*.[86] On another occasion 'the Mayor's officer' was paid 12d.,[87] and in yet another search during this period he had 8d. 'to go with us to see what Tallow [one]

---

d   His name appears in our Yeomanry quarterage list for 1518-9 (see p. 126).

e   Commentary, p. 237.

f   Commentary, p. 238.

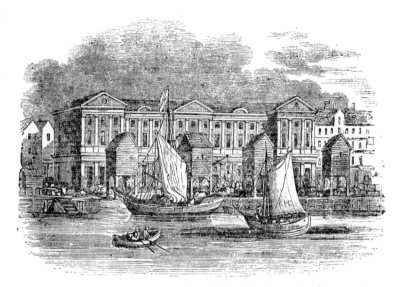

Fig. 12. The Custom House, London, before the Great Fire, from a print
by Hollar (1607–1677).

Hunt *in Southwark* had'.[88] In the accounts for 1551–3 a sum of
32*s.* is entered as having been 'received of *strangers* when we went
to search for candle',[89] a subject to which we shall return. There
is also a payment of 15*s.* 'to Master Recorder for his counsel in
overseeing the Bill exhibited to my Lord Mayor *for to get the
tallow into our hands*'.[90] This minute seems to be linked in some
way with an entry of the Court of Aldermen in July 1551,
recording that 'a certain Byll touching the Talowe hytherto
delyvered by the Bochers of Saint Nicholas Shambles*g* was red
and respyte taken for ordering of the matter in varyaunce between
the Taloughchaundelers and the Bochers'.[91] A two-day search
for candles is recorded in the accounts for 1553–5 when 2*s.* was
paid to 'the officer'.[92]

In May 1557 there was an order for a *general search*,[93] when our
Wardens received directions from the Court that they should

frome hensforwarde frome tyme to tyme *takynge alwayes with them one of the
Lord Mayors officers* diligently searche all theire hole Company and also all and

---

g   One of the recognized flesh markets of the City, on the North side of Newgate
Street.

singuler other persones of this Cytye that nowe do or hereafter shall make and put to sale any maner of tallouge candells within the same cytye . . .

and should view and try whether they

do truely observe and keape the good and laudable Acte and order of this Court here taken and made *sexto die Maij in Reportorio tempore maioratus Martini Bowes militis.*

The order made in the Mayoralty of Martin Bowes was, of course, the Thomas Cuttle recognizance of 1546, the terms of which are again recorded, and the decree goes on to direct that 'the saide wardens shall alwayes take a note in wrytinge of all suche tallough as they at any tyme in theire saide searche shall fynde in the possessyon of any suche offender' above the permitted quantity, 'so that the same Corte may thereupon take order for the distribution thereof accordinge to the Lawe . . .'[h]

We have seen how on more than one occasion our officers had been forced to enter into an obligation *binding on the Company* to abide by the various regulations for the sale of tallow and candles. On 6th October 1558,[94] accompanying the setting of the prices of cotton and wick candles, there is an order of the Court commanding our Wardens to keep 'the severall prices', to make proper candles, and 'to see the Cytie well served of the same & not to lak'. Then comes a direction

that an obligacion shalbe drawen & devysed by Mr Towne clerk wherin the hole companye of the seid Talloughchaundelers shalbe bounde in cc li. to the chamberleyn under their common seale for observyng this order which the wardeyns of the seid Companye promysed to seale/And the lyke order was taken with dyvers others of the candlemakers of this cytie beinge *free men of dyvers other companyes* who were also contentyed (sic) to be bounde by obligacion for performans of the seid order/And agreid that Mr Towne clerk shall drawe obligacions wherein iij or iiij at the leste/beinge of one felowship or companye/shalbe bounden iointly & severally in x li. with lyke condicion as the Talloughechaundlers shalbe bounden in.

Our Company brought in its obligation,[95] but there was evidently grave trouble with some of the other companies, for on the same day[96]

---

h   *Commentary,* p. 238.

yt was orderyd that the Towne clerk shall cause as menye of the candlemakers of this Cytie not beinge free of the felowship of the Talloughchaundelers as shall refuse or denye to seale their obligations . . . *to be sente to ward att the comaundement of this hole Courte there to remayne tyll they wyll wyllinglye do the same.*

In our accounts for 1561–2,[97] there is a payment of 2s. to '*Foster our officer* for going two times abroad with us to see the price of candles kept'.[i] The accounts at this time also afford evidence of our right to supervise the weighing of our tallow. We learn from the record for 1561–2[98] that 10s. has been paid

to Parker My Lord Mayor's officer for his pains at Leadenhall for six days at our *beginning to weigh* our tallow at Leadenhall/according to a Proclamation to us granted.[j]

In a minute dated 25th June 1562[99] we read that

this Court day it is fully agreed and determined that all such persons of our Company as hath or shall have any tallow at Leadenhall shall pay to our Common Beadle for the weighing of their tallow every week one penny, so that it be not under half a wey a week and this order to continue henceforth.

This entry is followed by another recording the payment of 10s. 'to Thomas Priest, our Beadle, for a Triangle'[k] and a 7 lb. weight of Lead,[100]

which is occupied at Leadenhall and to remain in the house.

On the 19th November of the same year (1562)[101] the Court of Aldermen directed that

all defective talough candells that the wardeins of the saide felowship of the taloughchaundelers have now in their hands which they lately found and seised upon their serche/shalbe by theym equally distributed to the house of the poore St Thomas Hospitall in Southwerke[l] & Bridwell[m] by even porcions.[n]

---

i   *Commentary*, p. 238.

j   *Commentary*, p. 238.

k   The name for a kind of large tripod comprised of three poles or spars joined at the top, bearing a pulley for hoisting heavy weights, or for weighing. O.E.D.

l   St Thomas Apostle, on the north side of St Thomas Street. (See *Commentary*, p. 238.)

m   See Volume III, p. 85, note *k*.

n   *Commentary*, p. 238.

At the same time the Wardens were bound by recognizance for themselves and all other persons free of the said Company to keep the prices of candles. It had not been the practice for many years to give the Wardens' names in the memoranda books, but, doubtless on account of the importance of the occasion and the nature of their bond, our four officers are named as Hugo Bennynge, Willielmus Hycks, Johannes Balis and Johannes Shorte 'gardiani artis sive mistere de les Taloughchaundelers London'.[o] We have met Hugh Benney before and shall hear of him again. John Bales was an Assistant of the Court in January 1570 when he was fined for 'misusing of himself' against John Myntes (p. 95), then Renter Warden, Myntes himself being fined for 'his unseemly behaviour'.[102] Bales and his wife, Elizabeth, owned three gardens with tenements in Horse Alley,[p] purchased in 1558, of which he was tenant,[103] and in the following year he acquired the lease of property in St Dunstan-in-the-East.[104] In 1574 he appears to have taken a lease from the Company of property in St Nicholas Shambles[105] and next year to have purchased several tenements and gardens in the parish of St Giles, Cripplegate.[106] John Short was Governor of the Yeomanry in 1568. He was one of our Wardens in 1569 and Master in 1577-8. We shall hear more of him later in the City, but nothing seems to be known of his private life. William Hicks' name does not occur again in the memoranda books. It does not appear in our books and nothing else seems to be known of him.

Evidence of searches both for tallow and candles is again found in our records for the next ten years, including searches resulting in 'distresses'. Evans, the Mayor's officer, was paid for enquiring of Butchers' names[107] and our Clerk (Robert Davison) 'for his travail and pains about search days'.[108] We spent money at divers times when search was made at the commandment of the Wardens,[109] and on two occasions we received search money.[110] On 4th October 1569[111] we paid and spent 3s.

---

o   An interesting mixture of Latin and French!

p   or 'Horsey Alley', which seems to have been on the east side of Coleman Street. Harben.

at the Castle*q* about searching for tallow at the commandment of the Lord Mayor,

and we see from the accounts for 1574–5[112] that another 3s. was paid

to Priest the Beadle for money lost by candles that we bought when search was made who sold candles above the Mayor's price.

The first of those two searches was followed, two days later, by our Wardens' attendance before the Mayor and Aldermen,[113] to receive their commands.

In the summer of 1568 the Court ordered the first of two sixteenth century searches by more than one member of our Company by name,[114] when directing that Stephen Rogers and Rychard Pynfold, tallow chandlers,

shall make a serche and newe viewe and surveye within this Cyty & the libertyes therof truely therby to lerne and knowe what store of talloughe remayneth within the same Cytye and in whose hands the same remayneth/ and that John Launde *Butcher* Nicholas Spenser *Merchauntt* and Rychard Lychefeyld one of my Lorde Mayor's officers shall go with them makinge the same serche for better credytt & countynaunce of the matter and as wytnesses therein/and that the sayde Pynfold & Rogers shall make a booke declaringe in whose hand the sayd tallowghe remayneth & deliver the same to this Courte . . .

The names of both Pynfold and Rogers appear in one of several lists of candle-makers, including many members of our Company, purchasing tallow in 1573.[115] Rogers was to follow Walter Westmoreland (p. 45) as Master of the Company in 1576, although there seems to be no evidence of his having served previously as Governor of the Yeomanry.*r* He and his wife, Barbara, had recently purchased from another tallow-chandler a 'messuage, etc., in Holborne Crosse Street and Turnegaine Lane,*s* near Holborne Bridge, St Sepulchre'.[116] Of Pynfold (or Pynfolde) nothing else is known, apart from his purchase from the Company,

---

q See Vol. III, *Appendix B*, note *a*.

r *Commentary*, p. 238.

s 'There lyeth a strete from Newgate west, to the end of Turnagaine lane, and winding north to Oldborne Conduite. This Conduit of *Oldborne Cross* was first builded 1498'. *Stow's Survey*, edition of 1603. (See *Commentary*, p. 238.)

when Master in 1582, of 'an old bedstead and an old chair' for
10s.,[117] which seems a fair price compared with the purchase of
'the Queen Majesty's Picture for the Hall', for which the Company paid at that time[118] only one pound'![t]

As we learnt when reading of searches among soap-makers in
the winter of 1573, a single tallow chandler, Thomas Redknight,
was also given power of search throughout the City and Liberties
for tallow and candles. Such merchandise, if destined to be conveyed out of the City or to be sold to 'forreyn or strangers', he
was authorized to seize[119] and bring to the Chamber.[120] He was
also to[121]

learne & serche out what Tallowchaundelers doe at any tyme hereafter sell
any candells above the price heretofore or hereafter to be set by the lord maior
of this Citie/and to present the names of thoffenders & the offences furthwith
to the lord maior . . .

We hear no more of Redknyght as an official of the Company,
but he is mentioned again in a May 1580 when we learn from
an award of the Court of the Yeomanry[u] that, as a member of
the Company, he was dealing at that time in candles as well as
soap.

In November 1574, little more than a year after our first meeting with Redknight, we learn that *three* tallow chandlers, Anthony
Alderson (or Adderson), Richard Bell, and Arthur Lye (Lee),
were sworn

to searche what tallowe ys at this presente in the hands of any Tallowghe
Chaundler or candlemaker or any other within this Cytie,

and to make report, and two officers of the Court were 'appoynted
to attende on them in their sayd searche'.[122] It is difficult to understand why it was thought necessary to engage another search
party when (as we have seen) Redknight was still employed. The
names of all three men appear in the contemporary list of tallow
chandlers already referred to.[123] Nothing is known of Alderson's

---

t   *Commentary*, p. 238.

u   See Appendix A.

private life and he does not seem ever to have held office in the
Company. He had an unfortunate record of quarreling with his
associates.[v] Bell (or Bill) seems at one time to have been a property owner.[124] He died in 1578[125] leaving his Company, 'for
thair pains' taken in coming to his burial, 40s. Among a number
of specific legacies, he left his brother Rafe (or Ralfe) his *second
livery gown faced with budge*,[w] which may be an indication that
he also possessed a 'foyne gown' (Appendix C), but it does not
appear from the Company's books that he ever took office on
the Court. Lee was Master in 1578-9. He had been a Warden
in the early 'sixties, when he was arrested 'at the suit of' one
Dodson, *a currier*,[126] but nothing seems to be known of the
incident. In 1575 he and his wife, Margaret, purchased from John
Bales and his wife the gardens[x] and tenements in Horse Alley[127]
which, as we have seen, the latter had acquired some sixteen
years before. Lee appears to have succeeded Bales as tenant. A
still earlier occupant was another tallow chandler, Humphrey
Nalson,[128] whom we have yet to meet. It seems likely that this
succession of tallow chandlers as tenants indicates that the premises were used for business. Lee lived until 1595 'aged in body
but of perfect mind and memory'[129] leaving to his son George
Lee 'and to his heirs for ever' all those his tenements lying in the
parish of St Botolph without Aldgate, which he and his wife
appear to have acquired jointly some twenty years earlier,[130] but
which have not been identified. He left to another son, Cuthbert[y]
'and his heirs', the Horse Alley tenements and gardens, together
with other properties in the parishes of St Botolph without
Bishopsgate and St Giles without Cripplegate. His gift to the
Company was £3 'to make merry withal at their discretion'. In
the early 'seventies father Lee, when a Warden, played a prominent part in the carrying out of improvements to the Hall, to
which reference is made in Appendix D.

---

v   *Commentary*, p. 238.

w   For the significance of this gift see Appendix B.

x   Then two only.

y   Master, 1605-1607.

Fig. 13. Church of St Giles, Cripplegate.

An effective way of securing the enforcement of civic laws was through the Wardmote inquests, and it became the practice to include directions that inquiries should be made at these meetings as to the observance or otherwise of price regulations. There is a good example in December 1568,[131] when the Court ordered that

for dyvers verye necessarye causes and consyderacyons movinge ye same there shalbe an article drawen and devysed to be added and put vnte ye chardge of *euery wardmote enquest of this cytie* amonge ye other vusuall artycles of theyr charge vpponn ye daye of St Thomas thapostle now nexte ensuynge (21st December)/dyligentlye and truely to enquire and present whyther any tallow chandeler or other maker and seller of tallow candles to be put to sale within this Cytie or ye libertyes thereof *hath transgressed or offended or broken* ye severall pryces of tallow candle latelye sett and stalled by ye Lorde Maior and ye courte of Aldermen of thys Cytie ye or naye,

and the respective prices of the different sorts of candle were stated. This was followed in January (1569)[132] by a *Precept* in simi-lar terms to the Aldermen. In the Spring of 1575[133] it was ordered that another Proclamation should be

drawen and prynted and after[wards] proclaymed of the pryces of talloughe
and candells assessyed and sette at the laste Courte holden/to thentente the
pryces thereof maybe observyd accordingly,

and in October an inquiry as to whether tallow prices were being
kept by the butchers and to whom the tallow was being sold, was
to be included in the Wardmote inquest,[134] this being an occasion
when the use of tallow in soap was under attack. In the usual
Precept to the Aldermen which followed[135] an investigation, was
ordered to be made as to what 'chaundelers', candle-makers and
others

use any *false & untrue weights* eyther to buy or sell withall within the seyd
cytty or the liberties thereof,

a subject to which we shall return.

IV

The matter of tallow melting is one which merits consideration
in the present chapter.

The Act of Common Council directed against the Wax Chandlers and ourselves jointly in 1509 has been noticed,[a] as also our
'bill' giving the names of tallow chandlers occupying melting
houses 'very perilous for fyre' in 1518[b] and the command given
in the same year to the *Curriers* engaged in melting tallow in the
City (p. 16). The existence of melting houses in the square mile
at a very early date is well known, of which the classic example
is the occupation by our forbears, the oynters (or melters), in
1283 of 'selds' in West Chepe, from which they were ordered to
remove their belongings.[c] In June 1521 our old friend Robert
Silver (or Sylver), Master of the Company three years earlier,[d]
was found guilty of melting his tallow in the City contrary to the
Act of 1509.[136] In February 1525 Robert Heron, later an Assistant

---

a   Volume III, p. 71.

b   Ibid., p. 70.

c   Volume I, p. 52.

d   Volume III, p. 70.

of the Court[e] who, as we have seen, had been sent to prison two years earlier for breaking the price of herring (p. 49), was again in trouble when a Wardmote inquest presented him[137]

for noyng greuously his neyghbours with meltyng & stenche of flotyce & Talugh within his house contrary to the goode ordre of this Citie.

His defence was that he

vseth noon otherwyse than all other Talughchaundelers does/that ys to sey he melteth talugh only for makyng of Candell & noon otherwyse,

which some observers might consider a reasonable excuse, but it availed him nothing. He was fined[138] and bound by recognizance not to repeat the offence.[139] Heron, or Herne, as he is described in his two wills, proved in the Commissary Court of London in 1551,[140] owned a 'tenement' with shops, cellars, sollers (or solars),[f] warehouses and the like in the Poultry.[141] His son Henry (also a tallow chandler),[142] was a principal beneficiary.[g] In April 1526[143] Humphrey Nalson, like Heron, an Assistant of the Court in 1538, confessed

that he hath molton Talugh within his dwellyng house in Colmanstrete contrary to the lawes and ordynaunces of this Citie/And theruppon hathe submytted hym and putt hym in the grace of the Courte/and after this the Chamberleyn brought forthe a greate maser[h] whiche the said Nalson delyuered to hym as plegge for his fine,

which was later fixed at xxs.[144] In June 1526[145] John Priour, tallow chandler, bearer of a distinguished name,[i]

whiche hath molton Talugh within Warwyke Inne[j] *within the walles of this Citie* contrary to the ordennaunce of Commen Counsell in that case ordeyned

---

e   See Volume III, Appendix F, Group I.

f   Upper Chambers (see Volume I, p. 58).

g   *Commentary*, p. 239.

h   Mazer. See note *z*, p. 232.

i   Master in 1476. One of the four 'Wardens' who obtained our Grant of Arms in 1456. See Volume III, p. 41-2.

j   Stow says that Warwick Lane (formerly Old Dean's Lane—*Harben*) took its name 'of an ancient' house there builded by an Earle of Warwicke, and was since called Warwicke Inne.

. . . hath brought yn to this Courte the somme of xl s accordyng to the tenour of the said Acte*k*/And the Courte considerynge his good obedience and his lowly submyssion in this behalffe hath remytted five nobles thereof And soo hath taken for his fine but onely vj s. viijd.*l* And iniunccion is geven to hym that he hereafter nowise melte eny Talugh there *or yn other place within the liberties of this Cite* vppon periell that wille falle theruppon.

We have seen how, in October 1531, in the case of John Sampson, salter (p. 30), the rules were relaxed to the extent of permitting him to melt *at night,m* after which the memoranda books are strangely silent on the subject for over twenty years, when in November 1553 one Anthony Sylver lodges a complaint against certain un-named tallow chandlers 'for meltinge of talowghe',[146] with what result we are not told. The Court records are again silent for another forty-five years, except for an Order in 1569[147] directing

that a precept shalbe made to the wardens of the buchers that they shall cause their tallowe to be delivered to the chaundelars and others that they sell ther tallowe unto *to be melted out of hande everie mondaie that they kill all the weke before.*

They are 'not to kepe and suffer the same to corrupt and putrifie as they now doe'.

There is very little to be learnt from our own records in the sixteenth century. In 1551 there was a dispute as to ownership of a melting house, the location of which is not stated.[148] It is true that in our Yeomanry accounts for 1561-2[149] there is an entry of a fine of 3s. 4d. for melting tallow *'in a Butcher's House* contrary to our Ordinances'.*n* But some important events of the years 1598-9, which are recorded in the City memoranda books, pass unnoticed in our minutes. They commence with the record of an information having been laid against a merchant taylor for 'melting of tallowe in Meere Lane in the parish of St Giles *without Creplegateo* . . . contrary to an Acte of Commen Councell

---

k   The Act of 27th September 1509.

l   Noble. A former English gold coin first minted by Edward III. (See *Commentary,* p. 239).

m   Volume II, p. 71.

n   *Commentary,* p. 239.

o   Location unknown.

in that case made & provided *Anno primo Henrici octavi*',[150] that is to say the Act of 27th September 1509, which, as we have seen, related to melting *within the City*. A few days later it was ordered that two Aldermen and the Common Sergeant should draw a bill to be preferred to the Common Council 'for reformation of abuses commytted by those that melte waxe and tallowe within this Cittie and the liberties thereof'.[151] Further evidence of 'abuses' at this period is afforded by a letter from the Lord Mayor dated 24th February 1592 contained in the record known as *the Remembrancia*, from which we learn that one Peter Clemens has submitted a request to the Lord Treasurer that a collection should be made in the several Wards to recompense him for the loss he has sustained through fire. In his reply the Lord Mayor expresses the view that 'it is very undesirable to tax the citizens, first, because the said Clemens is a *stranger*, second, because he, being a Tallow-chandler, ought not to have used the trade of melting tallow *within the City* contrary to the orders made in that behalf, thereby firing his own house and greatly imperilling his neighbours, and third, because the collection would be used by him to pay his creditors'. Nevertheless, if the Lord Treasurer still thinks it 'desirable, they will for his sake make the collection'.[152]

In November 1598[153] it was ordered at a meeting of the Common Council that a committee, led by an Alderman, sitting with an ironmonger, a grocer, and three merchant taylors (all named) should have

present consideracion of a bill drawen and exhibited to this Courte towchinge meltinge of tallough grease and kitchen stuffe within this Citie and the liberties thereof to the annoyance of the Inhabitants of the saide Citie, and to make reporte . . .

The Act, of which a copy will be found in Appendix H, followed on 5th December 1599. The reference to 'divers good lawes, constitucions and acts of Comen Councell' and to 'acts, orders and ordinaunces' then in force will be noticed. These references contrast with the mention in the 'information' respecting tallow melting in Meere Lane, which cites only the Act of 1509, and if there were in fact any other Acts, etc. they have not been traced.

It would seem that, after 90 years, it was high time that the law was brought up to date, but we hear of no effective steps for the enforcement of the new Act. The next entry is in the first decade of the next century when a Committee meets 'to consider the conveniency of the late Act of Common Council prohibiting melting houses of Tallow and complaints against the same',[154] which is followed by an Order of the Court of Aldermen in 1614 that a suit against one Thomas Coxon 'for using a melting house in Portsoken Ward' shall be stayed.[155] The law was evidently still being broken, for there was an Order soon afterwards forbidding the melting of tallow 'within the City'.[156] Four years later it was ordered that *a note was to be made of melting houses*.[157] We read at this time of a payment of 14s. 'about the suit touching the melting of Tallow in London',[158] and from the next account we learn that £16 12s. was 'laid out touching business *done by a Court of Aldermen for melting Tallow*, selling of candles, etc.'[159] We read in our minutes[160] that on 2nd July 1636 an Order was made by the Justices of the Peace of Middlesex, in compliance with commands from the Lords of the Council, for the 'Prevention and dispersing the Plague within the County of Middlesex near to the City of London *which is now visited therewith*'. This order directed

that during the time of this Visitation *only* all Tallow Chandlers that have any Melting House or Houses in any place *within or near the Suburbs of the City of London* shall by themselves or any other use the same for melting [save] only [for] once in every week and that to be *in the night* and not in the day and to be on the Friday night in every week when the Tallow is *new and sweet* by reason of the ordinary slaughters upon the Thursdays/and that to be for six hours only on that night of every week/And upon God's blessing to cease and withdraw the sickness/*to be at Liberty as before* . . .

We note that in due course £1 each was paid to certain Tallow Chandlers 'towards their charges *in procuring liberty for the melting Pans*'.[161] The final record in the memoranda books seems to have been made at or about the same time, when '*a melting house in the Old Bailey*' of one Thomas Wallis, *against whom an information had been exhibited*, was directed to be viewed[162] and a report was made.[163]

We may deduce from these various entries that the civic authorities found themselves quite unequal to dealing with this problem of tallow melting, although by the third decade of the seventeenth century they had been partially successful in banning melters to the suburbs. If the City required a supply of candles to be maintained, then the makers required the tallow to be melted somewhere near at hand. The only effective action that the Court could take was to minimize so far as possible the annoyance to the public and the risk of fire. The problem doubtless became easier of solution as the tallow trade itself ceased to be confined to the City.

V

We feel bound to record the commission of many different offences by members of our Company, as well as by other candle-makers, during the sixteenth century, particularly in the 'seventies, in marked contrast to the good behaviour observed amongst most of our men in earlier years.[a] In March 1523,[164] nearly two years after Robert Sylver himself was in trouble for tallow-melting (p. 83), his servant, Laurence Tunstall, tallow chandler,

aswell for sellyng of candell for jd ob. (1½d.) the lb. as for other certeyn mysdemeanours by hym doon ys commytted to the gaoel of Newgate[b] . . .

In November 1526, Henry Nortryche (p. 13), several times a Warden of our Company,[c] was sent to the prison of the Compter[165] for putting candles to sale

whiche lakketh a quortorn of an vnce in euery pounde contrary to the Lawe, etc.,

and the candles, which were stated to have been 'presented to this Courte' were 'forfeytd to thuse of the Chamber'. In November 1529 Robert Heron, the convicted tallow melter (p. 84), was

---

a   See Volume II, pp. 24, 25.

b   *Commentary*, p. 239.

c   See Volume III, pp. 73, 75, 78, 126.

accused of paying a butcher 12s.[166] a wey for tallow when the set price was 10s. In March 1530[167] the Court was 'credibly enfourmed' that John Hone (p. 10), another of our Wardens[d]

> hath made moche candelles of naughty & evyll stuff whereof example was shewed in this Courte to the seyd Hone Whereuppon the seyd Hone/examined/ seyd that *he cowed not denye yt* And theruppon putte hym in the grace of this Courte,

for which offence he was fined xl s.[168] In August 1531[169] James Quyk (or Quycke), one time tenant, as we have seen, of 'the Dolphin' (p. 26), was commanded, along with another man, apparently a cook, to bring into Court the sum of five pounds

> & theruppon to stand to suche ordre & direccion as this Courte shall sette & ordre concernyng their mysdemeanours of bying & sellyng of Talough contrarye to an Acte of Commen Counsell.

The precise nature of their offence is not stated (although the Act referred to is probably the Standard Edict of 1474.) As well as disposing by his will of 'the Dolphin' and its contents Quyk left 'to the company and clothing of the craft or mistery of tallowchaundelers in London 40s. to be for a potation or banquet for those attending his mass or requiem'.[170]

In the winter of 1545,[171] nearly twenty years after his earlier melting offence (p. 84), we read that

> the fyne of Humfrey Nalson, Taloughchaundeler/who lately contrarye to the laws & ordenaunces of this Cytie hath solde to be conveyed over the see out of the same Cytie a grete quantytie of molten talough bestowed in barrels/ys assessed by the Courte here at x.li. Sterling,

a fine which was afterwards reduced to xl s.[172] In the Spring of 1549 John Haynes (or Heynes) was committed to ward for 'transgressynge of the lawes of the Citie in byinge and sellynge talloughe before eny price gyven by the Lord Mayer'[173] and also fined.[174] We hear of him first in March 1545 when concerned in a dispute with an Antwerp merchant regarding a bargain of 'eleven cwt of Garlick' which the parties submitted to our Master and

---

[d]   See Volume III, pp. 67, 76, 77.

Wardens for arbitration, as a result of which the bargain was declared void on payment of a penalty of £3 by Haynes.[175] Four or five years later he and another Liveryman were together fined 5s. 4d. 'for misordering themselves',[176] and later still we shall see him using false weights. On his death in 1554 he was living in the parish of St Mary-at-Hill, and we see from his will that he had lands and tenements in 'Bexleigh', Kent, which he left to his wife Elizabeth and her heirs. He made a gift of 20s. each to the prisoners of Ludgate, Newgate, Kings Bench, and the Marshalsea, and did not forget to provide 'a recreation' for his fellow members of the Company attending his burial.[177] His name appears in the Yeomanry list for 1538–9 and in the third group of Company members in 1537–8.[e] Another offender sent to ward with Haynes was probably the William Stephens (or Steven) whose name is seventh in the second group.[f] We know that in November 1551[178] this man was fined forty shillings 'for sellynge Candle above the pryce of theym appoynted by my lorde mayer and this courte, and otherwyse dysobeyinge the orders of the same courte'.[g] He died in 1558 (having only recently completed a three-year term as Master) leaving the lease of his dwelling-house in the parish of St Mary at Hill, by Billingsgate to his wife. He also left her his house called the 'fawcon' (or falcon) in the parish of St Sepulchre without Newgate[h] and the lease of the houses and gardens in Houndsditch 'within Woolesacke Alley[i] in the right hand of the same Alley within St Botolphs parish at Aldgate', the whole lease of which he had 'bought of the Cutlers'.[179] One of his gowns 'furred with budge' was among his specific legacies.[j] In August of the same year (1551) 'John Robynson, taloughcaun-

---

e   Volume III, Appendix F, p. 126.

f   Ibid.

g   A fellow culprit on this occasion was one Robert Kychen, salter, the third guilty man in April 1549.

h   The Falcon Inn (or tavern) in the adjoining parish of St Brides which is known to have existed in Henry VIII's time may be intended. (See Falcon Court, *Harben*, p. 222.)

i   or Cutler Street. *Harben*.

j   See Appendix B.

Fig. 14. The Falcon Inn. One of several taverns of this name (see footnote *h*).

deler', brought in 'hys xl s. in pawne accordynge to the order here taken the last Court day,[180] whiche was delyveryd over to Mr Chamberlyn'.[181] All we know of this man is that the Wardens' accounts for 1551–3 show that he paid the Company 2s. 'for leaving his prentice *to work in the science of Candle making* with Robert Kychyn,[182] *salter*'[k] and that two or three years later he was fined for keeping an apprentice three years 'and not presenting him' to the Chamberlain.[183] From the accounts in the early 'fifties we learn that John Heynes, *the younger*, paid a fine of 10s. 'for selling of a Wey of Tallow to a *Currier* for £3, *contrary to his Bond to the House*',[184] when the set price, as we know, was from 19s. to 20s. the wey (p. 62).

During the twenty years commencing in 1547 there are entries in our minutes which relate to the use of *false or faulty weights* and to the sale of candles (and in one case soap) *lacking in weight*,

---

k   Note *g*. He is wrongly described in our minute as a Saddler. (See *Commentary*, p. 239.)

offences with which, in the main, the Court appears to have left our Company to deal until the late 'sixties under regulations contained in our Ordinances. We note in the Wardens' accounts for 1549–51 the receipt of a fine of 4d. from one William Bodoway 'for that his weights were too light'.[185] About four years later Roger Pylfold (or Pynfold), whom we have met as a searcher for eager wines (p. 42), paid a fine of 20s. 'for that he had 12 strings of candle too light and not full weight'.[186] At the same time John Haynes, the elder, was fined 12d. 'for that he had two weights of lead in his house too light',[187] and Walter Westmerland (p. 45) paid the same fine 'for that his Soap Scales were one far heavier than the other'.[188] In February 1562[189] our Court agreed:

that Mr Barton[l] shall forthwith go to ward or imprisonment for lack of weight of his candles and for selling the same above the price decreed for the same and that he shall also put away Farther Thomas/now his servant/within 14 days next coming after this order.

We note also in the accounts[190] the receipt from 'John Barton' of 5s.

for a fine for lack of good weight of his candles and for naughty making of the same candles with kitchen stuff.

In January 1565[191] we read that a fine of 10s. imposed on Harry Lambert, one of the Yeomanry, by reason of a faulty weight of lead, was remitted, he being 'a young man', but for the *next fault* he should pay his whole fine.

We are able to report, with some degree of satisfaction, that in the same period, apart from the commission of the above offences by a few members, serious as they doubtless were, our men appear, from the Corporation records, to have been on their best behaviour. The same cannot be said of some members of other companies, including the butchers, and it is only fair that their misdeeds should also be recorded.

In July 1547[192] the bill presented in the previous month by our Company was read again and 'largely debated' and it was agreed

---

l   *Commentary*, p. 239.

that 'proces' should be awarded against Thomas Marshall, *the salter* (p. 18), and others who '*occupye makyng of candells*', and that they should be 'bounden by recognizance' in the same terms as those imposed upon our members in the Mayoralty of Martin Bowes (p. 72).

for the true makyng of the same (candles) & for the observance of certeyn other poynts mencyoned within the condycion of the same recognysaunce *for as muche as they have observed almost no poynt of the sayd condycion.*

Among those fined for breaking the price of tallow were a number of butchers,[193] while a grocer[194] and a haberdasher[195] were both committed to prison for breaking the price of candles. Butchers were found guilty of conveying tallow out of the City.[196] A haberdasher was brought before the Court for conveying 'a barrel of candles into the country',[197] and the candles were ordered to be sold for the poor.[198] A wax chandler was reported for a like offence,[199] which prompted the Court to charge *all citizens* 'who commonly do make talloughe candells . . . to leave sellinge of their candle into the countrey'.[200] A feature of these unruly times was the manner in which candle-makers were forced to make payment to butchers 'to obtain their favours'.[201] In September 1558 the Wardens of the Tallow Chandlers were ordered to bring in their names,[202] when it was recorded that Hughe Benney (p. 42), Walter Westmoreland (p. 45) and Henry Eve (p. 43) had all been compelled 'to pay or forgive' their butchers money.[203]

We now enter upon a period of nearly nine years during which we have to confess that misdeeds among our own men were rife.

In May 1567[204] a tallow chandler by the name of Nortrige[m] bought tallow from a butcher, who 'of his own confession' had offended the law by selling twenty-three weys 'before any price geven and appointed by the lord mayer and court of Aldermen'.[n] A little later a Precept was issued to the Aldermen to inquire if any chandler 'transgresses or offends' in the price of candles,[205]

---

[m] His Christian name is omitted, and he has not been identified.

[n] Commentary, p. 240.

and Thomas Astell, Nicholas Hawkesworth (or Hawkesford) and John Warren, three well known tallow chandlers, whose names appear in contemporary lists of candle-makers, were among those required to enter into recognizances.[206] This was followed by a notice for a Special Court to be attended by the Wardens of the Butchers and Tallow Chandlers 'with certayne others of the best of theyse Campanyes with others that use the makinge of candells',[207] of which there seems to be no record, but at a meeting on 7th December 1568[208]

the wardeyns both of the butchers and also of the talloughechaundelers after the readinge of the auncyent lawes of this cytye touchinge and concerninge them & eyther of theyre companyes/*which lawes they could not denye but that they had offended & transgressed*/did humbly submyt themselves for theyre offences therein to the grace of this courte/wherupon they were all streightlye comaunded by the sayd courte not to fayle personally here to apeare from *courte to courte* tyll they shalbe clerely discharged thereof by the same courte.

The Wardens of the Tallow Chandlers were further commanded to charge all their Company *and the other candlemakers of the City* to observe and keep the several prices set by the Lord Mayor and the Court for the current year upon their candles 'at theyre uttermoste perills', but later that month[209] they again attended Court with the Butchers, when the Wardens of both companies

did upon theyre earnest examynacions not deny but playnely confesse and acknowledge that both they and their sayd severall felloweshippes *have hooly transgressed . . . the several prices of tallow and tallowcandle* here sett stalled and apoynted by this Courte . . .[o]

In the same month further recognizances were required, including one from our friend John Bales.[210] Then on 4th February 1569[211] we learn that at a meeting of the Court that day

all the Tallowchaundlers and other candelmakers and sellers of tallow caundells who lately were presented and indicted by the Wardemot Inquests in the severall wards wherein they do dwell for the not kepyng of the severall prices of their said candells . . . *dyd appere and playnely confesse their said offences.*

Each man was fined 6s. 8d., and it was ordered that the fines

---

[o]   *Commentary*, p. 240.

should go and be applied 'for the use of the pore in the Citie's hospitals'. The Aldermen were *to commit to ward* all those tallow chandlers and other candle-makers 'indited in forme aforesaid for the like offences', who had failed to appear, and each such offender was also to be fined. Every offender making 'humble suite' for the mitigation of this fine was, nevertheless, to receive 'such grace as seemed to the Court reasonable & convenient'. John Bales was among the guilty parties and Thomas Astell (p. 94), whom we recognize as a buyer of tallow on a substantial scale,[212] and (like his co-wardens Richard Clerke and Robert Atkinson in 1572) as a searcher for 'eger wines' (p. 47), was to await the pleasure of the Court, but we do not know his fate. He was Governor of the Yeomanry from 1575 to 1579 and Master from 1585 to 1587. Early in January 1558, when the fall of Calais was imminent, he had been a contributor with other members of our Company,[213] towards the charges of finding soldiers for the muster 'before the Queen's Grace at Greenwich',[p] the total sum recorded being £15 15s.[214] The soldiers were usually paid 12d. each as 'prest money'.[215] Another contributor was John Mynts, who joined one Peter Carlyle a little earlier[216] in paying 6s. 8d. a piece 'towards the finding of two men *in their stead* to go for soldiers beyond the sea.'

Next month (March 1569) three tallow chandlers were 'commaunded to Newgate' for their disobedience in the Court,[217] probably for breaking the price of candles, including John Mynts. There were other (un-named) offenders, of whom '*all the Tallowe Chaundlers*' were to go to ward 'thone halfe to one counter (compter) and thother halfe to thothe counter'. Soon afterwards[218] Richard Bell (p. 80), together with a grocer 'dwellinge in Tower Ward' are reported to have been

presented by the wardmote enquest *for light weights* which matter was by them confessed,

and the culprits, having submitted themselves to the order of the

---

p   *Commentary*, p. 240.

Court, were fined. In November of the following year[219] the Court agreed that

my L. Mayor shall commytt to ward as many of the Tallowchaundelers of this Cytie as shall refuse to be bounde by recognizance.

We hear no more at this time, but on 14th June of the following year (1571)[220] we read that

this daie *the Wardens* of the tallowchandlers of this Citie for there refusall to obey the price set upon there severall sorte of candell by the Courte here were commytted to warde in Newgate,

an entry which is followed in just over a fortnight by a report that three very well known tallow chandlers together with their wives, servants and 'assignees' have been bound by recognizance to keep the price.[221] The first two were John Shorte (p. 78) and Arthur Lee, or Leigh (p. 80) and the third was Thomas Armstrong, Governor of the Yeomanry from 1571 to 1575 and Master in 1583–5, having served as a Warden in 1569.[222] Nothing seems to be known of his private life, although he appears in *the Husting Rolls* as a co-grantee in reversion of Richard Syberye's messuages and cottages in St Andrew, Baynard's Castle sold prior to the latter's death in 1596 (p. 36).[223]

In the summer of 1573[224] Robert Wainwright, tallow chandler, another well known candle-maker and buyer of tallow,[225] was bound in the sum of £10 to keep the price of candles within 'this Cityye & liberties thereof' and also not to

convey awaye or sell out of this Cytye any kinde of Tallowe not beinge made into candell.

In July 1567, when a Warden, he had been reported as a buyer of tallow from a butcher 'at such excessive price as might grow to the great hinderance and discommodity of the whole Company, and that before the Lord Mayor had set the price', *for which he had been committed to ward.*[226] For this offence our Court was unanimous in dismissing him from 'his office of Wardenship and as one of the Assistants' until he should have 'reconciled himself and be thought meet to be admitted to his room again'. He made a second

te IV.   A section of Ogilby and Morgan's map of London dated 1677, showing the situation of Tallow Chandlers Hall (c. 22).

appearance later that day and, on 'acknowledging his said fault and repenting of the same' and on 'his promise of amendment was placed in his room and Wardenship again'. He died in 1578 leaving a will disposing of his 'goods, chattels, leases and household stuff' to his wife and providing for 'a repast or drinking on the day of his burial'.[227] About a year earlier he had taken part in discussions with representatives of the City as to the validity of our Elizabeth Patent of 1577, a question which, as we shall see, was of immediate concern to our Company.

In October (1573)[228]

straight commandment was geven to the wardens of Talloughchaundelers not only to serche and ponyshe *such as have already offended* of their company in sellyng candells contrarye to my Lord Maior's price but also to geve order to all the sellers of candells *of theire said company*

to keep the price. On the same day Precepts were to be addressed to the Aldermen[229] that they should '*out of hand* charge their inquest of wardmote to inquere of' all

sellers of tallough candalls within the Cittye and liberties thereof that have sold contrary to my Lord Maiors price *and under weight* and presente their names with theire offences . . .

and, in the following January, Nicholas Hawkesworth (p. 94) was committed to prison 'for sellinge candells lackinge weight, there to remayne untill this court shall take further order for his delyverence'.[230]

In the late Spring of 1574 a number of prominent tallow chandlers, including Anthony Skinner, John Foster, Nicholas King, John Warren, and our old friend Hugh Benney, were required to enter into recognizances for keeping of the price of candles and for all their stocks of tallow to be used for candlemaking.[231] Skinner was Governor of the Yeomanry in 1567-8 and Master in 1581-2. On his death in 1595 he left 40s. to the Company, and, among a number of specific bequests, he left his 'gown faced with satin' to his brother and his gown faced with bugg (budge) to his son Anthony. (See Appendix B). He left 5s. to 'the Clerk of our Hall' (at that time Francis Kydd) and a like amount to Pris (Priest) the beadle.[232] The testator's son inherited

G

his 'freehold land in the parish of St Mary Mat fellon'.[q] Foster figures on two occasions in the accounts as having been fined, first for 'checking the Master and Wardens', which cost him 2s. 6d., and secondly 'for a pound of brass faulty, 12d.'[233] King, who was Governor of the Yeomanry from 1579 to 1581, had fined for Renter Warden of the Company many years before,[234] and we do not recognize him as a member of the Court. Warren was Governor in 1569–70. He was an Assistant of the Court in April 1565,[235] when he was summoned before his colleagues by Henry Beche, then one of the Yeomanry

for getting away a Butcher called Booker who served the said Henry Beche this last year and for delivering him fifty pounds in money aforehand, *wherby the said Henry Beche lost his said Butcher*

The Court's order is a little difficult to follow, but it involved Warren in paying a fine of £5 *if the butcher refused to serve either of them.*

That summer (1574) Anthony Aldersonne (p. 80) was committed to Newgate 'for mysbehavinge himselfe in speache in the open Courte, there to remeyne untill this Courte shall take other order for his delyveraunce', and the notorious John Mynts was committed to the Compter 'for that he refused to be bounde *accordinge to the ordere lately taken in this Courte* for the utteringe and sellinge of candells'.[236] It had been thought necessary a little earlier to extend to butchers and chandlers, who sold 'candells, tallow and other chaffer' at higher prices than those fixed by the Court of Aldermen, the penalties prescribed for the illegal sale of 'victuall and fewell' by an Act of Common Council passed over twenty years before in the mayoralty of Sir Richard Dobbes. A new Act had accordingly been passed,[237] and the Court of Aldermen doubtless had this Act in mind when imposing these sentences.[r] In the winter of 1574 further Precepts for Wardmote inquests were ordered, including an inquiry respecting the use of any *'false and untrue wayghtes either to buy or sell'*.[238]

---

q   The old name for St Mary Whitechapel. Various suggestions as to its derivation have been made, but none seems to be entirely satisfactory. *Harben.*

r   *Commentary*, p. 240.

Before the end of the year matters had come to a head, by which time at least fifty members of our Company had been fined varying sums from 6s. 8d. to 40s. according to the gravity of their offences,[239] one member being called upon to pay as much as £5 for breaking the price of candles, while Thomas Parker, later to become Master, was fined £3 6s. 8d. for a similar offence.[240] Like earlier culprits many of these men figure in the contemporary lists as buyers of tallow in considerable quantities.[241] The ten men who were first to appear before the Court in company with a number of butchers included Henry Beche and Nicholas Hawkesford, together with John Mynts, all of whom were convicted of breaking the price.[242] They were accompanied by one Thomas Gawsell, 'Chaundler',[243] who was convicted as

a common ingrosser and buyer of tallowe of a grete number of Bochers within this Cytie at prices farre more deare then are sett and appoynted by this Courte/ and for that he sellythe the same tallowe agayne to dyvers at excessyve pryces not being convertyed and made into candles/and also for sellynge of talloughe candells above the pryces sett and appoynted by this Courte to the great dysceipte of the Quenes Majesty's people and muche agaynst the commen wealth.

The offender was ordered on the morrow to be

sett on the pyllorye in Chepesyde with a paper over his hedde declaringe his sayde offences/there to continewe from eighte of the clockke untyll xj and then to be recomytted to pryson agayne/there to remayne untyll this Courte shall take further order for his delyverie.

The remaining forty or more offenders included Thomas Armstrong (p. 96), John Foster and John Warren (p. 94). The first two were found guilty of breaking the price of candles and of 'not usynge good and true weights to buye and sell', for which they were fined.[244] The third, having been found guilty of breaking the price,[245] refused to pay the fine and was sent to prison. Among the others, all of whom were found guilty of breaking the price and fined,[246] were John King (p. 46), Nicholas King (p. 97), Robert Huchenson (Governor in 1593-4), Robert Jarrate (Governor in 1596-7 and Master from 1607 to 1609), and Christopher Nodding. Huchenson was co-grantee with Thomas Armstrong and Thomas Lambert (Master from 1601 to 1603) of Richard Syberye's messuages and cottages (p. 96).[247] He died in 1602 leaving 20s. to Francis Kidd, scrivener, 'in respect of such pains' as he should take with his wife as one of the overseers of his will. He also released and forgave his apprentice, John Gates, 'the eighth and last year of his term of apprenticeship'.[248] Kidd, who was Clerk to the Company from 1568 to 1607, received on his retirement £11 3s. 4d. 'for seven quarters wages and pension' and 'for his benevolence sithence he left serving the Company'.[249] Nodding, as we have seen, was a Warden in 1588 (p. 53). Ten years earlier one Christopher Donkyn was found guilty of 'buying of his butcher out of his (Nodding's) hands, for which offence our Court imposed a fine of 5s.[250] That same year[251] the Court of the Yeomanry, with the consent of the parties, considered a complaint made by Nodding against William Jesson, one of the sociates, for sundry evil speeches and 'reviling the said Warden contrary to the order of the House to the evil precedent of others', for which Jesson was fined.

Most of the offenders were bound by recognizance[252] not in future to break the price of tallow or candles, to use good and lawful weights and measures, and to convert all tallow that they might buy into candles. A few unconvicted tallow chandlers were also bound, and many butchers guilty of breaking the price of tallow were fined and bound.

Early next year (1575) a number of 'Bochers and Chaundelers' were 'taxed and assessyd' for their sundry offences,[253] among whom were Walter Westmoreland, Thomas Lambert, and John Noye. Thomas Priest, our Beadle, was also fined but pardoned shortly afterwards.[254] Lambert's will has not been traced and we do not know when he died, but there are entries in our minutes recording a gift in 1603 of £20 'to be lent to young men of the Mystery gratis by the appointment of the Master and Wardens'.[255] Noye, a lesser known tallow chandler, while a member of the Yeomanry in 1567, was concerned in a dispute with Nicholas Hawkesforde (p. 94) 'one of the Livery' who, he complained, had 'misused him to his customers', for which Hawkesforde was fined, while Noye himself was fined 'for his dis-

obedience used to his Master in the Hall'.[256] Recognizances were
required from several members[257] and from the Beadle, Thomas
Priest,[258] at this time.

After a brief respite another bout of price breaking commenced
early in the year 1576. Several lesser known tallow chandlers were
fined for the second time after presentation by the Wardmote
inquest of the Ward of Tower.[259] John Foster and three lesser
known men were presented in Bishopsgate and all were fined.
Foster, as we know, had been fined before and so had one of the
others. All confessed to having 'solde tallowe candells above the
prices heretobefore set and appoynted by this Courte *and contrarye
to the condycion of theyre severuall recognizaunces*'.[260] On the same
day seven more tallow chandlers, including Thomas Lambert, all
previously fined, were presented by the Wardmote inquests of
several Wards and all again paid the penalty.[261] In February a
total of sixteen of our men were presented by Wardmote inquests
and fined varying sums from iiis. iiijd. to xls.[262] They included
Warren, Hawkesford, Nicholas King, Hutchenson and Nodding,
all of whom, as we know, had been previously imprisoned or
fined. Among the others were Walter Westmorland and Francis
Styche. The fines of all these men were directed to be 'imployed
towards the releyfe and settynge on works of roages & masterless
men in Brydewell'. Francis Styche had been fined by our Court
in the 'sixties for 'unclean and naughty vinegar'.[263]

By this time the Court of Aldermen appears to have obtained
the upper hand. Candle-makers in our Company and in other
Misteries practising our 'art', as well as our suppliers, the butchers,
seem to have learnt their lesson. The advent of the Elizabethan
Patent happens to co-incide with the cessation of any serious
trouble among our members in the candle and tallow trades, and
there, in the last quarter of the sixteenth century, with the end
of price control in sight, we bid them farewell.

Cresset Light

I

WE relate in this chapter what we know of '*cresset light*'. We have seen that as early as 1378 *cressets* were being used for the 'Marching' (or going) watches, as they came to be called, on the eves of the nativity of St John the Baptist (24th June) and the feast day of S.S. Peter and Paul (29th June).[a] The cresset used on these occasions[1] is believed to have been a metal vessel—probably some kind of iron bowl—fixed to the top of a long pole or stave, the bowl being provided with a central spike. This was certainly the type used at the Tower of London early in the eighteenth century.[b] There are entries in our 'Wardens' accounts for 1566–7 of 4s. 6d. paid 'for three *cressets* and mending of two other' and 2s. 6d. paid 'for 5 cresset staves';[2] in an inventory in 1576 there are entries of '*six whole cressets with staves*', three others without staves, and two whole cressets[3] and in another inventory, dated 9th July, 1599, we read of 'six cressets and three *spits*', which were kept in the 'garret and armoury' at the Hall.[4] But, in practice, cresset lights seem to have been used only on the two festival days.

We hear first of *night watches* proper in 1285, when the Statute of Winchester was passed,[5] and thereafter there are frequent references to these nightly watches, when *lanthorns* are known to have been used. In a Wardmote Precept or 'Warrant' issued in 1437[6] the Aldermen are ordered to see that during the Feast of Christmas 'covenable watch be kept & *lant'nes light* be nyght'tale'

---

a   Volume II, pp. 81–3.

b   *Commentary*, p. 240.

in the '*manere accustomed*', and an Act of Common Council passed in 1705[7] recites the necessity

for a strong and sufficient watch to be kept *every night* within all and every the wards of the said city and liberties thereof, with men of strong and able bodies *provided with candles and lanthorns* . . .

Fig. 15. The *Repertories* contain the following sixteenth-century Order of the Court of Alderman:
Rep. 16, fo. 439. 27th January 1569.
Belmen. Item yt was this Day agreed by the courte here that the cytyes ij Bellmen admytted and apoynted the xxij[th] of this instant moneth of January shall nightly in theyre watches pronounce with a lowde voyce in every strete and lane wherein they shall watch these wordes ffollowinge videlicet/*Remember the clockes/Loke to your Lockes fyre and your light and god geve you good night for/nowe the bell ringeth.*

The orders for the nightly watches were often combined with orders to *householders* to hang out lanthorns. We have seen how in the 'thirties of the sixteenth century command was given that all persons, both spiritual and temporal, should find lanterns with light in them nightly to hang out on the street side.[c] The same Precept (dated 27th November 1537),[8] required also that

all persons aforesayd, *all Excuses sett aparte*, shall from hensforth kepe watches nyghtly within theyre wardes where they dwell and inhabit when theyre corses and turnes shall happen to come and fall/orels fynde *suffycient Deputye or Deputyes*[d] in hys or theyre Rowmes or stedes and places/to awayte upon the constables of the said warde according to the auncyent lawes customes and usages of thys citie.

As a general rule the *Aldermen of the Wards* were made responsible for organizing the daily and nightly watches throughout the City.[9] In January 1539 they were reminded that watches were

---

c   Volume III, p. 84.

d   *Commentary*, p. 240.

necessary for the 'deprehension & taking of myghtie strong & valyant beggars, russelers,[e] theves, vagabonds, with ale other unthriftie persons'.[10] The Precept in November 1570 that constables should see that 'lanthorn light' was 'hanged forth' according to 'ancient custom'[f] required also that 'suspect persons' should be apprehended and committed to ward, as well as 'masterless men and idle vagabonds'.[11] But there were frequent occasions when the duty to watch was laid upon the *crafts* (or misteries), of which an early example occurred, as we have seen, in 1370.[g] On 19th July 1549, at the time of the insurrections which took place against the reformed religion, when the City had been put into a state of defence, twenty of the 'companyes and felowshyps', among which were the 'talloughchaundelers', were ordered to keep a day and night watch over the gates and 'posternes'.[12] The number of men employed varied from two to seven according to the venue. It was our duty to watch with two of the Saddlers at 'Rome Lands', Billingsgate.[h] In the early 'seventies[13] ten men were appointed from each of twenty-two companies, our teammates again being the Saddlers.[i]

Two early sixteenth century records of the midsummer watches (so called) are to be found in the City memoranda books. The first of these entries is in the *Journal*, where we read of a Precept to the Aldermen in 1527 directing that certain 'honest and comely persons with *bows and arrows*, and clean harness, arrayed in jackets of white, having the arms of the City', are to come to Blackwell Hall[j] '*and there set forth*'.[14] The second is in the *Repertory* Book and is dated 18th June 1528. In this entry it is ordered that, because

---

e   Rustlers. A name more often used to denote cattle-thieves. *O.E.D.*

f   Volume III, p. 86.

g   Volume II, p. 59.

h   Romeland. A large open space at the head of Billingsgate Dock, in the parish of St Mary at Hill, Billingsgate Ward. In 28 Henry VIII 'le Romland' is said to have belonged to the parish church of St Mary at Hill. *Harben.*

i   *Commentary*, p. 240.

j   On the west side of Basinghall Street with a passage west to Guildhall and south to Cateaton Street (Gresham Street). In Bassishaw Ward. *Harben.*

Fig. 16. Military costume in the time of Henry VIII.

of the deadly pestilence known as 'the sweating sickness', said to be 'now reignyng', there shall be '*no goyng watche* with men in complete harnes *attendyng uppon my lorde mayr in his circuite* as afore tyme hath been used'. The constables 'with certeyne honeste persons, householders or their lawful deputies', are nevertheless 'to be in harneys in maner accustomed and ther to watche and kepe the sayd Wardes contynually from x of the Clok in the evenyng un to thre of the Clock in the mornyng'. The 'lorde mayr with masters (sic) and the sheryffs attendaunt uppon hym, in harneys apperelyd as afore tyme hath used to be, with all their officers harnesyd in their jackets of newe lyverys, with *Torches lyght* afore my lorde mayr and *cressetts lyght* before thofficers attendyng uppon theym', are to 'ryde and surveye all the seyd Watche'. The Lord Mayor is to have attendant upon him 'xl cressets lights att the costs of the chamber' and the Sheriffs are to have 'other xl cressets'.[15]

We have no clear evidence of what this cresset light consisted, although we know something of its cost. In our accounts for 1567–8 there is an entry recording the payment of 21*s*. 'on midsummer night for three hundred of cresset lights'.[16] In 1570–1 we find a payment of 15s. 'for 36 stone of cresset light at 5d. a stone',[17] with which we may compare the cost of rough tallow in 1574, namely, 32s. the wey, or 2s. the stone (p. 69). As we shall see the 'lights' were carried in a bag and, when required, the combustible material was evidently placed on the spike in the cresset bowl.

We read in an entry in the *Repertory* Book dated 27th August 1538 of a proposed motion to 'common counsuyll' that ten of the Great Twelve Companies shall 'provyde certeyn *Cressets* to serve at mydsommer and saynt peters tyde'.[18] Two days later[19] there is an Order of the Court of Aldermen reciting that in these vigils it has happened that the watches 'have lacked lyght by the mysorder and neglygence of *Cresset men*' to their 'greatt emblemys-shyng and decay'.[k] A command is accordingly given that

yerely from hensforth on everye of the said nyghts there shall be *a standing light of Cressetts* in every place accustomed where the seid watche shall goo and passe by, *for the honour of this Cytie,*

and it is ordered that sixteen companies, headed by the Great Twelve whose names are given in their order of precedence,[l] shall provide five hundred cressets 'to be prepared in A redynes under the marks of their severall companyes on thyssyde the Feast of Easter nowe next comyng'.

From a memorandum (so called) in the *Letter Book* dated 27th April 1539 we learn, however, that there has been a change of plan. We read that the duty of supplying the cressets '*for the hole waye which the watch shall go on mydsomer nyght*' has now been imposed upon a total of sixty-eight crafts, again headed by the Great Twelve. The 'Taloughchaundelers' occupy the seventeenth place and are required, along with the Ironmongers and Leather-sellers, to find ten cressets, some of the leaders having to find more than twice that number, and those that follow having to find eight or less. The cost of each cresset is given as 2s. 4d. 'little

---

k *Commentary*, p. 240.

l as settled in the year 1516. See Volume III, p. 45.

more or less', and the number required is 500, making a total outlay (according to the record) of £58 13s. 4d.[20] The directions are repeated in the *Journal* on 16th June of the following year,[21] preceded by an entry in the *Repertory* Book that two Aldermen have been appointed to assess the rates 'that the Crafts shall doe for provyson of Cressett men, *Cressetts and lights* and *hatts*' for 500 marchers.[22]

The first we hear of our Company supplying the *lights* is nearly a year later, when we learn that, at a meeting of the Court of Aldermen on 31st May 1541,[23] it was decreed '*by the assent*' of our Wardens

that my lorde Mayer, Mr Shreves (sic) & *all Craftes* shalbe well seruyed of good cressyt lyght for iis iiijd the hundred,

a decree which is followed, on the same day, by an order directing the route to be taken 'as well on mydsomer evyn as on seynte peters evyn from hensfyrth for ever'. We learn from an entry dated 20th June 1564[24] that

the wardens of the Talloughchaundelers were here this day streightlye charged by the Courte to take ordre with their hole companye that they and every of them doe honestly & reasonably use the constables of this cytye & *all other* in the pryce of their cresset lights/*which they muste have at their hands*/not exactynge or takynge for the same more than good reason woulde that they shoulde doe.[m]

This is followed some three years later by an order that our Wardens shall 'appear for the provision of cresset light'.[25] It seems reasonably certain, therefore, that our employment as sole purveyors of cresset light had long since become an established practice. As it happens, we have to wait until the late 'sixties before hearing anything more about cresset men and their equipment. The route (or circuit) for the march in May 1541 was

first from the Guyldhall in to Wodstrete (Wood Street) and then into Chepe and so alonge through Cornehyll (Cornhill) unto Algate (Aldgate) and up Fanchurchestre (Fenchurch Street) unto grasse church[n] and about the Condyte

---

m   Commentary, p. 241.

n   The earliest form of the name is seen to be Garscherche (later Graschirche) from which the street took its name. See *Harben*.

there and then up grassechurchestrete (Gracechurch Street) into Cornehyll
and so into Chepeside ageyn up unto the lyttle condyte att pauls gate,[o]

and there the watch was to 'breke'.

Fig. 17. The Watch with 'cresset' and beacons (Hollar).

II

Whatever may have been their origin,[a] the marches soon became
an occasion for pageantry. The word is used by Ludovico Spinelli,
Secretary of the Venetian Ambassador in England in a letter dated
1st July 1521[26] to his brother in France describing what the writer
has seen. His account[b] confirms our belief that all the elements of

<hr />

[o]   St Paul's Gate, otherwise St Augustine's Gate, on the east side of the Church yard·
      Named after the Church of St Augustine, Watling Street, *Harben*.

[a]   *Commentary*, p. 241.

[b]   *Commentary*, p. 241.

pageantry associated with royal entries, but not otherwise heard of at this period,[27] were present. John Stow, writing near the close of the century, gives a long and picturesque account of these 'vigiles of festivall dayes',[28] telling us of 'bone fires' and banqueting in the streets and of other festivities which accompanied the event. The standing watch also, of which we shall hear more later, was often a colourful affair.

The antiquary informs us,[29] mistakenly, that 'this Midsummer watch was accustomed yearly time out of mind *untill the yeare 1539*', when it was 'laide down', and 'not raysed till the yeare 1548'. He writes of 'a great muster' that took place on the *8th May*, made by

the Cittizens, at the miles end . . . which passed through London to Westminster and so through the sanctuary and round about the Parke of S. James and returned through Oldbourne (Holborn),

and it is to this event that he attributes the banning of the march 'provided for at midsummer for that yeare', for which action he informs us (mistakenly) King Henry VIII was responsible, because of 'the great charges of the cittizens for the furniture of this vnusuall Muster'. It is true that the march did not take place, as usual, in 1539, but the King was not to blame,[c] and, as we have seen, the necessary arrangements for the event were in hand in April.[d] Stow goes on to say that it was Sir John Gresham who, in 1548, when Mayor, 'caused the marching watch both on the Eve of Sainte John Baptist, and of S. Peter the Apostle *to be revived and set forth*, in as comely order as it had beene accustomed'. No record of this 'revival' has been found in the City's memoranda books, although it is referred to elsewhere.[e] We know that on 16th June 1540 the same sixty-eight crafts as were concerned in 1539 were engaged in furnishing cressets for 'the hole way whiche the watche shall go' on Mydsommer',[30] and (as we have seen) the

---

c   *Commentary*, p. 241.

d   *Commentary*, p. 241.

e   *Commentary*, p. 241.

Fig. 18. Henry VIII and his Council.

precise route was laid down in the following year. We have no reason to suppose that the march was suspended during the next seven years, although it is true that the midsummer watch had a somewhat chequered career. In a Precept addressed to 'thalderman of the Warde of Cheape' on 12th April 1564[31] command is given that the constables of the Ward are not to

prepare appoint or ordeyne eny maner of cresset light, dromeslate*f* or other minstralsie to be used or occupied in the watch which they were latlye appointed by you . . . to kepe on S. peters even nowe next comynge.

Instead they are to 'prepare and appoint good, sad and substancial double (standing) watch that night' to be kept within the Ward *'in such and like maner as in tyme past hath byne used and accustomed*

---

f   Dromslade—a drum, or some form of drum. *O.E.D.*

to be kept'. Again in the following year there appears to be no
mention either of a going or a standing watch with cresset light.
We read only[32] that the Chamberlain is to provide 'at the cytyes
charges' and deliver to the Lord Mayor 'as meny staff torches*[g]* . . .
as it shall please his lordship to call for, *to bewtyfye and set furth the
watche'*.

It seems that the Mayor and Aldermen were not always free
to make their own arrangements. On 10th June 1567[33] a command was addressed by the Mayor to the Wardens of the Mercers
Company *'on the Quene our soveraigne ladies behalf'*, charging them
to

provide and prepare in perfect redynes xx^te faire and comely cressetts with good
and sufficient lights for the same for the necessary muster and shewe of the
Standinge Watche which we have appointed *and are fully determined and mynded
(god willinge) to kepe and make* within this our said sovereigne lady the quenes
majesties cittye of London upon the Vigill or even of the feast of the natyvytie
of saint John Baptist nowe next comynge.

The Wardens are also to find

xx^ti honest apt and hable men to beare the same cressetts

and to prepare

for every towe Cressett bearers *one bagge bearer to beare cresset lights in,* with
strawen hatts upon their heads

having the Company's 'armes in paper thereupon', and the
Wardens are to cause all these men and cressets

with so many good lights as shalbe sufficient to serve duringe all the tyme of
the same Watche to be brought and conveyed to *leaden hall* within the said
Cittye before vij of the clocke in the afternone of the said Vigill or eve of St
John Baptist now next comynge.

That a similar order was given to the other companies is borne
out by a number of entries in our Wardens' accounts for 1566–7.[34]
We read there that 2s. 6d. was paid for 'nine hats and bands
belonging to them', while 18s. was paid 'for painting the Arms

---

g   Tall, thick candles used for ceremonial purposes. *O.E.D.*

upon the Hats', and 6s. was given to the Cresset bearers 'for their pains'. 12d. was laid out in 'bread and cheese at Leadenhall and our Hall for the creset bearers'. 'Four ells and three quarters of soutwitche (soutage)ʰ to carry cresset light' cost 2s., and 4d. was paid 'to the Beadle's wife for making the Bags'. 'Three hundred and four stone of cresset light' cost 21s. at this time and the Beadle's fee was 16d. 'for watching the cresset light'. In June of the following year the same command was addressed to the Wardens of the Brewers Company (and others).[35] We see from our accounts for 1567–8 that, like the Brewers, we employed six cresset bearers, who, with three bag bearers, received a total of 6s. Nine straw hats cost us 2s. 3d., while 3d. was paid for tape for the hats and 14d. for nine bags. 8d. was expended for bread and drink.[36]

These commands (as we see) were for a *standing watch*. We cannot rely, therefore, on an entry dated 1st August 1567[37] giving directions for a 'going watch'. The heading, indeed, records that what follows is '*the effect* of a Precept *to be directed to thaldermen of everie warde*'. We can only suppose that, for some reason, the Queen preferred a standing watch in both these years. It is interesting to note, nevertheless, that the Court of Aldermen was prepared for a going watch with all its customary glamour. The Alderman of each ward, or his deputy 'in his or their own person' is to

take charge that the hole nomber of Constables of his ward *with the hole number of their watches*, well appointed in faire white corseletts with pertisonsⁱ and holberdsʲ faire and clene, do begynne their watche in the vigill of St John Baptist next cominge by the houre of viij of the clocke that night at the furthest and that all the said Constables *with their severall watch men* shall repaire at the same houre to such convenient place within the said warde as the said alderman or his deputie shall appoint,

and, upon view and muster taken, the Alderman

---

h   Coarse cloth or canvas used especially for packing or as material for bags. Of obscure origin. *O.E.D.*

i   *Commentary*, p. 241.

j   *Commentary*, p. 242.

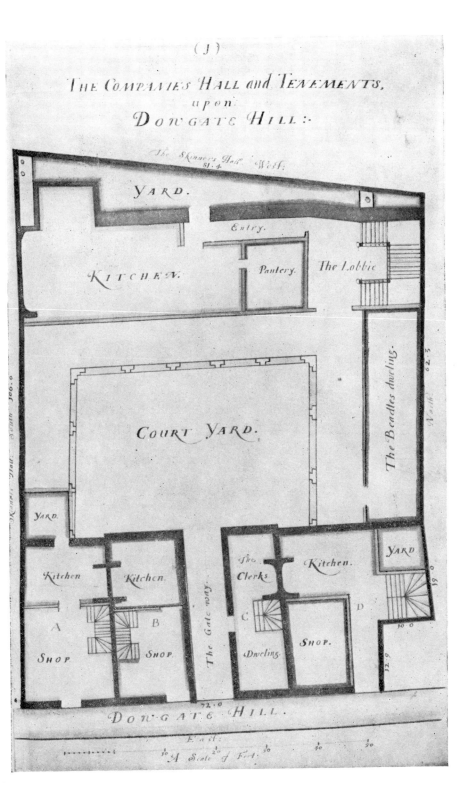

(J)

THE COMPANIES HALL and TENEMENTS,
upon
DOWGATE HILL:-

Plate V. Ground plot of the Company's 'Hall and Tenements upon Dowgate Hill' in 1678 (Appendix D).

shall electe and take out of the constables of said warde [of] the best trimmed and appointed with their henchemen and musical instruments

and shall also elect and choose

out of the said constables' watches [*of*] the tallest and best appointed men armed in faire white corseletts and weaponed with faire white (sic) partisons and holberds,

all which constables, with their watches

together with sufficient *cressets and lights* with men attendinge uppon the same to endure the time of the hole watche do repair to the Guildhall by the houre of ix of the clocke in the same night at the furthest/and there to attend *to be set furthe for the furniture of my lord maior in his goinge watch* by such direction as my lord Maire shall appointe,

and the *residue* of the constables with their watchmen, being in any case well armed,

to repaire to their place that they have byn accustomed to stand in, so it be betwixt the little condite in Cheape and Algate *in the sight of the goinge watche,* with sufficient lights with them/and that they departe not from their said standing untill the lord Maior and his goinge watche be broken up and one houre at the leaste.

The record continues with particulars of the number of constables from each Ward and the number of their corselets 'presented' and the number of constables appointed to the going watch with the number of their cressets,[k] and concludes with the information that four clerks from 'my Lord Mayor's Court' and a representative of the Bridge House are to receive the constables and armed men 'into the Guild Hall and set them out againe' and that forty wislers (whifflers)[l] are to guide the watch, including eight clerks of the Sheriffs' Court and ten representatives from each of the companies of Goldsmiths, Salters and Ironmongers. From two separate entries we also learn that the Chamberlain had to provide four silk flags for the use of the Lord Mayor[38] and four handsome doublets of white satin for the 'comely persons' who shall bear the flags.[39]

---

k   *Commentary,* p. 242.

l   *Commentary,* p. 242.

Fig. 19. Whiffler.

Strype, in his edition of Stow's *Survey*, which appeared in 1720,[40] inserts a passage in which he relates that

this Watch affording a great cavalcade and splendid show, brought abundance of all Degrees of People together, and not a few of the lighter sort; such as Rogues, Pickpurses, Quarrellers, Whoremongers and Drunkards. Which was found to have inconvenience. Therefore *in the year 1569* Sir Thomas Row, maior, with the universal Consent of the Aldermen, agreed to lay it aside, for that year at least: *and in the Room thereof to have a substantial Standing Watch for the Safety and Preservation of the City.*

He refers to the danger of 'dispersing the Plague into the Country' and mentions that the Mayor himself 'was so weak that he could not go in his own Person'. He then tells us that

the Recorder acquainted the Queen and Council with this Resolution. But it was signified back that the Queen disliked it and that it was her pleasure to have a going watch. Whereupon the Maior sent the Recorder to Sir William Cecyll the Secretary, earnestly desiring his interest with the Lords, that this Order might at least that year take Place upon the weighty Reasons aforesaid. And from henceforth it began to be laid aside.

There was, in fact, a double standing watch on midsummer eve that year (1569)[m] 'without musical noise of instruments' or lights

---

m   Volume III, p. 86.

'saving lanterns and candle light'. The watch was to consist 'both of constables and watchmen, being honest and discrete house-holders' of the Ward 'well and defensible harnesed and wea-poned'.[41] In the following year there was again a standing watch,[42] but on this occasion the direction given to each Alderman was to

cause all the constables of your said ward to appoint themselves to watch and that in as comely apparell or Armor as they in habilitie be able/with a double standing watche of everie of their precincts,

also that

your said watch [watchman] be of the comliest persons of your said warde well harnised in fayre and bright corseletts with faire and clenlie weapon/three parts of which your saide watche to be brought to stand (and) furnishe the highe strete of this citie *betwene Ludgate and Algate*[n] as they shalbe appointed/the same Con-stables to remain in the highe streats and the rest to furnish your saide Warde/ *everie constable to have his cresset light and bag bearer* to furnish his said watch with lighte/the same watch to be kept on the vigill of Saint John Baptist nexte cominge and to begin at ix of the clocke in the eveninge and to contynue till iiij[er] of the clocke in the morninge.

A command was issued a few days later to the Great Twelve Companies, with the addition of the Leathersellers[43] to provide 'cressets with lights' and also 'apte men to beare the same' and bag bearers with straw hats (as in the order of 10th June 1567), 'sufficient to serve during the time of the same watche'. The men with their supplies were to be brought to 'leaden hall' between four and five in the afternoon and the Alderman was to appoint

one or two discrete persons to see those cressett bearers and lightes well ordered and guyded during the tymes of their service.

Other Companies, including the Tallow Chandlers, were evi-dently ordered to join in the watch, for we read in our Wardens' accounts for 1570–1 of a payment of 12*d*. 'for nine badges for the cresset bearers' and '8*d*. a piece' to the men.[44]

The absence of any reference to a 'going Watch' for the past four years will have been noticed. On 12th June 1571[45] the Court of Aldermen ordered

---

n   *Commentary*, p. 242.

that my lord maior shall take order at his pleasure for the watche now at mydsomer next/aswell for Cressyt light to be had of the Companyes of this Citie and out of the Chambre/as also for other orders and Charges touchinge the same watche,

and it was agreed that the Chamberlain and others should 'attend upon the Lord Mayor for the same'. The result of these delibera-tions is not known, but in June 1574[46] we read that there is to be '*a good and substantial standing watch both of constables and watch-men*' who are to be 'harnessed and weaponed', again without any musical noise of instruments or lights, saving lanterns and candle light '*in such quiet manner as at other times in the year is commonly used*'. In the following year the order is repeated with the added requirement that the watchmen shall be 'honest and discrete householders of the Ward'.[47] Identical orders are known to have been made in the years 1578, 1582, 1583 and 1584.[48]

Stow concludes his account of the midsummer watch by telling us that since Sir John Gresham's time (p. 109) the *marching watch* 'hath not been vsed',[49] which may be correct, but, in view of the elaborate nature of some of the standing watches, the pro-nouncement is somewhat misleading. He observes, nevertheless, that 'some attemptes haue beene made thereunto,[o] *as in the yeare 1585* a book was drawn by a grave citizen, (John Mountgomery)[p] and by him dedicated to Sir Thomas Pullison, then Lord Mayor, and his Brethren the Aldermen, conteyning the manner and order of a marching watch in the Cittie vpon the Euens accustomed . . .'.[q] There seems no doubt that an attempt was made in 1585 to revive the marching watch, and that the citizen to whom Stow refers was not alone in this endeavour.[r] It is known that, in the same year, the Queen had the matter of the midsummer watch on her mind, but we cannot say whether the two events were related.

---

o   Commentary, p. 242.

p   The name appears in the margin of the edition of 1603. According to Kingsford, John Mountgomery's book is still preserved in the City archives at Guildhall. (*John Stow*, op. cit. Vol. II, pp. 284–5.)

q   Commentary, p. 242.

r   Commentary, p. 242.

The *Journal*[50] contains a record on the 24th June of a command addressed by William Sebright, the Town Clerk,[s] to the Aldermen, in which he informs them that he has 'of late received from the right honorable the Lords of her Majesty's most honorable privie counsell' a letter 'signifying Her Majesty's pleasure that there shall be on the eve of St John the Baptist next *a convenient and double standing watch in all parts of this City*'. Each Alderman is called upon to appoint *half the constables* of his Ward with their whole watches, whereof '*most of them* to be householders, being all harnessed in white bright armour with fair halberds, are to be in some convenient place' within the Ward in readiness by seven of the clock at night. 'Every of the said constables' appointed by the Alderman is to be there '*in such, decent and comely apparel as they will themselves*', having each of them a cresset together with the light (the cresset bearer and bag bearer both having straw hats), and each constable is to have one whiffler to attend upon him. But in the matter of music, the watch is to have '*one drum and no more*'. The directions are accompanied by an Order that there be 'candles and lanthorn light hanged out on the said eve at night *in all the lanes and other bye places*' within the Ward '*for the better passage of the people that shall go abroad*', and (presumably) to minimize the risk of disorder. The command is repeated in almost identical words in the following year,[51] after which a much shorter Precept is issued and,[52] by the turn of the century, the midsummer watch seems at last to have been abandoned.

---

s   *Commentary*, p. 242.

The Ordinances of 1538 and After
Quaterage
and the Conflict with the Salters

I

WE have mentioned the provisions contained in our Ordinances of 1538 for the making of bargains (p. 31) and also for the use of true weights (p. 92). These Ordinances constitute the earliest known regulations for the government of our Mistery, but it is most unlikely that they were the first.

Apart from the entry in the *Early Mayor's Court Rolls* in the year 1300 of an *ordinance* made by the men of the craft,[a] the first actual mention of 'Ordinances' occurs in the recital in our Grant of Arms of 1456 that our 'Mistery' is a Fellowship 'with Wardens and other officers authorized to make and enforce among themselves *rules and good ordinances* quite independently of other trades'.[b] The third Article of our Ordinances of 1538 speaks of 'certen persons' of the Company having been punished and corrected in the past 'for theyre defaulte as makynge vntrewe stuf, or other trespasses by them doon againste *the ordennaunces and constytucions* in the sayd Crafte made and vsed'. We may reasonably assume that we had a set of Articles at the date of our Charter of Incorporation in 1462, and may suppose that these are the 'ordennaunces and constytucions' referred to in 1538.

---

a   Volume I, pp. 61–2.

b   Volume III, p. 41.

The mention of an Assize of Candles[c] in the entry of 1300, as well as *the reported enforcement of an ordinance*, and the punishment of an offender for his trespass against *the officers of the Craft*,[1] are all strong pointers to our having been one of the fifteen crafts with known ordinances prior to 1327.[d] It is significant that the Wax Chandlers—the other purveyors of man-made light—had their ordinances recorded in 1371, and that by that date more than forty other crafts were in a like position.[e] Nor should we overlook, in this connection, the events which took place early in the fifteenth century, the first of which concerned our conflict with the Salters, and the second our claim to a portion of the 'issues' arising from our searches.[f] The Salters' development as a craft guild was a good deal later than ours, and it was not until 1465 that their first known ordinances[2] were made.[g] Nevertheless, there is a strong presumption that *both* companies had ordinances in 1419 when there was the so-called 'settlement' of our claim to assay the Salters' weights and measures,[h] supported in their case by the marginal note *Ordinacio de Salters* in the *Letter Book*;[3] and again in 1427, when it is our turn to gain recognition in the marginal note *Ordinacio Mistere de Talugh-Chaundellers*.[4]

It is worth noting that there are many blank pages in the *Letter Books* covering the years 1291 to 1497,[i] and the poor condition of the last few pages of *Letter Book* H (circa 1375–90) has already been referred to.[j] There is, moreover, a known case of a *Letter Book* having been tampered with. In a sixteenth century insertion in *Letter Book* K it is recorded that a certain ordinance made in 1447 on the petition of the Master and Wardens of the Mistery

---

c   Volume I, p. 61.

d   Volume III, Appendix A, p. 117.

e   See Volume III, Appendix A, pp. 117–19.

f   Volume III, pp. 55–6, and 24–5, respectively.

g   *Commentary*, p. 243.

h   Volume III, pp. 55–6.

i   *Commentary*, p. 243.

j   Volume II, p. 96.

Fig. 20. Royal procession, temp. Henry VI (Harleian collection).

of Drapers had been 'surreptitiously cut and taken away', which ordinance at the request of their officers 'was again inserted'.[5]

Some importance may also be attached to the fact that by a Statute of 15 Henry VI, c. 6 (1436–7)[6] not only were the Masters and Wardens of corporate bodies required to produce their Charters and Letters Patent and to cause them to be recorded by the appropriate local authority,[k] but, by the same enactment, *all ordinances had also to be approved before being put into force*. We have seen[l] how craft after craft, beginning with the Loriners in 1261, attended before the Mayor and Aldermen to record their ordinances, although some of the greater misteries, such as the Grocers in 1376[m] and the Fishmongers at a much later date,[n] appear to have considered that they were exempt from regulations which had been generally accepted. The Statute, therefore, did not greatly affect the London guilds,[7] and there is only one recorded case of disobedience at that time. when the Pewterers in 1438

---

k   In the City of London, the Mayor and Aldermen.

l   Volume III, p. 10.

m   Ibid., p. 17.

n   *Commentary*, p. 243.

were required to answer a charge of having made ordinances 'against the profit of the City'. They confessed their fault and the illegal ordinances were 'annulled and utterly reiecte'.[8] Nevertheless, there were evidently a sufficient number of offenders some fifty years later to cause the Court of Aldermen to take action. In 1475, for instance, a fine had been imposed on certain butchers for having made ordinances 'contrary to the liberty of the City.'[9] The Mayor and Aldermen accordingly made an Ordinance, entered in the *Letter Book* on 14th December 1487,[10] directing that

Wardens of the Misteries should thenceforth make no ordinances in their Misteries unless the same be approved by the Aldermen for the time being

with a rider that

thereupon Wardens of divers misteries brought in their books of ordinances that had not been approved by the Court of Aldermen *and those ordinances were cancelled*, and the leaves of the books on which they were recorded were cut out (*abscisa.*)[o]

Among these 'divers misteries' were the Wax Chandlers, whose wardens were 'enjoined that from henceforth they should not make any ordinances unless they were confirmed by the Mayor and Aldermen',[11] and it was agreed 'that their book in which the ordinances made by them, both on the authority of the lord King[p] and on their own authority, were registered, *should be wholly condemned* and remain in the Chamber of the Guildhall and never be returned . . . and that all the pages on which such ordinances were written should be torn out of the said book . . .'[q] Again, nearly three years later, we learn that 'the Wardens and other good men of the art or occupation of Saddlers have come before the Mayor and Aldermen and shown that, in times past, ordinances had been made for the rule of the Craft that had not been authorized within the City'. They had, therefore, 'brought in

---

o   *Commentary*, p. 243.

p   *Commentary*, p. 243.

q   *Commentary*, p. 243.

their book of ordinances before the Mayor and Aldermen, as commanded, and those that were not authorized had been cancelled, and thus they had been left without ordinances wherewith to govern the Craft'. Accordingly they prayed that the new ordinances set out in the *Letter Book* might be authorized,[12] a plea which was accepted.

In an endeavour to discover when our first Ordinances were made and to account for their absence from the *Letter Books*, it seems, therefore, that our problem is fourfold. Had ordinances actually been drawn up but not recorded prior to the year 1300; or were ordinances made and approved by the Mayor and Aldermen at a later date, and were they, either by the carelessness of a clerk, or by misfortune, omitted from the record; or were our Ordinances lost by the accidental or deliberate mutilation of the record; or did we simply fail to record them and escape detection? The puzzle is one which is not likely ever to be solved.

II

On 3rd October 1538, in the Mayoralty of Richard Gresham, two Aldermen were appointed 'to viewe the booke of Tallowghchaundelers touchyng theyre Ordynances of theyr Mystery & make reporte thereof to thys Courte',[13] and three weeks later the Wardens are reported 'to have exhybytted a supplicacion most humbly desyryng that the same and theyre peticions and ordynances *here vnder wrytten* may be entered of recorde'.[14] It is surprising that the Salters should apparently have raised no objection in April 1524 to the allowance of the Tallow Chandlers' 'bill' respecting the search for tallow and candle (p. 9), but the new Ordinances[15] contain, as will be seen, several articles which they must have found distasteful and one which, for obvious reasons, they were bound to oppose, namely the twenty-fourth[a] article relating to 'quarterage'.[b] This article comes straight to the point

---

[a]   For convenience the writer has numbered the articles 1 to 32 inclusive.

[b]   A brief reference was made to quarterage in Volume III, p. 35, when David (or Davy) Tompkins is mentioned as a member of the Yeomanry. His payment of 4*d.* in the Yeomanry list for 1518–9 was for half a year.

in the marginal note 'THE QUARTERAGIS of *other companies occupying ye crafte of Taloughchaundelers*', and its first part, including the recital, from which the object of the edict is at once apparent, reads as follows:

For asmuche as there be dyuerse & sundrye persones of *other occupacions* which occupyeth the crafte of Taloughchaundelers *& for bycause* that thei bere theim selfes of the occupacion that thei be made free of & wolle not be serched by the wardeins of the Company of Taloughchaundelers *nor bereth nothyng to the same Company* Therefore it is now ordeyned by the lorde Mayere of this Cytie of London & his bretherne the Aldremen of the same Cytie nowe for the tyme beyng & for their successours for euermore that *all suche persones what so euer thei be aswell within this Cytie as in the lyberties of the same that doth occupie the seyd Crafte of Taloughchaundelers* shall bere & paye *quarterage* to the same Companye/that ys to sey xvjd sterling/quarterly iiij.d.

There seems to be no recorded instance of a craft guild calling upon its members for the payment of quarterage, as such, until early in the fifteenth century. Its imposition on non-members comes later, and is comparatively rare. The Mercers' earliest known ordinances of 1347[16] in fact contain an article requiring 'that all of the mistery should be clad in a suit once a year . . . and that no charge should be put upon the livery beyond the first subscription, except only for the priest and the common servant'.[c] The Drapers may have been the mistery to lead the

Fig. 21. Women's costume in the time of Henry V.

---

[c]   Afterwards called 'the beadle', or in some companies the 'common beadle'.

field with an article in their new ordinances of 1418 directing the payment by every brother (of the mistery) of twelve pence a year in quarterage (related to his wearing of a livery) 'and though he be wedded he shall pay for him and his wife but xiid'.[17] Twenty years later we read in the Pewterers' ordinances[18] that

euery persone houshoulder of the saide craft that holdethe open shope by the strete side within the saide Cite or in the suburbs therof from this tyme forward paie yerly to the relef of pouer men of the same Craft xijd./to be disposid by the discrecions of the masters and goode men of the same crafte in tyme of necessite in peine of dowblinge/to the chambre.

In 1440 there is an article in the ordinances of the Writers of Court Letter (Scriveners) directing that 'every person enfranchised of the Craft and holding open shop in the City or suburbs shall pay yearly twelve pence *towards the support of the craft*'.[19] In 1451 a distinction is drawn for the first time in the Barbers' ordinances, between those of the clothing and those not of the clothing. The 'brothers' in the first group are to pay quarterly iijd, those in the second jd, in both cases 'to the Almes of the craft'.[20] In the Painters' ordinances of 1466 the quarterly charge on 'every brother being of the clothing' is 4*d*. 'to the alms', those out of the clothing are not called upon.[21] The article in the Bakers' ordinances of 1476 reads simply 'that every brother pay *his quarterage* of 3*d*.'[22] The Turners' ordinances of 1479 impose a quarterly charge of '4*d*. more or less' to pay the Common Beadle's salary.[23] The Masons' ordinances of 1481 require 'that certain days be kept for payment of *quarterages*, viz. 3 pence a quarter', an extra payment of 2 pence being made towards any recreation provided on those days by the Wardens.[24] Then—in the following record of the ordinances, or 'articles' as they call them, of the Brown bakers, made on the same day as those of the Masons—we find this, the first, reference, to *outsiders*.[25]

15 Oct., 21 Edward IV [1481] came likewise good men of the *Mistery* of Brounbakers before the Mayor and Aldermen/complaining that persons of divers other crafts use the Craft [trade][d] of Brounbakers *to a greater extent than*

---

d   *Commentary*, p. 243.

freemen of the Craft [*Mistery*] and refuse to obey the Wardens of the Craft in assize[e] and past (paste)[f]/pay no quarterage/neither bear lot nor scot.[g] They therefore prayed that certain articles for the regulation of the Craft might be approved and recorded to the following effect:

That every one occupying the Craft [trade] of Brounbakers in the City shall obey the Wardens in their search and observe the rules touching the assize and paste/under penalty of paying 6s. 8d.

That every brother [of the Mistery] or *occupier* of the Craft [trade] pay every quarter day 6d./besides 13d. to the Beadle/and every journeyman 2d.[h]

The matter of 'searches' is discussed later when we examine the second part of our Article 24. These articles of the Brown Bakers are followed in 1482 by 'Articles for the regulation of the Craft of Bruers',[26] among which is an article

that every person keeping house and being a Brother of the Bruers *and* occupying the craft of brewing pay quarterage towards the great charges of the Craft and Fraternity,

which seems to exclude outsiders. In the same year the ordinances of the Glovers provide that 'foreyn' are to obey the rules and ordinances of the Craft, but only those taking 'wages for their work' are required to pay quarterage.[27] The ordinances of the Cutlers in 1488 require 'that every freeman of the Mistery, being in the clothing, shall pay quarterly four pence to the Master and Wardens for their search, and every freeman not being of the clothing, and occupying a shop, two pence'.[28] Presumably 'Freemen not being of the clothing' means 'Freemen of the Company', and accordingly excludes outsiders. On the other hand the ordinances of the Bowyers[29] made on the same day expressly provide that 'every householder of the City *using the Craft* is to pay quarterly 3d. to the common box for the maintenance of a light before 'the Rode and Seint George' in the Chapel of St Thomas on London Bridge.[i] In the ordinances of the Hurers, or

---

e   The well-known 'Assize of Bread' regulating weight and price.

f   dough.

g   Volume II, p. 34, footnote 1 gives the supposed meaning of these words. (See Commentary, p. 243.)

h   Commentary, p. 244.

i   See Volume II, p. 52.

Cappers (1488),[30] the Coursours (horse-dealers) (1488),[31] the Founders (1490),[32] and the Leathersellers[j] (1493),[33] the payment of quarterage is confined to *members*, including the Founders' journeymen, while the Painters (1491),[34] in contrast to their earlier ordinances, bring in '*every one using the Craft*', and the Pastelers (1495), complaining that they have hitherto been 'deprived of their living by vintners, brewers, innholders and tipplers', require the payment of quarterage by '*all persons that seethe, roast, or bake victuals for sale in the City*'.[35]

Our earliest accounts to survive are contained in a book kept by *the Wardens of the Yeomanry*[k] commencing in 1518, and it is apparent from this book that it was the Wardens' duty to collect all quarterage money, which accordingly formed an important part of their revenue. The first account is that of William Knight and William Bradfote (p. 18) 'late Wardens of the Yeomanry' compiled on 1st August 1519 and presented in their 'A Compte' before 'Robert Sylver, Master, John Benet, John Hampton, John Laane and John Clerke' (all of whom, except Clerke, being well known to us[l]) 'and other *as well of the lyveray as owte of the lyveray*'.[36] While it is evident from these words that Liverymen are intended to be included,[m] the distinction is not clear from the list itself, and we cannot account for the absence of the Master and Wardens' names. The names of Choppyn (or Master Choppyn)[n] and Sylver (Mr), occur in subsequent accounts, and, when we come to the account for 1530–1,[37] we find it headed by the name of Stephen Astell, which occurs in Group I of the list in the Public Record Office of 1537–8, and that there are a number of names in Group II.[o] By the year 1534 the distinction has become

---

j   The Leathersellers' regulations included women members.

k   For an account of this junior organization within the Company of Tallow Chandlers see Appendix A.

l   See Volume III, pp. 62–78.

m   *Commentary*, p. 244.

n   Volume III, pp. 33, *passim*.

o   Volume III, pp. 77–8 and Appendix F.

clearer. The account starts with the heading 'Receytts of the Quarterage', with a long list of names, followed by the heading '*Quarterage receyved of the Lyvery*', [38] with only four names which all occur in Group II.[39] Eight years later the order is reversed. The first heading is 'Quarterage', in which list there are twelve names, four of which occur in Group II, and the others are to be found in Group III,[40] from which we deduce that, since 1538, all those in the earlier list who were not then Liverymen had since attained that status. The second heading is 'The yeomanry', in which there are no less than ninety-six names.[41] The same plan is adopted in the following year.[42] Then, in 1544, we get an even clearer picture. The first heading is '*Quarterage of the Clothing*', with nineteen names. The second is again '*The yeomanry*'[43] with one hundred and thirteen names.[p] In subsequent years the word 'Livery' is sometimes used, as it was earlier, instead of 'Clothing'.

It is to these accounts then that we turn for information regarding the 'diverse and sundry persons of other occupations' using our craft. But first we observe that the fee payable by members and strangers alike was for many years only *half* the amount stated in article 24. We do not know how the higher figure came to be inserted or why it was not corrected before the Ordinances were finally approved.

For the first fifteen years, the entries for outsiders are not very clear. We meet a few 'forens'[q] and four or five men of designated crafts.[44] These include in 1523 a tailor in 'Fletestret', in 1531 a skinner, and in 1533 a grocer, a salter and a brewer.[45] In 1534 there are again a few outsiders—a glazier, a salter, a saddler and a leatherseller, each paying the yearly quarterage of viij d, and a 'forren' paying ij, evidently for one quarter.[46] In 1535–6 there are two salters, a brewer, a tailor, a leatherseller and a girdler.[47] In the following year[48] the men of different alien crafts appear to have numbered seven.[r]

---

p   *Commentary*, p. 244.

q   *Commentary*, p. 244.

r   Two salters, a brewer, a saddler, a tailor, a leatherseller and a girdler.

From time to time there were 'detters', of which an early example occurs in 1528–9, when there were twenty-five. The defaulters are classed in two divisions; first, 'Here aftar foloythe the namys of sarten dettars'; secondly, 'The namys of them that be on payd (unpaid) of all ther holle quarterages & *wyll pay none*'.[49] In the memorable year 1531 that Richard Choppyng was Sheriff of London (p. 26) there were, alas, thirty-four.[50] In 1536—the year of his death—there were fifty,[51] when a climax was reached. On 30th June 1537[52] 'the moste parte of the *Brethern of the Company*', considering that

the Wardeyns of this Fraternyte of the yomandry of Taloughchaundelers before this tyme haue taken great Payens and Busenes in gooyng quarterly A brood for the gatheryng of their quarteragis of the Brethern of the same Company and hathe lost great labour and hathe spente moche tyme in vayen to their great Charges

and,

for A good order and usage w^t loue and faveo^r emonge theym selffes/to be hade maynteyned and contynewed in the same Fraternyte/

it was established that 'every Brother of the said Fraternyte', should come quarterly 'to the Taloughaundelers Halle' to pay his quarterage, failing which he was to forfeit 'vj d. sterlyngis or a lb of on wroughte (unwrought) waxe for the Mayntenance of the same Bretheren', having no 'scowes (excuse) lawfull or Reasonubyll'. That year there were no debtors!

Appended to the list for 1538–9,[53] which we have previously compared with the list in the Public Record Office (an entry which contains one hundred and seven names) are those of four persons individually described, viz. a 'taylour', a 'saddler', a 'bocher', and a 'letherseller', who are listed together for the first time as '*strangers*'.[s] In this list the Wardens reverted for some reason to their earlier practice of not distinguishing between those 'of the lyveray' and those 'owte of the lyveray'. We notice, nevertheless, the name of 'Maister Nalson' (p. 84), who occupies

---

s   *Commentary*, p. 244.

the last place among the Assistants in 1537–8, and eight names in Group II. In the list for the following year (1539–40) two men, set down as 'strangers', are inadvertently counted as part of the Company proper.[54]

Quarterage accounts continued to be kept by the Wardens of the Yeomanry, but after 1548 the names of strangers disappear from these accounts. The earliest 'Livery' (or Wardens') accounts to survive commence in 1549, and in the records for 1549–51 we find an entry of 36s. 'received of strangers for 2 years Quarterage',[55] which seems to represent the total receipts from twenty-seven persons paying at the rate of viijd a year. Again in the Livery accounts for 1551–3 we learn that 25s. has been 'received of the Companies not being free of the Mistery of Tallow Chandlers occupying the selling and making of Candles, for their Quarterage'.[56]

Turning now to the second part of Article 24, we read the following:

And also shall peasably & quyetly suffre the wardeins of yᵉ seid companye of Taloughchaundelers to come & entree into their shop house or houses & gardein/to serche for Oyelles Sawse and Weyghtes/Talough & Candyll/according as thei may aunswer for theim And he or thei that doth withstande the contrary/euery tyme so doyng to pay xxx sterlinges to be devyded as ys aforesaid [that is to say the one half to the Chamber of London and the other half to the mayntenaunce of the reperacions of the house].[t]

Powers of search, such as these, amongst outsiders, were quite common, and (as we have seen,[u] in the case of the Drapers and Tailors) they sometimes resulted in disputes which arose from privileges conferred by Letters Patent from the Crown.[57] By the Leathersellers' Charter of Incorporation of 1444 their Wardens were given 'full power of search throughout England',[58] subject, in London, 'to the survey of the Mayor', which meant that in practice the searchers must be accompanied by a Mayor's officer.[v] Seven years later it became necessary for the Leather-

---

t   Commentary, p. 244.

u   Volume III, p. 51.

v   Commentary, p. 244.

sellers and Glovers to join in presenting a petition to the Court of Aldermen. It was stated that 'members of the said Misteries often encroache upon each other's work, *and would not obey the search of the Wardens of the craft to which they did not belong'*, illustrating—as the learned author of the History of the first-named company pertinently observes—'the inconvenience which arose from the conflicting jurisdiction of two companies intimately related in manufacture and trade'.[59] The result was the allowance by the Court of joint ordinances, of which a feature was the appointment as searchers of two Wardens from each company,[60] an arrangement reminiscent of the Court's order made in 1518 respecting our searches, jointly with the Salters, of persons of both companies dealing in candles and sauces.[w]

By contrast, the Wax Chandlers obtained an order of the Court in 1569[61] that 'the Master and Wardens shall have their search & quarteridge *according to their charter'*. Their original charter of 16th February, 1 Richard III (1484) in fact makes no reference to quarter-age, but provision is made by an article in their *ordinances* of 1514[62] that

noo man use exercise or practise the sayd occupacion of Waxchaundelers within the sayd citie [of London] or liberties thereof/but that in all thyngs concernyng the same craft be obedient to pay *and to be contributorie* in every behalf as the other bretherne of the same occupacion.

This is doubtless the provision referred to in the Court order, which goes on to direct that they (the Master and Wardens)

shall from hensforth have the search of all suche as do sell utter or occupie any wax or other stuf readie wrought/concerninge the mysterye of Wexchaundlers *And that they shall paye quarterlye to the saide companye for the same search iijd*[x] *viz. xijd by the yeare*/And they to *commytt to prison* at my L. Mayors commaunde-ment all suche as shall refuse to paye the same accordinglye.

In one important respect the position of strangers in our Company differed from that of our own members. Article 30, containing 'the othe for the Fremen, as well for prentyzes as for

---

w   Volume III, p. 69.

x   *Commentary*, p. 244.

redempcyoners' that '*desyre to be free*', requires them to be 'true & faythfull' not only to the Sovereign and to 'the mayster & mynysters of this Citie', but also to the Master and Wardens of the Craft. The next Article (31) containing '*the othe of the bretherne that cometh into the same company*', which, in the context, can only relate to outsiders, requires only allegiance to the Sovereign. Both Articles require attendance on summons, but here again there is a difference. Each freeman is to be 'obedyent to all suche summons' that he be 'laufully warned vnto'. (Article 30.) Outsiders are warned only to come 'to the seyd mayster & wardeins att all tymes *for such causes as shall concerne the weale of the same Crafte* [or trade]' (Article 31). Freemen are compelled to keep 'the Actes & rueles' of the Company (or of their occupacion as it is called) and its '*Secrettes*', of which presumably only they will be fully aware (Article 30), while outsiders are bound to observe only 'the good ruelle & ordre of the same Crafte [or trade] of Taloughchaundelers'. (Article 31.)

Article 25 empowers the Master and Wardens to impose a penalty on 'any persone or persones of the seyd Felowship, *or that occupyeth the seyd Crafte of Taloughchaundelers*, of what degree or condycion he be, that offendeth in any Artycle Acte or ordenaunce in this boke expressed'. And, if he fails to pay,

then yt shalbe leefull to the sayd mayster and wardeins for the tyme beyng att euerye laufull tyme to entre into the howse or shopp of him or theim so denying or refusing to paye And there *to take a dystres or dystresses* convenyent for the same/ & those dystres or dystresses so taken laufully to leade dryve & beare away and kepe to the vses aforesaid,

with power 'to prayse & make sale of the seyd dystres or dystresses to the full contentacion of the forfeytures' and so on. We may assume that the 'Articles, Acts and Ordinances' for the breach of which *strangers* could be punished, were confined to those which concerned 'the weale' of the Craft (Article 31), but even so this is a stringent regulation for non-members, and, under one further article, number 10, which remains to be mentioned, they appear to be placed in a worse position than our own men.

The other two articles (apart from number 10) to which the Salters may well have objected are numbers 8 and 9.

Article 8, reads as follows:

FOR WEYGHTES   ALSO by yt ordeyned that
                                          all men aswell of the said
                                          Companye of Tulloughe Chaundelers
as of any other Company/whiche vsethe the Crafte of Talloughe Chaundelers/
shall vse and occupye true ballans and weyghtes after Haberdepoyes marked
with the Kynges marke/that is to say with the letter of H. crowned and true
measures also/And also that vseth the contrary/as ofte as yt may be proued and
founde fawtye/shall pay to the vse aforesayd x.s sterlinge/to be devyded as ys
abouesayd,[y]

The importance attached by the Salters to this subject of weights
was seen in the 1419 memorandum, when they were given the

Fig. 22. Henry VII's trial of weights and measures (Harleian collection).

exclusive control of measures and weights *within their own mistery.*[z]

Article 9 reads thus:

SAWSES   ALSO Be yt ordeyned that
                                         no man of the sayd Fellow-
ship/*nor of none other companye*/make or do to be made any venyger but yf yt be
of clene wyne swete and holsome for mans body[aa] Nor also no mustard[bb]
nor verges[cc] but yf yt be of good stuf swete and holsome as yt ought to be for
mans bodye/upon payne of vjs. viijd sterlinge where as yt shalbe founde the
contrarye/to be devyded as ys aforesayd.

We know that the Salters were concerned in the making of sauces from very early times, and we have seen them in conflict with our Company over *the right of search* little more than twenty years before.[dd]

These two articles give point to the second part of Article 24 with respect to searches. It may seem strange that 'Oyelles, Talough & Candyll', which like 'Weyghtes' and 'Sawses' figure in that article are not also given articles to themselves. Possibly the regulations respecting tallow and candles were so well known as not to need clarification while large-scale dealings in oil were, on the other hand, as yet comparatively rare.

Finally, Article 10, which is concerned with goods taken in *distress*, should be read in conjunction with Article 25. The marginal note reads 'Rescewe[ee] agaynst the Maister & Wardens *in Serchynge*', and the article falls into two distinct parts. First, it imposes a penalty of xx s. sterlinge on '*any Talloughe Chaundeler whatsoeuer they be*' who 'make any rescue' at any time that the Master and Wardens make search

and wyll not suffer theyre wares & stuf perteynynge to the said occupacion

---

z   Volume III, pp. 55–6.

aa   *Commentary*, p. 244.

bb   Mustard was used in the making of sauces. See the reference to a mill (mola) for grinding in Volume II, p. 80.

cc   Vinegar.

dd   Volume III, p. 69.

ee   The forcible recovery (by the owner) of goods distrained. O.E.D.

to be seyn and habeled*ff* laufull/or will not suffre them (the searchers) to take a dystresse for amendement of the same/and *to come to theyre commen Hall* at all tymes to make aunswere to suche thinges as shalbe laid to theyre charges touchinge the same occupacion.

This direction can relate only to members of the Company, for, by the *second* part of the article, it is ordained that 'yf any other person or persones that vseth the feate or crafte of Chaundelers *and yet in dede ys no Talloughchaundeler, but free of another companie*', makes any rescue against the Master and Wardens for any such lawful search

then he or they that soo shalbe founde fautye thereof [shall come] *before the Chamberleyn of London* for the tyme beinge and before the sayd Maister and Wardeins there being present,

and 'the same partie so founde faltye' is to incur the same penalty as our members. It seems likely that the requirement that strangers should attend before the Chamberlain was inserted by order of the Court of Aldermen to protect offenders against persecution by our Master and Wardens, but in practice it may well have imposed upon them unnecessarily the indignity of a public trial.*gg*

III

Having had their attention drawn to our Ordinances, the Salters took a little time to lodge their protest, but when it came it was very much to the point. The Ordinances appear from the entry in the *Letter Book* to have been approved by the Court of Aldermen on 24th October, 1538. By June of the next year our rivals were in the field. There is a warning in the *Repertory* Book on the 12th[63] that 'thordynances of the Talough Chaundelers shalbe redde the next Courte day, & to be here . . . to answer to *the petition of the Company of Salters*', and we read on the 17th,[64] that

---

ff   See note *jj*, p. 233.

gg   *Commentary*, p. 244.

the peticion of Salters hath bene redde/fyndyng theym selffes *grevyd* that ye Talowchaundlers shuld have serche of ye Salters for Sawse Talow candelles oyles or Sauce (sic)^a/ & that y^{ey} shuld have iiij d for quarterage of suche as occupye that same feate . . .

But the Court was in no hurry. On 28th October 1539—over four months later—comes the entry[65]

Item. the M^r & Wardeyns of Talowchaundelers desyred [that] others of other companyes that vse makyng of Candelles shall be contributuryes to pay theyre quarterages with the seyd company of Talowchaundelers, & ys agreed that the decre made yn the tyme of Mr Gresham^b *shalbe advysedly loked vpon*/ & the salters to be harde what they can say yn thys byhalf.

We can picture the clerk to the Court conscientiously 'looking upon' the record book, but we are told nothing of the Court's deliberations or what more the Salters had to say on the subject, assuming they were heard. It is fairly obvious that notwithstanding the high reputation attained by the Salters Company, of which five members had already held office as Lord Mayor,[66] the Court was reluctant to interfere with existing arrangements for employing our Company as a police force to secure an adequate supply of tallow and candle for the inhabitants of the City. The Mayor and Aldermen were doubtless quite content also that weighing should be in our capable hands, despite the early decree which was probably long since forgotten, and they may have looked upon *sauce-making*, as they did *the search of oils* (p. 133), as of minor importance. As an indication of the continuing attitude of the Court to the part that our Company was expected to play in the task of maintaining supplies, the *recognizance* dated 16th May 1538,[67] to which we have referred more than once,^{c} reiterated earlier commands to our men that they should

sell no candell out of thys Cyte And also make all suche Talloughe as shall come to theyre severall handes in candelles.

---

a   Probably a mistake for 'weights'.

b   The decree which gave approval to the Ordinances (*supra*).

c   See Volume III, p. 70 and p. 57 (*supra*).

Next, by a decree of the Court dated 4th December 1543,[68] the 'articles' (so called)[d] were read

aswell as to the Wardeyns & dyuerse other of the same fellowship

as also to five men of other crafts, who are, for some reason, particularly mentioned, and of whom it is said that they '*occupye Chaundelers craft & vse to make Candelles*'.[e] Lastly, '*commaundment*' was given to our Wardens

dylygently to serche bothe thurrough out theyr owne felowship & all other vsyng that feate Whither they observe the seyd artycles or nott/And truely to present to this Court the names of theym that they shall fynde to make defaute.

Notwithstanding these directions, our Company had to wait until 28th May 1549 for the Court's solemn adjudication on the Salters' complaint, but when at last it came, we see that, in the matter of quarterage at least, it was entirely in our favour. This is how the first part of the order reads:[69]

ITEM for certeyn reasonable consyderacion movyng the Courte yt is this daye ordered & agreed by the same that fromhensfurthe *all suche persons as nowe are or herafter shalbe free of the Companye of the Salters & shall vse & occupye the crafte & occupacion of the Talloughchaundelers* shall be truelye & quyetlye contente & paye to the Wardeyns of the seid fellowship of the Talloughchaundelers all such quarterages as they, by the acte of this Courte made in the tyme of the Mayeraltye of S[r] Richard Gresham knight (Article number 24 of our Ordinances), are appoynted to paye.

The decree goes on to repeat the directions contained in the order of 27th April 1518[f] that two of the Company of Salters and two of our Company should join in the search, which would not have pleased us, but to which we might have found it difficult to object.

But, alas, we were doomed to disappointment. On 13th February of the following year (1550), with a new Mayor in office, there comes another order. Notwithstanding the marginal note

---

d   *Commentary*, p. 244.

e   *Commentary*, p. 245.

f   Volume III, p. 69.

'Salters & Talloughchaundlers *for the accustomed search*', it is plain from the order itself that our practice, long since approved by the Court, of conducting our searches without interference, is confirmed, but in regard to our claim to quarterage, we see that it is quite a different matter.[70] The new order tells us that 'after the full & delyberate herynge & debatement of the matter' in variance

yt was fynallye agreid & orderyd by the Courte that the seid wardeyns of the Talloughchaundlers . . . for the tyme being *shall dyligentlye & truely make & contynewe their seid serche* from tyme to tyme from hensforward in suche & lyke maner as they hertofore have vsyed to doo/so alweyes that they or eny of theym *do not take eny maner of quarterage or other exaccion for their seid serche* of enye maner of person or persons so by theym serched *other then suche as are & shalbe free of their own ffelowshipe*/or that *wyllyngelye shalbe contentyed to paye vnto theym suche quarterage or exacion*/eny lawe vsuge acte or ordeynaunce hertofore made had or vsyd to the contrarye notwithstondyng/

So ended a fight which, considering the relatively small reward, we might have been wiser never to have begun. The subject is not mentioned again in the City records until the winter of 1560,[71] when we read that the Court has

agreed to examine thoroughly the matter moved by the Salters agaynst the Talloughchaundlers concernynge the quarterage that the wardeyns of the Talloughchaundelers do clayme to have of suche of the said company of Salters as do occupye the trade of the talloughchaundelers & make an ende thereof before candlemas next,

and it is ordered

that the said wardeyns of the talloughchaundelers shall not onely redeliver unto every of the said company of the Salters suche money & gages *as they have already takyn of late of theym for quarterage* but also quyetly cease from the claymynge of eny more such quarterage of any of the said company of Salters in the meane season.

We are puzzled to account for this entry, for there seems to be no evidence in our books of quarterage having been paid by strangers at the period or of any refund of monies having been made in pursuance of the order. Nor has any further entry been found in the Corporation records. The next we hear of strangers' monies is in the accounts for 1565–6, which contain a record of payments by 'divers strangers of other companies for search

money',[72] and again two or three years later we learn from the
same source that our Wardens have 'received of Candle-makers
for search money' 40s. for 'the first year' of their time and the
same amount for 'the last year'.[73] We do not know if any Salters
were included, but, if they were, it is strange that no complaint
was made, for 'search money' would surely have been an 'exacion' within the terms of the Court Order of 13th February 1550.
Distresses, taken in the search for which provision is made, as we
have seen, in Article 10, were in a different category. In March
1565 we learn of three pieces of mayling (mailing) cord[g] being
taken in a distress from a salter 'for a year's search',[74] and, on
the same day, of distresses taken from another salter for two
years' search.[75] Again in November 1575, a cake of wax of $2\frac{1}{2}$ lbs.
was taken in distress by our Wardens from a salter 'for denying
of a duty of 16d for search', a sum which, (according to the
minute) was payable 'by order of the Court of Aldermen'. The
wax was 'praised at 2s. 1d., leaving a surplusage', which the
culprit disdainfully refused.[76] These cases support the view that,
while strongly objecting to paying quarterage, the Salters had
decided not to resist the search. As for quarterage from strangers
in general, nothing more is heard on this subject until 1589, when
we obtained new Ordinances.[77]

IV

There is a record in the accounts of a dinner at the Hall in February 1588 when 'the Wardens and certain of the Assistants' met
'about setting down of our Ordinances and for agreement of the
same to be confirmed',[78] and, among other disbursements, 30s.
was later paid 'to Mr Daniell (p. 151) for his counsel'.[79] A great
many of the articles deal with domestic matters, such as assemblies, elections of officers and assistants, the keeping of accounts,
and the wearing of a livery, to mention only a few, but there are

---

g   Used for tying or wrapping up.

Fig. 23. Westminster Hall from the River, temp. Henry VIII.

several which are concerned with *quarterage* and '*the search*'.[a] Notwithstanding the rebuff which we had received at the hands of the Salters in 1560 and the order of the Court that they should no longer be molested (p. 137), there is an article (number 35) directing that every person of the 'Cominaltie of the Crafte or misterie of Tallowechaundelers, of what Crafte or mysterye soever he may be, and all persons *not being freemen of the same Cominaltie*, inhabitinge or dwellinge within the said Cittie of London or suburbes of the same, Southwarke', including 'places priviledged and exempt', and within one mile compas aboute the saide Cittie

that at anie tyme or tymes hereafter dothe or shall trade use and exercise aniethinge concerninge the Crafte or misterie of Tallowchaundelers *shall paie*

a   *Commentary*, p. 245.

unto the maister and wardens for the tyme beeing to the common utilitie benefite and maintenance of the Cominaltie . . . all that and suche portion of money as hee is or oughte to pay *for quarterage* by reason of this ordinance . . .

The payment is fixed at 4*d*. a quarter, as it was in 1538, and a penalty is imposed for disobedience. The *search* is covered by two articles (numbers 36 and 37). The first directs that it shall take place quarterly and be conducted by the Master and Wardens 'or their deputies or some of them, callinge unto them some of the assistauntes . . . *amongest all manner of persons whatsoever* inhabiting or dwellinge' within the stated area

whiche shall occupie the trade of the said Crafte or mysterie of Tallowe-chaundelers/to the intent that no person or persons shall occupie the same trade but suche as shalbee sufficiente able and skilful in the said Crafte . . .

Power is given to the searchers to enter the premises of any persons occupying the trade in order to inspect 'the weights & measures and all the wares, goodes and merchandizes and commodities' in their hands, and to 'searche all the workers, makers, sellers', and so on, within the stated area. The declared object is to discover whether the wares 'be made, used and wroughte withe good, true, commendable, profitable and holsome stuffe' as they ought to be; with power to carry away defective goods. The second of these articles directs that none shall refuse the search and that every person 'of the liverie' of the Company shall pay towards the charges of the search quarterly 4*d*. and those 'not beinge of the liverie' quarterly 2*d*., '*in the name of search money*'.

There is very little evidence of these powers having been enforced, and, as with the Elizabethan Patent with which we deal in the next chapter, it may seem surprising that they were ever sought. As we should expect, such offenders had to be brought before the Court of Aldermen, and there are known cases, one of which we already have noticed in 1575 (p. 138), of this having been done. In November 1589 there is an entry in our accounts of our Wardens having dined, when they attended the Court *about their 'distresses' taken in their search*,[80] but these attendances were rare, and no case of a demand for quarterage from strangers under our new powers has been found.

Fifty years later, when obtaining yet another set of Articles, we made no specific claim to make searches. These Ordinances, which are dated 19th September 1639[81] (and are our last) contain only a brief reference to 'search money' and 'quarterages', with no claim at all on strangers. Article 38 provides only for the payment to our Master and Wardens of

all the pains, penalties, fines and forfeitures, search money and quarterages to be due by these ordinances or Laws, not being otherwise appointed or disposed of

(which monies are to be employed and bestowed to the utility, benefit and maintenance of the Commonalty), but no precise charge is mentioned. Some may think that the action of our officers was less wise when, as we shall see, they applied to Charles II, for still further powers in 1676.[82]

Letters Patent of Elizabeth I
(Tyler's Patent)
Soap, Vinegar, Barrelled Butter, Oil and Hops

I

O N 15th April 1577 our Company obtained from Queen
Elizabeth I the Letters Patent which were to become a
bone of contention with the City for many years.[1] By
this grant the Master, Wardens and 'Comynalty' of the Art and
Mistery of Tallow Chandlers of the City of London and their
successors were appointed to be 'searchers, waighers, examyners,
viewers and tryers of all '*sope, vyniger and barrelled butter*' (with
the duty to weigh every firkin of butter) and also of all '*oile and
hoppes*'.[a] The Company's powers were not confined to the City
and liberties. They extended to the Borough of Southwark,[b] to
'St Katherens nere the Tower of London,' and to 'White Chappell, Shorditch, St Jones (John's) Clarkenwell', and to 'St Giles in
the field Westmynster'.[c]

Strype (writing nearly 150 years later)[2] tells us that 'in Queen
Elizabeth's reign, about the year 1576 *and before*, abuses and deceits
were daily used and increased in this (the Tallow Chandlers')
trade, concerning which the *chief of the Company* had divers con-
ferences in their Common Hall', and he goes on to relate how

---

a   Commentary, p. 245.

b   Southwark, Borough of, on the south of the Thames, long known as The Borough,
     takes its name from being originally the fortification of London on the South.
     Wheatley.

c   Commentary, p. 245.

Fig. 24. St John's Gate, Clerkenwell.

we petitioned Her Majesty 'for a new Grant to search and destroy corrupt wares, etc.' Our own minutes are in fact silent as to the circumstances under which we came to approach the Crown, and although it becomes clear later that, as Strype says, Roger Tyler (p. 26) an Assistant of our Court, was the prime mover in the affair, the first contemporary record is to be found in a minute of the Court of Aldermen only a few days after the date of the Patent, coupled with two brief entries of expenditure in our Wardens' accounts. From the Court record[3] we learn that an order has been given to five Aldermen and two Commoners

that, callinge before them the Wardens of the Company of the tallowe-chaundlers of this Cytie,

they shall

consyder of the valydyte of the lettres patent lately granted by the Quenes Majestie to the sayd Wardeyns[d] concerning the searche of all manner of hoppes, oyle and suche lyke merchandyzes brought unto this Cytie,

---

d   Commentary, p. 246.

and that they are to take such order therein 'as to their dyscreacions shall seame good, and thereof to make report unto this Courte'. From the account book we learn of a payment of 5*s*. 2*d*. 'for charges of the Wardens going to Greenwich by water and for their dinner *when they went about the Letters Patent*'[4] and of 50*s*. paid '*for answer making to those Articles that my Lord Mayor objected against our last Patent* . . .'[5] No copy of this answer seems to have been preserved. We know only that a few days after the Court's order for a consultation 'Mr Chamberlyn' was ordered to 're-payre unto Mr Secreatary Walsingham[e] with a lettre dyrectyd to him from this Courte, wherein shalbe conteyned the answere of the wardens of the Company of the tallowe chaundlers concearninge the Lettres patentes grauntyd unto them by the Quenes Majestie'.[6]

Fig. 25. Elizabeth I surrounded by her Court.

We have already considered the Patent's opening recital, in so far as it relates to soap (p. 38). The like 'unmeete devises' are said to exist in the

---

[e]   *Commentary*, p. 246.

makinge of *vynegar* of corrupt beare and ale, myngled with unholsome dredges for the coloringe of hit, where it ought to be made only of perfect eger wyne.[f]

It is also said that

dyvers *oyles and hoppes* brought from forraine partes and uttered in this our realme have byn and yet are oft founde myngled and impayred by sundry great abuses from their naturall goodness.

And also that

the like abuse is used in the packinge of *barrelled butter* by mynglinge of corrupt and musty butter in parte of vessels of butter, and soe not meete to be uttered to our subjects to be eaten, and alsoe [in] the lacke of waight in dyvers firkyns of butter,[g]

which abuses (it is said)

are like to contynue and moe devises deceivable and hurtfull to our people, if good remedy be not by us in this behalfe provided.

For the reformation of which abuses the Queen has

thought it very meete to appoint some discreete and skilfull persons to have the perusinge and tryinge of those things . . . And *consideringe* that none for many respects can be thought meeter to have the care and charge therof *than the Master Wardens and Commonalty of the art and mistery of Tallowe Chandlers of our citty of London,*

Her Majesty, of her special grace . . . confers upon the grantees the above recorded powers of search, and,

for the better doeinge and executinge of this charge,

she gives and grants to them

and to *their sufficient deputy or deputies* full power and authority by virtue hereof and of the said office *to enter and goe into all manner of sope houses, shoppes, cellars, sollers, warehouses, wharfes, keyes, gardeyns and to all other place and places where any sope, viniger or barrelled butter shall be made, kept, layd or putt to sale, or where any oyle or hoppes shall remayne or be kept to thintent to be sold,* and from tyme to tyme *to make viewe and tryall of the same* where any such shall be found.

There are other provisions, which, very briefly stated, are as

---

f   Commentary, p. 246.

g   Commentary, p. 246.

K

follows. *First,* the grantees are to publish the Letters Patent and, after allowing sufficient time, offending wares are to be 'consumed by fyre in the sight of the people'.

Secondly, an 'outward mark is to be placed on all wares', those that are good to bear the 'roase and crowne imperial, and those that are corrupt to bear the letter C', betokening 'coarse'.

Thirdly, sellers are not to use fraud or deceit in weighing, allowance is to be given for lack of weight, and the 'abusinge' of marks is to be punishable with imprisonment.

Fourthly, no wares are to be sold until the grantees, or their deputies, have 'searched, etc,' and 'marked the same'.

Fifthly, certain fixed rates may be charged for executing the searches, etc., according to the nature of the wares.[h]

Sixthly, buyers are to be recompensed for false markings.

Seventhly, all justices of the peace, mayors, etc. are to be 'aydinge and assistinge' unto the grantees.

Lastly the Grant may be revoked for good cause.

Hops, as we see, are the *last* of the five commodities mentioned in this Grant, for the search of which we were to be responsible. On 3rd September 1551 there had been an Act of Common Council (as recited in the *Journal* in October of the following year)[7] that

> from thensforth there shoulde be vj sadde & dyscrete commoners of the severall & dystincte Companyes herunder wrytten That is to saye *ij Grocers, ij Salters and ij Berebruers* yerely aboute the feast of Saint Mychaell tharchaungell (29th September)... newly nominated & appointed by the lorde Maire & Aldermen of this Cytie ... to survey & serche all suche hoppes as then ware or from hensforth shuld be brought & conveyed to the said Cytie & lyberties therof to be sold ...[i]

In May 1569 there had again been six searchers consisting of two grocers, two salters, a mercer and a brewer.[8] In May of the following year[9] a salter, a mercer and a grocer had been named with '*thother,*[j] that before this tyme were assigned to serch the hoppes

---

h   Commentary, p. 247.

i   Commentary, p. 247.

j   Perhaps a brewer.

within this citie and liberties thereof', to make search with speed

of all such hoppes as they shall finde within this Citie to be defective,

and they were to cause the same

to be conveyed to the guildhall to be ordered ther *according to the lawes and ordinances of the same citie,*

with the command that Mr Chamberlain should 'assigne an officer of the chamber to attend upon them in their serch and to call them together'. In September 1574 several salters and two brewers were sworn, with the like powers.

These long-standing arrangements with other companies for the search of hops had been made at a time when beer-brewing was, as we know (p. 48) one of our rarer occupations. This being so, our appointment as searchers in 1577 seems as surprising to us now as it must have seemed then to the Mayor and Aldermen. That hops, although mentioned last in the Patent, should have been mentioned *first* when the Court first met to consider its implications may not be without significance. Note also that the second commodity to be named in the Order was *oil*, in which the Court had lately begun to take a new interest (p. 32).

This was not the first occasion on which alleged abuses in the hop trade had attracted the attention of the Crown. On 30th January 1564 there had been a Royal Proclamation[10] reciting that

many marchantes as well of her owne subjects as strangers seking their singular gayne and advantage contrarye to all and the commone wealthe of her Majesty's good naturall subjects/and *directly agaynste thauncyent lawes and statutes of this realme*/have of late gathered into theyr handes greate quantities of hoppes making such a *monopolie* of the same hops as the hundreth weyghts of hopps which hath bene usually solde within these fewe yeres at xiij s. iiij d. or xx s. at the moste for every hundreth be now solde for syxe poundes and more.

It was said that this 'ill' example

mighte bringe the lyke monopolies of other wares and merchaundies to the greate losse of the multytude of marchauntes using the trade of marchaundyze and *to the greate decay of the commone of this her Majesties realme.*[k]

---

k   Commentary, p. 247.

Charge and command were accordingly given that after the 1st February next no merchant should put to sale any hops 'in grosse or by retayle' at more than 'fourtie shillings for every hundreth'.

In July (1577) it became necessary to raise the sum of £10 from among our members 'for the redemption of Roger Tyler . . . from an execution wherein he lay in the King's Bench', for the repayment of which sum Tyler appears to have been made personally responsible,[11] and a further £10 was laid out at this time 'towards the Letters Patent' by Walter Stone, described in the account book as 'our Warden'.[12] He died in November of the following year[13] leaving £6 13s. 4d. to the Master and Wardens 'to the use and comfort' of the Company and 'willed' that his wife Johan should 'occupy and enjoy for the space of one year next' after his decease his 'messuage called the sign of the Holly Lambe situate in the parish of St Botolphs without Bishopsgate'.[1]

Fig. 26. Women's headdresses, temp., Elizabeth I.

We do not know upon what charge Roger Tyler was imprisoned and we have to wait until 28th September (1577) for any more news about the Court's deliberations. On that date a meeting was planned to take place at Guildhall[14] of 'the learnyd councell of the City', including the Recorder and several Alder-

---

1   No house called the 'Holy Lamb' has been traced in this locality. There was a Lamb Alley west out of Bishopsgate in Bishopsgate Ward Without, which is said to have derived its name from the sign of 'the Lamb Tavern'. *Harben.*

men, with two representatives of the Company of Grocers, two of the Company of Salters, several members of our Company (although not so designated) and some others—among whom we note Thomas Hunt, the soap-maker (p. 38)—who were to have

consyderacion of *the Validity* of the Lettres Patentes lately grauntyd by the Queens Majestie to the Companye of the Tallowechaundlers.

We recognize four only of our own representatives, namely John Shorte (p. 78) then Master, Stephen Rogers, his immediate predecessor (p. 79), Thomas Astall (p. 47) and Robert Wainwright (p. 96). The result of the meeting is not known. On 10th October another meeting was called[15] which 'all the learnyd councell' were to attend as well as representatives of the Brewers and the Fishmongers

for certeyn cawses betwyxte this Cytie and the Company of the Tallowechaundlers,

to which gathering we do not seem to have been invited, and again we are left in the dark as to the result.

In November comes the search for vinegar and *presentation by our Wardens* with the resulting Inquest of office (p. 48), and a little later in the month we read that one Charles Hobson, a tallow chandler, has persuaded the Court of Aldermen to restore to him 'xxxvij pypes and hoggeshedds of evil and corrupt vinegar' on his recognizance to 'transporte and carry the same viniger into partyes beyonde the seas'.[16]

II

For several years the records of the Court and our minutes are unaccountably silent. Then, in the Summer of 1580, it seems that our Company has become aware of the need for action. We read in the Wardens' accounts for 1580–1[17] of a payment of 6s.

to the Town Clerk for preferring the *supplication the Company exhibited to the Mayor and Aldermen* about the Patent Roger Tyler procured, and of a payment of 2s. to our Clerk[a] 'for making the supplication'.[18] On 23rd June we went to my Lord Chancellors about 'Tyler's Patent',[19] and we made a second visit on 15th July 'about Roger Tyler, *his deputation*'.[20] No record has been found of the 'supplication' in the minutes of the Court of Aldermen, but we know that on 3rd October 1580 *'a deputation to search'* was granted by the Company to Roger Tyler for life *with power of nominating a successor*,[21] and that this grant was confirmed several years later.[22] A second 'deputation' appears to have been made in 1581, for we read in the accounts of a payment of 15s. to Mr Weeks (named as 'Counsellor') 'for perusing our *second Book* which was drawn between the Company and Roger Tyler',[23] and of 20s. having been paid to our Clerk[24]

for drawing our first and second Deputation which is to pass to Roger Tyler and for copying one of them out and for his travail and pains to my Lord Chancellor and to Counsel with us about the same matter.

The next we hear of 'Tyler's Patent' is about a year later. We read in the accounts of 'supper' at the 'Cardinal's Hat in Lombard Street,[b] when we went about Tyler's matter'.[25] We learn also at this time of a payment to Mr Weeks 'for his travail *to my Lord Chancellor's* about Tyler's matter'[26] and of 12d. 'for boat hire when we went with Mr Weeks to my Lord Chancellor'[27]. On 15 May (1582), according to our accounts, a meeting took place *before the Lord Mayor and Aldermen in the Inner Chamber of Guildhall,[c]* when we were represented by Mr Weeks,[28] and, on the following day, there was a consultation with the Lord Chancellor, attended by the Recorder and several Aldermen.[29] Naturally there was a 'drinking', and our Clerk was paid 10s. 'for his pains-taking' and 'for writing out divers things'.[30] In February of the following year our Wardens were charged and sworn to

---

a   Francis Kidd (see p. 100).

b   A tavern which gave its name to Cardinal Alley (Leake 1666), later Swan and Hoop Passage, south out of Cornhill. *Harben*. It is called *Cardinals Hat Tavern* by Stow. *Survey*, text of 1603.

c   Volume II, p. 32, note.

make search for 'all suche oyles and vyneger as ys wythin thys Cyttye and the freedome and lybertyes of the same',[31] which suggests either a compromise or that the parties were marking time. A report was made and an Inquest of office was ordered.

But that same year we became engaged in an action in the Court of Chancery, referred to in our minutes as 'Tyler's process',[32] or 'Tyler's suit'.[33] This was probably 'a friendly action' made necessary by the City's opposition and embarked upon with a view to establishing our title under the grant as well as Tyler's right under his 'deputation'. It originated in a 'Bill of Complaint'[d] by Tyler[34] and there are numerous disbursements shown in the accounts, including the fee (6s. 8d.) 'paid to Mr Pott of the Chancery to be our Attorney against Tyler'[35] and to his man (12d.) 'to put his master in remembrance',[36] a fee (10s.) 'to Mr Owen for his Counsel *in our answer to the Lord Mayor concerning Tyler*',[37] and our Clerk's fee (4s.) for copying out the answer.[38] There is also an entry in the *Repertory* Book of an order requiring the Recorder,[39] Mr Danyell,[e] and Mr Owen to 'conferre with Mr Solycytor Generall for a case to be agreyd uppon emongest them selves concerninge the controversye betwyxte thys Cytie and the Companye of Talloughchaundelers and Roger Tyler theyre deputye'.[40]

On 16th April 1583[41] we paid 20s. 'to Mr Serjeant Gawdy for his pains *in pleading in the Chancery at the hearing of Tyler's matter*'.[f] Mr Pott 'our attorney' received 6s. 8d.[42] and 'his man' 2s. 'for his pains',[43] while 'the porter of the Court of Chancery' was paid 16d.[44] We breakfasted at Westminster[45] and afterwards Mr Owen was paid 30s. 'for his Counsel and for being for us before the Master of the Rolls *when we heard my Lord Chancellor's order concerning Tyler*',[46] which order was 'viewed' by Sergeant Gawdy on 26th April.[47]

We have no record of the proceedings, but Strype has a great

---

d   *Commentary*, p. 247.

e   Later 'Sergeant at lawe'.

f   *Commentary*, p. 248.

deal to say on the subject.[48] He tells us that in October 1583 (a date which, as we see, does not agree with our minute) 'The Lord Maior and Court of Aldermen resisted the execution of this Patent, and made a declaration *why it ought to be stayed and utterly void*', citing an Act of 12 Edward IV, cap. 8, respecting *the surveying of all Victuals* and the correction and punishment of offenders, a task which belonged (so it was urged) to 'the Maiors, Bailiffs and other like Governors of every City, Burgh and Town of substance within the Realm'. It was argued that

by this Charter made to the Tallow Chandlers they (the Governors) are to be disinherited for ever . . . *In all the Places mentioned in the Patent* where the Tallow Chandlers have their Power of searching *the Lords of the Liberty* have *Leets or Law Days* . . . so that there was [is] no place left where the Tallow Chandlers might exercise the said office of search, but where other men were [are] justly inheritable in the same.[g]

Another argument against the Patent, according to Strype, was that

the Maior and Aldermen of the City, and all other the chief Governors thereof, and their Predecessors, always, time out of mind, had and used to have, the View, Search and correction of *all Mysteries and Crafts within the City*, for and concerning all manner of Deceits and Defaults in all things touching their Mysteries . . . and, besides the general Usage and Custom, there were *special Grants and Charters* made to the City touching these things in question; as Butter, Hops, Vinegar, etc.

He tells us that 'these were *the Arguments and Pleadings* of Fleetwood Recorder, Thomas Wykes (p. 150) and William Daniel (p. 151), all learned Lawyers, who urged also 'that the Imposition contained in the said Letters Patent was against the Common Law, *and the Liberty of every subject in his Goods; and against the free Traffick of the City of London, granted by Charter* . . .' and that

there was *no need of this Patent* for the Tallow Chandlers searching these Commodities; because *the Lord Maior* was bound by his Oath taken in the *Exchequer* to perform the said search . . .

Strype does not inform his readers of the result of these proceedings in Chancery and unfortunately we have no copy of the

---

g   *Commentary*, p. 248.

Fig. 27. Great Seal of Elizabeth I.

Order, but it is evident from a letter calendared in the *Remem-brancia*[49] that it favoured our cause, although, as we shall see, this document appears to have made little impression on the Court of Aldermen. We read that after the hearing, 'a letter from the Lords of the Council had been received

stating that a supplication had been exhibited to them by Roger Tyler, on behalf of the Tallowchandlers of the City, requesting them *to inform his Lord-ship* of a certain grant by Letters Patent lately given by Her Majesty . . .

with which the Lord Mayor and his learned Counsel had been made acquainted. '*Upon* [*the*] *hearing of the matter in the Court of Chancery*' the Lords could see no objection, and desired that, upon the consideration of the contents, the Lord Mayor should either publish the Letters Patent or advise the Council of a lawful or sufficient cause to the contrary.[h]

On 29th April (1583) only three days after Sergeant Gawdy had viewed the order in the Chancery suit, our Wardens, elated no doubt by the successful conclusion of the action, paid Mr Owen 'for his Counsel' in drawing yet another deputation in favour of Roger Tyler,[50] and on 10th July his original deputation was confirmed by deed, '*but without account to be rendered to the*

---

h   *Commentary*, p. 248.

Company'.[51] If, however, they were hoping for the immediate collapse of the City's case they were disappointed. On 10th October[52] several Aldermen in company with two lawyers, one of whom was Mr Wykes, were ordered by the Court to

treat with Wyllyam [Roger] Tyler Tallough chaundler/touchinge lettres patent by hym procured for the searchinge of vinegar hoppes and other things.

In the accounts for 1583–5 there are two entries, the one recording a payment of 12d. 'for writing of a copy of *the last order* in the Chancery between the Company and Tyler' and the other a payment 'to our Clerk for his attendance at Guildhall about *delivery of answer to the Lord Mayor, and for making of certain Bills concerning the same*'.[53] Apart from these entries our own records and those of the Court of Aldermen contain nothing on the subject of our claim until 4th November 1585 when we learn from the *Repertory* Book[54] of an Order directing that

the several companyes of Grocers and Salters of this Cyttye shall appoynet certayne honeste and discrete persons of bothe theyre sayd Companyes to be sworne for the searche of suche *hoppes* as shalbe brought to this Cyttye.

The searchers when appointed and sworn twelve days later were two grocers, two salters and two brewers, thus following the precedent of the old Act of Common Council (p. 146), their duty being 'to search truly and indifferently' and to 'present' such hops as they should 'finde to be corrupte, defective or not wholsome for mans bodye'.[55] Strange to say we seem to have made no protest, and the next we hear of any of the five commodities mentioned in our Patent is in October 1587, when the reported meeting of *soap-boilers* and Wardens of Butchers and Tallow Chandlers takes place (p. 38); followed by an order directing one William Ravenscrofte[i] to have 'the search and oversight of all the sopeboylers'.[56] Not until November of the following year do we hear of the City taking any further interest in the affair of our Patent[57] when the Court orders a number of Aldermen, with the Recorder, *Mr Owen*, and another official to

---

Commentary, p. 248.

have consideracion of the cause touching the guaggynge of wynes and oyles.

This is followed in March 1589 by the swearing in, as before, of a sextet of grocers, salters, and brewers for the search of defective and unwholesome hops 'for the space of one whole yeare next insueinge',[58] but it seems then that a new era is about to commence.

We learn from our few original documents of the period that have been preserved that on 25th June 1589 Roger Tyler assigned to Sir George Carey, who was later to become Lord Chamberlain, the 'deputation of search' granted to Tyler for life by the Company in 1580[59] (p. 150)[j] and that on 4th November (1589)[60] *the Company appointed Carey their deputy to search during Tyler's lifetime.*[k] On the same day Carey entered into a Bond in the sum of £600 for observance of the covenants,[61] and the Company granted him a like deputation *for ten years after Tyler's death,*[62] Carey again entering into a like Bond.[63] On the 5th our Master, Wardens and *'certain others'* were present at the examination of 'the four Books of Indentures' and dined together.[64] It is doubtful if any of those attending the meeting of Common Council which took place only nine days later were with us at that dinner, for the event was not one for them to celebrate. But the minute of the meeting[65] makes it certain that by the 24th the Court knew very well what had been going on. We are told that six Aldermen, among whom were three past Lord Mayors[l] and six Commoners, representative of the Great Twelve Companies,[m] were appointed

presentlie to meete and to resolve what course is best to be taken touching the patent procured by [them (sic) and] the wardens of the companye of Tallow-chaundlers for search of oyle, viniger etc. nowe assigned over to Sir George Cary Knight, Knight Marshal of England/and to make reporte before Saterdaye nexte to my Lord Mair and Courte of Aldermen what they thinke good to be done therein.

---

j   *Commentary*, p. 248.

k   *Commentary*, p. 248.

l   Sir Rowland Heyward (1570), Sir Wolstan Dixie (1585) and Sir George Barne (1586).

m   Two grocers, a goldsmith, two merchant tailors and a haberdasher.

No copy of the report has been found, and it seems that the meeting was followed by an uneasy truce which lasted for over eighteen months. We read that on 9th December (1589)[66] two of our men were appointed to make an old-style search of wines 'latelye presented by the Vyntiners in theyre serche to be defectyve'.[n] They were Thomas Parker (p. 99) and Thomas Lambert (p. 100) whose duty it was to certify to the Court whether the wines 'or any parte thereof be fytt for sawce or not'. Nearly a month later they made a detailed report[67] of which a copy will be found in Appendix I. In February 1590 our Master and Wardens present in Court promised to search in all shops, cellars and warehouses 'for all kynde and sort of false chaundlarye wares',[68] with what result we are not told. On 4th March we learn that the Court of Aldermen has made arrangements for a deputation to 'repayre unto the right honorable the Lord Chauncellor of England to aunsweare his Lordshipps lettres towchinge the serche of hoppes, oyle, vinegar, barreled butter, soape and suche lyke'.[69] The party consisted of four Aldermen[o] and the Recorder, and the visit produced an immediate result, although not the one that might have been expected, for the powers of search granted to Sir George Carey by Deed in November 1589 *were passed over* (presumably with the knowledge, if not the consent, of the Lord Chancellor) and on 8th March the Court of Aldermen ordered that

the wardens of the severall companyes of the grocers, salters, brewers, *and talloughchaundlers* shall at the nexte courte present two sufficient persons of theyre sayd severall companyes to be sworne for the serche

of the five commodities.[70] Finally, on 15th July 1591 the Court at last appears to recognize our interest as searchers of *soap*,[71] when appointing two salters and *two well known tallow chandlers*, Hugh Ingram (who had already served as Master and was to serve again) and Christopher Noddinge (p. 100)

---

n   *Commentary*, p. 249.

o   *Commentary*, p. 249.

for the searche and trial of all suche soape as shalbe made or putto sale within this Cyttye and the freedome and liberties of the same for the space of one whole yeare next ensuynge, *whether the same be made good sweete and marchauntable* according to the late acte of common councell or not, and thereof to make presentement, etc.

No copy of the Act of Common Council has been found, but it will be seen that, in appointing searchers *for one whole year*, the Court was following the precedent established for the search of hops in 1589 (p. 155). Ingram was another co-grantee of Richard Syberye's messuages and cottages in St Andrew, Baynard's Castle.[72] Soon after Sybery's death, when the Company obtained vacant possession of the premises, Ingram made an advance 'for the clearing of the encumbrances about the houses'.[73] By his will, proved in March 1614, he left each of his sons, one of whom was a 'Doctor of the Civil Law' and the other a knight, £10 'to make him and his wife mourning gowns'. Others received the same or smaller legacies for the same purpose. The children in Christ's Hospital in London[p] received a legacy of 40s. to accompany his corpse to the Church, and 'the poor at church' at his burial received 20s. He left the lease of the house[q] in which he lived to his wife for life with reversion to his son-in-law.[74]

III

The eighteen months truce came to an end soon after the company search, by which time it seems that Carey had decided not only to take belated action on his own account, but that the Crown should take steps also to curb the City in its interference with our Patent rights. We read in our Wardens' accounts of a payment to one William Malory 'with the consent of the Court of Assistants, for his satisfaction of losses alleged to be sustained in a boiling of soap *made at the request of Sir George Carey, knight*',[75] and on 19th October (1591) we learn indirectly of a

---

[p]   The 'Blue Coat School'. On the north side of Newgate Street on the site occupied by the Grey Friars Monastery (Ordnance Survey Map, 1894). *Harben* (see *Commentary*, p. 249).

[q]   *Commentary*, p. 249.

suite prosequited by *Quo warranto*[a] in the Exchequer *in the name of Sir George Carey Knighte* touching the searche of hopps oyle vynegar and other things within this Cyttye and the Borroughe of Southwork.

This information is contained in an entry in the *Repertory* Book,[76] which records 'that *the Bridgemaster* shall beare and paye an equall thirde parte as well of all charges heretofore layde out as hereafter to be assessed (and) disbursed in defence' of the suit. We are left in ignorance of the result of these proceedings, but, to judge from subsequent events, it seems most likely that they failed.[b]

During the next four or five years our participation in 'the search' followed much the same pattern as before. In the winter of 1591–2 we learn (again from the *Repertories*) that two salters, a mercer, a grocer, *and two 'chaundlers*[c] have been sworn for the search of soap'.[77] In April 1593 the same two men, on being appointed with one of the two salters and one of the two mercers, reported that they 'doe finde none to be defective'.[78] In March 1594 an ironmonger, a salter and a grocer were sworn *in company with two chaundlers*[d] for the like purpose *'according as in tyme paste hathe been accustomed'*.[79] In January 1593 'the wardens of the several companyes of the Grocers, Salters and Brewers were ordered to appoynte a suffycient nombre of discrete persones to be sworn for the searche of hoppes'.[80] The intervention of *Wardens* was unusual, but the appointment, which followed, of named representatives of these three crafts was in accordance with precedent.[81] Again in December 1595 there was yet another old style search of wines *by our Wardens*,[82] when they had supper 'at the Emperor's Head by the Three Cranes in the Vintry'.[e]

A great change, however, takes place in June 1596 when a search is ordered *in which not a single tallow chandler is named.*

---

a   Commentary, p. 249.

b   Commentary, p. 249.

c   Commentary, p. 249.

d   Commentary, p. 249.

e   The Emperor's Head has not beenl ocated. There was an 'Emperor's Head Lane Alley' later 'Bell Wharf Lane' in Vintry Ward. 'The Three Cranes' in the parish of St Martin Vintry in the same Ward was a famous tavern. *Harben.*

We learn from the Court records of the appointment, as searchers of *'soape, hoppes, butter, vinegar and oiles'* within the City and liberties, of two *'soape boylers'*, a saddler, a salter, and a grocer *'for the space of one whole year'*.[83] We could not be expected to accept this affront without a fight. Our own records are silent, but we learn from a minute of the Court of Aldermen of 10th March 1597 of an order given to 'Mr Recorder', three Aldermen, two Commoners and 'Mr Doctor Fletcher', the Remembrancer,[f] that they should meet together *'to consider of the suyte commenced in the name of the Master and Wardens of the Company of the Tallow Chandlers against this Citty'*.[84] During June and July what were described as *private meetings* were arranged to consider the matter of 'Tylers patent', what 'answer to send *privately* to Lord Hunsden, the *Lord Chamberlain*' (who appears to have written more than one letter) and what course to take *'in the cause between this Citty and the grauntee of Tyler'* (Sir George Carey);[85] and on 8th August there was a meeting of Common Council when it was agreed that a number of Aldermen and Commoners, together with the Recorder and the Remembrancer, should meet to consider what course was best to be undertaken 'on the City's behalf'[86]. In July Sir George Carey had again been active, entering into an agreement to which Thomas Harris, serjeant-at-law, and others were parties[g] In December it appears from our accounts that we made a search of corrupt beer.[87]

The Committee's Report does not seem to have found its way into the minutes, and no decision seems to have been taken. We hear no more of our Company's suit, and on 16th March 1598 we again see *two tallow chandlers* being sworn among the searchers. This time we head the list with our Beadle, John Barnes.[h] He is accompanied by Edward Lightfoot, whom we recognize as Governor of the Yeomanry some sixteen years later, and they are followed by two salters and a grocer.[88] Their search is to cover

---

f   See *London and the Kingdom*, Vol. II, p. 2.

g   *Commentary*, p. 250.

h   See *Commentary*, c.

all suche oyle, soape, vinegar, butter, hoppes and *other chandelary stuff* as shalbe or remayne within this Citty and the liberties thereof,

and the engagement is for one whole year. But in February of the following year,[89] when the same commodities are mentioned, the searchers are headed by *two salters*, and we take second place with William Mee and William Hewett, no mention being made on this occasion of 'chandlery stuff'. Nothing seems to be known of Mee, but Hewett was to become Governor of the Yeomanry, and later Master. We recognize him also among the men presented at one of the Wardmote Inquests, along with Thomas Lambert, and fined for breaking the price of candles in February 1576 (p. 101).

Early in the same year (1599) it becomes apparent that more trouble is in store for us[90] when it is ordered that a Committee of Aldermen with the Chamberlain of the City and 'Mr Doctor Fletcher' shall have

present consideracion of the contents of a lettre written to this Courte from the Right Honourable the L. Chamberlyn *of her Majesties most hon. household.*

They are also 'to call before them all such sopeboylers, sellers of hoppes, butter, oyle and such like persons whom the contents of (the) same letters maye any waie concerne'. The next thing we hear is that there is a further meeting of Common Council on 28th July when another Committee is appointed to consider the validity of the Letters Patent[91] and on 5th October yet another 'to consider what course in their opinions is fitt to be taken *in the cause betwene the right honorable the Lord Chamberlain*' and '*the state of this Citie* . . . to thend that such further order maye be taken in that cause as shalbe convenient'.[92]

The conclusion jointly reached by the various Committees was, in essence, that the Lord Mayor and Court of Aldermen should treat with the Lord Chamberlain (Lord Hunsden), as the Queen's representative,[93] *for the surrender of the Patent to the City,*[i] and that 'all such Companies and particular persons as use to sell' within

---

i   *Commentary,* p. 250.

A View of CHELSEA.

Vûe du Village de CHELSEA.

Plate VI. A drawing made in 1744 showing the river front from Chelsea Old Church to the ground of the Royal Hospital, with barge houses near the centre of the picture (See Appendix K).

Reproduced by permission of the Kensington and Chelsea Public Libraries.

the City any of the commodities mentioned in the Letters Patent should be called upon to attend and that they should be dealt with 'in such sort as to the Lord Maior and Court of Aldermen shalbe thought meete'.[94] The Court accepted these proposals and power

Fig. 28. Men's headdresses: sixteenth century.

was assumed 'in the name of the City' to treat with Lord Hunsdon,[95] but a certain lack of purpose is evident in future dealings. Early in the new year (1600) the committees were called together again[96] and a number of Aldermen and Commoners were ordered to treat with the vendors of commodities.[97] Meanwhile two tallow chandlers, Thomas Winton[j] and Edward Lightfoot (p. 159), acting (surprisingly) on their own, were sworn 'to make due search and triall of al manner of *hoppes, oyle and vinegar*' within the City 'and *to make true presentment*' to the Court.[98] And *within a few days* we see Christopher Nodding 'one of the wardens of the companie', with Thomas Armstrong (p. 96) and Cuthbert Lee (p. 81), 'both of them free of the same companie', making a promise of the utmost importance.[99] Speaking 'as well for themselves as for all the rest of the Company of Tallow Chandlers' they 'promised and undertook' that

the Master and Wardens of the said Company shall at all tymes hereafter when and as often as the Courte of Lord Maior and Aldermen for the tyme being shall

---

j   Winton succeeded Lightfoot in 1615 as Governor of the Yeomanry and became Master in the following year, serving again in 1622–3.

L

thincke meet *joyne with the saide Courte* in the nomynacion of such & so many persons as the said courte shall thincke fitt/being men of experience & skill/ to make searche & tryall for all manner of oyle sope vinegar salte butter hoppes and such like as shalbe brought to this Citty to be solde/the same to be performed *under the Commen Seale of theire Company.*

A separate Committee, acting with the Common Serjeant, was to consider what covenants 'were fitt to be devised',[100] one such covenant (as stated in the undertaking) being that our Company would not 'nomynat or appoint any other persons for the searche of anie things conteyned in the lettres patentes for search but such as the said Courte shall first like & allowe of'. We were not to revoke the letters patent, nor to 'do any thing therein without consent of this courte first had & obteyned'. Here, surely, was an ideal way of solving the City's problem which was also our own, but, alas, other counsels prevailed.[k]

It is evident from the Court minutes which followed during the Spring and early Summer of 1600 that, notwithstanding our solemn undertaking, it was at length decided to put into operation the scheme accepted in the previous autumn. On the 15th March it was agreed that all sums of money disbursed by the City '*for anie composition or agreement* to be made by the Lord Maior & Court of Aldermen with the right hon. the lo. Hunsdon, Lord Chamberlayn', should be borne pro rata by the various companies rated to contribute towards the provision of corn for the City.[101] On the 24th April the delivery to the City Chamberlain of 'severall writings' is recorded.[102] These included a deputation from Sir George Carey (now Lord Chamberlain) to *four mercers* granted only six days before, the two indentures between the Tallow Chandlers Company and Carey dated 4th November 1589, 'divers paper writings concerninge suits prosecuted by the said Sir George Carey', and one writing dated 18th April 1600 'signed and not sealed whereby the said (sic) Lord Hunsdon promised to discharge suits heretofore prosecuted'. The next entry[103] records the allowance to Mr Chamberlain for money advanced 'towards the procuring to the Citties use of her Majesty's lettres

k   *Commentary,* p. 250.

patentes granted to the Company',[1] and is followed by the appointment of a Committee to consider what course should be taken for putting into execution of the Patent 'granted to the Company *and by them deputed to this Citty*'.[104] In July it is ordered[105] that two new members (a goldsmith and a mercer)

shall ioyne with the Commyttes (sic) appointed by this Courte on the third June last for order to be taken *for the due execucion* of Her Majesties lettres patentes for searche of oyles, soape and such like within this Citty and libertyes thereof.

The events of the next few years are poorly documented and it is sometimes difficult to follow their thread, but it seems certain that procrastination continued to be the order of the day. A new committee 'calling unto them the *Soape boylers* and such others as they shall thinke meete' was appointed to 'consider of a convenyent course to be undertaken touching searche' of the five commodities within the City and liberties.[106] On 8th September (1601) '*the Master(s) and wardens of the fower principallest of the twelve Worshipful Companies*',[m] were brought in, their instructions being to certify to the Court 'two fitt and sufficyent persons' of each said company to be appointed by the Court 'for searche of soape, oyle, butter and suche like' *according to the Letters Patent*.[107] There seems to be no evidence, either in the City records or in our own, that such delegates were ever named. On the contrary, we read a year later that *a single mercer* has been sworn in for a general search,[108] to be followed two months later by two *haberdashers*, who are to 'ioyne with others heretofore appoynted'[109] and two days later a party of *Vintners* were to make a search of defective wines 'according as in former tymes hath bene accustomed'.[110] Our ancient right to inspect these wines for *vinegar* is not mentioned. On the same day[111] George Foster, who, like his name-sake Richard, (p. 21) was evidently an officer of the City, was ordered 'to attend from tyme to tyme upon such

---

l   *Commentary*, p. 250.

m   The Mercers, Grocers, Drapers and Fishmongers. See Vol. II, pp. 64, 65 and Vol. III, p. 45, referring to the order of precedence established in January 1516.

cittizens as are appoynted by this Corte' and sworn for the searche
. . . of such things 'as are conteyned in her Majesty's letters patent
graunted to the Companie of Tallow Chaundlers'.[n]

There is a record in our Wardens' accounts for 1603–4[112] of
3s. 6d. 'spent at the Mitre in Cheap[o] *when the Wardens had been
before Mr Chamberlain about Roger Tylers Patent*', but we have no
means of knowing whether this visit occurred before or after the
delivery by Sir William Ryder, Alderman,[p] to Mr Chamberlain
of the Letters Patent, which event, according to the minute in
the *Repertory* Book, took place on 1st February 1603.[113] Nor do
we know at what date the grant had come into the possession of
the Court of Aldermen.

We hear no more until November (1603) when a skinner, two
goldsmiths and two fishmongers are sworn to make search
'according to thentent, purpose, true mennynge and effecte of
the lettres patent' for the space of one whole year.[114] The appointment is followed in quick succession by the swearing in of a
single goldsmith,[115] a single skinner[116] and two 'merchaunttes',[117]
so called, for a like purpose.

IV

Neither the Queen's promise in the last Parliament of her reign
to repeal or suspend some of the 'monpolies' that had raised
such an outcry,[118] nor her death on 24th March 1603, is thought
to have deterred the Court of Aldermen from its purpose. Our
interest is certainly aroused when we read in January 1604 of an
order[119] that

Sir John Watts and Sir Henry Rowe, knyghts[a] shall have consideracon of *the
cause informed to this Corte* by the searchers of soape, oyle, hoppes, salte butter,
and such like And to make reporte to this Corte *of their opinyons therein.*

---

n   *Commentary*, p. 250.

o   Mitre Court. South out of Cheapside The Mitre Tavern stood here. An old tavern
      in existence in 1475, burnt in the Fire and not rebuilt. The Court commemorated its
      name. *Harben.*

p   Lord Mayor in 1600.

a   Sir John Watts: Lord Mayor 1606, Sir Henry Rowe: Lord Mayor 1607.

But we have to wait eighteen months[120] for the news, which is indeed surprising, that the

> Wardens of the *Companie of Tallowchaundlers* and such others as they shall think fit shall consider what course is best to be undertaken *for putting in execucion* of the letters patent . . . and they to make report to this Court of their opinion in wryting under their hands.

We have no explanation to offer for this change of front on the part of the City, but our Master and Wardens may have felt encouraged to continue the battle by the fact that only a few months earlier we had, as we shall see in the next Chapter, obtained a new Charter from James I *renewing the powers of search* conferred by our Charter of Incorporation.[b] We read of a visit by the Wardens early in October to the 'Salutation' at Billingsgate[c] 'concerning the search of Hops *and the patent*'.[121] We learn of an account being taken on the 29th 'of *hops seized, recovered and sold*[d] by Edward Lightfoot, Warden' (p. 159),[122] and there is a record of money received of one Robert Greenwell, *salter*, 'for *hops delivered* from the Company'.[123] We paid Counsel 20s. 'about the *Deputation* for Tyler's patent'.[124] A search was made 'in the Crown office for the Quo Warranto brought against the City'[125] (p. 151) and a 'warning' was given to the Aldermen by the Mayor's officer.[126] A copy of some document 'concerning the search of hops' was also obtained by our Wardens.[127] But we cannot account for the absence of any further information in the City records at this time. All we know is that in the Autumn of 1607 a Petition was 'preferred' to the Court by our Master and Wardens and that this was referred to a committee of Aldermen and Commoners 'to make report'.[128]

On 26th November 1607 *Roger Price* 'the elder', as we know him, was chosen Clerk 'for the tearme of his naturall life',[129] and on 10th December he took 'his oathe for the due execucion of

---

b   See Volume III, pp. 48–52.

c   A tavern situated in Salutation Court, north out of Lower Thames Street, between Love Lane and St Mary Hill in Billingsgate Ward . . . The Court was demolished for the formation of Monument Street, which now occupies the site. *Harben.*

d   *Commentary*, p. 250.

his place . . . and likewise the oath of supremacy'. His first duty
was to procure (if he could) from the Court of Aldermen the
Letters Patent which the said Court *detaine in their custody*, or
elles to procure the same pattent to be exemplified under the
great seale of England againe at the charges of this house'.[130]
Evidently the Court could not be persuaded to surrender the
document, for on *1st March 1608* we read in our minutes that
'this daie the Letters Patent . . . being exemplified[131] was brought
in by our Clerk and laid up in the treasury.'[132] We know that
discussions had taken place prior to that date with representatives
of the Court and suspect that they had been protracted, for the
accounts record a payment of £12 'to our Clerk for charges
about the patent by order of Court',[133] and on the very day of
our meeting the Court of Aldermen also met,[134] when 'William
Jesson Tallowchaundler, (p. 100) Edward Lightfoote Tallowchandler and Robert Shelton *Saddler*' were sworn

for the true and indifferent searching and sealing of all soape oyle hoppes
vinegar and barrelled butter according to the lettres patents (sic) made and
provyded.

On that same day our Court had ordered that '*a deputacion*' should
be granted to Jesson, Lightfoote, *Roger Price* & Shelton 'for x yeres
from Candlemas last they yeldinge a fourth part of the proffittes
thereof to this house yerely'.[135] The absence of Price's name from
the Court order will be noticed, and there seems to be no evidence
that the deputation itself was in fact granted.

There is little more to tell. Roger Price was elected to the
Court of Assistants in July 1615,[136] and, among our documents,
there is a counterpart indenture dated 4th June 1618 between the
Company of the one part and Francis Michell (whose description
is 'esquire'), together with four 'citizens and tallow chaundlers'
(including Price) of the second (or other) part,[e] reciting the
letters patent, and appointing the grantees as the Company's
'*deputies*' for a period of ten years with the benefit of 'all fees, etc.',

---

[e]   *Commentary*, p. 250.

for which the consideration was £10 per annum.[137] This indenture was executed pursuant to a resolution of our Court on 19th March 1618[138] ordering the deputies 'by all possible means' to procure that the letters patent 'might be strengthened & confirmed by order of lawe *for that heretofore the same hath bin opposed*',[f] and was sealed on the 6th May,[139] but it seems unlikely that the grant was ever put into operation. We note that in August 1622 the Court of Aldermen made an order that *two salters*, (in the presence of two of the Lord Mayor's officers) should 'indifferently garble the hoppes of Mr Hussey *late seized*',[140] and that in November 1625[141] an *ironmonger* and a *salter* were appointed

searchers of soape and guagers of vessells for soape.

In the accounts for 1623–4 there is a payment of £40 to the four Assistants mentioned in the 1618 grant,[142] and a payment of £10 'to our Clerk *in part* that he hath laid out for the Patent' is shown in the accounts for the two following years.[143] Then in August 1627 we read that £12 has been paid to three of the Assistants out of the House Stock *in full* for such monies as they have laid out for and about the Letters Patent 'viz., to every of them £4 *which they were well pleased to accept*'. Considering those minutes and accounts together, we are left with the impression that this final payment marked the conclusion of a long and costly experiment.

---

f *Commentary*, p. 250.

The Stuart Charters
The Candlemakers
and the End of Searches

I

THE earliest surviving confirmation of the Charter of
Edward IV, (8th March 1462)—our Charter of Incorporation*—is dated 16th February 1548 and bears the endorsement 'a corporacion from Edward Sixt vnto this Company'.[1]
It followed a patent from Henry VIII, dated 15th November 1516,
and was itself followed by two further patents,[b] both of which
are inspeximus charters like the first two, and none of the four
contains any new powers. These formal ratifications by the House
of Tudor were in turn succeeded by the lengthy charters of the
Stuart Kings, with which the present chapter is mainly concerned.[c]

Our sixth Royal Charter was granted by James I on 6th March
1606.[2] After reciting our first charter, the King, on the humble
petition of the *now freemen of the mystery or art of Tallow Chandlers*,
'wills' that

whether heretofore they shall have been incorporated or not or by what name
or names of Incorporation soever,

they shall be

---

a   Volume II, pp. 48–52.

b   *Commentary*, p. 251.

c   Appendix L, Part I, includes the companies to which the Stuarts granted incorporation, in addition to renewing the grants of many of the early craft guilds listed in
Appendix D of Volume III.

by virtue of these presents one body corporate and politick (unum corpus cor-
poratum et politicum) by the name of the Master Wardens and Commonalty
of the Mystery of Tallow Chandlers of the City of London (misterie de
Talloughchaundelers civitatis Londonie).

The power to elect a Master and four Wardens to govern the
mistery is repeated. So is the right to a common seal, the power
to purchase and hold land, and the right to plead. There is a new
power to make Ordinances, and the power to inflict penalties is
wider. The most important extension is in the matter of searches
(p. 129). The Charter directs that

for the better rule and government of all persons who do now exercise or hereafter exercise the mistery or art of Tallow Chandlers within the said City of
London and the Suburbs of the same,

the Master and Wardens for the time being or any two or more
of them

shall have survey, search, correction and government of *all and singular persons
occupying, exercising or using the mistery or art of Tallow Chandlers* within the said
City of London, the liberties and suburbs of the same, *and within two miles of
the same City,* and within all liberties, franchizes, jurisdictions and places as well
exempt as not exempt . . . ,

with power to punish 'all delinquents for their offences in the
false, undue and insufficient occupation or execution' of the
mistery. We have seen how the grant of this Charter preceded by
only a few months a change of front by the City in the matter of
our rights under the Elizabeth Patent (p. 165). In the accounts for
1605–7 there are payments relating to 'the first and second years
searches'[3] which could relate to either Patent.

Perhaps the most important reason for securing this Charter
at a cost not far short of £100,[d] was the need to re-establish our
right both to acquire and to hold land. As we have seen, our
Company, in common with the other craft guilds, had been compelled to redeem, at a heavy cost, the rent charges created by the
second Statute of Chantries in 1547.[e] The monies due to the King

---

d   *Commentary*, p. 251.

e   Volume III, pp. 38–9.

Fig. 29. Coronation of James I.

were paid into His Majesty's Exchequer, and, in exchange, it was agreed that the King should, by his letters patent, grant 'all such rentes, revenues and sommes of money as were given, devised or appropriated to superstitions use or uses' to trustees on behalf of the City, who in turn would release to the companies those for which they had individually compounded.[4] On 18th August 1550 we obtained our discharge, which was duly endorsed 'a deed of release for the purchase of the obyt money',[f] but it failed to name 'the Bowyers House' and 'atte Vine' (which alone of John Steward's Bishopsgate properties remained to us), a mistake which was to cost us dear.

Later, another error, which concerned all the companies, was discovered. In or about the year 1578 (to quote from Roger Price's narrative) 'a question did arise amongst the Lawyers of the Land whither the assurance passed to the City of London . . . *were good or not, and whither there remained anie interest in the Crowne of or in the said landes, yea or no'*,[g] seeing that the King had granted

---

f   For a copy of this release and endorsement see *T.C.C.R.*, pp. 156, 157.

g   See *T.C.C.R.*, p. 167.

'the rentes superstitiously ymployed', but not the Lands or Tenements out of which the same did arise.[h] For 'the further triall thereof' the Queen made a grant of these 'concealed Landes' to nominees, but 'upon the commencement of some sutes in Lawe' the City compounded with the patentees, and they 'did convey to certain feofees such right and interest' as they had therein.[i] Thereupon (according to Price)

the City were at quiet, and the severall Companies held their severall Landes till the iiij[th] yere of the reigne of King James, about which tyme . . . at the humble suite of the Citizens of London, and for avoydance of further questions in Lawe . . . yt was enacted That the severall Companies of London & their Successors and assigns should respectively and severally hould and enjoy such Landes and Tenements as were mencioned in the letters Patentes of Kinge Edward the sixt (14th July 1550) and the rentes and proffites of the same w.[th]out anie lett or interrupcion of the saide Kinge James, his Successors, officers or assigns.[j]

The Act, which was a private one, was passed a few months after the grant of our Charter,[5] and must have brought some degree of comfort to the Company, but the matter was by no means settled. Price continues his narrative by reciting, first, a bargain struck in 1619 between the City and John Murray of the King's bedchamber, involving 'assessments' on the companies according to the value of their 'concealed lands', to which our Company refused to consent or contribute,[k] and secondly—this being the principal cause of our dissenting—'a grant procured by the Countess of Sussex under the great seale of England from Kinge James'

of all the said Landes given by . . . John Steward to the . . . Company of Tallow-chaundlers and lyeng in the said parish of St Ethulburgh the Virgin as given and held for maintenance of superstitious uses.

He explains that, by virtue of this grant, legal proceedings were brought against the Company's tenants

---

h   Ibid., p. 166.

i   Ibid., pp. 167–8.

j   Ibid., p. .168

k   Commentary, p. 251.

as against others that held Land of the same title, which the Company had heretofore sould away, and for the enjoyenge whereof the said Company had made severall *warranties* to the purchassers thereof.[l]

In our Wardens' accounts for 1615–6 there is an entry recording the payment of £9 'in suit of Law touching our Lands within Bishopsgate'.[6] In the accounts for 1617–8, we read that £82 13s. was spent 'in defense of our Lands[7] and that a further £15 4s. was paid for counsell about the Information'.[8] Price tells us how, 'by mediacion of frendes on both sides', an agreement was made between the Countess of Sussex and the Company[m] and, from the accounts for 1618–9 we learn how this unhappy affair was at last brought to a conclusion.[9] We read that £166 13s. 4d. was paid

to the Countess of Sussex upon the Arbitration of Sir Henry Yelverton, Attorney General for a *Quietus est* from the said Lady for certain Tenements within Bishopsgate which she had gotten assured to her from the King's Majesty as forfeited uponn the Statute of Chantries.

A dinner at 'the Sealing of the Writings'[n] cost us £1 6s. 6d., and Mr Attorney General was paid £22 'for his pains therein and for his counsel'. A Mr Beal, who presumably represented us, 'his Chief Clerk and other his clerks', received £11, while the cost of 'enrolling the Deed and other charges' amounted to £2 10s. 6s., and £14 12s. was paid in the Crown Office.[10] Thus (in the words of our narrator) after much trouble and costes with great charges & expenses *the said landes were settled upon the said Company*, which was 'enjoyned for ever to preserve the guift and delivery of the said xxv quarters of Charr coles to the poore of the said parishes of St Buttolph without Bishopsgate and St Ethelburgh the Virgin *within Bishopsgate . . .*'[o]

Price describes the final step taken by our Master and Wardens to make the Company secure, in which we may be certain that he played a major part. 'Afterwardes', he writes

---

l   T.C.C.R., p. 171.

m   T.C.C.R., p. 172.

n   Commentary, p. 251.

o   Volume III, p. 37.

the said Company of Tallowchaundlers haveinge undergon many troubles and sutes in lawe for preservacion of their landes, Vpon theire humble peticion to the saide Kinge James and in consideracion of a certen somme of money paid into his Exchequer: The said Kinge James was graciously pleased to graunt vnto the said Company, . . . and to theire successors, a confirmacion vnder the great Seale of England of all such landes, tenementes and hereditamentes as the said Company were then seazed of To hold to them and theire successors for euer.

These Letters Patent, of which he gives an abstract, cost us £115.[11] They are dated 20th October 1619 and are described in the endorsement as 'a Perpetuity granted to the Mr Wardens & Commonalty of the mistery of Tallow Chandlers of London'.[12] Thus equipped we would have learned with no more than academic interest of the final settlement in 1624 which secured for the City and the companies 'quiet enjoyment of their possessions'.[13]

II

During the next ten years it is evident that, with a wider area to cover, the conduct of searches among offending candle-makers was assuming a growing importance. That these searches continued to meet with resistance is seen from the accounts for 1634–5 in which we hear of a 'warning of divers chandlers before the Justices of Middlesex',[14] and in December 1639 we learn from the Court minute book of action being taken nearer home.[15] We read that

wheras our Master and Wardens being in their search in and about the City, the 19 November, for the discovery of bad wares and light weights *according to their Ordinances*, came to the shop of John Gazeley, *a Brother of this Company*, to try his wares and weights and demanded 8*d*. for search money, which he refused to pay. Now, for as much as due proof was this day made unto the Court that the said Gazeley in a peremptory and contemptious manner refused to pay the said search money, and called one of the Wardens, "Knave and long shag haired fellow": it is this day ordered that the said Gazeley shall pay for his several offences aforesaid the several fines hereafter following, viz: for refusing to pay search money 3*s*. 4*d*. and for miscalling the said Warden £6 13. 4.

In punishing him for his failure to pay search money our officers were doubtless relying upon the new powers conferred by the first of the Jacobean charters (6th March 1606), since only a brief reference to this command is made in the Ordinances so recently obtained (p. 141), but, when imposing a penalty for *resistance by a member of the Company*, it is to Article 44 that they would have turned, this article providing, as it does, for the punishment of refractory and disobedient persons of the 'Commonalty'.[a] £2 14s. 8d. was paid for prosecuting the offender 'for refusing to pay search money and for giving our Master and Wardens ill language in their search'[16], and, on 22nd January 1640[17]

the said John Gazeley refusing to submit himself to the demands of this Company and to pay the Fines, etc. was *committed from this Court upon the command of the Lord Mayor to the Poultry Compter* by Peter Stedman, one of his Lordship's officers.

But this was more than he could bear. Next day he appeared (presumably under guard)[18]

and made submission, acknowledged his offence, and paid the fines and was enlarged: the Court accepted of his humble apology, and, that it might appear this Court aimed more at government than at money, freely gave him his whole fine again, whereof he thankfully accepted and acknowledged the favour of this Court *to be far greater than he deserved*.

A Court minute of the mid-forties affords evidence that the searches were continuing. On 28th November 1645 it is recorded that there were two applicants for the position of 'butler or officer' to the Company 'for the drawing of beer and *attending them in their searches* and at other times', and of these two, David Williams was appointed to have 'the said place with such allowances as formerly have been given'.[19] In the Wardens' accounts for 1653–4 we read of one Richard Hill, a member of the Company, incurring a fine of 2s. 6d. 'for having light weights and uneven scales'[20] and of a payment of 11s. 8d. to 'the Lieutenant of the Tower' in prosecution of two persons '*that refused the search*'.[21] Light weights again figured in the minutes in April 1664, when it was resolved that the Master and Wardens should take such action as they judged 'the likeliest way' to make offenders comply with the Ordinances of the Company in that behalf,[22] resulting

---

[a]   *Commentary*, p. 251.

in a payment of 10s. for two *warrants* from the Recorder of London.[23] Next year, our Court, on being informed that one John Gale, 'a chandler' in Cursitors Alley[b] 'gave abusive language unto the Wardens and Assistants in their search, and refused to pay search money, directed that a *Recorder's Warrant* should be obtained 'for to bring the said Gale before the Lord Mayor, there to answer for his contempt'.[24] In the accounts for 1667-8[25] we read that 13s. 4d. has been paid to

the Lord Mayor's officer for warning 9 persons that had been refractory in the search last year *and for his Lordship's warrant for some that did not appear on the summons,* and for a porter

for the carriage of Charters. Further summonses to 'refractory persons' followed in the next few years.[26] In June, 1669 several offenders submitted and paid their dues to the Company without appearing before the Lord Mayor. In another case on the same day, John Cooper, candle-maker in Whitechapel, paid 6s. 8d. by order of the Lord Mayor 'for his candles being false and made of mixed stuff' but his Lordship 'looking on him as a young man', remitted the 3s. 4d. forfeited for non payment of search money.

Meanwhile we were coming under pressure from the Trade. In July 1650[27] two practising tallow chandlers presented a Petition to our Court 'in the name of the Tallow candle-makers of London, touching some grievances in their trade', viz:

some useing the trade not having served apprenticeship, and other forestalling of markets, in buying of melted and rough Tallow, and other things specified.

A Committee was appointed,[28] which (in conjunction with the Master and Wardens) was ordered 'to consider *who are fit to be taken into the clothing* of this Company'. We are not told the result, but a year later our Court was again approached[29] with a request for assistance in procuring some way whereby

those who use the trade of candle-making and have not served seven years apprenticeship thereto might be suppressed and not have the like liberties and benefit as those who have served the same.

---

b   The earlier name for Cursitor Street, east out of Chancery Lane. *Harben*.

There were two meetings,[30] at the second of which a number of those attending, some of them members of the Company, desired that the Charter might be read, and there was talk of consulting Counsel.

In July 1663 a further Petition, this time from 'the candlemakers inhabiting in London', was presented.[31] It was addressed to 'the right worshipful the Master, Wardens and Assistants of the Company of Tallow Chandlers' and was evidently of some importance, but the Clerk omits to acquaint us with its contents. All we are told is that there is to be a meeting, our representatives being six candle-makers who were members of the Company, to discuss means for redressing grievances.

We hear nothing more of the affair until April 1669,[32] when there is a Court Meeting at which 'divers candlemakers, as well free of this Company as of several other companies', put forward proposals for the renewal of our Charter of James I *with enlarged provisions*. According to the minute these proposals did not appear to us of 'much weight' at the time. Nevertheless, we wished to show our 'readiness to promote *the good of the trade*'. We accordingly made our Charter and Bye-Laws available for inspection to the visitors, and our Clerk, John Maxfield, was instructed to provide them with a copy of 'such *branches* as they should judge would tend most' to its advancement.

Nothing further seems to have been heard of the matter at that time, but, from contemporary records, it is evident that we were not feeling at all happy about our powers. It is true that the Charter gave us a right of search over all persons exercising the art or mistery of tallow chandlers within the City and Liberties and two miles beyond, but, as we have seen (p. 141), our *Ordinances* of 1639 contained very little on the subject of searches. A copy of the opinion of Mr John Howell, the Recorder, dated 3rd May 1670, has been preserved, in which he advises, in effect, that the search probably extends only to those who can be said to use the trade of tallow chandlers, and not to sellers of candles *per se*.[33] At a meeting just over a year later[34] it was ordered

that the Master, with such other persons as he shall think fit to take with him, shall consult and advise with some or more able Counsel about the *Book of Ordinances*, what may be thought to be the best and safest way to bring refractory persons to yield due obedience . . .

We paid £2 to 'Mr Simpson, Counsel, for advice upon the Ordinances . . . and giving his opinion large in writing under his hand'[35] but unfortunately the paper has not survived.

Organized searches, nevertheless, continued. Following the minutes for 20th December 1669 there is an entry[36] recording that

on Tuesday, Wednesday and Thursday the 22nd, 23rd and 24th day of March 1669 [1670] the Master, Wardens and Assistants of the Mistery of Tallow Chandlers of the City of London made their search in and about the said City and Liberties thereof and within two miles compass of the same *according to the ancient custom and usual manner*, and received for, and in the name of, search money over and above all charges £12 11s.

A like entry follows the minute for 19th January 1671[37], reporting a three-day search in March, and a Recorder's Warrant was issued on 4th January 1672 'to arrest persons free of the Tallow Chandlers Company, or using their trade'.[38] A similar warrant had been issued 'from the Recorder's Chambers in Lincoln's Inn' in the previous year.[39]

At a Court held on 30th January 1673[40] it was ordered that those who had refused or delayed to pay search money on a recent search

shall with all convenient speed be legally proceeded against in manner following, viz.: all such as are *freemen* of the City shall be warned or summoned by some one of the officers of the Right Honble the Lord Mayor . . . to answer unto such matters as shall be alleged against each of them respectively by the Master & Wardens of this Company, and *all other persons* so culpable as aforesaid being *foreigners* [non-freemen] shall be served with Recorder's Warrants to appear before the said Right Honble the Lord Mayor *or some other of His Majesty's Justices of the Peace* in the City of London, Westminster, counties of Middlesex, Hertford, Essex, Kent & Surrey upon the account above expressed. . .

In March 1674 there was a two-day search, when the net receipts were £8 17s.[41]

In November 1674 'divers persons exercising the trade of Tallow Chandlers, as well Freemen of this and other companies',

M

appeared before our Court and requested the Company to 'make a penal order prohibiting all persons using the said Trade and living within the City of London and Southwark and within two miles compass of the same City from giving or bestowing unto or amongst their customers any candles, wrought or plain, for *Christmas candles*, or to make any allowance whatsoever for or in lieu thereof'.[42] A paper was drawn up[43] in which it was alleged that

by many years of observance it hath been found that vaine use of Tallow Chandlers giveing of candles to many of their Customers at Christmas hath beene very prejuditiall and produced many inconvenyenties to the members of the said trade as

1.   By the grete dissattisfaction it gave to most Customers, they not thinking them according to theire deserts

2.   These beeing cheefely desired by those whose custom was very small and many times did give the Giver much trouble and disturbance

3.   And thirdly, many going frome one shop to another pretending to bee customers purposely to gett a candle when they have never been in the shop before.

Attention was drawn also to 'the little or no advantedge the customers received thereby, nay rather to most considerable customers a disadvauntage and charge'. To prevent such inconveniences, the giving of candles, or other thing in lieu thereof, was to be forbidden, and a copy of the order was to be put up in every shop. Our Court decided that 'they did not judge they had such a coercive power as to restrain any person from disposing of their own goods and commodities as he thought meet', and it seems unlikely that the order was ever issued.

Fig. 30. Crown of Charles II.

In March 1675 we were again approached by representatives of the trade.[44] At a meeting of the Court on the 18th there was presented 'the humble petition of the Candlemakers inhabiting in London and the parts adjacent thereto', containing a number of proposals, of which the first, and most important, was that

all the Candlemakers within the City and suburbs who have duly served seven years as apprentice to the said trade or, as masters, have followed the same for seven years last past, *may be admitted members of the Company*.

It was proposed also that all admitted members who were members of other companies should be admitted 'in the same capacity' as they then stood in those companies, and that care should be taken to relieve them of the double burden of belonging to two companies. A further proposal was that provision should be made for the admission to the freedom in due course of apprentices already bound in other companies. There were other proposals for the regulation of the trade and the remedy of abuses.

This request by the candle-makers that they should be admitted to the Freedom of the Company as of right seems to have come without warning. Admission by Redemption had anciently been regarded as a privilege, and there are examples in the first quarter of the century of candle-makers, who had not been apprenticed to Freemen-members of the Company, making presents (when admitted), which usually took the form of a piece of silver.[45] A Committee[c] was appointed[46] to 'treat, consult and consider' with eight persons nominated by the petitioners

how far this Company may legally & safely answer & comply with the petition and proposals aforesaid.

The Court was reluctant to grant the petitioners' request to be supplied with a copy of the Ordinances of 1589.[47] An oblique reference was made to a recent 'Ordinance',[d] and we were faced by a fresh deputation, whose applicants asked to peruse the Company's Charter and Ordinances and to be supplied with copies

---

c   *Commentary*, p. 252.

d   *Commentary*, p. 252.

to th'intent they thereby might be enabled to draw upp such further instruments & authority for ye reforming of abuses & better regulacion of the Trade of candlemaking as with the consent of this Courte and advice of Councell to be had therein should be advisable.

They were at first refused permission on the ground of expense, but this was later granted,[48] and they came back on 20th July,[49] when there was read

a petition presented to this Courte *by the Candlemakers* directed to the King's most excellent Majesty . . . And also a paper annexed to the same entitled the Additions and Alterations humbly desired to be added *to the Tallow Chandlers Charter*.

It was decided that the advice of Counsel should be taken and, at a meeting of our Court on 11th August,[50] a lengthy draft was submitted, of which two clauses were left for further consideration. It is evident that the Court then decided to take legal advice. The accounts[51] record a payment 'to Sir Francis Winington, Solicitor-General, and to other Counsel for advice about the Company's Charter', and money was spent 'at several meetings about the same'. A sum of £5 was also paid

for transcribing several copies of the Company's Charter and Ordinances and attending on Counsel about renewing the Charter and the Clerk's pains and service therein.

We have no copy of Counsel's opinion, but, on 18th January 1676,[52] '*The King's Warrant to the Attorney-General*' was issued to prepare a Bill confirming the powers contained in existing Charters and granting fresh privileges, which, in general, were aimed at compelling *all persons* in and near the City, *including those in other companies*, exercising the trade of a tallow chandler, to be made free of the Tallow Chandlers Company. Fresh powers of search were also to be conferred upon us.

Further meetings with the candle-makers took place, and their proposals were discussed in Committee.[53] At a meeting in February they submitted a fresh paper 'importing their desires' and, in the following month, a lengthy draft was considered by 'Mr Steele'. In a paper in which they set out (in anticipation)[54] the 'severall priviledges agreed to be granted to the candlemakers' they refer to their proposals for the better management & benefitt of the trade & for the weale & profitt of the Company, all of which . . . (in regard of the great charge & expence the Company hath of late yeares been at in building of their Hall, and other occasions, by reason of the late dreadfull fire of London) they freely proffer to doe at their owne proper charges.

On 20th April[55] it was agreed 'at a full Court of Assistants' that a Committee of the Court 'shall forthwith attend Sir Francis Winnington, Her Majesty's Solicitor-Generals, and advise with him concerning the said drafte *and to endeavour the settlement thereof*'. It seems that the Lord Mayor, Sir Thomas Davies, was also concerned in the discussions,[56] and that he asked for an assurance that, in presenting our petition, we did not intend

to disturbe or offend anie other Companies of London by takeing anie of their members forceablie from them, but that they may remaine as members of them, and beare place & charge amongst them as formerlie, *as in the case of The Distillers & other Companies.*

On 2nd June 1676 the whole Livery was summoned 'by tickets' to meet together with the Master, Wardens and Assistants at the Hall, in order that they might be acquainted 'with the late trans-actions' and our Court's decision 'to renew the Company's Charter to the good of the Trade of the Candlemakers and the benefit and profit of the Company'.[57] The draft was 'openly read in the Common Hall and approved'[58] and on 6th February 1677 the Letters Patent from the King, dated 29th July 1676[59] (Plate I) were enrolled amongst the Records of the City,[60] at a cost of £5 7s.[61]

'The divers inconveniences and abuses' to which we had been subjected since the granting of our earlier Charters were given as the reason for our Petition to the Crown. It was pleaded, first, that the City had been 'much enlarged', and that the number of tallow chandlers in and about the same had been *greatly increased*,

partly by reason of divers persons resorting (there) from remote parts . . . and partly because very many persons who were originally educated and brought up in other Arts and Mysteries *yet have and do exercise and use the said Art or Mystery of a Tallow Chandler.*

Our second plea was that 'the greater part' of the freemen tallow chandlers are members of *other corporations*, and are not free or enfranchised of, or in, the Corporation or Commonalty of the Mystery of Tallow Chandlers,

on which account, as also by reason of the great falling off of the members of the Company,

due scrutinies cannot be made of bad, false, dishonest and adulterated stuff, Wares, Tallow and Manufactures of and belonging to the Art or Mystery, nor the irregularities and abuses thereof be discovered, corrected or rectified

as the same ought to be,

whence it happens that very bad stuff, wares, Tallow and Candles are daily made and sold, and great quantities of candles *are brought from remote parts to the said City of London* and are there disposed of and sold,

to the great injury and prejudice of the King's faithful subjects, 'and likewise to the great impoverishment and discouragement of the Corporation or Commonalty of the Mystery of Tallow Chandlers'.

The remedies provided by the new Charter were threefold. First, that all persons exercising the Art or Mystery of Tallow Chandlers in the City of London, or within three miles thereof, shall be made 'free and enfranchized of and in the said Corporation' within a period of twelve months, and that all persons afterwards exercising the trade shall become free of the Company *as soon as they begin to exercise the same*, with appropriate penalties for disobeying. Secondly, that all persons exercising the trade within the prescribed area shall make their apprentices free of the Company after they shall have served their respective times, *or at least before they shall exercise the trade*, again with appropriate penalties. Thirdly, that the Master and Wardens,

calling to their Assistance *such persons being candlemakers* of the said commonalty as they shall think fit for the making of due searches . . . of . . . all persons who shall use and exercise the said Art of a Tallow Chandler or shall make or sell Tallow Candles or shall melt any Tallow within the City of London aforesaid or within three miles thereof, shall once in every year hereafter . . ./and oftener if occasion shall require/make and grant *one or more Deputation or Deputations under their Common Seal* to authorise twelve or more such persons/being *Candlemakers*/of the Assistants or Livery . . . to make and execute such searches,[e]

---

[e]   *Commentary*, p. 252.

which said twelve or more such persons . . . or any four of them

shall . . . make and execute due searches in all and singular places [as aforesaid] for and concerning all bad false dishonest mixt and adulterated stuff/ work/Tallow Candles/Goods/Wares or Merchandise whatsoever in any wise relating to the Art or Mystery aforesaid,

and, if they shall find or discover any such . . .,

that then it shall and may be lawful . . . all such stuff manufactures Tallow candles goods and merchandize whatsoever . . . *to break destroy throw away and make uncapable and unfit for sale* by such lawful ways or means as they may think fit.

Because of the action of persons dwelling in parts remote from the City hitherto unpunishable the searchers were to take special care in searching for, and viewing, candles brought into the prescribed area and in breaking and making unfit for sale all such as were found to be 'bad or fraudulent'.*f*

At the meeting of the Court of Aldermen in February 1677,[62] it was resolved that

all persons using the said trade within the City or three miles thereof who have served apprenticeship thereto and are not freemen of this City *being by the direction of the said Charter admitted into the said Company*, shall also upon presentment of them to the Court by the Wardens of the said Company *be admitted into the freedom of this City by redemption* for such moderate fine as the Committee hereunder named shall think fitting.

But, on the advice of the committee,[63] which met a week later, chaired by Sir Joseph Sheldon,*g* the Court made an order restraining our Company from taking away any former apprentices of freemen of any of the Great Twelve Companies and directed that former apprentices of freemen of 'the inferior Companies' might be made free of our Company (on payment of a fine of 3*s*. 4*d*.) *only upon their petition to the Court*. 'Foreigners' also, who had served apprenticeship to the trade within the prescribed area *and should by petition desire to become members of the Company and to*

Commentary, p. 252.

g   One of our great benefactors (see Appendices D and K). He had become Lord Mayor in 1675 after translation to the Drapers Company.

take their freedom of the City by redemption, *might be* so admitted (on payment of £3 6s. 8d.). Restrictions such as these illustrate the continued resistance by the City to Royal Charters. (The affair of the Distillers Company, referred to by the Lord Mayor, is a case in point.)[h] Having supported the candle-makers so far in their demands, we must have been disappointed with this decision, notwithstanding the final direction that apprentices who had served their full term with any freemen of the City using the trade (except freemen of the Twelve) might *and ought to be* free of our Company *only*.

Warnings were sent out by our Court calling upon candle-makers, not numbered among our members, to take their Freedom with the Company. No copy has been preserved, but the summons (so called) printed in 1678 at a cost of 17s.[64] is given in Figure 31. A number of Freemen's oaths were printed at this time, for which, and for a supply of paper, we paid 9s. 8d.[65]

By March 1677 at least thirty tallow chandlers by trade from

SIR,

YOU (being a Tallow-Chandler by Trade) are (by Vertue of his Majesties Charter, Dated 29ᵗʰ of *July*, 1676. granted to the Company of Tallow-Chandlers, *London*) Required within one year then next coming, to take your Freedom of the said Company. And although you have had often Notice thereof, and many Warnings given you within that time, you have neglected to accept thereof, and have elapsed the time given you, contrary to his Majesties Grant under the great Seal of *England*; Yet notwithstanding the Court of Assistants have thought meet once more to Require you to appear at the Tallow-Chandlers Hall at *Dowgate, London*, on   the   day of   1678. in the   then and there to take your Freedom of the said Company, which if you shall fail or neglect to do, they will put in execution that Power which is given them by the said Grant, and thereby leave you without excuse: Whereof you are desired not to fail, as you will avoid the trouble and charge which thereby will ensue.

Fig. 31. Seventeenth century Summons to take the Freedom in the Tallow Chandlers Company.

---

h   *Commentary*, p. 252.

other companies had been admitted to the Freedom of the Tallow
Chandlers Company. Some of them had been immediately
clothed with the Livery and admitted as Assistants of the Court,
a step which is recorded as having been taken 'according to
agreement formerly made upon renewing the Company's Charter'.[66] The candle-makers had failed to secure the inclusion of
this condition in the new Charter. They had also failed in their
claim that entrants should be admitted 'in the same capacity' as
they stood in their parent companies. On 5th March a member of
the Salters Company, having been admitted to the Freedom of our
Company, was taken into the clothing and chosen as an Assistant,
'leaving it to himself what he will wish to give to the Company
upon his admittance, he having passed all offices in the Company
of Salters'. Another Salter taken into the Livery and chosen as one
of the Assistants, paid 40 shillings for the Livery and a fine of £5
'for passing the place of Steward'.[67] Apart from these two men,
we have no means of knowing what positions the new freemen
had previously held, but it is clear from a minute of 13th March[68]
that they were given a degree of seniority on the Court.[i] In the
same period a few candle-makers residing outside the City boundary had also been admitted to the Freedom 'all of whom promised to take their freedoms of the Cittie'.[69] In the next six
months another forty or more tallow chandlers in other companies became freemen of our Company,[70] some of them being
admitted 'gratis'.[71] Five of the Great Twelve Companies[j] and at
least eleven of the lesser companies[k] were represented among the
men admitted during the period March to September 1677.

At a meeting on 11th July 1678[72]

the Tallowchaundelers by Trade declared that they had beene with Councell
concerning those persons who refused to come in to the Company and to be
made free thereof according to the Charter in that behalf.

---

i   Commentary, p. 252.

j   Commentary, p. 252.

k   Commentary, p. 252.

It was agreed that their names should be given to the Court of Assistants and that a 'Speciall Sumons' should be drawn up, whereby they should be required to appear before the Master, Wardens and Assistants. In case they should not appear 'or should refuse to accept thereof', proceedings were to be commenced against them 'by information in His Majesty's Exchequer[1] at the charge of the Company'. The next we hear of the matter is in October, when ten persons (by name) were 'nominated' to be proceeded against 'for not submitting to the Charter', and it was decided to go to Counsel.[73] At the following Court[74] it was agreed that 'writs be forthwith taken out' against some of the offenders and that others should be proceeded against by 'information'. The addresses of these persons, some of which were outside the City boundary, are given,[75] but no company designations are stated, and it seems probable that they were foreigners, or non-freemen. In view of the restraint imposed on us by Order of the Court of Aldermen when our new Charter was enrolled (particularly in the case of members of the Great Twelve Companies) it is unlikely that we would have run the risk of prosecuting Freemen. In January 1679[76] it was ordered that three tallow chandlers by trade should be 'further proceeded against' by bills of information in the Exchequer

for not submitting to his Majesty's charter lately granted to this Company and refusing to take their freedom of this Company in that behalf,

after which these prosecutions seem to have been discontinued and, during the next fifteen years, candle-makers in other companies were left in peace.

III

Commencing in January 1682 Charles II became engaged in a struggle with the City concerning the election of the Sheriffs and control of the Common Council. A writ in the nature of a *Quo Warranto* was issued to the Sheriffs, calling upon them to summon

---

1   *Commentary*, p. 252.

'the Mayor and commonalty and citizens of the City to appear in the Court of King's Bench to answer by what warrant they claimed divers liberties, franchises and privileges', including the right to elect sheriffs.[77] By the end of the year Charles, having been successful in obtaining the election both of a royalist mayor and royalist sheriffs, turned his attention to the Common Council. He issued a command to the Mayor to enforce on the electors the obligation of electing as members on St Thomas' day (21st December) only men who had conformed with the provisions of the Corporation Act.[a] By this means he hoped to secure a Common Council which might make a voluntary surrender of the City's Charter instead of forcing matters to an issue at law.[78] But this having failed, he resolved to proceed with the *Quo Warranto*, and judgment was pronounced against the City on 12th June 1683.[79] A few days later the Common Council presented a petition to the King asking pardon for their late offences, and declaring their readiness to submit to anything that he might direct. His terms included what amounted to a complete surrender of control over the election of the Mayor, Sheriffs and other City officers, in exchange for which His Majesty was willing to confirm the City's charter.[80] In September the Lord Mayor, Sir William Prichard, laid before the Common Council drafts of a surrender of the City's franchise to his Majesty, and a re-grant prepared by the Attorney-General, but, after much debate, a majority voted against sealing the deed, whereupon judgment was entered against the City. The Recorder was dismissed, and eight Aldermen were removed from the Court, their places being filled by nominees of the King.[81]

Having thus reduced the Corporation of London to submission, Charles proceeded to take similar action against the livery companies, with the object of getting into his hands the power of appointing and dismissing their officers.[82] In April 1684 our Company received a writ of *Quo Warranto* out of the Court of

---

[a]   *Commentary*, p. 253.

King's Bench[b] demanding by what right we exercised our privileges and commanding our appearance, and on the 9th May the Court of Assistants met 'to consider the method of a Petition and submission' to be presented to the King.[83] This petition was settled in consultation with the Attorney-General, and on Sunday 11th May our Wardens delivered it to the King at Windsor, by whom 'it was graciously received'.[84] But less than a month later[85] it became necessary to call a special Court[c] to consider

the surrender of the powers, franchises, privileges and authorities of the Tallow Chandlers Company to the King and imploring his Majesty *to regrant unto them* the naming and choosing of such officers who shall manage the governing part of the said Company under such restrictions, qualifications and reservations as his Majesty shall think fit.

This humiliating document (bearing date 9th June 1684) was engrossed, sealed, and delivered on 29th June into the hands of 'Sir George Jefferies, Knt, Lord Chief Justice of England'.[86] The usual salutation with which the Surrender commenced was followed by the gentle reminder

how much it Imports the government of this City and the Companyes thereof to have persons of *knowne Loyalty and approved Integrity* to beare offices of trust therein,

and on the same day 'a list of the names of the Master, Wardens and Assistants, such as had passed Stewards, and the whole Livery of the Company' was delivered by the Clerk to Mr Graham of Clifford's Inn, with which action the Lord Chief Justice was acquainted.[87]

Charles II died on 6th February 1685 without having granted us a new charter, in which respect we differed from some other companies.[d] His death was quickly followed by a proclamation of his successor's wishes that all persons in office at the time of the decease of the late King should so continue until further notice.[88] On the same day as the surrender of our liberties, our Court had

---

b   Commentary, p. 253.

c   Commentary, p. 253.

d   Commentary, p. 253.

Fig. 32. Portrait of James II. From a painting by Sir Godfrey
Kneller (1649–1723).

agreed,[89] on the petition of Gilbert Brandon, 'that he be recommended to his Majesty by the Attorney-General as Clerk, vice John Marsh resigned,[90] for approbation and confirmation of the said place'.[e] On 27th June 1685 we obtained James II's Charter[91] at a cost of £177 2s. 4d.[92] of which we had to borrow £100 under our common seal.[93] The minute of the meeting of the Court of Assistants which took place on 14th July[94] records the reading of the Charter, by which, 'amongst other things, his Majesty is graciously pleased to create, constitute and appoint for present Master, Wardens, Assistants and Clerk' of the said Company, the persons named, that is to say Nicholas Charleton 'first and Modern Master' the four Wardens, twenty-four Assistants and Gilbert Brandon, Clerk.[f] Nicholas Charleton's name heads the list of Assistants in 1681 and he was present as 'Deputy Master' on many occasions in 1684–5. On 22nd October (1685) James

---

e   *Commentary*, p. 253.

f   *Commentary*, p. 253.

Woods (appointed first Warden by the Charter) attended on the Town Clerk with the Bill for registering the new Charter 'amounting unto £5 12s. 6d., and requested that he would be as kind to the Company as he could, whereupon the Town Clerk accepted £4 12s. 6d . . .'[95] On 17th September, by Order of the Court of Aldermen the Company was granted a new *Livery*.[96] A copy was delivered to the Master and Wardens on 6th October,[97] and 6s. was paid for an 'Order of the Court of Aldermen, for their *approbation* of the list of the Clothing'.[98]

During the next three years the King proceeded to exercise the power reserved to him in the various new Charters granted to the Companies in 1685 to remove their officers by Order in Council[g]—a policy aimed at eventually packing these assemblies with men favourable to the Roman Catholic cause. On 10th February 1688, for instance, the Drapers Company received an order removing nine members of their Court,[99] and, on 5th March following the Master, two of the Wardens and six Assistants of the Butchers Company were removed.[100] On 10th February 1688 James Woods (elected Master of our Company in June 1687) and others were removed 'by order of the King and Council'.[101] On the 14th an Order was made for a new list of our Master, Wardens, Assistants and Livery to be delivered at the Town Hall and this was done on the 29th.[102] William Wickins was chosen Master in Woods' place for the remainder of the year.[103] He was re-elected in June 1688, and, at a meeting of the Court (when in the Chair) on 19th July, he produced an order *whereby Gilbert Brandon was removed from the office of Clerk*, 'for which said office so vacant no candidates or Petitioners to this Court appeared'.[104] The office seems to have remained vacant until 6th September[105] when the Court (after serious debate)

chose William Dodington, gent, to be Clerk to this Company so as he be approved of and confirmed in the said office by his Majesty according to the meaning of this Company's Charter in this behalf.

Dodington's term of office was short lived. Seeing, when it was

---

too late, that the patience of his subjects had been over-taxed, and, in a last effort to avoid the loss of his throne, the King resolved to make amends by restoring the City's cherished 'liberties'. On 7th October (1688) the Court of Aldermen issued a Precept[106] which recited that his Majesty had been 'graciously pleased to restore to this City its ancient franchises' and required, 'by his Charter lately given for y^t purpose, that this Court should cause to be restored to their respective places all such Liverymen of the severall companies of this City as were of the Livery of the s^d companies at the time of the late Judgm^t given ag^t this city upon the *quo warranto*'. It was accordingly *ordered*

that all such members of the respective Livery Companies now living as were of ye Livery at the time of the Judgm^t be forthwith restored to their s^d places in their respective companies . . .[h]

To complete the operation it was necessary that the Surrenders executed by the companies should be made void, and each Company was separately informed of this intention. The Drapers' instrument of Surrender was handed back to their Master at Guildhall on 20th November 1688.[107] Three days later the King had fled the country. Our minutes for the 21st contain the following entry.[108]

This day was received from the Lord Chancellor Jeffreys a note desiring the Master, Wardens and some of the Assistants of this Company to attend him to-morrow at 3 p.m. at his house in Duke St Westminster, pursuant to which the Master and others a tended and received from him this Company's Surrender under their Common Seal[i], who assured them that the same *was never enrolled*, and in that regard *the patent or Charter granted to this Company by King Charles II in the 28th year of his reign is not Surrendered and made void nor any part thereof*, no more than if the same surrender had never been made or executed, and his Lordship advised the persons attending to cancel the said surrender,

an assurance which our learned Clerk caused to be endorsed, and himself signed, on the back of the document.[109] On 29th November[110]

---

h   *Commentary*, p. 253.

i   See Volume III, Plate III for the original Common Seal of the Company (15th Century).

Mr William Dodington lately chosen Clerk to this Company appeared and delivered up to this Court or General Assembly a surrender under his hand and seal of the office of Clerkship, after which Gilbert Brandon late Clerk, upon his humble petition, by this Court is most unanimously chosen, restored and admitted to the said place of Clerk.

It only remains to add that, by one of the first statutes of the reign of the new King and Queen (2 William & Mary c. 8, s. 12), the companies were restored 'to all and every the lands . . . liberties . . . and immunities which they lawfully had and enjoyed' before the Judgment in the *Quo Warranto*, and it was enacted that 'as well all *surrenders* as *Charters*, Letters Patents and Grants for new incorporating any of the said companies . . . made or granted by *the late King James* or by the said King Charles II, since the giving of the said Judgment, shall be void . . .'[111]

IV

Returning now to the subject of our searches.

On 21st June 1677 a copy of the first Deputation 'drawn up by Councell' under the new Charter was read to the Court of Assistants and approved, and it was ordered that it should be 'engrossed in parchment and sealed with the Company's seal'.[112] These deputations (p. 194) are addressed by the Master, Wardens and Comminalty to 'all Christian People' and each contains a lengthy recital of the Company's powers. A number of persons named in the grant, 'being all Candlemakers by Trade and Members of the said Company', or any four of them, are authorized, as often as occasion shall require, to

make and execute our searches in all and singular places as well within the City of London as within *three miles* of the same or of any part thereof and for all bad, undue, mixt, false, and adulterate stuff, works, Tallow Candles and other goods or Merchandise whatsoever touching or anywaies concerning the said Mistery or Art of a Tallow Chandler,

with power to 'break, deface, destroy' and render 'uncapable and unfitt for sale' all false goods and merchandise 'by whatever lawful waies and means shall to them seem good'.

The searchers are authorized and enjoyned to take special care 'in searching and supervizing' as well all candles made in places '*without the said City*' and three miles thereof, *and brought unto the City* or other places, and in breaking and rendering unfit for sale such candles found in any manner bad or deceitful. All mayors and other officers, ministers and subjects are strictly charged to be aiding and assisting as often as need shall require, and the Deputation is to continue in force for one whole year.[113]

At the meeting in June (1677) when the first Deputation was read, 'the names of several persons, candlemakers by Trade, were presented according to the Charter', out of which there were chosen sixteen persons to be searchers for the year ensuing, and it was ordered that there should be three 'Deputacions'.[114] For the next two years the same persons were appointed and there were to be three 'several commissions' on each occasion.[115] The accounts for the years 1678–9 record a payment of £3 'for drawing and engrossing in parchment the Tallow Chandlers Commissions for the search for two years'.[116] In June 1681 it was agreed that the same persons named in the Commissions granted for the *Tallow Chandlers searches* the last year should be continued for one year longer.[117] In February 1682 it was agreed that '*the Master and Wardens* with the assistance of four others should search amongst the Mistery of Tallow Chandelers onlie'.[118] This was evidently not a candle-makers' or tallow chandlers' search like the others, but was 'a general search', so called, of which we are to hear more shortly.

The minutes for a time are rather rough, and the Clerk does not trouble to record the searches. In May 1684 there is a great improvement, and we read in the minute for 13th January 1686[119] of an order for a search 'according to custom' on the first Monday in March next

and to continue for such further dais as shall be found requisite And that two years arrears for that duty be demanded.

In June of that year[120] there were chosen and appointed twelve persons, including two of the Wardens

being all of them Candlemakers by Trade *and of the Livery and Assistants of this Company* according to direction of this Companies Charter.

N

Regular appointments are made in June of each of the next four years.[121] Then, in February 1691[122] we read that

for the future foure Deputacions be made and granted under the Common Seal of this Company for the making of searches in and amongst the Candlemakers.

£3 is to be allowed to the searchers and for the future 'all reasonable expenses and disbursements' may be charged not exceeding 20s. for each Deputation. The order goes on to direct that

a *General Search* be had and made in the month of March next.

The original deputations (some of them with their seals still attached) for most of the years 1678 to 1709 have been preserved.[123] About the year 1688 the searchers appear to have been divided into what were known as 'the Eastern and Western Clerk's and Beadle's walks', and the accounts for 1691–2 record the expenditure of £4 13s. 7d. 'by the four divisions of searches at sundry times this year'.[124] No alteration appears to have taken place in the manner of conducting the searches when the new Charter was granted. Several earlier search books are extant, the first of which covers four days and contains the names of over four hundred and thirty persons, each of whom paid 8d. search money.[125]

In February 1692[126] a *general search* was again ordered to be made

according to ancient *Custom* and for that end and purpose the Master and Wardens are desired to obtain the Recorder's Warrant or any other matter or thing that may corroborate that service of duty.

It is probable that the main object of these general searches was to look for non-freemen improperly carrying on the trade. The minutes contain very little information on the subject, but it may well be that some of the 'complaints' of which we read resulted from the visits. In April[127] it was reported that, according to Mr Munday of Counsel, a Recorder's Warrant lacking a name is not legal, but that it would be 'easy enough' from time to time to obtain one for a particular offender. Counsel, having read our Ordinances, also advised that none of our members who did not

actually make or sell candles was liable to pay search money 'in
such capacity, neither could this Company warrant the receipt of
any search money so taken of them'. Yet, they were obliged to
pay towards the charge of such searches as members. The Clerk's
marginal note reads 'Concerning the Generall Search'. It took
place that month,[128] and in June a Committee of the Court, all
of them candlemakers, was appointed to inspect the offences of all
such persons found 'as well on the private and public searches of
this Company and to make such proceedings against them as shall
be fitting'.[129] Apart from the record of fees to the staff to which
we have yet to refer, this appears to be the only time that the
distinction is drawn between 'private' and 'public' searches, but
it seems that private searches were those for which deputations
were required. The reader is referred to Appendix M for further
details.

The Committee appointed to inspect offences,[130] having met[131]
and well considered the Ordinances and 'perused the names of
divers offenders therein, as well Candlemakers as Retayle Chandlers', unanimously ordered

that (as a tryall or Experience of their success herein) but two of them (the
offenders) at this present shall be summoned before the Rt Honble Sir Thomas
Stamp, kt Lord Mayor of this city for refusing to pay the duty of search
monies, namely Baptist Mead, a Tallow Chandler or candlemaker, and Thomas
Penn, a Retayler

Penn, on being summoned 'complied'. Mead, 'refusing to pay
the said duty was by the Lord Mayor referred to the Court of
Aldermen who made an Order thereupon',[132] of which we shall
hear more in the next chapter.

To judge from the record kept by our Wardens for the year
ended June 1696[133] they were beginning to have misgivings about
continuing the searches. They observe that the duty of search 'is
as uncertain as the rest and has scarcely ever produced anything
like so little as within the last year, which, clear of all charges,
came unto but £2 4s. 5d'. The searches (as had happened before)
were sometimes meeting with resistance. In February 1692 a man
named John Ellars was reprimanded by our Court 'for his great
rudeness and misbehaviour towards the searchers at the time of

viewing his candles',[134] and there was an occasion in March 1701[135] when proceedings were threatened by the steward of the manors of St Giles in the Fields[a] and Bloomsbury.[b] As we shall see, the legal position was uncertain, and the end came only a few years later.

Fig. 33. Queen Anne farthing.

On 5th September 1709[136] a report was made

that Mr William Mayne and divers other members of this Company stand indicted[c] at Hickes Hall[d] for breaking the candles of Lewis Nicholls at his shop in 'Pick a Dilley' at a search by them there lately made, pursuant to a Depucon under the Common Seale of this Company executed in the year 1708

A Committee of the Court waited on the Recorder, Sir Peter King, who, having perused 'their case and queries', gave them 'good encouragement' to believe that the Defendants might be acquitted of the *Indictments*, but warned them that they must be prepared 'for tryall' of Nicholls' claim for the breaking of his candles at the Queens Bench Court, Westminster.[137] The Committee's Counsel advised them to obtain from the Attorney General a stay of the Indictment,[138] but this was refused,[139] and, notwithstanding the Recorder's early optimism, Counsel, having perused the Company's Charter, advised them 'not to try the cause'.[140] The prosecution's costs were taxed at £8 13s. 4d. and these were paid at the Crown office on 3rd February, 1710.[141]

---

[a]   At the east end of Oxford Street there was originally a village separated from London and Westminster by broad fields, and its church was so designated to distinguish it from St Giles, Cripplegate. *Wheatley.*

[b]   The district lying between the north side of New Oxford Street and High Holborn. See *Commentary*, p. 253.

[c]   *Commentary*, p. 253.

[d]   The Sessions House of the County of Middlesex. See Volume III, p. 112, note *l.*

Three days later[142] it was announced that the case in the Queens Bench Court was to be heard and, after being twice deferred because of the non-appearance of the Attorney General,[143] it was duly heard on the 9th February by Lord Chief Justice Holt, Mr Justice Powell and Mr Justice Gold[144] when, after arguments on both sides,

it was adjudged and ordered that the *persecutor* Lewis Nicholl should have full Costs and Satisfaction for his candles broke by the said defendants . . .

The costs of the indictment amounted to over £170,[145] and on 9th May 1710 the costs and damages in the Queens Bench Court were 'taxed by the Master in the Crown office' at £30.[146]

It had been decided at a meeting of the Court on 5th July 1709 that the Clerk should provide (as usual) four Deputations of search which were to be ready by the 9th August,[147] but not surprisingly, there is no record of their having been sealed. The last of the search books covers the period 15th to 29th March 1708. It contains over two hundred names, and Lewis Nichols' name, with 'pickadilly' as his address appears in the list for the second of three days searches.[148] Each day's list is signed by the searchers taking part, among whom is William Mayne. The Minute for 28th June 1710[149] leaves us in no doubt that his duties and those of his colleagues in this field are ended. We read that

for this present year and for every year hereafter yearly shall be paid and allowed unto the Clerk, Beadle, under Beadle or porter, and Butler of this Company for the time being the several and respective yearly sums hereafter particularly mencioned.

The Clerk was to receive four pounds yearly 'in lieu and recompence of the Fees Antiently paid him for attending the publick search and makeing four deputacions for executing private searches for this Company yearly which is now suspended'. The Beadle was to receive twenty shillings yearly 'in lieu and recompence of the Fees antiently paid him for attending the *publick search now suspended*'. The recompense of the Under Beadle and the Butler for the loss of private searches was to be ten shillings each yearly.

Wind of Change

I

THE collapse of our settled policy of conducting searches marks the end of an era, but the practice had been under attack ever since a decision of the courts in 1599,[1] when the confiscation of goods during the search was declared illegal in a test case against the Dyers' Company.[a] Most of the Great Twelve companies had already abandoned the search[b] as part of their policy of phasing out a craft monopoly no longer suited to the times.[2] Many of the lesser companies did not share that view, and were determined to continue searches as part of a plan to enforce the bye-laws which they claimed were still binding on those who 'occupied' their trades. In 1571 a petition had been presented to the Court of Aldermen by fourteen[c] crafts, including the Tallow Chandlers,[3] 'praying for a return of the condition of ancient times when each company had the sole exercise of its art or handicraft'[d] but it is probable that, notwithstanding their Wardens' plans, most company searches were by now being reluctantly carried out by the operators and were meeting with increased resistance.[4]

The decision against the Dyers at the close of the sixteenth century came at a time when the expansion of business in the suburbs, resulting from the rapid extension of the built-up area around the old square mile, was beginning to cause the Corpora-

---

a   Commentary, p. 254.

b   Commentary, p. 254.

c   Commentary, p. 254.

d   Commentary, p. 254.

tion grave misgivings. Strype quotes from a Royal Proclamation against new buildings made in 1580,[5] reciting that

the Queen's Majesty, perceiving the state of the City of London . . . and the suburbs and confines thereof to encrease daily by access of People to inhabit the same, in such ample sort as thereby many inconveniences are seen already . . . Doth charge and straightly command all Persons of what Quality soever they be to desist and forbear from any new Buildings of any new House or Tenement within three miles of any of the Gates of the said City, to serve for Habitation or Lodging for any Person, where no former House hath been known to have been in Memory of such as are now living.[e]

The traditional control exercised in the City jointly by the craft guilds and the Corporation over handicraft production and retail shop-keeping was showing signs of breaking down.[6] At the same time the ordinances drawn up by the guilds for the regulation of their respective trades, which in the main had Corporation support, were declared valid only so long as they were consonant to law and reason.[7] The Dyers' case has been cited as affording evidence that trade privileges in general could now be successfully challenged in Courts of law, and, indeed, in two provincial towns[f] even the right to compel the enrolment of un-freemen practising a trade was soon to be questioned.[8] In 1592 we are reminded of the outbreak against *alien* craftsmen that had found expression on 'evil May day' 1517.[9] It is recorded in the *Journal* that complaint had been made by '*Chandlers* and sundrie other artificers and Freemen against sundrie strangers borne owte of the Realm for intruding themselves into their trades and manual occupacions' and 'the cause' had been referred to a committee[10]

which shall heare the griefes of all such citizens and receive from them such instructions for proof thereof as they shall thinke needful.

The maintenance of an adequate supply of candles at a fair price was, as we know, vital to the City's needs. In the same year[11] another committee was accordingly ordered to consider

what cause is most fytest to be taken in the Cytye's behalf against all suche Dutchmen and other strangers as use to make and sell candells within the City

---

e   *Commentary*, p. 254.

f   Ipswich and Newbury.

and liberties of the same, contrarye to the Libertye of the said Citye.

In 1610[12] it was shown to Common Council

that freedoms and liberties of the City are at present impeached and violated by strangers borne and forreyns (un-freemen) as well as merchants as tradesmen and artizans/whereby the freemen are hindered in their trades . . .

A Committee of Aldermen and Commoners was therefore appointed to consider all grievances *and some means of redress*. In 1623 when a Royal Commission *concerning strangers* was appointed, a committee bemoaned the presence of the 'multitudes' then present in the City and prayed for an opportunity to state 'what they conceive to bee the likeliest and fairest means to reduce them to better order'.[13]

The conclusion cannot be avoided that, notwithstanding the efforts of the lesser companies to retain the image of craft control, the old craft guilds, both in their *origin* and in the manner of their *constitution*, had proved themselves unsuited to manage any larger area than that to which they were accustomed within the City walls, and that the growth of the great suburbs, particularly those of Westminster and Southwark, was seriously interfering with their efficiency as superintendents of production.[14] The continuing search for a solution which thus faced the Common Council and committees was later intensified by the Great Fire and by the Crown's attack on civic rights in the eighties.

It had long been a basic principle that not only must a man who wished to carry on a trade in the City of London have been admitted to the Freedom of the City, but he must also have been apprenticed to a trade for at least seven years. The normal method of admission for such applicants was by 'servitude'. The Corporation was opposed to admitting by 'patrimony' those who had served a term of apprenticeship. This policy was endorsed by the Court of Aldermen in 1560, (when an applicant made free of the Dyers' Company by his Father's 'copy', though he had served his time as a stationer, was directed to be 'set over' to the Fellowship of Stationers)[15] and made law[g] some forty years later.[16] Persons

---

g   *Commentary*, p. 254.

accepted for admission by *Redemption* were bound by recognizance to exercise only the nominal trade of the Craft or Mistery
in which they were admitted.[17] In 1495 the Chamberlain was
ordered 'to sue such Freemen by Redemption as had broken their
recognizances',[18] and a little later those who had been 'complained
of for occupying other crafts than those to which they are free'
were sent for by the Court of Aldermen to be examined 'whether
they will abide by the order of the Court or by the extremity of
the law'.[19] In 1537 there was an order that 'if anyone desire to be
free by redemption, he shall be examined and be free of that craft
in which he has the best skill',[20] and when, in 1548, the Court
agreed to admit a group of Painter-Stainers, it was on condition
that the admissions should be void 'if they do not occupy such
Art'.[21] There were times when the procedure of admission by
Redemption was suspended[22] and in 1588 there was an order
prohibiting admission 'but it be made by the balloting box'.[23]

Fig. 34. Male costume in the time of Henry IV.

The ban on 'foreigners' in general[h] had existed as a 'custom of
London' without interruption for close on two hundred years[i]
when, on 15th April 1606[24] the law was declared by an Act of

---

h   Commentary, p. 254.

i   Commentary, p. 255.

Common Council enacting first, that

> no person whatsoever, not being free of the City of London, shall . . . by any *colour*, way or means whatsoever, either directly or indirectly, by himself, *or by any other*, shew, sell or put to sale any wares or merchandize whatsoever *by Retail* within the City of London or the Liberties or suburbs of the same . . .

and secondly that

> no person whatsoever not being free of the City . . . shall . . . directly or indirectly by himself, *or by any other, keep any shop or other place whatsoever inward or outward* for show, sale, or putting to sale any wares or merchandize whatsoever by way of *Retail*, or use any Art, Trade, Occupation, Mystery or Handicraft whatsoever within the said City or the Liberties or Suburbs of the same,

and the Act imposed a penalty of £5 for every infringement.

The 'colouring of a foreigner's goods' (for which the first part of the Act made provision) had for many years been considered a serious offence. It was decreed by an Act of Common Council in 1526[25] that

> if any Freeman or Freewomen . . . colour any Foreign Goods, or . . . buy or sell for any person . . . being Foreign . . . cloaths, silks, wines, oyls, or any other Goods or merchandize . . . he [or she] shall for evermore be disfranchised,

and apprentices guilty of dealing in such goods for their masters were also penalized. A freeman disfranchised in 1528 for 'colouring wine between two foreigners', was only restored to the Freedom on payment of 40s. with the consent of the Common Council,[26] and in 1551 another freeman, disfranchised 'for untruly colouring foreigners' goods and selling them in the City as his own proper goods',[27] was lucky to be re-instated. A second man, on admitting his offence, had part of his fine returned, but was told that if he colour any other foreigners' goods, he would be '*de-facto* disfranchised',[28] and there were later cases. From the *Repertory* Book in 1614 we learn that 'a petition of the Tallow Chandlers against foreigners was referred by the Court of Aldermen to a committee',[29] but we do not know the result. In 1628 it was reported that 'complaint has often been made that divers merchants and others not free of the City do frequently buy and sell and trade . . . as freely and amply *as any freeman*.'[30] In 1646 there was an Act of Common Council[31] reciting that

> forrein buying and selling, and colouring of foreigners' goods . . . are of late yeares more used and practised than in former times,

and awarding to those persons who seize and present such goods to the Chamberlain 'for their paynes and labour' one half of the forfeitures less expenses. In 1696 the Town Clerk was ordered to deliver to the Comptroller 'such copies of books as may be necessary to prevent foreign buying and selling within the City'.[32] Regulations expressly forbidding the sale of tallow to foreigners have been noticed in an earlier chapter.[j]

Fig. 35. Shilling of Mary.

The penalty for *employing* foreigners was fixed in 1555 by Act of Common Council at £5 a day.[33] In our Wardens' accounts for 1563–4 we find a payment of 12d. to an officer of the Chamber for warning a foreigner in Redcross Street[k] that used our science 'to shut in'.[34] Our Ordinances of 1589 (p. 138) contained an article (No. 56)

> that no person or persons nowe beinge or that hereafter shalbee an householder and of the cominaltie of the said Crafte or Misterie of Tallowechaundelers, nor anie other person or persons occupyinge, usinge or exercisinge . . . the said crafte or Mistery of Tallowchaundelers shall from henceforth sette to worke in the said Crafte or misterie within the Cittie of London or suburbs of the same, Southwarke . . . or within one mile compas of the same *anie Jorneiman beinge a forenner or straunger* if he may have a Jorneiman, not a forrener or stranger, beeinge a skilfull and a competente workman in that Crafte or misterie, to worke for reasonable wages . . .

---

j   See pp. 37, 59, 80.

k   See p. 44.

While there seems to be no evidence in our Court books of the breach of this ordinance, we observe from an entry in the *Yeomanry Accounts*[1] that early in the next century a fine of 5*s.* was incurred by a yeoman member for employing foreigners.[35] This problem of their illegal employment in the City continued to baffle the Corporation for many years. The Feltmakers were actually authorized by an Act of Common Council in 1556 to employ non-freemen,[36] but in 1661 the Company itself petitioned the Court to repeal the clause and it was repealed on the advice of a committee.[37] The question of whether or not foreigners should be 'tolerated' (as the Feltmakers put it) continued to be a source of trouble until 1750, when (as we shall see) a system of licensing was introduced.

Having been admitted to the Freedom, a man was expected, as a general rule, to reside with his family in the City, and thus contribute to its charges, failing which he ran the risk of disfranchizement. But there were exceptions. In 1515, in the Mayoralty of William Boteler, an Act of Common Council was passed requiring every Freeman found to have dwelt with his household out of the City 'by the space of a year' to be disfanchized.[38] In the 'forties a man was warned 'to repair to the City with his family on pain of loss of Freedom',[39] in the 'sixties an order was made for persons to return with their families or be disfranchized,[40] and some citizens living in Exeter, who had been warned to return, were ordered to be so dealt with.[41] On the other hand there is early evidence of certain Commoners having been 'appointed to communicate together whether they think it *convenient* that persons being Freemen and dwelling out of the Liberties nigh the City, as Westminster, Southwark, etc., shall be disfranchized according to the Act of 1515',[42] and precepts were 'directed to the Wardens of misteries, where persons of the same be dwelling out of the Liberties, to assess the substance of such persons *and rate their fines*'.[43] In the late 'twenties of that (the sixteenth) century a man was 'licensed to dwell out of the City for five years' on

---

1   *Commentary*, p. 255.

payment of forty marks, and to be bound in five hundred marks to return at the end of that term,[44] and the freedom of another man, who had been licensed to be absent for two years, was 'reserved' pending his return.[45] Some thirty years later the Clerks of companies were told 'to declare on oath the names of persons free of their companies not resident within the City',[46] and search was directed to be made for Freemen absenting themselves,[47] but there seems to be no evidence of offenders having been punished at that time. On two occasions in the 'sixties precepts were issued and certificates were brought in,[48] but again there seems to be no record of any action having been taken. In the 'seventies[49] precepts were directed to be made 'to the Wardens of companies touching Freemen abiding in the country' and not having repaired to the City and made their abode, *bearing scot and lot*.[m] Apart from the mention of a hearing in 1629 'of a cause touching Freemen of the City in the Town of Exeter',[50] this seems to be the last entry in the *Repertories* on the subject of non-resident Freemen until the year 1665, when we read that the question of 'taking the suburbs into the Freedom' is *under discussion*.[51]

The Great Plague and Fire in successive years, which drove many of the inhabitants and traders into the suburbs, settled the issue. While the Court of Aldermen made determined efforts to entice those who had departed from the City to return and to encourage un-freemen to take up residence, the practice of *requiring* Freemen to reside in the old City had to be abandoned.

The duty of apprenticeship was governed by two sections of a Statute of 5 Elizabeth, Chapter 4, (1563).[52] It was enacted, first, by Section xix, that householders in Cities 'using and exercising any Arte, Misterye, or *Manuell occupacion* there' might take apprentices 'to serve and bee bounde after the custome and order of the Citie of London for seven yeares at the leaste', and, secondly, by Section xxiv, that

it shall not be lawfull to any person or persons to set uppe, occupie, use or exercise any Crafte, Misterye, or Occupacion, now used or occupied within

---

[m]   Volume II, pp. 34, 87.

the Realme of Englande or Wales *except* he shall have been broughte uppe therein seaven yeares at the least as apprentice in maner and fourme abovesaid,

and a man might not

set anye person on worke in such Misterye, arte or occupacion . . . *except* he shall have bene apprentice as ys aforesaid, orels, having served as an Apprentice as ys aforesaid, shall or will become a Journeyman, or be hyred by the yere . . .

The penalty 'for every default' was forty shillings 'for every month'.

In practice—apart from a few redemptioners in breach of their recognizances—there were three distinct classes of person trading in the City. First, non-freemen, or 'foreigners', trading illegally, secondly, those who had been admitted to the freedom by servitude but openly carried on a trade other than that to which they had been apprenticed, and, thirdly, Freemen carrying on, legitimately, the nominal trade of the company to which they belonged.

It was declared 'a good custom', in 1614 in the case of J. Tolley,[53] a London wool-packer, turned upholsterer, that a man, having once been apprenticed for seven years,

may well and lawfully relinquish that Trade and exercise another Trade at his will and pleasure.

Twenty years later, on the records being searched by order of the Court of Aldermen,[54] the opinion was expressed

that there is *no such custom for manufacture or handicrafts*, but only for merchandising and trades.

The Recorder was ordered to 'certify',[55] and in 1638 his certificate was cited in the Court of King's Bench[56]

that there is no such custom for one who useth a manual trade but there *is* such a custom concerning trades of *buying and selling*.

The defendant in that case was sued by one, Applenton, for the sum of twenty-two pounds 'because he used within London the trade of a point-maker,[n] not being brought up as an apprentice

---

[n]   *Commentary*, p. 255.

for seven years', in which action the plaintiff was successful, but only because the defendant's occupation was manual. Nothing was heard for a time of the candle-makers request in 1651 (p. 175), but it becomes increasingly clear that the decision in Appleton's case that the custom 'doth not concern *all* persons in London' was unacceptable to many. In November 1658[57] our Court of Assistants received notice that 'a committee appointed by order of Common Council for Trade' intended to meet shortly in Guildhall to consider drafts of Acts lately presented by the Companies of Founders, Cordwainers, Upholders, Clockmakers and others

to the end to enioyne all persons exercising those several arts to bind their apprentices *to the respective arts they use.*

We were advised that we might, if we thought fit, be represented at the meeting to offer reasons against the proposal, an invitation which our Court (in its wisdom) decided to accept. It was resolved that our Clerk, John Marsh, should attend and signify to the meeting

that there are divers members of this Incorporation who doe exercise some of the above-mentioned arts, And that this Court does consider it will prove very prejudicial unto this Company if these should be enjoyned to binde and make free their apprentices of and to anie other company then now they are [of] ...,

Marsh was to point out that there were 'many helpfull branches' proceeding from this membership

which, if taken away, will weaken the Company and disable them from bearing that public Charge of the Citie and Company as is required of them ...

It seems that, while we (as a company) might be willing to accept as apprentices outsiders engaged in the tallow trade, it was quite another matter when it came to releasing our own members' apprentices because they did not happen to be so engaged. Marsh observes (in parenthesis) that there were 'divers of the Livery who are candle-makers by Trade' present in Court when our reply was sent, but he does not state how they voted!

The next step in this campaign to confine every trader to a particular mistery or guild came in August 1660 when Edward

Sole, a member of our Company, exercising the trade of a *baker* complained that he was 'much molested' by the Company of Bakers. He was threatened, so he said, with being sued for using that trade and told that he should not continue 'unless he were translated⁰ unto them', to which proposal we consented on payment of a fine of 40s.[58] The Bakers may have had the support of the Court of Aldermen in making this approach. It would not have been the first time that the issue had been raised in the City. As early as 1613 the Broderers had petitioned the Court (albeit unsuccessfully) for an Order 'that apprentices bound to others using their mistery should be translated' at the expiration of their apprenticeship to the Broderers Company'.[59]

Our surrender to the Bakers was followed in June 1664[60] by a summons to our Master and Wardens to appear before the Lord Mayor and Court of Aldermen 'for to translate from this Company to the *Company of Innholders* all such of the members of this Company as have Inns or use the profession of an Innholder *according to an Act of Common Council in that behalf'.ᵖ* Our Clerk,

Fig. 36. The Tabard (or Talbot) Inn. c. 1780.

---

o *Commentary*, p. 255.

p *Commentary*, p. 255.

John Maxfield, relates that, on appearing before the Court of Aldermen, our officers refused to give their consent 'for the translation of any member of this Company unto another Company' without an order of our Court of Assistants, whereupon they were directed to obtain the necessary authority. Later the same day[61] he records that the matter has been referred to a Committee in the belief that

it would greatly redound to the prejudice of this Company if such persons, members of this Company as keep Inns, should be translated . . .

The Committee was directed to consult with 'any other Company who have members that use the trade of Innholder and are required to translate them' to that company and 'to consider what action might be taken to prevent it'.[62] At the same meeting, one of our members—Robert Briscoe—who kept an Inn 'did publicly declare that he was unwilling to be translated from this Company'. We hear nothing more until September[63] when we learn from the minutes that our friend, then described as '*a member of this Court*' has been required to appear before the King and Council

as a person refractory to the duties enioyned in the Innholders Charter (sic), for that he has refused to be translated from this Company unto the Innholders.

We are told that he duly appeared on 31st August, 'to show cause why he would not condescend to be so incorporated into the Innholders *as to be quite taken off this Company*', but, notwithstanding his Counsel's arguments to the contrary 'his plea was over-ruled, and the Lord Chancellor told him that, if he would not be translated . . . his inn doors would speedily be shutt upp'. A copy of the Order of the 'Counsell Board'*q* was read to our Court, reciting 'the complaint of the Master, Wardens and Assistants of the Company of Innholders . . . shown unto Robert Briscoe att the syne of the Ram in West Smithfield*r* and to

---

q　Commentary, 255.

r　On the north side of West Smithfield in Farringdon Ward Without (*Ogilby and Morgan's Map of London*, 1677, and *Lockie's Topography*, 1816). The site now covered by Smithfield Market. *Harben.*

William Gale at the White Horse in Fleet Street',[s] and directing that the offenders do

> forthwith translate themselves into the Company of Innholders and submitt unto that Government, otherwise due course wilbe taken to compell them thereunto . . .

Two days later[64]—in obedience to the 'Act' and *by my Lord Mayor's order*—the translation of Robert Briscoe and several others[t] duly took place. We cannot but admire Briscoe's loyalty to the Tallow Chandlers Company. As a member of our Court his position in the Innholders Company was assured. To quote from the 'Act', he was to take his place 'according to his quality and degree' and 'the precedence and dignity of the Company from which he was translated'. But he wanted to remain with his friends.[u]

Translation, as a means of securing within our own Company the allegiance of those in other companies, does not seem ever to have been seriously considered. The fact that so many members of the great Company of Salters had been our trade rivals for so long would have placed us in some difficulty. Few Salters would have been willing to be translated to an 'inferior' company, although some, as we know, were willing to belong to both companies notwithstanding the additional expense. This question of expense was considered by the Court of Aldermen in November 1687 when William Pettever, a member of the Curriers Company, complained, (as Edward Sole, the baker, had done in 1660) that he was 'threatened to be molested' if he did not change his company. Pettever, being a wheelwright by trade, petitioned the Court that he might either be translated to the Wheelwrights Company 'or permitted to follow his trade'. It appeared, on investigation, that he was *already a member* of the last mentioned company, as well as being a Currier, but the Court decided that he should, nevertheless, be translated from the one company to

---

s   An inn, north out of Fleet Street in Farringdon Ward Without, east of Wine Office Court, west of Shoe Lane (Ogilby and Morgan's Map, *supra*—Strype, 1755). *Harben.*
t   *Commentary*, p. 255.
u   *Commentary*, p. 255.

the other, to save him from bearing 'the burthen and charges of both said companies'.[65]

Matters came to a head for us in 1692, when, as we have seen (p. 195), Baptist Mead, 'a tallow chandler or candle-maker by trade' was summoned before the Lord Mayor for refusing to pay the search money demanded of him by our Company. On 16th June[66] the Court of Aldermen, having considered the complaint, ordered that our Master and Wardens should attend upon Mr Recorder

and produce to him their Charter and Bye-Laws, who is to consider thereof and give his opinion therein unto this Court . . . and that Mr Town Clerk do inform himself of the Jurisdiction of this Court over Artificers *and especially Tallow Chandlers within this City.*

Nothing further having been heard of the matter for some months, two of our Wardens with three others, taking with them Mr Munday, 'the Company's standing Counsel', waited on the Recorder who promised to draw up his report.[67] This he did in due course, and, the report having been accepted by the Court of Aldermen, their Order[68] was found to contain a direction

that Baptist Mead, tallow chandler, do appear before this Court . . . to show cause why hee should not be *translated to the Company of Tallow Chandlers.*

He was told that he must first make an appearance before our Master and Wardens.[69] This he failed to do until 21st July,[70] when the tribunal (a committee of members) complained of his obstinacy

in refusing to pay search money *and to become free of this Company,* to their great damage and to the evil example of others.

He was asked 'whether he would not comply with this Command and *become free of them'*, which he 'utterly refused' to do, where-upon, the members of the Committee and Mead having with-drawn, and the culprit having returned alone, it was later announced[71]

that hee would for the future Pay unto this Company the Duty of search money *but would not become free of them,* and so this Committee was dismissed, Mr Town

Clerk acquainting them that *noe order of this Proceeding in that Court would be made* (!)

After a delay of two months we learn[72] that, having again been summoned before the Court of Aldermen at the complaint of our Company, he

addressed himself to this assembly and freely submitted himself, promising not merely to pay the said Duty of search money now due *But also for the future* . . .

We get the impression from reading these minutes that no one was sorry that the idea of 'translation' had been finally abandoned.

To return to the proposal of the Founders and others in 1658 (p. 207), it appears from an entry in the *Repertories* that their efforts to secure the binding of apprentices 'to the respective Arts they use' had been followed by similar proposals in other companies resulting in an Act of Common Council. The entry is dated 16th July 1672[73] and records that the Court of Aldermen is of the opinion that *the Act should be repealed* 'as likely to be very prejudicial to several of the Principal Companies'. Whatever the result of this advice, we read less than a year later[74] that the traditional right of freemen of the City to retain their membership of those companies in which they have been admitted is recognized (indirectly) by the Court when making an order that

all persons exercising any Handicraft or other inferior trade that now are, or here-after, shall come to be free of this City in any of the twelve companies/*or any other than the company whose trade he professes*/shall duly observe and keep all the Rules and Ordinances *of the said company whose trade he useth*/for and touching the number of apprentices and other matters relating to the trade, *as if they were members of the said company*

A new approach to the problem of 'regulating' the Companies (as it became known), for which the newly formed Company of Coachmakers appears to have been responsible, was made in the 'nineties. In the summer of 1693[75] we petitioned the Court of Aldermen for an Order compelling all persons using our trade 'as well within as without the City' to take up their freedom in our Company 'at a small fine'. The reason we gave was that 'tho they (the Company) have a power in their Charter' to compel such persons, yet they are 'rather willing to have *an Order* . . . as

. . . lately granted to the Company of Coach and Coach Harness Makers'.[v] It was our case that 'persons who would be willing to come in upon payment of 3s. 4d., or some small fine', will not take up their freedom at the standard fee of 46s. 8d.,

and especially since the Company is poor and not so well able to goo to Law as their Charter directs.

The result was that on 23rd November (1693) the Court of Aldermen, on the recommendation of its committee, made an order[76] directing

that all persons useing the said Trade . . . and having a right to their freedoms in any other Company shall be made free in the said Company of Tallow Chandlers onely, being first presented to and allowed by this Court and paying to Mr Chamberlain, to the Cities use xiijs iiijd. a piece.

The Coachmakers had been associated in this venture with the Wheelwrights and the Glaziers,[w] and our action in following these three companies was itself followed within a year by the Masons[x] and the Plaisterers,[77] both of whom obtained Acts of Common Council, and, in 1699, by the Barber Surgeons.[y] All decrees were designed to achieve the same object, namely to secure the enrolment *in the petitioners' companies* of all persons practising each such company's nominal trade and having the right to admission to the freedom in *other companies*. This right could exist, as we know, either by patrimony or by servitude. The Plaisterers added, for good measure, 'redemption' by virtue of the father's freedom.[z] Our Order included those using our trade 'as well within and without the City'. The area specified in other cases was 'the City and liberties'. The Masons' and Plaisterers' Acts imposed penalties for non-compliance. Our Order, after a slow start, was reasonably successful in bringing in applicants who had been apprenticed,

v   Commentary, p. 256.

w   Commentary, p. 256.

x   Commentary p. 256.

y   Commentary, p. 256.

z   Commentary, p. 256.

or turned over, to men in other companies, and occasionally, those apprenticed in other companies, turned over to members of our Company. A private order made by our Court in August 1698[78] for '*the incouragement*' of all persons using our trade and having the right to their freedoms in other companies, seems to have made little difference. This order directed that such persons should in future be admitted into the freedom of our Company

without paying unto them any money or makeing unto them any offering or other consideracion whatsoever, onely unto their Clerke and Beadle for their fees and for the Duty of Stamps.

Apprentices, who are quite often stated to have come in 'by order of the Court of Aldermen' continued to be admitted. A few freemen in other companies were also admitted by Redemption by order of the Court and one such an applicant is entered as having been 'made free by Charter'. Those coming in by Order of the Court were usually admitted without payment of a fine and, in such cases, the customary 'free gift' was also waived.

In September 1700 the Glaziers and Tallow Chandlers together presented petitions to the Court of Aldermen which recited their earlier Orders,[aa] and, on 19th November,[79] a new Order was made

that the Petitioners shall have the respective privilege of making all persons who by Trade are either Glaziers or Tallow Chandlers *and do inhabit within the City and liberties thereto and that have a right to the freedom of the City in other Companies* made free of the said Companies respectively upon the fine of 3s. 4d. apiece as hath been granted to the Company of Barber-Surgeons the 23rd November last, *they being first certified unto this Court by Mr Chamberlain* to be so qualified as aforesaid.

The Order followed a Committee report, in which the Court was informed that, in requiring the certificate of the Chamberlain,

we are rather of this opinion because the Petitioners were/by the first recited orders/to have such persons so qualified made free . . . upon the respective certificates of their *Clerks only*/but the same being now desired to be done by Mr Chamberlain we conceive this Honble Court will be the *less liable to be imposed upon by untrue or false certificates.*

---

aa   *Commentary*, p. 256.

Four days later our Clerk, Gilbert Brandon, received from the Town Clerk, (with the Order) a copy of the Report![80]

II

In the 'eighties of the seventeenth century we began to turn our particular attention to the complaints received from various sources against persons carrying on our trade illegally. The first recorded instance of a *non-freeman* being charged occurs in August 1682,[81] when the Clerk (John Marsh) was directed to inquire 'what proceedings there hath beene against Weeks in Fetter Lane, a tallowchandler, for useing the Trade *not being free* and to take care that some prosecution be made against him at the Companies charge concerning the same'. In June of the following year[82] a Mr Miller and others, tallow chandlers by trade, complained at a meeting of the Court 'that several persons use the Trade of Tallowchandlers not having anie right so to do', when it was agreed that the Master and Wardens 'would direct their officer' to summon the offenders to appear. At a meeting a fortnight later[83] it was agreed that one John Burnham, tallow chandler, should be 'prosecuted at Law' by the complainants and that if 'the said Burnham be found guiltie, then this Company will allow them the reasonable charge of such prosecution therein'. We have no record of these prosecutions, but there seems little doubt that the offenders, like Weeks, were 'un-freemen'. In April 1687,[84] however, we read of one Bradford 'exercising, with his wife, the trade of making and selling candles in Fleet Lane,[a] to which he hath no right, being by trade *a joiner*', and of another offender 'in Bethelham,[b] exercising the said trade having no right thereto, she being the widow of a wyre-drawer'. All three were summoned to appear to answer charges.

---

a   West out of Old Bailey. In Farringdon Ward Without. Perhaps identical with 'a lane without Newgate going towards the Fleet', 49 H.III (Anc. Deeds, A.2328). *Harben*.

b   The houses built on the site of the Church and Chapel of St Botolph without Bishopsgate in the reign of Elizabeth later formed the street known as 'Old Bethlem' or 'Old Bethlehem', which took its name from the Hospital founded by Simon Fitz Mary, Sheriff in 1247. The site is now occupied by Liverpool Street Station, etc. See *Harben*.

In March 1689[85] comes the first report of proceedings against William Collett, 'by trade *a baker*', whose misdeeds, as we shall see, were the Company's special concern for over six years. Commencing in October 1691[86] we also became involved in the case of Richard Milner—a member of the Tallow Chandlers Company *not apprenticed in the trade*. He was first summoned to show

by what Right he doth follow and exercise to his owne use the art or mistery of a Tallow Chandler having never served a due apprenticeship to the same.

He appeared at the same meeting at Katherine Caseby (Appendix M) on a charge of exercising the trade 'not having any Legull Right thereto, *and for making false and adulterate candles*', but was not heard. When attending again in the following April[87] the Court 'would not proceed to fine him for his frequent making of adulterate candles lest it might be a prejudice to the intended proceedings against him for exercising the Trade having noe Legal Right thereto'. We were, nevertheless, advised two days later[88] by Mr Munday, 'one of the Judges of the Sheriffs' Court' that he might be prosecuted 'upon the Statute of the 5th Elizabeth (p. 205), notwithstanding that he was a member of our Company', and he was duly charged at Guildhall on 26th November[89] with

exercising the Art or *Manuall occupacion* of a Tallowchandler having not served thereto as an apprentice/contrary to the Statute

That the charge should be that of exercising 'a manual occupation' and not the trade of a tallowchandler (which involved 'buying and selling') is not without significance. It was on the 'manual occupation' charge that he was tried, and found guilty by Sir John Holt, Lord Chief Justice of the King's Bench. It was established that he had 'followed the said Art or manual occupation for the space of three months and more'. The verdict against him was for 'two of the said three months', for which he was ordered to pay 40s. for each month 'according to the penalty of the said Statute' (p. 206). The Attorney General moved to arrest judgment,[90]

for that a Generall custome was in London that a Freeman of London might exercise *any Trade* within London.

There were legal arguments,[91] resulting in the case being referred to the Judges of King's Bench.[92] On 18th May, 1693[93] it was

Fig. 37. Westminster Hall, where the old Law Courts were held until removed to the Strand in 1882.

decided that 'the Judges' Opinion concerning the verdict obtained against Richard Milner bee not at the present moved nor sought for', after which the record is unaccountably silent.

Proceedings against William Collett of Newport Street[c] had been authorized by a resolution of our Court of Assistants on 21st March 1689 on 'the complaint exhibited' by two members of the Company 'in behalf of themselves and others'. It was alleged[94] that Collett, being by trade a baker, had for some years

exercised and practised the art and mistery of *candle making* having not served an apprenticeship thereunto, and doth still follow and exercise the said art of *making Tallow candles*, to the great diminutation and prejudice of the said art.

Gilbert Brandon, our clerk, was 'licensed, ordered and impowered to solicit this cause'. It will be seen that the offence charged was that of carrying on a manual occupation as in Milner's case and it seems likely that the 'Appleton' ruling (p. 207) was under con-

---

c   West of Long Acre; derives its name from 'Newport House', the London residence of Montjoy Blount, created Earl of Newport by King Charles I (d. 1665). *Wheatley.*

sideration in 1689 as it evidently was a little later. An account of Collett's trials (and tribulations) ending in his acquittal, will be found in Appendix N.

There are occasional references in the minutes to other persons being accused of exercising our trade without having been apprenticed,[95] notably in a case which came before our Court of Assistants in 1694 involving John Smith, a member of the Company,

against whom it was alleged that he did countenance and protect Alexander Hallowes in the exercise of the Trade of a Tallow Chandler (having no right thereto).

Smith affirmed 'and was ready to make Oath that the said Alexander was his apprentice . . . and produced his Indentures'. It was claimed that the stock and shop in the Strand was really Smith's 'without any fraud or collusion and [that he] did provide for and maintain the said Alexander as his apprentice'. The latter affirmed and was ready to swear 'that he was the said Mr Smith's apprentice *to all intents and purposes*' and that he had no manner of interest 'either in profit or loss in the said Trade or shopp, whereupon the said John Smith and Alexander Hallowes were for this time excused and dismissed'.[96] We hear of no further prosecutions, and the matter of the wrongful exercise of our trade does not appear to have been raised again until 1723,[97] when two of our Liverymen, being candle-makers by trade, appeared before our Court

and alleged that their Trade and mistery was very greatly invaded by many persons who had no right thereto and, hoping to find out some remedy for the same, they therefore requested that they might have the perusal of this Company's Charter . . . and to have copies thereof.

The request was granted 'on their reasonably paying for the same', but we hear nothing more, and a certain lack of interest in trade matters at this time is apparent from the minutes. The subject was raised again in 1732 when the Opinion of Mr William Chapple, of Counsel, was taken in the matter of Mary Fontaine, a widow, whose late husband, a freeman of London, was an Upholder by Trade.[98] This Mary Fontaine (to quote from the 'case')

kept a tallow chandler's shop and caused to be made in her house
great quantities of candles, which were entered in the Excise
Office in her name. She sold them in her shop and gave bills and
receipts in her own name. But the journeymen employed and
set on work by her to make the candles were persons who had
served seven years as apprentices to the candle-making trade.
Counsel advised that, in his opinion, this lady 'is within the
intent' of the clause in Anno 5, Elizabeth, Cap. 4, and that she is

liable to be prosecuted for exercising the trade of a tallow chandler, for the
persons she employs are but as her servants and their having served as apprentices to the Trade will not exempt her from the penalty.

There is, however, no record in the minutes of any action having
been instituted by the Company. It is clear from a minute in 1703
(when our Court agreed to make a contribution of £12 out of
the Company's stock),[99] that the Collett prosecutions had been
largely financed by persons in the Trade, and it seems likely that,
as in 1723, the burden, as well as the expense, of proceedings had
again been placed upon the Trade.

The next approach came in December 1775[100] when four tallow
chandlers by trade attended our Court 'on behalf of themselves
and the rest of the Committee of the Trade' and delivered a
Petition setting forth

that for several years past divers persons not duly qualified by law nor being
Free of this Company Have taken upon themselves to exercise the said Trade
to the Great Injury of this Company and of all Persons legally authorized to
carry on the same, and in direct violation of the Statutes in that case made and
provided, several of which Illegal Traders have been prosecuted to Conviction
by the said Committee *in their own private capacity.*

The Petitioners prayed the Court of Assistants 'to authorize the
said Committee to carry out such prosecutions as should be necessary in the name of the Company'. They asked that our Beadle
should

summon all such persons as shall be judged illegal traders before the Court to
prove their right to the said trade . . .

in an endeavour 'to preserve inviolate *the exclusive rights of such*

persons as are by law entitled to carry on the same'. This appeal was
followed by 'the Humble Petition of the Trade of Tallow Chandlers at large' for the prosecution of illegal traders, signed by one
Joseph Flight, as Chairman.[101] The Petitioners were 'encouraged
by the favourable reception' which their former Petition had
received 'and the known practice of most other companies who
constantly protect their rights and privileges *at the companies'
expence'*. They were recommended 'to inform the Clerk of such
persons as have no right to exercise the trade, in order to summon
them before the Court or Committee' to show cause 'by what
right they carry on the same',[102] whereupon a request was made
that four persons might be summoned to appear.[103] At a meeting
of the Committee eight days later the number was increased to
six.[104] Four of these persons satisfied the Committee that they
were innocent of the charge, one of them, practising in White
Cross Street[d] showing that he had served a term of apprenticeship in Yorkshire.[105] A fifth,[106] in Petticoat Lane,[e] agreed to
desist from exercising the trade.[f] A sixth was prosecuted more
than once and apparently convicted.[107] A seventh, attending on
28th May, promised to withdraw his entry at the Excise Office.[108]
He 'had not sold a single ounce nor ever intended it, and would
not presume to enter or make any more candles without inform-
ing the Master and Wardens'. Of three more persons (including a
woman) summoned to attend at the next Court, two were apparently found not guilty, while a third was proved to be a
journeyman who had 'nothing to do with the business'.[109] A
memorial from the Trade was presented on 23rd December
1780,[110] stating

that they were very much aggrieved by illegal traders *and under-sellers* and
praying leave that their Attorney might inspect the Company's books and
Charters relative thereto,

---

d   North from Fore Street to Old Street, in Cripplegate Ward Without, except for
the northern portion, which is outside the City boundary, in the Borough of Finsbury. Named after White Cross (see *Commentary*, p. 256). Harben.

e   Later to become known as Middlesex Street, north out of Aldgate High Street to
Bishopsgate. (See *Commentary*, p. 256.)

f   *Commentary*, p. 257.

after which it is reported that an Information had been filed against Richard Foster, 'an illegal trader' by order of a former Court, and that he had been tried and convicted.[111] But in February 1782 we find an entry 'that in future no Informations against illegal Traders shall be prosecuted at the expense of the Company without an Order of the Court',[112] which is the last record in our minutes relating to prosecutions.

III

Two Acts of Common Council in the eighteenth century relating to the activities of *foreigners* remain to be mentioned.

The treatment of 'foreins' had continued to be a problem. In April 1673,[113] the Court, having been informed

that divers persons that have taken houses and inhabited within this City are *prosecuted as foreigners* . . . it is ordered . . . that all prosecutions shall be stayed against the said persons until further order.

Fig. 38. Costume of the Commonalty in the time of Charles II.

As might be expected this command was opposed by many free retail traders and handicraftsmen. In July 1675[114] we read that

upon the humble petition of the journeymen handicraft Taylors, freemen of this City therein, complaining of great injurys occasioned them and their families by the imployment of great numbers of foreigners in the said trade within this City, and desiring that they may be prosecuted at the suit of Mr Chamberlain *according to the laws and customs of this City*/This Court doth refer it to Mr. Chamberlain to doe therein for the relief of the said petitioners as he shall so cause

A little later[115] the Fishmongers petitioned against 'the employment of Foreigners unlicensed and engrossing fish and selling in the streets'. No record has been found of the 'prosecutions' mentioned by the Journeymen tailors; nor do we know whether the City Chamberlain thought fit to take the steps suggested by the Court, or whether the Fishmongers' (or any other) petition at that time was successful. On the contrary, in 1675, we read of the wife of a resident foreigner being permitted to follow a trade,[116] and two years later the widow of another foreigner was permitted 'to exercise her husband's trade'.[117] In 1678 we read of a non-freeman's petition for the Freedom 'and he to appear again *and not to be prosecuted for exercising his Trade*',[118] but it seems that the Corporation lacked a settled policy. Two years later a trader was prosecuted 'for not being a Freeman'.[119] The prosecution of another man 'not free of the City' was ordered to be stayed',[120] but he was later prosecuted.[121] Such proceedings were, nevertheless, infrequent, and in 1685 the prosecution of a woman keeping a shop, not being free, was stayed 'on her intention to take her freedom'.[122] In 1687 there comes a sudden burst of energy, for which it seems that James II was responsible. On 15th February[123] the Court of Aldermen is reported to have

lately received anew a commission from His Majesty the King whereby all persons not free of this City are prohibited from keeping shops, selling by retail or following any trade within this City or the liberties thereof And command is therein given that all such be effectually prosecuted.

The Court accordingly made an order

that both Mr Chamblen (sic) and all officers . . . do take especial care that noe such unfreemen be tolerated,

with a direction to prosecute all such as should be discovered. This was followed very soon by an Order[124] directing the prosecution of 'suits against inhabitants of Blackfriars', and we learn that action has been taken 'against a woman not being free for keeping a seamstress shop'.[125] Yet, in the same year 'a labourer employed in rebuilding London' was permitted to exercise his trade 'though not free',[126] and next year 'part of a debt and costs for working at a trade not being free' was remitted.[127] In 1689 'license' was granted to one William Scriven, 'lately come over from Ireland on account of the troubles, to work his trade till he become of age to take his freedom'.[128] During the next few years a number of applications from non-freemen to carry on their trade were referred to the Chamberlain and at least two licenses were granted.[129] Commencing in the early 'nineties there are numerous cases of masons and carpenters who had worked for seven years and upwards in the rebuilding of the City after the Great Fire being permitted 'to follow their trades pursuant to Act of Parliament',[130] but for many years there were prosecutions and threats of prosecution for working at trades 'being foreigners'. In 1696, for instance, the Town Clerk was ordered to deliver to the Comptroller such copies of books as may be necessary to prevent foreign buying and selling in the City,[131] and a year later a foreigner was allowed two months in which 'to move out of the liberties'.[132]

The first of the two Acts is dated 4th July 1712.[133] In essence it recites the provisions of the Acts of 1606 (p. 201) and 1555 (p. 203) respectively, 'the which Laws and Customs' notwithstanding,

divers Persons not being Free of the said City do use and exercise sundry manual occupations or handicrafts . . . and several other Artificers and Handicrafts-men and other shop-keepers and Traders by Retail, being freemen of this City

(not regarding 'the same Lawes and Customs', nor the oath which they have taken . . .)

have of late not only willingly employed, hired and set on work . . . divers foreigners from the Liberties of the same City, in divers and sundry handicrafts and manual occupations, and in buying and selling, and exposing for sale by retail, divers Wares and merchandize . . . but have also refused to take, employ, and set on work in their Trades and occupations

the 'honest, poor citizens and Freemen' of the same City

to the great Hinderance, Loss and Prejudice of the said Poor Citizens, and to the *utter undoing* of a great number of the said poor handicrafts men, and other

Persons bred to Trades, and not of ability to set up the same, (being Citizens and Freemen of the said City), unless some speedy Remedy be herein provided.

For the reformation of which abuses the provisions of the Act of 1606 (in relation to the exercise of any trade or occupation and the sale of goods by retail in the City), and of the Act of 1555 (in relation to the employment of foreigners) were re-enacted.

Fig. 39. General costume of the time of George I.

This Act, although passed in response to numerous petitions for clarification of the law,[134] brought opposition from some of the companies, which took exception to the grant of an exclusive right to monopolize the handicraft and retail trades.[135] The problem was how to modify the Act, so as to satisfy its critics without abandoning the principle of guild regulation.[136]

An answer was found in the second of the two Acts, namely, an Act of Common Council dated 22nd November 1750,[137] being

an Act to explain and amend two several Acts of Common Council the one passed the 15th April 1606 and the other the 4th July 1712, concerning Foreigners.

The relevant provisions of the two earlier Acts were recited, followed by an explanation that

several of the mysteries, occupations and handicrafts exercised and carried on
within this city and liberties thereof cannot at all times be supplied with a
sufficient number of fit and able journeymen, being Freemen of the said City;
in which cases the restrictions in the said in-part recited Acts . . . may be
prejudicial to the trade and manufacturers of the said City.

For remedy whereof it was enacted that 'the Court of the Lord
Mayor and Aldermen' may give or grant licence or authority to
any person or persons, being free of the said City and residing
within the same or the liberties thereof . . . to hire, retain, employ
and set to work . . . so many foreigners from the liberties of the
said City . . . as . . . shall seem fit and necessary'. *And* . . . that the
Lord Mayor . . . may . . . by warrant . . . give licence and authority
to any such persons as aforesaid

(who shall make it appear to the satisfaction of the said Lord Mayor that he,
she, or they respectively hath or have used their best endeavours and cannot
procure a sufficient number of fit and able journeymen, being Freemen of the
said City . . .)

to hire, etc. , . . so many foreigners, as aforesaid, under such restrictions . . . 'and for and during such time or times (so as the
same do not exceed the space of six weeks) as to the said Lord
Mayor . . . shall seem fit and necessary'. . . . No persons to whom
such licence was granted, and no such foreigner hired, etc., was
to be liable to any of the earlier penalties. Each applicant had
nevertheless to prove, either that he had at least one resident
apprentice with him, or had had with him one such apprentice
within twelve months prior to his application. Full particulars
had to be registered with the Town Clerk, and licences might be
revoked.

On the whole this system of licensing worked well and helped
to prevent earlier enactments from being brought into contempt
by non-observance. Moreover, the year following the passing of
the Act of 1750 saw the beginning of a series of Acts for 'regulating' (as formerly) most of the companies which were still active
in their nominal trades, that is to say, to secure the enrollment of
all practitioners within their ranks. These companies numbered
twenty-two, of which the first in the field was the Scriveners
Company. The Leathersellers came last but one, to be followed

P

eight years later by the Tallow Chandlers.[a] The reason for a delay (of eight years) is not easy to understand. We had made a beginning in 1693 when we had been partially successful in our efforts to capture those using our trade, who, on completing their indentures of apprenticeship, were entitled to their freedom in other companies (p. 212). Between 1776 and 1781 we had (as we have seen) successfully prosecuted those using our trade illegally. But by now we had urgent need to take action *for a different reason*. The draft petition submitted for approval to our Court on 15th October contains a recital that, notwithstanding the Charter of Charles II, many persons who now exercise the Art or Mystery of a Tallow Chandler have not been made free of your Petitioner's said Company, but have obtained their Freedoms of other Companies by Redemption or otherwise' . . .

by means whereof the said Company of Tallow Chandlers are so greatly diminished in number that for some years past they have not been able to fill up the vacancies as they have happened, by which means the Livery of the said Company . . . notwithstanding every exertion . . . consists only of eighty-four, and your Petitioners have reason to apprehend that in a few years, without the aid and assistance of this Honourable Court, they shall not have a sufficient number of Liverymen whereout to elect and keep up the usual number of Assistants to hold Courts and manage the business of the Company.

We were not alone in experiencing this decline. By the early eighteenth century the economic benefits of admission to the freedom of a London Company had become far less evident than in former years. Most of the guilds were passing through a period of transition, when the Freedom offered neither the economic advantages of earlier centuries nor the honorific significance (as it has been called)[b] of more recent times. In spite of the encouragement given by the Act of 1712 the intake of new members had fallen significantly by 1750.[138]

The Act 'for Regulating the Master, Wardens and Commonalty of the Mystery of Tallowchandlers of the City of London' was passed by the Court of Common Council on 14th May 1784.[139]

---

a   *Commentary*, p. 257.

b   *The Breakdown of the Gild and Corporation Control over the Handicraft and Retail Trades in London*, by J. R. Kellett, pp. 387–92.

Fig. 40. Halfpenny of Charles II.

After briefly reciting the relevant passage in Charles II's Charter and the harm done to our Company by the failure of so many persons exercising our trade to become members, and by binding their apprentices in other companies (and the need for a remedy) it was enacted, *first*

that ... every Person (not being already free of this City) using or exercising ... the Trade, Art of Mystery of a Tallowchandler within this City and Liberties thereof shall take up his or her Freedom and be made free of the said Company ... And that no Person using or exercising ... the said Trade, etc., shall ... be admitted by the Chamberlain ... into the Freedoms of this City of or in any other Company ...

with a proviso limiting the amount of the fee payable by those entitled to the Freedom of any other company by Patrimony or Service, and *secondly*,

that if any Person (except as aforesaid) doth ... use the Trade, Art or Mystery of a Tallowchandler within this City and Liberties not being free of the said Company ... then such Person ... shall forfeit and pay the sum of £5 ... for every such offence

The manner in which the penalties made payable by the Act were to be recovered was stated, and provision was made for indemnifying the City Chamberlain, in whose name proceedings were to be taken, as also for the disposal of penalties.

The various other Acts for compelling enrollment took much the same form, but while, in some companies, litigation to enforce the provisions of the Acts was not un-common[c] in many companies (including our own) peaceful persuasion was the order of

---

[c]   *Commentary*, p. 257.

the day. We find evidence in our minutes of the Company having advertised for some years in several newspapers,[140] but it seems that the Clerk did not think it necessary to enter any further details.

The eventual breakdown of craft and retail trade monopoly in the City could not be indefinitely postponed. In theory the system of guild privilege remained unimpaired until after the beginning of the nineteenth century, but Corporation and company records both tell us that in practice it was slowly disintegrating.[141] Occasional entries in our minutes serve to remind us of the fact. In January 1792, for instance, we read that 'the Committee delegated by the Trade of Tallow Chandlers at large' have requested the Company's *assistance* in defraying the cost of defending proceedings for nuisance brought against a member. The Court's action was significant. It decided to defer its answer until hearing that the Committee had received the whole of their collection from the Trade'.[142] Only in very rare cases was the occupation of a craft still limited to the freemen of a particular company,[143] and in 1835 it became possible to be free of the City without being associated with any of the handicraft or trade guilds.[144] For trade purposes the freedom became no more than a civic licence. Citizens who did not take up this licence or who employed 'foreigners' as hired servants in their shops were still liable to the penalties of the Act of 1712, but in 1821 the Chamberlain was instructed to give two months' clear notice to offenders before issuing a summons.[145] In 1827 the Court of Common Council adopted a Report recommending that persons professing to be wholesale dealers who make 'a constant practice of openly exposing their goods for sale, and selling by retail', should be compelled to take up their freedom,[146] but in 1836 the institution of any proceedings against foreigners was forbidden without the written permission of the Chamberlain,[147] and in 1856 all laws and customs preventing persons 'other than freemen of the City from carrying on business by retail or exercising any handicraft' were formally abolished.[148]

By the mid-nineteenth century most of the companies had indeed become transformed. From close communities possessing a practical connection with their trades they had gradually changed to corporations largely concerned with managing their properties and trust estates and engaging in various charitable and educational activities.[149] Their heyday as craft guilds was nearly over by the mid-fifties of the sixteenth century. Thereafter the period of their new and vastly different life, no less interesting in its slow development, commenced. That many of the companies should have succeeded for so long in maintaining an effective contact with their trades was due in large measure to their own efforts. Quite a number—the Tallow Chandlers among them—retain to this day links which it is their policy to strengthen and preserve. We must also remember the new guilds founded during the present century which take pride in carrying on the craft tradition.[d]

---

[d]   See Appendix L, Part III.

Commentary

EARLY SEARCHES

THE CURRIERS AND THE SOAPMAKERS

SAUCE, HERRING AND CHEESE

Page and
footnote

I

9   *b*   The petitioners refer to themselves as '*your poore oratours* the Wardeyns' a form of address to which the recipients were not unaccustomed. The first mention of this 'bill' was in March 1520, when the Wardens were commanded by the Court to bring in the names of 'all suche as occupye the occupacion [sic] of Talugh-chaundelers & [are] not free of the same and howe many apprentices every of them hath'.[1] The matter was again referred to in June 1523 when several Aldermen were appointed to oversee 'the ordynances' (so called) of the Tallow Chandlers and to report to the Court.[2]

9   *c*   The Wardens were to '*serche in the houses of all & every parsone or parsonees as vsen to make Talugh Candells to sell*'.

10   *d*   At the same meeting one Marten, a butcher, was ordered to bring in a pledge for selling tallow above the set price 'contrary to an Acte of Common Council made Anno xiiij° E[dward] iiij,[ti] that is to say the Standard Edict of 5th October 1474 (Volume III, p. 58). The pledge, which had to be of the value of £10, took the form of 'iij gobblettes with a couer parcele [part] gylte in a whyte bagge the couer havyig in the Top an image of an oxe enamelyd with letters S LUC in the oon syde & a merchaunttes marke with the letters IR & a merchaunttes mark on ther [? other] syde'.

15   *n*   The accounts contain the following entries. For the year 1530–1, 'paid to William Wyldys' wife for her husband's labours for making this accompt 14*d*, and to *Martyn Gowsse*, scrivener, for the fulfynyshyng thereof 6*d*.,' and for the years 1549–51 'received of Martyn Gowse *our Clerk* for coming too late to the Hall for a fine 4*d*.'[3] William Wyldys appears to have been the first of the Company's Clerks of whom there is any record.

II

16   *b*   An entry a few days earlier records the names of 'suche persones Talughchaundelers as occupye meltyng houses' in Flete Street and

elsewhere, which be very perilous for fyre'[4] (see Volume III, pp. 70–1).

17 c This provision is unusual. Tallow melting by butchers was forbidden by the Standard Edict of 1474 (Volume III, p. 59) and was, as we shall see, the exception in the sixteenth century.

17 d We learn from this record that Girdlers and Cordwainers as well as Curriers were interested in tallow. Cordwainers, as boot and shoe makers, were closely allied with Curriers, and they are mentioned later in this chapter (p. 19). Girdlers used leather, as well as other materials, but information regarding their employment of tallow appears to be lacking.

18 g Like so many other testators of this era he seems to have put off making his will until almost on the point of death. He bequeathes to his son-in-law, Richard White, a brother tallow chandler, on the death of his wife, 'the feather bed I now lie in'. Most of his other chattels are left to his wife, accompanied (perhaps) by a memorandum of wishes, for we find 'a brass pot' included as his gift in the Yeomanry Inventory very soon after his death.[5]

18 h It is possible that this order and the order *of the same date* (*infra*) relating to 'kitchen stuff' were in some way related (see note *j*). We may note *en passant* that according to our *Livery* (*Wardens'*) *Account Book* about this time one of our younger members was fined 10s. for selling a wey of tallow to a *currier* at the exhorbitant price (even for molten tallow, so called) of £3, 'contrary to his bond to the House'.[6]

19 i This price of xxxv s. for molten tallow compares with xxvj s. viij d. for rough tallow, fixed by the Court a few months earlier 'for the yere ensuing'.[7]

19 j It seems clear from the order dated 11th January 1574 (p. 22) that 'flotts' has this meaning. Compare also the use of the word 'flotice' (flotis or flotesse), which is thought to be synonymous with *grease*, in the order dated 24th September 1473 (Volume III, p. 57) and to refer there to the surface scum in boiling rough fat.

20 k It is evident from the paragraph in *Rokesle's Assizes* of 1277 directing that 'no foreign butcher sell meat in the City except in the manner accustomed' that the 'standings' of these butchers had been regulated for centuries. The reader is referred to the version printed as an Appendix in Volume I at p. 76.

20 l After 1546 there appears to be no record of 'foreign' butchers operating lawfully elsewhere than at Leadenhall Market. It seems likely, therefore, that the references to 'other markets' or 'elsewhere' which we find in the orders were inserted by the clerks *ex abundanti cautela*. But it seems that the orders were frequently broken. In a proclamation dated 4th June 1573 'the forren Butchers who bringe fleshe to this Cittie to be solde' are accused of 'having regard onlie to there owne pryvat lucre & gayne without anny respect to preserue *the common market at Leaden Hall within the said Cittie* or to releue the poore of the same' and of bringing 'to the same markett only fleshe/keping from the same markett the hides tallough',

etc., '*whereof they make secret marketts at home* to the greate hurte or the comon markett, and raysing of the prises of Hides and *Talloughe* . . .'[8]

21   *n*   This was the ancient means of identification of those who had been admitted to the freedom of the City, which still prevails. Its use here makes it certain that Redknight was a member of our Company.

24   *s*   AD 1754, May 23, ZOMER, Peter.—'A method of extracting and making from the tails and fins of whales, and from such sediment, trash, and undissolved pieces of the fish, as were usually thrown away as useless and of little or of no value by the makers of train oil, after the boiling of the blubber of such fish, *a sort of black train oil* . . .'.

24   *u*   Stow's readers are given this information for the first time in the second edition of his *Survey of London*, which appeared in 1603, containing the following passage correctly transcribed by C. L. Kingsford,[9] 'I haue not read or heard of Sope making in this Cittie till within this fourescore yeares, that John Lame (sic.) dwelling in Grassestreete set vp a boyling house'. His reason for introducing the subject of soap-making was to disprove what he conceived to be the popular misconception that the road formerly known as Soper's or Sopar's Lane (corresponding to what at the present time is the northern end of Queen Street, Cheapside) took its name from the soap-makers conducting their business there. His theory, which he states as a fact in his first edition printed in 1598, and repeats, is that one Alen le Sopar was responsible. The reader is referred to Appendix G of Volume I for an alternative explanation.

26   *z*   Among his specific bequests he left the Yeomanry 'a mazer with a band of silver and gilt with a boss (raised ornament) in it graven with an image of St Katherine', a gift which was entered in the *Yeomanry Account Book*.[10] The testator's interest in the Fraternity of St Katherine, founded in 1517, is not known. A mazer is a bowl, drinking cup, or goblet without a foot, originally made of 'mazer' wood, often richly carved or ornamented and mounted with silver or other metal. *O.E.D.*

27   *cc*   The testator expressed a wish to be buried in the parish church of St Botolph, without Bishopsgate, where he was a parishoner, and, among other legacies, he left to 'the Yeomanry' of his company twenty shillings 'in respect of their pains to be taken accompanying his corpse to the grave'.[11]

27   *dd*   See *The Compleat Cook* (Rebecca Price) compiled and introduced by Madeleine Masson, p. [6].

27   *ee*   Stow refers to 'grey soap, speckled with white, very sweet and good from Bristow (Bristol)' in his comments on soap-making referred to in note *u, supra*.

27   *ff*   From this title given to him by the testator, it seems probable that the legatee was our Fourth Warden, who was one of the Vendors in 1482 of John Bracy's property 'Le Nonne', which he had left to the Tallow Chandlers Company (see Volume III, p. 39).[12]

27   *hh*   See Volume III, p. 38. The devolution of the property is traced in *T.C.C.R.*, Appendix C, pp. 215–53. Original deeds at Guildhall Library, Ms. 6180, Boxes 1 and 2, Nos. 1–58. It appears from the final document (a mortgage dated 27th July 1648) that it was 'the Crane' which was the 'soap house'.

28   *jj*   A rare use of hable (or habile)= fit, suitable (*O.E.D.*) as a verb. Another requirement was that, after being 'habled', the soap should be 'marked with the Armes of this Citie and the markes of the houses where the said sope shalbe made, the marker thereof takyng for hys labour for the markyng of every laste of sope three pence.'

29   *kk*   See for instance the following records cited in Volume II, viz., the inventory of goods in the house of Emma Hatfeld made in 1373, including a barrel of Seville oil (Appendix G), and the will of John Busshe made in 1398 leaving conditionally to a fellow chandler a cask, or two pipes, of best oil (p. 91).

32   *nn*   'An enquiry made by the King's Officer . . . or by commissioners specially appointed, concerning any matter that intitles the King to the possession of lands or tenements, *goods or chattels*. This is done by a jury of no determinite number . . . *Commentaries on the Laws of England*, by William Blackstone (1723–80), Fifth Edition, Book III, Chapter 17, p. 258.

33   *qq*   Strype tells his readers that, because of the Act, much oil was destroyed 'that might have been employed to good use'. Nothing we have learnt so far supports the assertion, and this passage seems to disprove it. He goes on to say, however, that since 'no fee was granted for the execution, it was neglected', in which he could well be right![13]

35   *rr*   The entry in the *Repertory* Book records an agreement that a Mr George Wynter 'shall carry away xvij fatts of tallowe alredy shipped which were brought from Muscovia upon his promise to do as moch as in hym is to brynge so much more into this Cytty agaynst wynter next for the furniture of the same Cytty'.

36   *uu*   In the winter of the year following his 'presentation' of a soap maker (supra), Sybery was paid £20 2s. 'for to follow the suit for the Company in the Parliament House'.[14] This may have been the Act anno octavo Elizabeth regina (1565–6) regulating the prices of barrels of various sizes for the sale of ale, beer and *soap* in the Cities, Boroughs and Towns.[15] In December 1574 he is on record as one of over thirty chandlers required to enter into recognizances to keep the price of candles.[16] A number of these men were, as we shall see, fined on the same day for breaking the price, but Sybery's name does not appear among them.

38   *xx*   A judicial court in the palace of our Kings at Westminster, commonly said to have been erected by Henry VIII, but which was in fact, as Hallam pointed out, the old *Concilium Regis* or *Ordinarium*, and the object of Statute 3 Henry VII. c. 1 was to revive the Council and place its jurisdiction on a permanent and unquestionable basis . . . Under the Tudors the Star Chamber formed a terrible instrument for the punishment, short of death, of any who had fallen under the

Page and
footnote

displeasure of the Government, but its full capacity in this respect only became manifest under the Stuarts, when, by its means, as Macaulay remarks, 'the Government was able to fine, imprison, pillory, and mutilate at pleasure' . . . *Wheatley.*

40 *zz* It will be observed that the use of whale (or trane) oil, which as we have seen, was expressly forbidden by the Ordinance of 1510, (p. 24) is now permitted in second grade soaps. Further provisions of this long Report are given in Appendix F, Part III.

III

41 *d* In the Company's accounts for the years 1549–51, there is an entry recording the payment of 10s. 'for our Dinner and to the Lord Mayor's officer at the search for wine', and another entry recording that 8s. 3d. was paid 'to the officer for his Fee when he went in search for wine and for expences'.[17]

43 *h* The Vintners' mark ⚭ which often appears in the *Repertories.* In our accounts for 1551–3 there is a record of a fine for possessing 'a hogshead of liquor defective, and for causing of other to taste it, after the Wardens had set the King's mark thereon',[18] and another record of a fine 'for selling away 2 hogsheads of liquor found defective and after they were marked with the King's mark'.[19] There seems to be no other record of a King's mark for defective wine.

43 *i* He is not to be confused with the John Bedyll, citizen and tallowchandler, who died in 1515 leaving, among other bequests, 40s. 'to the marriage of poor maidens that dwell in the parish of St John Evangelist'.[20]

44 *l* There was a tavern called 'Redcrosse' in Barbican (L.C.C. Deeds, Harben Bequest, 1600–1700, No. 18), which may have occupied the site of an older house of the same sign, named from a cross there. *Harben.*

44 *m* This was evidently one of those cases noticed by Unwin[21] where control was exercised by the Mayor—as a rule over the lesser companies—in frequent interference in their domestic concerns. The incident in 1474 of three of the Butchers' Wardens being discharged by the authority of the Court and others being appointed in their place was mentioned in Volume III, p. 60.

45 *o* This was a customary requirement when the Court of Assistants (or appointed arbitrators) were engaged in settling domestic and other disputes between members of the Company who appeared before them. An early example occurs in 1454, when the contestants agreed 'to continue as lovers, and rancour to be laid apart'.[22]

45 *p* As the reader will have observed from Appendix B in Volume III, several 'dinners' are recorded, and in the accounts for 1563–4 there is a payment of 8d. 'to a carman for his pains and carriage of a Hogshead of unclean vinegar to Leadenhall'.[23] 50s. was also spent about the search of vinegar at St Katherines[24] (*query* St Katherine Coleman, Fenchurch Street, *Harben*), and other places.

46   *q*   As we know, the Master did not usually appear with the Wardens in an executive position (Volume III, p. 70). The clue on this occasion may be found in a contemporary entry in our accounts,[25] recording the payment of 3*s*. 4*d*. for making certificates and *supplications* to the Lord Mayor concerning the Company, which seems to be related in some way to our search for vinegar.

49   *x*   An Act of Common Council *temp*. Browne (William Browne, Mayor 1507) is referred to more than once,[26] but no copy of the Act seems to have survived.

52   *cc*   There is an entry in our Wardens' account for 1652–3 recording the purchase of 'An Act of Parliament concerning the Cheesemongers',[27] but it is not known to what Act this relates.

52   *dd*   The minute concerns a dispute between Richard Sibery (p. 36) and Mr King—probably John King (p. 32)—respecting 'three barrels and a half of butter, the price of which was fixed by our Court at 58*s*. the barrel.

TALLOW AND CANDLE

I

57   *d*   These officers were required to bring into court 'a suffycient wrytynge obligatorye vnder the seale of theyre corporacion to be made of the somme of cc li sterlinge suffyciently to bynde theyre successours'. This is the bond under the Company's common seal mentioned in Volume III, p. 70. They made an attempt to induce the Court to change its mind, asking that they might be handled as theyre predecessours have been vsed to be bounde by *recognysance*'.[28] but a peremptory command was given that they should obey the order,[29] after which we hear no more of the matter.

57   *e*   The 'bill' also contained a request that candle-makers should be required to 'occupye no *flottes* in theire Candelles', and this stipulation is made in both recognizances, where the word used is 'flottyce'. (See Volume III, p. 57.)

59   *k*   An early instance of this rule occurred in 1470, when it was ordered that butchers 'should not sell to strangers until the City be supplied'.[30] Again, as we have seen, (Volume III, p. 61) in April 1497 both butchers and tallow chandlers were forbidden to sell 'to no strangers nor out of this city withoute licence of this courte', a breach of which regulation made offenders liable to 'emprisonement and fyne'.[31]

59   *l*   An earlier instance of the relaxation of this rule was given in Volume III, p. 61, and another occurs in December 1550, when the Court agrees that several butchers who have been licensed to 'make their own Talloughe into candelles shall so be suffred styll to do, the denyer of the Talloughchaundelers not with stondyng'.[32]

61 *n*   The will of Thomas Stow (grandfather of the antiquary John Stow—Volume III, p. 62) citizen and tallow chandler of London, contains a direction that every one of seven altars 'in the Worship of the VII Sacraments' in the Parish Church of St Michael, Cornhill, was to have 'a wacchyng Candell burning from VI of the Clocke tyll it be past VII', which candle was to 'begynne to burne, and to be set upon the Aultar from Allhalowen day (31st October) tyll it be Candlemas day (2nd February) following', and to be 'wacchyng Candel of viii in the li'. Printed in John Strype's 1720 edition of Stow's *Survey of London*, First Volume, Book II, pp. 145–6.

61 *o*   His name was coupled with the name of Henry Eve (Ive) in the minutes of the Court of Aldermen for 11th July 1538 (p. 44) while that of Robert Fen (in group III of the list of 1537–8 and in the Yeomanry list of 1538–9) who is known from a list of the previous year to have been *Warden of the Yeomanry* at that time (Appendix A) is coupled with the name of John Burnet, then a Warden of the Company. (See Volume III, Appendix F.)

65 *q*   'Warnings' to the Butchers in the second half of the sixteenth century were of frequent occurrence. In May 1567 we paid 3s. 'to the Mayor's officer that warned the Butchers for the price of tallow',[33] and in the autumn the Wardens of our two companies were directed by the Court 'to consult on a reasonable price for tallow and candles'.[34] In the accounts for 1569–70 there is an entry recording a further warning to the Butchers' Wardens 'to come before the Lord Mayor for a price of tallow'.[35] We learn from the accounts for 1573–4 that our Beadle, (Thomas Priest) was paid 2s. 'for a proclamation between the Butchers and others',[36] and in October 1573 the Court of Aldermen agreed that a Proclamation should be drawn and made prohibiting butchers and others from selling tallow to 'foreigners' and requiring them 'to sell and utter the same onelye to the Chaundelers and other makers of candells'.[37]

65 *r*   Watching-candles are included in the order setting the price of candles in April 1562, but the price is left blank.[38] In the following November our Wardens are 'straightly charged by the Court' to see that the prices of 'the several sorts of candles are kept',[39] but in a recognizance entered into by these four Wardens later the same month they are bound only to keep the prices of candles 'made with cotton' and those 'made with weake'.[40]

65 *s*   In an entry in our Yeomanry accounts (or minutes) in 1563 we read of a 'bargain of candles' when the Governor (Walter Westmoreland) and others order one of two contestants to deliver 'every week till Shrove Sunday next coming . . . 4 dozen of *weke* candle and 2 dozen *cotton* candle, being good and merchantable ware'.[41]

66 *t*   According to John Dummelow, the learned author of *The Wax Chandlers of London*, a much heavier blow to the Wax Chandlers than the raiding of superstitious trusts was the loss of their principal markets the Church . . . In 1547 they (the Clergy) were . . . ordered to 'take awaie, utterly extincte, and destroy, all . . .

candlesticks, tryndilles or rolles of wax, and the commissioners appeared at St Paul's to see that the council's edicts were carried out: the Cathedral had already discontinued the use of candles on Candlemas Day ... The gloom was lightened, if for only a few years, by the return to the Roman dispensation under Mary ... With the death of Mary, candles disappeared again, though not altogether...'[42] The records of the Tallow Chandlers Company proper prior to the Reformation have not survived, but there are numerous references in the Accounts of the Yeomanry to their religious devotions at St Botolph's Church, Without Bishopsgate. (See Volume III, p. 34.)

II

66   a   There is an entry in the *Yeomanry Account Book* for 1549–51 of a prayer by the Wardens for 'allowance for loss of money after the Proclamation.[43] The 'fall of money' is again noticed twice in the next decade.[44]

66   b   For the views on this subject expressed by a number of modern writers see *The Price Revolution in Sixteenth Century England*, edited by Peter H. Ramsey (1971).

67   d   The Proclamation, which followed two disastrous harvests,[45] begins by reciting that 'God Almyghty off hys infynyte goodness, grace and mercy hath this present yere blessyd vs more plentyfully with store of grayne and other vyctualles for or comfort and sustentacion then of late yeres he hathe done'.[46]

69   g   This seems to be a rare instance of the punishment of the pillory being imposed on those breaking the price of tallow or candles. No copy of the Act of Common Council seems to have been preserved.

70   h   A fifteenth century statute ordained that 'the weight of a way of Cheese may contain xxxii Cloves, that is to say, every Clove vij li'.[47] Clove—a weight formerly used for wool and cheese equal to 7 or 8 lbs. avoirdupois. Recorde *Gr. Artes* (1575) 203. In Cheese ... The Verye weightes of it are Cloues and Weyes: so that a Cloue shoulde contayne *7 pounde*. O.E.D. See Volume II, p. 54 where the view is expressed that a different measure prevailed at the time of the standard edict of 1362.

71   i   Again based on the standard measure of $32 \times 7 = 224$ lbs. (2 cwt.) to the wey.

71   j   It is clear from the entries which follow that a Proclamation was issued, but no copy has been traced.

71   k   'Foreign' butchers, as we know, had to take their tallow with the carcases of the beasts to Leadenhall, and their price had sometimes been set lower than that of the free butchers.

III

74   e   Possibly his livery, as a servant of the Mayor and his 'clothing'

as a Liveryman of the Tallow Chandlers Company (Appendix B) for which members had to pay at cost price.[48]

74   *f*   A later instance of his handiwork occurs in 1527, when he was responsible for seizing five ways of tallow sold by two butchers to one John Danbury of Walden, Essex, for conveyance out of the City, contrary to the Act (Standard Edict) of 5th October 1474. The Court agreed that they should 'make restitucion to the seyd persone of Walden' of the purchase money.[49]

76   *h*   The following entries appear to have been made in our accounts about the time of this decree. First, a payment of 5s. 8d. 'to the Mayor, his officers for warning the Butchers and for a drinking'[50] and secondly 5s. 4½d. 'for a Dinner at the Castle (see Volume III, Appendix B, note *a*) at the search for tallow'.[51]

77   *i*   Richard Foster's name appears first in the accounts for 1557-9, when he is shown as the recipient of 2s. for arresting Thomas Belson, the defaulting tenant of 'the Lamb', formerly 'the Dolphin', (p. 26). Although referred to here as 'our officer', he was probably the same person as Richard Foster, 'one of the Lord Mayor's officers sent with our Wardens to Leadenhall Market in April 1562 (p. 21) and 'Foster, my Lord Mayor's officer' referred to hereafter.

77   *j*   This seems to be the Proclamation made in April 1562 as a result of our 'Bill', (p. 21).

77   *l*   The church of the dissolved Monastery or Hospital of St Thomas in Southwark, made parochial after the dissolution of religious houses . . . In 1521, the parish was known as 'the parish of St Thomas's Hospital' . . . The parish is the smallest in Southwark, but it included within it two magnificent hospitals of St Thomas and Guy's, until the former was removed to make room for the extension of the South Eastern Railway. *Wheatley.*

77   *n*   There seems to be no account of this search in the City memoranda books. In our accounts for 1561-2 there is a record of a payment of 5s. to an officer 'for the Proclamation for Tallow',[52] but this appears to refer to the weighing at Leadenhall'.

79   *r*   There is a hiatus in our record of Governors between 1539 and 1552, but Rogers is unlikely to have held office so early. Another blank occurs in 1557-8, when he could have served.

79   *s*   Turnagine lane. The name suggests Tindale's words in 1531, 'a turnagaine lane which they cannot goe through'. *Harben.*

80   *t*   It had been the practice to hang a portrait of the Sovereign in the Hall. There is a record dated 28th September 1563 in the Wardens' accounts of 'two pictures, one of Henry VIII and the other of King Edward VI, of the gift of Mr Benye,[53] and in 'an Inventory taken 9th July 1599 of all the Goods and Furniture belonging to the Company of Tallow Chandlers' are 'three pictures of King Henry, King Edward and the Queen's Majesty.[54] Unfortunately, none of these pictures has survived (see Appendix D).

81   *v*   He was the Liveryman found guilty of brawling in a tavern with Warden Crookes (p. 45), an incident which occurred in 1563,[55]

and six years earlier he had been involved in an argument with another Liveryman whom he had called 'villain with other approbrious words', although, admittedly, his opponent had been guilty of drawing his dagger on him.[56] Again, in the accounts for 1563-4, he is charged with 6s. 8d. 'for his disobedience and abusing himself to the Wardens'.[57] In the summer of 1574 he was, as we shall see imprisoned for causing offence to the Court of Aldermen. The choice of this tactless man as 'searcher' seems strange.

IV

84 g   In his will of goods, Robert Heron desires his 'wretched carcas and body to be buried in the parish church of Our Lady Woolchurch Haw' near the body of his wife. 'The clothing' of his Company are to receive 20s. 'for a recreation'. His 'Kinsman, John Herne, servant with the Duke of Somerset', is named as *'overseer'*, (a title given to a person—formerly—appointed by a testator to supervise or assist the executor or executors of the will O.E.D.) There are many such appointments in early wills.

85 l   The Act imposed a penalty of 40s. This passage accordingly fixes the current value at 6s. 8d. (see the O.E.D. for varying values).

85 n   It is not known to what regulation this record in the 'sixties relates. So far as we know the Ordinances then in force were those of 1538 (infra), which contain no specific reference to tallow melting. Apart from the occasions when butchers were (exceptionally) permitted to make candles, which involved the melting of tallow —see for instance Volume III, p. 61—there are two entries indicating that the restrictions against butchers themselves melting tallow were sometimes relaxed. In 1547 there is an order that they shall not be suffered 'to melt their own talough *without the especiall lycense of the Court'*.[58] Three years later they are 'lycensed to melt and make candells of their taloughe . . . *for that the Taloughe Chaundelers refuse to buy it of them*.[59]

V

88 b   The price of candles during this era had been as low as 1d. the lb., and only that year had been set at $1\frac{1}{4}d$.[60]

91 k   This is not the only time that candle-making is referred to as 'a science' in our records. Another instance occurs in December 1595 when the sum of 6s. 8d. was received from one Roger Garrard, dwelling in Southwark, near Horsley Down for *'opening his shop and using our science'*.[61] *Horselydown*—A district that extends from the eastern end of Tooley Street to Dockhead, and from the Thames to the Tenter-ground, Bermondsey. It was formerly an exercise and grazing-ground for horses—hence the name. *Wheatley* contains much other interesting information regarding this area.

92 l   Probably the same man as the John Barton mentioned in the accounts for 1561-2. Nothing further seems to be known of him.

93   *n*   Only the seller seems to have incurred any penalty. If the buyer was a Londoner he must surely have known that the law was being broken, and was lucky to escape punishment.

94   *o*   An order made in the previous May, when the price of rough tallow was set at 24s. the wey, is mentioned.[62]

95   *p*   Eight soldiers were sent forth receiving 12d. each prest money; for their conduct money 3s. 4d. was paid to each man by the Mayor's commandment; for 18¼ yards of watchet Kersey to make coats at 2s. 8d. the yard, 48s. was paid. 5s. 4d. was paid for two yards of red kersey to welt the coats and 8s. for making them, 8d. being paid for buttons.[63] Kersey—a kind of coarse narrow cloth, woven from long wool and usually ribbed. 'Watchet', a light blue colour; cloth or garments of this colour. *O.E.D.*

98   *r*   Another man to incur the same penalty was one William Corker, 'chayndler',[64] of whom nothing else is known.

CRESSET LIGHT

1

102   *b*   See Volume II, Plate V, for a picture of this cresset. There were, nevertheless, many forms. According to William O'Dea, Keeper in the Science Museum, London, beyond the fact that it was some sort of iron holder containing a *raised fire* 'it cannot be narrowed down by definition to anything very specific'.[65] Sir Thomas Hanmer, for instance, is quoted by Isaac Reed in the second *Variorum* (published in 1813) of the Johnson-Steevens text of Shakespeare's Plays, as defining the cresset as 'a great light set upon a beacon, light-house, or watch-tower: from the French word *croissette*, a little cross, because the beacons had anciently crosses on the top of them'.[66]

103   *d*   In the Wardens' accounts for 1553-5 there is an entry of 2s. 'received from John Shorte (p. 78) towards the payment of those that did Watch and Ward for that he was not there himself'.[67]

104   *i*   Two men from each company were to stand at each of the following ten gates, viz.: the postern gate by the Tower, Aldgate, Bishopsgate, Moorgate, Cripplegate, Aldersgate, Newgate, Ludgate, the Bridge and Billingsgate.

106   *k*   A Precept of 29th January 1539 gives another reason for the failure of the Watches. The Aldermen are informed that it has 'comen to the King's knowledge and his honourable counseille' that they (the Aldermen) have had 'but lytle regarde' to his commandments, having kept their watches 'with many unharnyssed & not as watchemen & not observing the houres' to them 'lymytted, as men not regarding' their duties.[68] Again in a warning to the Wardens of the Mercers (see p. 111) in June 1568 there is a reference to 'the disorder of the said Cresset bearers as have heretofore been by you sent', alleging that 'in the cheifest tyme of their service'

they have 'negligentlie loked to their charge and some departed before the said watch ended, so as loked for services have not be accomplished'.[69]

107   *m*   The price paid by our Wardens in 1567–8 was 7s. per hundred.[70] This compares with 2s. 4d. payable by *all crafts* in 1541, and the money was presumably owing to one of our members as the actual maker of the cresset light.

II

108   *a*   Riley gives what seems to be an unlikely reason for the institution of these watches, namely, 'the great necessity for the prevention of fires at this (midsummer) season, owing to the drought usually prevalent at the period',[71] for which he quotes no authority.

108   *b*   He tells us that, in addition to men in armour (bearing cressets), archers, pikemen, steel-clad halberdiers, constables in armour, and musketeers, there were morris dancers, several bands of musicians and numerous 'stages' (floats). On one of these stages was 'a very beautiful little girl under a canopy of brocade, representing the Virgin Mary, with four boys in white surplices, chanting 'lauds'. On another was Saint George, in armour, choking a big dragon.

109   *c*   The *Letter-Book* makes it quite clear that six weeks after the great muster held on 8th May 1539 the King, far from wishing to ban the marching watch in future, expressed a preference for it, although in letters to the Mayor, Aldermen, Recorder, and Sheriffs he left the decision to them. In August, having given consideration to the matter, they also expressed a strong preference for the watch.[72]

109   *d*   See Volume II, p. 284 of *John Stow, a Survey of London* reprinted from the text of 1603 with *Introduction and Notes* (1971) by C. L. Kingsford for (a) the editor's inclusion of a 'contemporary notice for 1538–9' of the exceptional muster in May 1539, 'apparently written by a citizen, and preserved amongst Stow's *Collections* (Harley Ms. 530, f. 119) and (b) the editor's note (regarding Henry VIII's supposed action in forbidding the marching-watch), which tells us that (according to Wriothesley) the sheriffs had made their preparations 'and had noe knowledge till two days afore Midsommer that yt should not be kept, which was a great loose to poor men'. (*Chronicle*, i. 100). The Editor also refers us to 'other accounts in Wriothesley's *Chronicle*, i. 95–7, and *Letters and Papers*, xiv, 940

109   *e*   See C. L. Kingsford's brief reference to 'Gresham's revival'. (*Chronicle*, ii. 3) in his notes on *John Stow* op. cit. *Supra*.

112   *i*   Partisan. A military weapon used (under this name) by footmen in the sixteenth and seventeenth centuries, consisting of a long-handled spear, the blade having one or more lateral cutting projections, variously shaped, so as sometimes to pass into the gisarme★

★ A kind of battle-axe, bill or halberd.

and the halberd; in some of its forms used also in boar hunting. O.E.D.

112   *j*   Halberd. A military weapon, especially in use during the fifteenth and sixteenth centuries; a kind of combination of spear and battle-axe, consisting of a sharp-edged blade ending in a point, and a spear-head, mounted on a handle five or seven feet long. O.E.D.

113   *k*   The constables are seen to number over two hundred for the twenty-five Wards and the Corslets to over three thousand. The constables appointed in the going watch are seen to number nearly ninety,★ and the cressets to number thirteen hundred and eighty.

113   Whiffler. One of a body of attendants armed with a javelin, battle-axe, sword, or staff, and wearing a chain, employed to keep the way clear for a procession or at some public spectacle. O.E.D.

115   *n*   Compare this area with the route prescribed for the marching watch in 1541.

116   *o*   He describes one such, made in 1564, in his *Summarie of Englishe Chronicles* for 1566 (f. 275) thus: 'This yeare, thorough (sic) the earnest suite of the Armorers, there was on the Vigile of Saint Peter a certayne kynde of a watche in the Citie of London, which dyd onely stande in the hyghest streetes of Cheape, Cornhyll, and so foorthe towardes Algate: whyche was to the commons of the same citie (for the most parte) as chargeable as when in tymes paste it was most commendably done, where as this beyng to very small purpose was of a small a number well lyked'. This is somewhat fuller than the notice as finally incorporated in the *Annales of England. See* the editor's note in Vol. II, of *John Stow,* op. cit., p. 284.

116   *q*   Stow continues as follows: 'in commendation whereof namely in times of peace to be used, he hath words to this effect. The artificers of sondry sortes were thereby well set a worke, none but rich men charged, poore men helped, old Souldiers, Trompiters, Drommers, Fifes, and ensigne bearers with such like men, meet for Princes service kept in vze, wherein the safety and defence of euery common weale consisteth. Armour and Weapon beeing yearly occupied in this wise the Cittizens had of their owne redily prepared for any neede, whereas by intermission hereof, armorers are out of worke. Soldiers out of vze, weapons overgrown with foulness, few or none good being prouided, etc.' We detect the hand of the Worshipful Company of Armourers (see note *o supra.*) in this appeal!

116   *r*   For what appears to be an independent attempt at revival in 1585, see *the Harleian Miscellancy, a collection of scarce, curious and entertaining Pamphlets and Tracts as well in manuscript as in print* Vol. IX, selected and prepared by Thomas Park, F.S.A., 1812, (Guildhall Library).

117   *s*   Or 'Common Clerk'. He came into office in 1574 and served for nearly forty years. Following the practice believed to have been initiated by his illustrious predecessor, John Carpenter, who was appointed Common Clerk in 1417, he signs with his surname only.

★ There is a discrepancy. The heading gives 86, but the list gives a total of 89.

THE ORDINANCES OF 1538 AND AFTER
QUARTERAGE
AND THE CONFLICT WITH THE SALTERS

I

119   g   The ordinances of 1394 referred to in '*A History of the Salters'
Company*' by J. Steven Watson, pp. 8, 9, were those of the *Fraternity*
as opposed to the Craft Guild.

119   i   As clearly shown in Dr Sharpe's Calendar, there are no less than
forty-five blank folios in *Letter Book C* (c. 1291–1309) which
contains the ordinances of the Fullers, Weavers, and Cordwainers
and an article of the Curriers, there are thirty-two in *Letter Book D*
(c. 1309–14), and twenty-five in *Letter Book E* (c. 1314–37),
which contains the ordinances of the Pepperers, Armourers, and
Tapicers, as well as a lengthy agreement between the Saddlers,
Fusters and Loriners. The folio in *Letter Book F* (c. 1337–52),
recording the ordinances of the Girdlers made in the reign of
Edward III is immediately followed by a blank folio and there are
ten other folios blank. *Letter Books G* (c. 1352–74), *H* (c. 1375–
99), and *I* (c. 1400–22) all have blank folios, and *Letter Book K*
(*temp.* Henry VI) has forty-three. *Letter Book L* (*temp.* Edward IV–
Henry VII) has one folio torn.

120   n   In March 1462 the Fishmongers 'who had made certain ordinances
on their own account' were ordered to show them to the Court,
and told that in future they should use no ordinances until they had
been confirmed by the Court.[73] This was not the first time that they
had been in trouble with the civic authorities. In 1382 they had
shown great reluctance in producing their charters to the Court,
but were forced to give in. (See Volume II, p. 88).

121   o   The date given in a similar entry in the *Journal* is 1st February
1488.[74]

121   p   This reference to the King probably related to the power conferred upon the Commonalty by *Royal Charter* in 1484 (see Volume
III, Appendix D) to choose officers 'after their custom, or better by
the advice *and Ordinances* of the same commonalty *hereafter to be
made*'.

121   q   The words 'and not returned with the said book', which followed,
seem to be meaningless, since the book itself was to be retained in
the Chamber.

II

124   d   Here we have a clear case of the word 'craft' being used to signify
the *trade*. Later in the same passage it denotes the Mistery (or Company) of Brown Bakers.

125   g   They may be used here to signify private, as opposed to public,
taxes.

Page and
footnote

125   *h*   It is not clear whether journeymen, as well as 'brothers', were to be responsible for the stated contribution to the Beadle's wages.

126   *m*   The late Mr Story Maskelyne (p. 14, note *l*), was misled by this and later references to 'the Clothing' into thinking that the Yeomanry had followed the example of the Company proper by developing a *clothing of its own*, failing to appreciate that *all* quarter-age receipts of the period are included in the Yeomanry accounts. Attention is drawn here to this mistake because Part II of 'the Records', for which he was responsible (containing an unfinished chapter on the Yeomanry) although never published, was printed, and a copy was deposited at Guildhall Library, where doubtless it can still be seen.

127   *p*   These accounts give a good idea of the Company's numerical strength, which may be compared with that of the Founders, during the first half of the sixteenth century. The learned editor of their *Wardens Accounts* from 1497 onwards shows that before 1524 the normal total of Livery and Yeomanry combined was between 80 and 90, and after that date was more often over than under 90. During the period ending in 1569, only in the three years of which 1530–1 was one, were there more than 100 names.[75]

127   *q*   As used in these accounts the word 'forrens' may relate to 'strangers', and does not necessarily mean 'non-freemen' of the City.

128   *s*   The word 'strangers', incidentally, occurs frequently in the Founders' accounts.

129   *t*   These words occur in Article 1, 'for the chosynge of the Wardeins', and requiring them to make their accounts by a given date 'vpon payn of xl s. Sterlinges' payable as stated.

129   *v*   See, for example, the ordinances of the Painters, dated 14th July 1467.[76]

130   *x*   The quarterage is given incorrectly as 3s. in the abbreviated version of this order in *The Wax Chandlers of London* by John Dummelow, p. 52.

133   *aa*   The words 'swete and holsome for man's bodye', were, as we have seen, usually reserved for *wines* that were fit to drink. Those suitable only for *vinegar* were called 'eager wines' for which it seems that the word 'sound' would have been more appropriate than 'sweet'.

134   *gg*   There are a number of entries in the Company's minutes of the second half of the sixteenth century of distresses having taken place, but there seems to be no record of any 'rescue', either in the minutes or in the Corporation memoranda books.

III

136   *d*   One of these articles, which it is a little difficult to understand, was that the Master and Wardens should from time to time 'delyuer *the moyte* of all suche Talloughe as shall fortune to come to theyre handes amonge theyre Companye to be made in Candelles'.

136   *e*   They were two salters, one of whom was Thomas Marshall (p. 93), two leathersellers, and one saddler, Robert Kytchyn (p. 91). After 'monycion & charge streyghtly gven' to every one of those to whom the directions were read that they should observe every poynt of the seyd condycion', the five 'were bounden by recognizaunce in xl li sterling for the juste obseruance of the Artycles mencyoned in the seyd Condyccion'.

IV

139   *a*   Note, however, the ban contained in Article 56 against employing foreigners (p. 203).

LETTERS PATENT OF ELIZABETH I
(TYLER'S PATENT)
SOAP, VINEGAR, BARRELLED BUTTER, OIL AND HOPS

I

142   *a*   The powers of search covered all goods in the first category 'made brought and kept' within the stipulated area 'with intent to be uttered and put to sale', and all goods in the second category 'brought thither from any forraine partes', or such as should 'growe to be made' or should 'in any way [be] kept' in the stipulated area.

142   *c*   (i) *St Katherine's by the Tower*, a royal hospital, college or free chapel, founded in 1148 by Matilda, wife of King Stephen, augmented 1273 by Eleanor, widow of Henry III, refounded by Eleanor, Queen of Edward I, and enlarged by Phillipa, Queen of Edward III. The hospital was suppressed with the other religious houses, but Henry VIII and Katherine his first wife, founded here a Guild of St Barbara of which Cardinal Wolsey and many of the chief nobility were enrolled as members, but it lapsed in the next reign, and Elizabeth by a charter of 1556, reconstituted the Hospital of St Katherine for the maintenance of a master, three brethren, three sisters and ten bedeswomen . . . The precinct or liberty of St Katherine extended from the Tower to Ratcliffe, and had its two courts in which actions were tried weekly . . . When the royal assent was given to the erection of St Katherine's Docks, the hospital was removed to Regent's Park.

(ii) *Whitechapel*, a parish lying east of Aldgate, originally a chapelry in the parish of Stepney, but constituted a separate parish in the seventeenth century.

(iii) *Shoreditch*, a manor and populous parish, at the north-east end of London . . . The old way of spelling the name is Soersditch, but the derivation is uncertain.

(iv) *Clerkenwell,* a parish extending northwards from St Andrew's Holborn, and Smithfield to the Pentonville Road . . . The original village grew up about the Priory of *St John of Jerusalem,* the site of which is marked by St John's Square . . . The parish derived its name from a holy well at which the parish clerks of London annually assembled to perform a miracle or Scripture play, or series of plays.

(v) St Giles-in-the-Fields, at the east end of Oxford Street, was originally a village separated from London and Westminster by broad fields, and its church was so designated to distinguish it from St Giles, Cripplegate . . . The hospital chapel became the parochial church when the parish of St Giles was formed and the building remained until 1623, when it was demolished. *Wheatley.*

143   *d*   As we know, the grant was in fact to the Company itself, not to the Wardens.

144   *e*   Sir Francis Walsingham, Secretary of state. Principal secretary to Queen Elizabeth I from 1573 to 1590. *Encyclopaedia Britannica.* (1968), Vol. 23, p. 178.

145   *f*   Strype continues his account of our petition to the Queen with a recital that 'whereas much counterfeit vinegar was made of *corrupt Beer and Ale,* and the same coloured and mingled with unwholesome Dreges, as well within the Liberty of London as also in St Katharine's, Whitechapel, Shoreditch, St Johns, Clerkenwell, and other such like places . . . and yet the same was sold into the City for good and perfect; the people thereby deceived besides the fear of great infection to be bred therewith'. He adds that 'the Dredges used for colouring Vinegar were Elder-berries, Privet-berries. Torne-sole★ and such ther like Dredges'. He does not tell his readers from what source he has acquired this information respecting 'counterfeit vinegar' and our records prior to the granting of the Patent contain no entries relating to searches for vinegar made from anything but wine.

145   *g*   Strype's recital continues as follows: 'And also Firkins of salt butter mingled and packed up with old musty butter in divers parts of the Firkins; and the like abuse used in Oil and Hops', in regard to which 'deceits' he adds: 'The musty and moldy Butter was packed in the heart of the vessels of Butter. The Sallet Oils were mingled with Lisbon oil. The old and musty Hops were packed in the heart of the Sacks of Hops, and great Quantity of Sand mingled with the same to make them weigh more. Which mingling was done in Flanders'. Again he quotes no authority. The allegations respecting the packing of salt butter, in which commodity tallow chandlers had an interest may, in rare cases, have been true, but again evidence is lacking. Dealings in 'salad oil', as such, do not figure either in the Corporation records of the sixteenth century or in our own minutes. His statement, which follows,

---

★Or turnsole, a violet or purple colouring matter obtained from the plant *Crozophorsa tinctoria.* O.E.D.

that 'for Reformation' of such matters 'the Master and Wardens of Tallow Chandlers of London, *who did retail these things* and finding daily these Deceits, were moved in conscience to procure Redress', should accordingly be given critical examination. The search of *Hops*, both before and after the Grant, is touched on in the text.

146   h   'For the Vewe searche wayenge and markinge of everye barrell of good sope twoe pence and of every halfe barrell a penny, and of everye firkyn* a halfe pennye and of everye halfe firkyn a farthinge, of everye tonne of good vyniger eighte pence, of everye ponchion (puncheon)† foure pence, of everye hogsheade twoe pence, of everye barrell of good barrelled butter markinge and wayenge twoe pence, of every halfe barrell a pennye and of every firkyn one halfe pennye, of everye tonne of good Civill (Seville) oile or trane oil eighte pence, of everye pipe foure pence and of everye hogshead twoe pence, of every barrell of good rape oil or whale oil twoe pence and of everye barrell of sallett (salad) oile twoe pence and of every sacke of good hoppes eighte pence and of every pockett (pocket)‡ of good hoppes foure pence'.

146   i   The record in the *Journal* is of an Act of Common Council dated 16th October 1552, which required only one Commoner, instead of all six members, to retire annually.

147   k   Strange words for a monarch whose reputation for *granting* monopolies was before long to become nationwide. But the 'monopoly' complained of here, created, as it was by the sale of hops by *'many merchants'* at excessive prices, differed greatly from the monopolies later granted by the Queen as rewards for faithful service or sold by her to the highest bidder.[77] These new monopolies gave the grantees the sole right to market and fix the price of certain articles of commerce. They had a disastrous effect on the cost of living and the general welfare of the community, and caused an outcry in Parliament near the end of the reign.[78] The powers of inspection and taxation granted to the Tallow Chandlers Company by the Patent of 1577 were again of a different kind, but it is easy to see how those powers might pass into monopoly.[79]

II

151   d   The first commencement of a suit in Chancery is by preferring a bill to the Lord Chancellor in the style of a petition; 'humbly complaining sheweth to your lordship your orator A.B. that, etc.' This is in the nature of a declaration at Common Law . . . setting

---

  * Originally a quarter of a 'barrel' or half a kilderkin. Varying in capacity according to the commodity. *O.E.D.*

  † A large cast for liquids. *Op. cit.*

  ‡ A bag or sack. Sometimes used as a measure of quantity, varying in capacity according o the commodity contained and the locality. *Op. cit.*

Page and
footnote

forth the circumstances of the case at length ... 'in tender consideration whereof' (which is the usual language of the bill) 'and for that
your orator is wholly without remedy at the common law, relief
is therefore prayed at the Chancellor's hands ...'. *Commentaries of
the Laws of England*, fifth edition, op. cit., Book III, p. 442.

151   *f*   There seems to have been a preliminary attendance, for we read
of a payment 'for the dinner of the Wardens at the hearing of Tyler's
Bill of Complaint' on 11th November 1582[80] and there is reference
to an 'Order'.[81]

152   *g*   Strype names 'the places' mentioned in the Patent together with
the 'Lords of the Liberty' in each case, as follows: In *Southwark*,
the Lord Maior and Commons have a Leet, or Law-Day. In
St Katharines, the Master and confreres. In *White Chappel*, the lord
Wentworth. In *Shoreditch*, the Dean and Chapter of Paul's. In
Clerkenwell, the Queen. In *St Giles in the Fields*, and in *High
Holbourne*, the Lord Mountjoy. High Holborn is not in fact men-
tioned in the Patent.

153   *h*   This record is the first of a number of entries calendared in the
Analytical Index under the heading 'monopolies'. See *Commentary*,
p. 247, note *k*.

154   *i*   He is called the servant of 'Mr Common Hunt', or 'Huntsman'
of the Commonalty, an office first mentioned in the City records in
1379, (Riley *Memorials*, p. 428), and seems to have taken the place
of Thomas Redknight (p. 21).

155   *j*   It appears that on 4th July (1589) he entered into some agreement
which is referred to in April 1600 as an Indenture between Sir
George Carey, Knight' now Lord Chamberlain and Henry
Huntley',[82] of which no particulars have survived.

155   *k*   After reciting in full the provisions of the Patent, the deed
declares that the grantors 'have ordeyned, deputed', etc. 'and in
their stede and place have put and by theis presentes Doe depute',
etc. 'theire welbeloved Sir George Carey Knighte his deputie and
deputies, assigne and assignes their true, sufficiente and lawfull
deputie and assigne, deputies and assignes for them, and in their
name and names, to take exercise execute' etc. 'and enjoye all and
singular suche powers, authorities, liberties, interests and other premisses whatsoever eyther by ye said ltres pattentes given and graunted or otherwise belonginge, or in anye wise apperteyninge, to the
saide Mr Wardens and Comynaltye of the said arte and misterie
of tallow chaundelers *together with all fees profittes benefites and
comodyties as doe, shall, or maie arise growe, chaunce, or happen to bee
exercised, used, had or taken* by vertue of the saide lettres pattentes in
or within the severall places or anie of them hereafter severallye or
speciallye mencioned, that is to saie [the stipulated areas] in as large
and ample manner and forme as the saide Mr Wardens and comynaltie' etc. 'have, hath, maie' etc. 'or ought' etc. to 'take, exercise' etc.,
'ye saide powers' etc. 'and other the premisses whatsoever conteyned
or mencioned in ye saide ltres pattentes *and without anie accompt to be
given or yeilden for the same or anie of them to ye saide Mr Wardens and*

Comynaltie', *etc.* 'To have, holde' etc. 'the saide Deputacion, powers'
etc. 'to the saide Sr George Casey Knyghte, his deputie and
deputies, assigne and assignes, or to anie of them, to his and theire
owne proper use and behoofe *for and duringe the naturall life of Roger
Tyler citizen and Tallowchaundeler of London'*. Covenants by the
grantors for title, quiet enjoyment, further assurance, and indemnity. Covenants by the grantee for himself, his executors, admini-
strators, deputies and assigns for good behaviour and indemnity.

156   *n*   'Charges in the search by us made for defective wines' amounted
to 6s. 10*d.* 'out of which was paid to Mr Town Clerk's man for
making the Bill of Report from the Vintner 12*d.*'[83]

156   *o*   Of these four, three were past Lord Mayors—Sir Rowland Heyward (note *l*), Sir George Barne (note *l*) and Sir George Bond
(1587).

157   *p*   The site of the monastery was granted to the Mayor and citizens
of London, 38 H. VIII, 1547, and in the reign of Edward VI, owing
to the King's efforts to cope with the increase of beggary in the
City, the buildings were repaired and furnished for the maintenance
of poor fatherless children, and were to be called Christs Hospital
(Tanner) . . . much damaged in the Fire. The hall rebuilt 1680 . . .
again rebuilt 1825–9 . . . School was removed to Horsham in 1897,
the Newgate Street gateway being re-erected there. *Harben.*

157   *q*   The testator gives no address and the property has not been
traced. His will directed that he should be buried 'in the parish
church of St Michael Huggin Lane in Wood Street'.

III

158   *a*   In discussing 'injuries proceeding from or affecting the Crown'
as part of his treatise on 'Private wrongs' Blackstone informs us
that 'a writ of *quo warranto* is in the nature of a writ of right for
the King, against him who claims or usurps any office, franchise or
liberty, to inquire by what authority he supports his claim, in
order to determine the right'. It lies also in the case of the non-user
etc.—The judgment on a writ of *quo warranto* (being in the nature
of a writ of right) is final and conclusive even against the crown . . .
(See *Commentaries on the Laws of England*, Book the Third, fifth
edition, by William Blackstone, Solicitor General to Her Majesty,
pp. 262, 263

158   *b*   It is true that in May 1593 there was an Order of the Court of
Aldermen that the Lord Treasurer (or Lord High Treasurer, who,
in the sixteenth century held office from the Crown) was to be
informed of corrupt hops seized within the City,[84] but the reason
for this is not apparent.

158   *c*   They were John Barnes, *our Beadle* (p. 159) and *William Cheston
(or Jesson), perhaps the under-beadle.*

158   *d*   They were Henry *Beadle* and John Hall, who was probably
under-beadle at this time, a Mrs Hall being mentioned in 1607 as a
creditor of John Barnes.

Page and
footnote

159   *g*   The Agreement, which was under seal and dated 11th July 1596, is mentioned in the inventory of deeds and documents handed to the City Chamberlain in April 1600(see p. 162). The parties were (1) Sir George Carey (2) Thomas Harris, Sergeant-at-law, and (3) John Ivone (?) and Richard Hewish, gent.[85]

160   *i*   The Committee appointed on 3rd (or 5th) October 1599 recommended that 'soe as' the Lord Chamberlain (Lord Hunsden) 'doe assigne his interest he hath (as the Queen's representative) from the Tallow Chandlers' in Her Majesty's Letters Patent and 'doe procure the Tallowchandlers to make the like assignment of their letters patent to the Maior and Commonaltie of the Cittie of London and that alsoe his Lordship doe procure Mr Wade, one of the Clerks of Her Majesty's privie counsaile . . . to assigne his interest which he hath or claimeth to have' in the things contained in the patent 'concerninge those severall places mencioned' therein (if so advised), 'that then some meete persons to be appointed by Acte of Common Counsayle to treate with his lordship and to compound with him for his interest in the sayd letters patents . . .'

162   *k*   It is true that, soon after the appointment of Winton and Lightfoot, the usual contingent from the companies of Grocers, Salters and Brewers had been sworn for the search of *hops* (as were our men) and that they too were to make presentment to the Court,[86] but there is no reason to suppose that this duplication had any sinister significance.

163   *l*   According to this entry the Saddlers Company appears to have played a part in what is called 'the redemption of the patent', for which they receive £6.

164   *n*   To avoid any possibility of doubt the Clerk adds the words 'and by them assigned over to this Citty'.

IV

165   *d*   The best hops after they were garbled weighed three hundred three quarters and 24 pounds and were sold at 34*s.* the hundred: the second hops after they were garbled weighed seven hundred and quarter and 14 lbs. and were sold at 24*s.* the hundred; the coarse hops after they were garbled weighed two hundred just and were sold at 20*s.* the hundred. Particulars of other sales are given.

166   *e*   Like Roger Price, the other three were probably Assistants. They were William Karver (or Carver), Jeffrey Merchant, and William Payne. Carver was Governor of the Yeomanry from 1624 to 1626, and Master in 1628-9. Merchant (or Marchant) succeeded him as Governor and also as Master in 1626 and 1629 respectively.

167   For some reason a second exemplification of the Letters Patent was obtained at the request of Roger Price on 28th April 1618.[87]

THE STUART CHARTERS
THE CANDLEMAKERS
AND THE END OF SEARCHES

I

168   *b*   The Patent of Edward VI contains a recital that a confirmation was made by Henry VIII by letters patent dated 15th November 1516, of which there appears to be no record of an exemplification. 'A General Pardon from Henry VIII of all offences committed by the Company' dated 27th November of the same year is, however, in our possession.[88] This pardon is in line with the Letters Patent granted by the King dated 9th June 1509 absolving the City of all trespasses committed before the date of his accession.[89] The Company also possesses the exemplifications of the Patents of Edward VI, Philip and Mary, and Elizabeth I.[90]

169   *d*   Among the payments made at this time were the following:

Sir Edward Cooke, the King's Attorney, for his fee about our Corporation	£20
His Clerk for drawing of our Corporation, containing 30 sheets at 2s. the sheet	£3
Engrossing the same for the King Majesty's hand	50s.
Signification of the Petition to the King and Bill signed by the King	£15
The Signet and Privy Seal and twice engrossing same	£15
The Great Seal to our Incorporation	£8 13s. 4d.
'Divident' and Enrollment	£4
Engrossing the Corporation and for 2 Vellum skins	£3 15s.
A Fine taxed by the Lord Chancellor for Confirmation of our Liberties	£8
Mr Raby for Prosecuting our Corporation	£13 6s. 8d.
Mr Wilbraine for Englishing our Corporation and writing	30s.

171   *k*   See T.C.C.R. p. 171. The bargin is referred to in *London and the Kingdom*, Vol. II, p. 88, and also in the *Analytical Index to the Remembrancia*, p. 116.

172   *n*   The precise manner in which the agreement was carried out, with a copy of the deed dated 14th December 1618, is given in *T.C.C.R.*, pp. 172–3.

II

174   *a*   'Every person and persons of the said Commonalty shall be of good and honest behaviour and bearing as well in their words as in their deeds towards the Master, Wardens and Assistants of the

Commonalty of the said Craft or Mystery and all that be put in authority over them in the said Company and be and show him and themselves tractable, conformable and obedient touching all and every their lawful constitutions, ordinances, causes and matters concerning the said Craft'. The article goes on to deal with wilful obstinancy, or disobedience and the 'let hindrance or disturbance' of the officers in their duties.

179   c   It included three members of the Company who later became Master, viz. Henry Hawkes (1692–3), William Gaunt (1696–7) and Josiah Ragdale (1703–4).

179   d   An 'ordinance' enjoyning members of other companies using the Art or Trade of candlemaking to bind their apprentices to a member of the Tallow Chandlers Company is referred to at this time, but it seems that it can only have been a draft. As early as July 1674, however, the Court of Aldermen had had under consideration a Petition of the Wheelwrights Company which included a provision that all apprentices to the Wheelwrights' trade should be bound in that Company.[91]

182   e   The twelve were to be chosen out of *twenty-four* Candlemakers of the said Assistants or Livery presented to the Court 'by such of the members of the said Company as shall for the time being be of the Livery'.

183   f   The Charter contains the following additional powers, viz. (1) power to 'the Master, Wardens and Commonalty and their successors' to make ordinances (2) All officers are to assist in the execution of the Ordinances, and (3) all Charters are to be construed in favour of the Company.

184   h   Before the grant of their Charter in 1638 members of the trade pursued their craft in London through the freedom of other companies. The Court of Aldermen refused to enrol the charter on the grounds that it would weaken other companies, of which distillers were then members. Even threats that failure would be regarded as contempt of the royal command did not move the City, and the charter was not enrolled in the Chamber of London until 17th March 1658.[92]

185   i   It was ordered that they should be 'placed and take their degrees' among the fifty-seven Assistants in positions indicated, which resulted in three of them taking the thirteenth, fourteenth and fifteenth places, while two took the twenty-second and twenty-third places, one took the twenty-sixth and one the twenty-eighth place.

185   j   The Drapers, Merchant Taylors, Haberdashers, Salters and Clothworkers.

185   k   The Barber-Surgeons, Blacksmiths, Bowyers, Broderers, Curriers, Cutlers, Farriers, Girdlers, Leathersellers, Shipwrights, and Stationers.

186   l   One of the oldest offices under the Crown, and usually attached to the palace of the Sovereign. *Wheatley.*

III

187   a   An Act passed in 1661 which prevented anyone from holding a municipal office unless he renounced the covenant, took the oath of non-resistance, and received the sacrament according to the rites of the Church of England.[93]

188   b   No copy of this writ is extant, but there is little doubt that it was in the same form as those writs served on other companies, of which particulars are available.[94]

188   c   According to the minutes the 'tickets' bore the following surprising message. 'Pray fail not. The business of the last Court could not be despatched for want of a full court'.[95]

188   d   The Drapers Company was one of these.[96]

189   e   John Marsh was first elected Clerk, on the retirement of Thomas Worseley, in 1645 and served until 1662 when he was succeeded by John Maxfield. He returned as Clerk in 1676 when Maxfield, who had misconducted himself, surrendered his office. He was elected to the Livery in 1655 and became Master in 1690.

189   f   After reciting the 'Surrender', which the King accepted, His Majesty willed that 'ever taking into consideration *the Improvement of the Company* . . . all and each of the Freemen of the Mystery . . . should be . . . one Body Corporate and politic . . . under the name of Master, Wardens and Commonalty of the Society of Tallow Chandlers of the City of London'. The Master and Wardens were to be subject to annual election. The Assistants were to number twenty-two, or, at most, thirty-one, and were appointed for life unless removed by the King for 'bad administration' or other reasonable cause. The appointment of the Clerk had to be approved by the King and he might be removed. The Charter included provisions for admitting to the Freedom all persons exercising the Trade of a tallow chandler within three miles of the City, and for the appointment of candle-makers as scrutineers, with power to destroy bad candles.

191   h   In a Precept dated 9th October 1688 addressed to each company, we were informed of the King's action in restoring the City's franchises and that he had 'directed that the Lord Mayor for the year ensuing shall forthwith be elected *in the manner heretofore accustomed before the Judgment upon the Quo Warranto*'. Sheriffs also remained to be elected 'by the Mayor & Comminalty & Citizens for the present year'. The Master and Wardens were, therefore, to cause all our Liverymen to come together in their Livery Gowns to Guildhall on Thursday morning next at 9 of the clock, there to make the said Eleccions in manner heretofore accustomed within this City And also to choose Chamberlain and Bridge Ma[rs] for this present yeare.[97]

IV

196   b   The name is a corruption of Blemundsbury, the manor of the De Blemontes, Blemunds or Blemmots. Blemund's Dyche, which

was afterwards called Bloomsbury Great Ditch, and Southampton Sewer divided the two manors of St Giles and Bloomsbury. *Wheatley.*

196   *c*   Indictment. A written accusation of one or more persons of a crime or misdemeanor, preferred to, and presented upon oath by, a grand jury. *Blackstone Commentaries*, Fifth Edition, Book IV, p. 302.

WIND OF CHANGE

I

198   *a*   Waltham & Austin's case, 'no forfeiture can be imposed on the goods of a subject'. 8th Part, Reports of Sir Edward Coke, 125a, Vol. IV, pp. 386–400.

198   *b*   The Goldsmiths' and Fishmongers' Companies were exceptions. The former conducted searches until the first quarter of the eighteenth century. The latter, at the beginning of that century, was 'an uneasy union' of City merchants, who held the high offices of the Company and the trading fishmongers, who were retail and wholesale dealers in fish.[99]

198   *c*   They consisted of eight of the older incorporations, viz. the Cutlers, Cordwainers, Girdlers, Tallow Chandlers, Dyers, Carpenters, Bakers and Coopers (Vol. III, Appendix D), the remaining six being the Stationers, Blacksmiths and Painters (Ibid), and the Upholders, Glaziers and Horners (See Appendix L, Part I.)

198   *d*   Not strictly accurate in the case of the Tallow Chandlers, as we know.

199   *e*   He goes on to relate that 'after all this, it was found that the Law was too short to pull down houses that were already built, . . . And all they could do was to inflict Punishment upon such as had built contrary to the Queen's Proclamation, . . . But such flocking there was notwithstanding to the City continually . . . that the Queen's successor, King James the First, in the first year of his reign, set forth his Proclamation dated 16th September 1603 'against Inmates and Multitudes of Dwellers in straight rooms and Places', which have been 'one of the chief occasions of plague and mortality', in which directions were given that 'no new Tenants or Inmates or other persons be admitted to inhabit or reside' in any place infected by 'Plague', and giving permission to pull down such dwellings. He also refers to an Act of Parliament in 1656 made for 'preventing the multiplicity of Buildings in and about the suburbs and within ten miles thereof'.

200   *g*   'Apprentices enrolled are not to be made Free by Patrimony'.

201   *h*   'Foreign' butchers had a privileged position for a time, doubtless in order to maintain an adequate supply of meat, but as we have seen, their activities were most strictly controlled.

201   *i*   The Statute of York passed in the Parliament of 1335 (anno 9 Edward III) permitted 'free trade to natives and foreigners alike, *notwithstanding previous charters*.[100] By letters patent of the same King (26th March 1337) the citizens were to have all their liberties and free customs uninjured and entire 'as before these times they more freely had the same',[101] but in 1351 the 'ordinance' of 1335 in favour of foreign merchants was confirmed, and their rights were again preserved by a statute passed in 1406 (anno 7 Henry IV).[102] In the following year the King 'willed (in response to a prayer to the Commons) that the citizens should enjoy *the same liberties as before the statute*, a privilege which Edward IV confirmed in the first charter of his reign.

204   *l*   The entry reads '1602 Aug. 31. Received of Thomas Shelton for setting a Foreigner at work contrary to the Ordinances of the House a fine of 5*s*.'[103]

206   *n*   A maker of 'point-lace'=thread lace made wholly with the needle. *O.E.D.*

208   *o*   Translation—The transfer of a freeman from one mistery to another (see Volume III, p. 23). Translations became popular about the year 1575 and they are recorded in the *Repertory* Book continuously for close on one hundred years, after which they became much less common.

208   *p*   1663 May 23. An Act of Common Council for the Translation of all Persons that keep Inns, Osteries* or Livery-Stables within this City and Liberties into the Company of Innholders.[104]

209   *q*   The Order is given in the minutes[105] with the following heading:

Att the Court att Whitehall
the 31st August 1664
Present
The King's Most Excellent Majesty

His Royall Highness ye Duke of Yorke	Earle of Anglesey
	Lord Bishop of London
His Highness Prince Rupert	Lord Wentworth
Lord Bishop of Canterbury	Lord Berkeley
Lord Chancellor	Lord Ashley
Lord Privie Seale	Mr Treasurer
Duke of Buckingham	Mr Vice Chamberlain
Duke of Albermarle	Mr Secretary Morrice
Duke of Ormonde	Mr Secretary Bennett
Lord Chamberlain	Mr Chancellor of ye
Earle of Berkshire	Dutchy

Sir Edward Nichols

210   *t*   For some reason William Gale's name is not included.

210   *u*   It is over forty years before we hear of another translation from our Company to the Innholders. In June 1708[106] we read that the

---

* Obs. ff. Hostry. A hostelry. *O.E.D.*

Master and Wardens, having been summoned to attend the translation of one Henry Woolhead 'a member of this Company which now keepeth the Bell Inn in Aldersgate Street',* appeared before the Court of Aldermen with the evident intention of lodging a protest, 'but, being well assured that ye said Company of Innholders had for many years past obtained an Act of Common Council for translating into their Company all persons who should keep common Inns' they remained to subscribe their names as witnesses to 'an instrument which was delivered unto Mr Thomas Allen, now Clerk' of that Company.

213   *v*   This Company, although not incorporated until 1677, appears to have led the field in obtaining one of the new Acts of Common Council which were to become so popular.

213   *w*   The Wheelwrights and Glaziers both received their Orders in 1692.

213   *x*   The Masons Act is dated 11th September 1694[107] and the Plaisterers the 19th October 1694.[108] The Tallow Chandlers Company received notice in July 1694 of a Bill presented by the Joiners, as well as by the Plaisterers,[109] but no copy of the Joiners Act is available.

213   *y*   See the order dated 19th November 1700 jointly in favour of the Glaziers and Tallow Chandlers (infra).

213   *z*   This provision seems to have been inserted to cover the absence of the Father's 'copy' to prove his son's entitlement. A case was reported in the early 'fifties of the sixteenth century of a son having been admitted 'by his Father's copy', though it could not be found,[110] but no record has been traced of a son having been admitted 'by redemption' in such circumstances.

214   *aa*   We regret having no explanation to offer for this joint action, unless it was to save expense.

II

220   *d*   In an Inquisition, 3 Ed. I, mention is made of water coming down from Smethefeld del Barbican in the Ward of Cripplegate towards the Moor over which an arch of stone had been erected at the White Cross, occasioning a stoppage of the water on account of its narrowness, quoted by Strype, ed. 1720, l. iii. 88 . . . Its position, as set out above, indicates that it may well have given its name to Whitecross Street. *Harben.*

220   *e*   The French weavers settled in this part when they came over in the seventeenth century during the religious persecutions, but they were followed gradually by Jews, many of them sellers of old clothes, etc., and the street at one time had a low reputation. From *Harben.*

---

* On the east side, south of Barbican (Ogilby and Morgan's Map, 1677).

220   *f*   The offender declared that he was advised 'by a member of the
Company, and a man of Fortune, to enter the shop in his own
name', as he might stand a chance in proper time to gain the privilege of exercising the Trade, 'tho at first he entered the House in
the name of Thomas Simmons a drunken journeyman'.[111]

III

226   *a*   Apart from the Tin Plate Workers and Upholders, for which
companies no reference in the *Journals* has been found, the order
in which the Companies obtained their Acts with the *Journal*
references, is as follows:

Scriveners	J. 59, fo(s)	38–40[b]	Blacksmiths	J. 63 fo(s)	109	
Bakers	,,	90	Poulters	,,	128	
Cooks	,,	92	Armourers &			
Founders	,,	93–5[b]	Brasiers	,,	299	
Brewers	,,	101–3	Clockmakers	,,	314–6	
Plumbers	,,	184	Cordwainers	65	237	
Cutlers	61	116–8	Saddlers	,,	256	
Apothecaries	,,	308	Distillers	66	132[b]	
Farriers	,,	314	Leatherellers	67	133[b]	
Feltmakers	62	17–19	Tallow			
Painter-Stainers	,,	145[b]	Chandlers	69	69–82	

Printed lists give Tin Plate Workers, 1750, and Upholders, 1759,
as the years in which their Acts were obtained.[112]

227   *c*   The cases of the Farriers and the Distillers in particular are cited
in *the Breakdown of Gild and Corporation Control over the Handicraft
and Retail Trade of London*, pp. 390–92.

Appendix A

THE YEOMANRY

Most of the early craft guilds had a number of members who, although householders, belonged to a separate body known as the Yeomanry.[a] But these more prosperous members—many of whom were later to become Liverymen—formed only part of the organization. It also comprised apprentices (recently out of their articles and now freemen), small traders (generally shop-keepers), and journeymen. The new freemen were usually encouraged to work at a trade as employees before setting up in business for themselves, when they might expect to be called to the Livery. The small men had little prospect of joining them, while the journeymen were likely to remain servants all their working lives.

The freemen were recognized in a special way in our Ordinances of 1589, Article 22 of which authorized the Master, Wardens and Assistants within one month before the Feast of St Simon and St Jude (28th October) yearly

to appointe electe and choose by their discretions out of the younger sorte of freemen of the Cominaltie of the said Crafte or Misterie of Tallowechaundelers certaine persons of the yeomanrie . . . viz. foure sixe or eighte for to bee *bachelers* to geeue their attendaunce and to waighte uppon the maister, wardens and assistauntes . . . at suche tyme as the Lorde Mayer of the said Cyttie of London shall take his oathe for that office at Westminster or els where.

It was the duty of these bachelors to contribute towards the charges of a dinner on the Lord Mayor's day, and those refusing to take office and to contribute were fined.

---

a   See Vol. III, pp. 77–8 and Appendix F.

In our Company's case, as with some others, this independent body was self-governing, having its own funds and keeping its own accounts. In the remaining companies the Yeomanry, although organized up to a point, appears to have stopped short of full government.[1]

It was from the last class of members—the journeymen—that a certain amount of trouble was experienced in some companies. The best known case is probably that of the 'yeomen-taillours', so called, who came before the Mayor and Aldermen in 1415 on a complaint of having 'consorted together in dwellinghouses, behaving in an unruly manner' and assaulting one of the 'masters' of the mistery. The Master and Wardens, on appearing before the Mayor and Aldermen 'to answer for their want of control over their servants and journeymen, expressed both their regret at the state of affairs *and their inability to put a stop to it*'! The offenders were ordered to cease consorting, and the Court ordained 'that henceforth the servants of the said mistery should be under the rule and governance of the Masters and Wardens, *like servants of other misteries*, and that *they should cease to use a livery or clothing* at their un-lawful assemblies'.[2] It is gratifying to relate that there seems to have been no case of insubordination in the ranks of our yeomanry of sufficient importance to be reported in the *Letter Books* or in our own minutes. It is true that in the summer of 1518 our Master and Wardens were presented with a number of proposals for regulating the conduct of members and the privileges granted to them by their superiors, and that an agreement setting out the terms was duly sealed by the Master and Wardens 'with thassent & consent of the holle clothyng' on the one hand and by the Governor and Wardens of the Yeomanry on the other. Of the fifteen articles, the first seven and part of the eighth have, unhappily, been torn away, but, in those that have survived, there is no evidence of revolt. The last article reads as follows:[3]

More over we dyssyuer and humble requere of your mastershipis to have lyberte to assemble at the hall at all tymes convenyent & nessessarye & in esspecyall to have *the chambre or galarye over the hall dores* severall to us with looke and key that we maye ther set out suche stoffe or goodes perteynyng or bylongyng to our brethered as, by the grace of god and the helpe and suportacion of your good mastershipis, herafter we shall have, *provyded all waye* that the Master or Wardens or ther wyffs for them and ther frendes *shall have the same chamber or galary at ther comaundment at anye tyme, ther to take ther plessers or comandmenttes*

The names of the Governors of the Yeomanry commencing with Richard Choppyn, who with the two Wardens, was a party to the agreement, are extant from 1518 to 1539. After this there is a hiatus until 1552, as from which date, with very few exceptions, the list is complete until 1695.

The Governor and Wardens presided over a Court of Assistants, in accordance with the pattern set by the Company proper. The men elected to be Master had in many cases served first as Governor, and, commencing early in the seventeenth century, Governors had frequently only a year or two to wait before assuming the senior office.

A number of associates, or 'sociates' (as they were known), were required to attend the Wardens in their duties. They were appointed by the Court of Yeomanry and could be fined by that Court for refusing to serve. They were provided with white staves and ribbons on ceremonial occasions.[4]

As we know, the Yeomanry had a close bond with a religious fraternity (distinct from that with which the Company proper was associated) known as 'the fraternity of our Lady and Saint Elizabeth' founded in the Church of St Botolph Without Bishopsgate, where their members worshipped (Volume III, pp. 34–5). There are several reminders of these members' piety in the early Yeomanry accounts, including payments for torches and for wax and to the priests 'for keeping the mass'.

In June 1660 a Committee was appointed by the Court of Assistants 'to advise and consider the business of the Yeomanry and of the usefulness, benefit and advantage which arises thereby, or whether it will not be more advantage to the Company to dissolve them'.[5] The organization was given a reprieve, but in March 1696 the conclusion was reached that the Court of Yeomanry should be 'suspended'.[6] It was accordingly ordered to be 'suspended and discontinued' as from the following 24th

June[b] and all quarterage money collected thereafter from 'yeomen members' was directed to be applied by the Master and Wardens for the use of the Company.[7] The services of the sociates were retained for the Company. In July 1711, however, the Court of Assistants had occasion to take notice of their 'great disorder and misbehaviour', particularly on Lord Mayor's day, with the result that eight Freemen of the Company 'of honest, sober and good report' were appointed 'to perform the said office on the Lord Mayor's day next', when they were admonished to be of good behaviour, carrying nothing such as victuals, pewter or linen out of the Hall! It would appear from this entry that the sociates, of whom we first hear in 1553, had later taken over the duty of the bachelors in contributing to the dinner.

---

[b]   The Clerk, Gilbert Brandon, was ordered to 'provide and make ready one large Book wherein shall be written the names of all the yeomen-members as well now or hereafter to be admitted, giving their Trades, places of abode and dates of their admission. (At Guildhall Library, Ms. 6164, Vol. I., 1694–1725.)

Appendix B

THE LIVERY OR CLOTHING

The term 'livery' originally meant the allowance in provisions and clothing made to the servants and officers of great households. It was gradually restricted to the gift of *clothing* as a badge of service, and this custom, which was copied by the religious fraternities, with which the early craft guilds were closely linked, later gave the guilds their name of 'Livery Companies'. The livery, in which their members came to be clothed, consisted of a gown and a hood, although in the earliest ordinances a distinction is drawn between those who only wore the hood and those who took the whole suit.[1] Stow tells us that 'in London amongst the grauer sort (I meane the Liveries of Companies) remayneth a memory of the hoodes of olde time worne by their predecessors: These hoodes were worne, the Roundelets vpon their heads, the skirts to hang behind in their neckes to keep them warme, the tippet to lye on their shoulder, or to wind about their necks . . .'[2] There are two recorded cases in our Wardens' accounts of the sixteenth century of Liverymen being *deprived of their hoods*. In May 1565[3] an Assistant's Livery Hood was taken away from him for 'a misdemeanour used against one of the Yeomanry'. Ten years later it was agreed that a Liveryman's 'Hood or Livery' should remain in the House, and he was dismissed of the Livery for contempt 'until that he shall appear to have reformed himself and become obedient as he ought'.[4] The liveries were traditionally of two colours which the companies were accustomed to change from time to time, the members of some of the wealthier guilds having a new livery every year. In 1476 the Goldsmiths and the Fishmongers appear to have consulted together about their respective colours.[5] There are infrequent records in our accounts of a change of Livery, the first of which occurs in May 1545, when the Wardens 'concluded upon a new Livery of the colour of puce' (presumably the principal colour),[6] the next ocasion being in April ten years later, when it was agreed 'that there shall be a Livery gown given (sic) to the whole Company against midsummer next'.[7] In our Ordinances of 1589 (Article 31) it was ordained

that euerie eighte yere at the furthest . . . euerie one beeinge of the liverie of the Cominaltie of the said Crafte or Mysterie of Tallowechaundelors shall *make him* a newe liverie gowne decentelie *accordinge to the usuall manner of wearinge of the Cominaltie* . . . and that the maister and wardens for the tyme beeinge or some of them, associate withe three or foure or more of the aunciente assistauntes . . . shall or maye at their libertie and pleasure *buy a whole piece or two of broade clothe or lesse then a whole piece, to thend that euerie person beeinge of the said liverie that will, and all other thereunto enabled, may come and fetche of the same a gowne clothe* at suche reasonable pryce as may bee afoorded. And yf hee or they *like not the clothe* so boughte, then hee or they to take a scantlyn thereof and pay to the maister and wardens for the tyme beinge for a fyne two shillinges of lawefull Englishe money to bee ymployed to the common utilitie benefite and maintenaunce of the Cominaltie . . . and thereuppon shall provide him a gowneclothe elsewhere against the tyme that shalbee to him or them prefixed

Furthermore (by Article 32) every person of the Livery was to keep 'two liveries or gownes allwaies togither . . . his best liverie, and his seconde, and one good and faire hood . . .' failing which he was to forfeit the sum of 3s. 4d. 'for euerie suche defaulte'.

The gowns normally worn by Liverymen were trimmed with budge, a kind of fur consisting of lambskin with the wool dressed outwards.[a] In February 1620 the Lord Mayor issued a Precept 'for reformation of some disorders used in wearing Livery gowns, that the *Master and Wardens* for the time being and all such as have personally borne the place of Master and first or second Wardens shall usually at all public meetings and assemblies wear their gowns faced with Fynes (Appendix C) in the Winter time, and the rest of the Livery shall wear *their gowns faced with Budge* in the Winter season, upon pain of forfeiture of two shillings for every time that any of them shall do the con-

---

a   The word 'budge', of which the etymology is obscure (O.E.D.) is perpetuated in Budge Row, (south-east from Watling Street to Cannon Street) . . . so called, says Stow, 'of Budge, Furre and of *Skinners* dwelling there'. *Harben.*

trary'.[8] In 1686 a Court order of our Company was issued that 'the Assistants and Livery shall, on the Lord Mayor's day and succeeding days of solemnity at their return from Westminster to their Common Hall, always keep themselves clothed in their Livery Gowns and Hoods and not take off the same for, during and until the Assistants and Livery shall have dined . . . under penalty of 12d.'[9] In the accounts for 1691–2 we read that 4s. 6d. was 'paid to three porters for their attendance on this Company to carry and re-carry their gowns at the time of this Company dining with the Lord Mayor'.[10] In 1785 there was an order that 'no person be admitted into the Barge (Appendix K) on Lord Mayor's day without his Livery Gown'.[11]

When warned to attend at St Paul's Church on Lord Mayor's Day and other ceremonial occasions the Company had to hire its own forms on which to sit. In March 1618 the place appointed for the whole Company was so small that the Beadle was directed henceforth to 'warn only half of the Livery at one time . . . except on the Lord Mayor's day' or 'by special order'.[12] At one period the forms were supplied by the bell ringer.[13] In 1628 the charge for the year was 12s.[14] On special occasions when, for instance, the Sovereign visited the City, the venue was St Paul's Cross.[b] In early days such events were given a special name, as mentioned in an Inventory of effects in the Hall in 1555, in which 'five pieces of timber' kept in the Hall yard are said to be 'for the Company to stand on at *Triumphs* in the City'.[15]

A call to the Livery was a command, and a modest fee (or fine) was imposed on acceptance. By Article 29 of the Ordinances of 1589 it was ordered that

euerye two three or foure yeares as occasion shall serue the said Maister Wardens and Assistauntes . . . shall or maie electe or choose into the liverie or clothinge of the Cominaltie of the said Crafte and Misterie of Tallowe Chaundelors suche and so manie of the *yeomanrie of the same Cominaltie* as shall seeme most meete and conveniente to them . . . And yf anie of the Cominaltie . . . so elected and chosen . . . *shall refuse to bee* of the same *liverie* . . . he shall pay for euerie tyme that hee shall refuse the same the somme of fortie shillinges of lawfull Englishe moneye . . .

---

b   As rebuilt c. 1450, this was a pulpit (Dugdale), which was pulled down in 1643 (Strype, ed. 1720). *Harben.*

By 1652 this 40s. fine for not accepting the Livery had been increased to £15,[16] an additional fine being imposed for refusing other offices, including the office of Steward, in which two Liverymen were appointed annually to provide dinner for the Company, as distinct from the Yeomanry (Appendix A) on Lord Mayor's Day. In 1685 there are entries in our minutes recording that delinquents were being brought before the Lord Mayor at that time and bound by recognizance to pay their fines.[17]

In 1772 a number of Liverymen presented a memorial to the Court of Assistants claiming that the Livery had the right to elect the Master and Wardens, as well as the Assistants as vacancies occurred. The dispute lasted for nearly five years and involved the Company in a suit in Chancery in which the claimants were unsuccessful.

Appendix C

THE COURT OF ASSISTANTS

The central and distinctive feature of the London Craft Guild in its fully developed form of a Livery Company was, as Unwin points out,[1] a Court. This body, which in course of time became known as 'the Court of Assistants' was, as we have seen, not just an executive committee. It had (as we know) actual jurisdiction over its members, and even outsiders who were engaged in the same trade.

One of the earliest references to a 'Court of Assistants' in all but name occurs in 1463 in the records of the Mercers Company in which we read that 'for the holdyng of many Courtes and congregacions' according 'hit is tedious & grevous to the body of the felyshipp and specially for maters of no grete effect . . . *hereafter shalbe chosen & associatte* to the Custoses for the tyme beyng, 'xij other sufficiant parsones . . . whan as ofte as they be duly requyred if nede be . . .'[2] The earliest record that we possess of an embryo Court of Assistants in our company is contained in Article 22 of our Ordinances of 1538 in which it was ordained that no man may be received into the Company by redemption . . .

but yf yt be . . . thought by thadvyse of the maister & iiij wardeins & *viij moo of the bodye of the same Crafte* that hath bein wardeins thynkyng by their dyscrecions that the seyd Crafte may be the better in all honestye by hym or theim that so cometh in by redempcion.

This passage supports the view expressed by the writer in Volume III, p. 78, that Group I in the list of members of our Company in 1537–8 consisted of the Master and four Wardens with *ten Assistants*. We read also of 'a Court' held in December 1544 when Thomas Cuttle 'was chosen, made and sworn High Master of the

Company',[3] and from 1565 onwards there are frequent records of Court Meetings. Then, in 1589, we are informed in our new Ordinances (Article 8) that it is 'convenient and necessary' that the Master and Wardens of the Commonalty 'should sufficiently be aided with the advice and good counsel of the grave and wise men of the same'. It is therefore ordered and ordained

That so manie persons of the said Cominaltie as heretofore have beene or shall hereafter beare the office of maister or wardens of the liverie of the said Cominaltie shall from henceforth bee Assistauntes and of the Common Counsell of the Cominaltie . . .

The next step was to bring in, as additional Assistants, others who had not yet served office. Our Ordinances of 1639 accordingly direct (Article 14)

that the Master, Wardens and Assistants of the said Commonalty or the more part of them for the time being shall and may at their free will and pleasure, so often and when as need shall require, nominate, elect and choose such, and so many, honest, able and discreet persons *out of the livery or clothing* of the said Company as they shall think meet to be Assistants to the said Master and Wardens of the said Mystery.

The gowns 'faced with Fynes', or foin gowns, (see Appendix B), in which the Master, Wardens and other senior members of the Court were ordered to robe in accordance with the Precept of 1620 were faced with fur.[a] Our Court order of 1686 contained the further direction that '*all and every the Assistants of this Company* do and shall respectively appear in and be clothed with a Foyne *and not a Budge gown* on the Lord Mayor's oath day next and on all other succeeding days of solemnity whatsoever, under penalty of paying to the Master, etc., for this Company's use, 12d.'. The reason for this decision was that 'it hath been often observed that divers of the Assistants upon their public walks and appearance on days of solemnity being clothed in Budge Gowns and frequently intermixing with the Foyne Gowns greatly lesseneth those other more graceful ornamental habits'.[4]

To advise the Court of Assistants and to keep a record of its proceedings the companies required a 'clerk'. Most of the

---

a   Foin: in *plural*, trimmings or garments made of fur . . . foins-gown, one trimmed with fur. *O.E.D.*

greater companies probably had clerks from the beginning of the fifteenth century, but in the majority of the lesser companies the need for a clerk was not imperatively felt till the middle of the sixteenth century, when weekly sittings of the Court began to require a regular record.[5] Our first Clerk, William Wyldys, appears to have been appointed prior to 1530. His office was recognized in our Ordinances of 1538, Article 26 of which required him to read such parts thereof as should be thought by the Master and Wardens 'most mete & convenyent to be redde . . . whereby no persone of the sayd fellowship shall pretende ignoraunce in the same ordennaunces . . .'. The Ordinances of 1589 required the election '(when and as often as yt shall seeme to them expediente and necessarie) of *some honeste discrete and sufficiente Clerke*' (Article 23) to perform the customary duties.

Of all this Company's Clerks the most notable figure is undoubtedly Roger Price the elder, whom we have met on several occasions. He was elected Clerk in December 1607[6] and became an Assistant in July 1615.[7] He resigned his Clerkship in 1635[8] and served as Master of the Company in 1638-9, having been Governor of the Yeomanry two years earlier. His father, John Price, a clothworker by trade,[b] had become our tenant of a house and shop in Fryers Alley (Appendix D) prior to 1575, when he had obtained permission 'to set and fasten a clothworker's press in such place there as may not hurt the same house nor the Common Hall therunto adjoining',[9] a privilege denied to his immediate predecessor.[10] By 1619 Roger himself had become the Company's tenant of 'a messuage (or dwelling house) in the Alley',[11] which he doubtless occupied, but in November of the following year he and his wife and family were permitted by the Court to 'inhabit and dwell within the Hall',[12] (Appendix D), and in June of the following year an order was made allowing him to 'dwell in the Hall for life, he having made a fit dwelling therein . . .' and having 'disbursed £80 and odd pounds' on the premises.[13] A few years earlier he had acquired a lease of the Company's

---

b   *The Compleat Cook, by Rebecca Price*, introduced by Madeleine Masson. (Family Tree of Rebecca Price, pp. viii, ix).

property in Soaphouse Alley, afterwards Sweet Apple Court, (p.27), which later became his family home.[15] He is believed to have been the first of our Clerks to reside in the Hall. On resigning his Clerkship in 1635 he agreed to deliver up possession,[16] but there appears to be no evidence of his immediate successor, Thomas Worseley, occupying the premises. A later successor, John Marsh, (when in his second term of office) was, however, living there at the time of the Great Fire.[17] John Maxfield (Clerk from 1662 to 1676) rented one of the Company's new houses on Dowgate Hill after the Fire, and he appears to have lived there until his death some thirteen years later. Marsh moved into the house vacated by Maxfield's widow,[18] and the Beadle (William Gurney), who at that time was living in another of the Dowgate Hill houses, was given accommodation in the Hall,[19] which became the Beadle's permanent home. (See Appendix D and Plate V.)

Appendix D

THE HALL

We know that in December 1464, less than three years after the Company's incorporation, we were occupying a Hall which bore our name, but which we probably rented, at the junction of Throgmorton Street and Old Broad Street, close to Austin Friars.[a] We do not know how long we had been there, nor do we know for certain when we left, but it seems a fair assumption that we remained there until ready to move to Dowgate Hill, where we have had our home for over five hundred years.

On 9th March 1476 John Seman and other citizens and tallow chandlers of London entered into a contract with Dame Margaret Alley, widow of Alderman Sir Richard Alley, and others (his executors) for the purchase of 'all the londes *and tenements*' etc. 'in the parish of Seint John upon Walbroke of London, which late were the said Richard Alley's *holy*, with all their appurtenances'.[1] The original contract and all the important title deeds commencing in the year 1335, some of them bearing the seals of the highest in the land (Plate III) are in the Company's possession.[b] The property cost us £166 13s. 4d., of which £100 was payable in ten annual instalments.

For its exact situation we turn first to the grant by which the legal estate was conveyed on 2nd July 1476 to John Priour (or Prior) and eight others, on the Company's behalf.[2] The southern boundary is described as 'the common hall belonging to the commonalty of the mistery of Skinners of London'. On the east is 'the king's

---

a   *Commentary*, p. 282.

b   For an abstract of these deeds see *T.C.C.R.*, Appendix A.

way of Walbroke' (better known as 'the highway leading
from the street of Wallebrok to the gate of Douegate'ᶜ while
on the west is 'the foss of Walbroke'. For the northern boundary
it is best to refer to two earlier records, first, a deed dated 18th
July 1441 made between Thomas Peverell and his wife of the one
part and members of the family of Thornbury (or rather their
'feofees')ᵈ of the other,[3] and secondly a deed dated 28th March
1452 of which the contracting parties were Richard and William
Thornbury and one Richard Peverell.[4] By the earlier deed the
Thornburys acquired

eight messuages and eight shops thereto adjoining and annexed, in the parish
of St John on Walbrook on the south side of the Church of St John aforesaid
extending from a certain great place called Skynners Halle to *Horshobrigge*
there.

The second deed is a conveyance *by the Thornburys* to Richard
Peverell of

five tenements . . . between the ditch called Walbroke at Horshobrigge on
the west and a street leading from the said church towards Dowgate on the
east . . . situate on the *north side* of the said tenements, and *opposite* lands and
tenements belonging to the said Richard and William Thornbury . . . on the
south . . .

The site purcased by our Company in 1476 was accordingly somewhat less than that acquired by the Thornburys in 1441.

Peverell's purchase deed contains a valuable piece of information regarding the property *retained by the Thornburys*, which was
later to pass into our hands. In giving the measurements, it mentions a Hall,ᵉ which was an essential feature of a London merchant's house of the period, and by a strange coincidence we have
a perfect example in the property known as Asselyn's (or Pake-
nam's) wharf in Thames Street, erected in or about 1384 by
Richard Willysdon (or Willesdone) *tallow chandler*, whom we
recognize as one of our earliest representatives on the Common

---

c   *Commentary*, p. 283.

d   or 'feeofees to uses'= trustees.

e   Thus in longitudine a dicto fossato (Walbrook) usque et *in medium aule* tenementorum
     nostrum dictorum Ricardi Thornbury et Willielmi versus orientem . . . *T.C.C.R.*
     Appendix A, pp. 189–91.

Council.[f] His lease required him to pull down existing buildings and to erect 'a chief dwelling-place, *to wit a Hall*, 40 feet in length and 24 feet in breadth, with a suitable parlour, kitchen and buttery', and on the rest of the site there were to be 'chambers and houses for merchandise'. These and other features, mentioned in a later deed, follow the usual plan of such houses, in which the street frontage was occupied by subordinate tenements with a gate-house giving access to the main Court, round which were grouped the Hall and other buildings.[5] The information to be derived from our own records is, in the main, confined to inventories of chattels in the various rooms, of which the earliest is dated 28th November 1549[6] and to entries of repairs and improvements. But this information, coupled with the mention of a Hall on our site in 1452, makes it reasonably certain that we acquired, with the land conveyed to us in 1476, just such a group of buildings as those erected on Thames side by Willesdone in the 'eighties of the previous century. We know that seven years later we were one of twenty-six craft guilds having halls, for a list of which the reader is referred to Appendix J. Stow, writing over a century later, names forty-six companies with halls, and the Tallow Chandlers share with the Goldsmiths[7] and the Founders[8] the distinction of having their Hall referred to as 'a proper house'.

The land retained by Peverell in 1452 extended *north* to 'the street leading from the Church towards Dowgate', which appears to have borne the name 'Horshewbridge', or Horseshoebridge, Street. *To the south was Cloak Lane* marking our northern boundary,[g] in which was Friar's, or Fryers, Alley with its gate-house (known earlier as 'Chaundellers Aley')[9] leading from the Hall. Here were several tenements, first mentioned in our earliest surviving rent roll in June 1555,[10] and an inn, with 'the sign of the Friar', from which the alley took its name.[11] In 1639 the well in the alley was replaced by a pump because of the danger to children playing there.[12]

---

f   Volume II, pp. 65, 79, 80, 115.

g   Commentary, p. 283.

We know from the Inventory of 1549 that the Hall then consisted of 'a Chamber', a Parlour, a Livery Hall (although not so
named), a Court House (or Masters' Court House, as it was sometimes called), a Kitchen, a Buttery and a Pastry;[h] as well as a dry
Larder or Larder 'House', and a wet Larder (where moist or
liquid provisions were stored), to which are added in an inventory dated 10th August 1551[13] a 'Compting' House and a Harness
Chamber. We learn from the accounts for the period 1544 to
1545 that the *Yeomanry* have lately contributed towards the Company's charges,[14] and when, in August 1545, we read of the
'*roofing* (or re-roofing) *of the chamber*',[15] it becomes apparent that
this was '*the chamber or gallery over the hall doors*' which they were
given permission to use in 1518 (Appendix A). Mention is made
in the accounts for 1561-2 of '*the great chamber over the parlour* and
of the stairs leading thereto, at the upper end of which, and in
the Chamber, were 'racks to hang links upon'.[16] In a minute
dated 22nd October 1569 there is a resolution for taking down
these two rooms, which were evidently situated on the north,
or '*masters*', side of the Court Yard (as it was called), and raising
them and building them new again.[17] The cost of these and other
works ran into several hundred pounds, most of the money being
advanced by Arthur Lee, one of the Wardens, whose 'gentleness'
was gratefully acknowledged.[18] While the works were proceeding the Cutlers Company, whose Hall was close by in Cloak Lane,
permitted us to bake in their ovens, for which they made a
modest charge.[19] It appears from the accounts that the Compting
House, which was evidently situated on the opposite side of the
Court Yard, was re-constructed at this time.[20] In 1572 'the removing of the kitchen and new building of the same and making a
Court House for the yeomanry' was undertaken.[21] This new
kitchen is later referred to as 'the Great Kitchen'[22] and was probably constructed below the Livery Hall, occupying the west end
of the site, adjoining Skinners Hall, as it does today. The Court
House, to the building of which the Yeomanry contributed,[23]

---

h   A place where pastry is made. *Obs. O.E.D.*

evidently replaced the Yeomanry 'Chamber over the hall doors' and it appears to have adjoined the Compting House. We hear later of an Armoury, or Armoury House,[24] and a Powder House.[25]

The cost of 'paving the street before the Hall', as well as the entry, fell upon the Company.[26] There is a brief reference in 1562 to a garden,[27] but the ground was probably quite small, as was usual with such houses, in which most of the open space was taken up by a court yard. Our yard was paved[28] and possessed a pump.[29] Two of the early inventories include 'a pair of stocks',[30] but their presence is not explained. It is evident from the accounts that good care was usually taken of the buildings, but there was an exception in 1662 when we read that the Court has taken notice 'that the tiling of the Hall . . . and the several rooms . . . is very much decayed . . . and that it doth rain into the Hall and other rooms'. The Renter Warden was desired to see that the necessary works were carried out,[31] and the accounts reveal the expenditure of over £20, which included breakfasts.[32]

We know that the Livery Hall was wainscotted, that the wainscotting was coloured,[33] and that the room had a white plaster ceiling.[34] It appears to have had an ornamental screen,[35] a familiar feature in livery company halls—but of this we have no details. The Court House—later enlarged and re-named 'the Court Room'[36]—and the Parlour, both had plaster ceilings,[37] both rooms were wainscotted, and the wainscot in the Parlour, like that in the Livery Hall, was coloured.[38] Under the Yeomanry Court House and the Compting House there appears to have been a covered 'walk',[39] the inside wall of which was wainscotted[40] and coloured,[41] the other side of the walk having pillars and being open to the Court Yard.[42]

There were four houses on the street—two on each side of the entrance to the Court Yard.[43] A Beadle's house is mentioned several times and it seems certain that he occupied the one immediately to the south of the entrance.[44] We know also that after the Great Fire, William Gurney, Beadle, was given temporary accommodation in the newly built house on that site.[45] (See Plate V.) It appears also that for many years the Company's Beadle had had the use of a shop,[46] and we read that immediately after the Fire it was ordered

that a shed shall, at the charge of the Company, be erected within the ruins of their Common Hall, wherein the said Beadle may dwell and inhabit during the pleasure of the Court, and may therein sell drink and chandlery ware during so long time as to this Court shall seem convenient.

The first we hear of accommodation at the Hall being provided for the Clerk is in 1619 (Appendix C), when the Court 'viewed the several rooms' and found that, if he would 'bestow some cost therein' a convenient house might be made 'on the Masters' side'.[47] The position chosen was the ground floor below the Parlour, where, after the Fire, the *Beadle* was to make his home (see Plate V). Price was encouraged to provide 'two double shutting doors' for this dwelling at his own cost[48]

because the way into the Hall lieth open for all passengers out of the gate, which is very inconvenient.

The various rooms do not appear to have been elaborately furnished to judge from the early inventories. In the Livery Hall in 1549[49] there was a long table called 'the high table', for which there were 'three trestles (meaning three legged stools or seats) and two 'joined' forms.[i] There was also a long side table having three joined feet, with 'two forms to that table' and another side table with two trestles, and there were several joined stools. 'A great carpet' was provided for the high table, which, being old and moth eaten (according to the inventory) was replaced two years later by a carpet of silk (so called) 'lined with linen'.[50] In the Parlour there were tables and trestles and one 'joined' chair, with a carpet for one of the tables. The window had two old curtains of buckram.[j] There were six 'quysshens' and hangings 'round about'. In the Court House there was 'an old long table with two trestles'. Two benches were provided, and there were 'two pieces of hangings'. The inventory mentions 'a great ship chest with a

---

i   Furniture made by a joiner. *e.g.* a joined (or joint) stool: a stool made by a joiner, as distinguished from one of clumsy workmanship. *O.E.D.*

j   In early times, a costly and delicate fabric, sometimes of cotton and sometimes of linen. *O.E.D.*

bar of iron' and another ship chest (in the Parlour), each with its
lock and key. In the Chamber there was a joined bedstead, with
two long tables, two trestles and two forms. In 1599[51] the Hall is
seen to be a little better furnished. In the Livery Hall, for instance,
a 'foot piece before the high table' has been added, and there are
curtains, one of 'green say'[k] and the other red, but we miss the
carpet. The Court House is better equipped and boasts a carpet
and twelve green cushions, as well as nine old cushions of tapes-
try. But it is not until 1645 that we read of the purchase of three
leather chairs.[52]

Notwithstanding the plainness of the furniture, the rooms were
not lacking in ornament. We notice in the inventory of 1549 (for
the first time) 'a gilt beam'[l] with five candlesticks[m] having 'an
image of our Lady gilt with a *dove* and four chains long and short'.
Six years later[53] we read of a 'scutcheon' (or shield) with three
turtles (meaning turtle doves!) in the Parlour. The doves figure
again in the Yeomanry inventory at the turn of the century.[54]
There is a 'fair new carpet of broad cloth', the gift of one of the
Wardens, 'which cloth hath embroidered upon it, in the midst,
the Queen's Arms, and at each end three pigeons (!) embroidered
with silk and silver, compassed within a border'; and 'it hath at
each end a fringe of blue silk and white silk'. At the same time
'the beam candlestick with pigeons' is 'repaired, gilded and bur-
nished'. Portraits of Henry VIII, Edward VI and Elizabeth are
mentioned in the inventories,[55] as well as various Coats of Arms
and armorial bearings. Frequent references are made to the Hall
windows, some of which undoubtedly contained heraldic painted
glass. The Parlour, in particular, is said to have had 'four panes
with arms standing in the window'.[56] The Arms of London figure
in a streamer in 1559.[57] In the accounts for 1597–8[58] there is a

---

k   Say: a cloth of fine texture resembling serge—in the sixteenth century sometimes
partly of silk, subsequently entirely of wool. *O.E.D.*

l   Candle-beam. 1. The name given to a beam between the chancel and the nave of a
church on which the rood stood with candles placed on each end of it. 2. *A suspended
beam of wood to support a number of candles.* 1552 Huloet, 'candle-beam, such as hangeth
in gentlemen's halles with socketts to set candels vpon'. *O.E.D.*

m   Later described as 'laten' candle-sticks. Latten: a mixed metal of yellow colour,
either identical with, or closely resembling brass.

payment of 4s. 8d. 'for a curtain of green say and for hooks to the same to hang before the Arms of the House'. In 1631[59] the Company was given a fair taffety[n] curtain as an ornament 'to cover the Arms of this Incorporation' which were fastened over the Parlour door, and the accounts for 1662-3[60] record the purchase of Charles II's Arms 'for the Hall'. It seems likely that prior to 1597[61] it had become the practice (as it is today) to record somewhere in the Hall the names of the Masters of the Company, for we read of a payment of £3 3s. to the Painter 'for new trimming the Arms of the House and *for trimming the letters of the names over the wainscot in the Court House with gold*'.

The Company was proud of its banners, streamers and flags. In the accounts for 1567-8[62] we note the purchase of blue and crimson sarsenet[o] and the payment of £11 'for staining the same silk', which made four long flags, two 'square banners being large', nine 'square banners small' and sixteen 'pencells'[p] of red and blue. The accounts for 1601-2[63] record the payment of 42 shillings for two ells of great taffeta and for fringe and fustian[q] for one of the banners, and in June 1603[64] a total of over £9 was spent on taffeta, sarcenet and fustian for 'the ensign belonging to the Company with their Arms' and for making the same. The charges for James I's banner, banner poles and staves, including twelve staves for the whifflers, again exceeded £9,[65] and further expenditure on streamers and banners is recorded in future years. In 1603[66] a place to hang 'the King's banner and others' was found on the west side of the Livery Hall. The accounts for 1651-2[67] record the purchase of a banner with the Commonwealth Arms at a cost of £5.[r]

The 'fair new carpet' acquired by the Yeomanry in 1600 was

---

n   Taffety (or taffeta): A name applied at different times to different fabrics. In early times apparently a plain-wove glossy silk (of any colour) O.E.D.

o   A very fine and soft silk material made both plain and twilled, in various colours, now used chiefly for lining. S.O.E.D.

p   Pencil, pensel: a small pennon or streamer.

q   Fustian: formerly a kind of coarse cloth made of cotton and flax. O.E.D.

r   On 21st May 1660 these Arms were ordered by the Lord Mayor to be taken out of 'all things' used by our Company (see T.C.C. C.B. 11. 1660, May 21).

not their only treasured possession. For many years they owned a pall cloth, which was permitted to be hired for funerals. The old cloth, first mentioned in 1519,[68] wore out in course of time, and was replaced in 1596[69] by

a Pall cloth of black velvet having on either side two escutchions, two pigeons and one angel and at either end one escutchion, all which are embroidered and have fringe of black silk and silver round about the edge of the same cloth with a piece of cotton to cover all the velvet.

This pall cloth 'lay in a fair square box of wainscot with a lock and key to the same'. The garlands, which are known to have figured in the election of the Governor and Wardens of the Yeomanry from the time when records begin, also played their part. We read in the accounts for 1563–4[70] of

three garlands of green velvet with six pigeons, three escutchions and three roses of silver all gilt weighing three ounces 3 quarters which garlands were of the gift of Walter Westmerland (page 45) then Governor of the Yeomanry, and the pigeons, escutchions and roses were borne out of the money in the Box.

The Company itself also had garlands for its officers, but we have no particulars earlier than 1551. We read then[71] of a payment of 3s. 4d. 'for a St Johns Head of silver and gilt for 4 garlands' and in 1555[72] (and later)[73] of a box with four[s] garlands of *crimson* velvet with twelve turtle doves of silver and four St John's heads of silver gilt engraved on escutcheons of silver.[74]

The old Hall, standing where it did, had little chance of surviving the Great Fire which started in the early hours of Sunday 2nd September 1666 in Pudding Lane, near the northern end of London Bridge. When the Court met on the 13th[75] the Assistants were told that 'part of the Hall wall and several of the chimneys were so much damaged that it was convenient to pull them down for preventing further mischief' and that it was 'necessary to bring a new mantle-tree[t] over the kitchen chimney to prevent it from

---

s   Why only four, when the Company's officers consisted of a Master and four Wardens?

t   Mantel tree: an arch or lintel over a fireplace opening. *Principles of the Planning of Buildings*, third impression 1953. Printed by the London Technical Press Ltd., Gloucester Road, Kingston Hill, Surrey.

falling'. At the next meeting on the 4th October[76] it was arranged that 'for the better preserving the lead, iron and other 'materials' within the ruins an enclosure should be made 'from the outer part of the wall, *which is yet standing* unto the further side of the house wherein the Beadle dwelt' (p. 274), and also on the south side of the adjoining house next Skinners Hall. It soon became apparent, however, that the buildings could not be saved. A minute of 18th October[77] lists the Company's properties destroyed by the Fire, among which are 'the Common Hall of the Company, the Clerk's and Beadle's houses, and all other buildings to the said Hall belonging'.

In the Company's collection of plate there were numerous standing cups of silver and silver gilt with covers, given mostly by candle-makers in the early seventeenth century on their admission to the Freedom (p. 179). In 1636 Roger Price, when a Warden, gave 'a standing cup of silver with a cover double gilt, desiring that the same may be used yearly in the choice of the Upper Warden'.[78] In 1640 the newly incorporated company of Distillers presented 'a fair tankard, with thankful acknowledgment of this Company's love unto them in accommodating them with the use of their Hall'.[79] In June 1643, our Court, faced by Parliament's heavy demands for money with which to carry on the war against the King, ordered[80]

that in respect of the great and urgent occasions of the Company's present use of monies and of their want and inability to procure the same otherways, and especially for the payment of their weekly assessment,

£100 worth of plate should be sold, excepting from the sale Price's cup, and one other. Numerous spoons[u] were sold later. All the silver that remained at the time of the Fire was removed together with the 'writings' and linen, to the Master's family home at Pinner[81] before the flames had reached his house in Golden Lane, to which they had first been taken.[82] The 'writings'

---

u   It was the practice at one time for each apprentice to present the Company with a silver spoon, or, in lieu thereof, to pay the sum of 1s., on being admitted to the freedom. (See the entry in the Court Book dated 1664, March 22, respecting this reported sale. T.C.C. C.B. 11 GL Ms. 6153, Vol. 3).

included our valuable Court minutes and Court and Yeomanry account books with a great many ancient deeds and documents. The linen (or napery)[83] included diaper and damask table cloths, table 'napkins' and towels.

Among other treasures was 'a little nut[v] garnished with scriptures and a fair deep foot with three lions, which had a fair cover' with 'a knob and a sceptre of silver, all gilt' presented to the Company in 1549,[84] 'a fair great cup with a cover of mazer tree[w] (presented in 1562)[85] and several silver cups. 'A fair great horn[x] garnished with silver and gilt' had been sold in 1573 to provide 'a joined table with a form and so many forms of wainscot as shall serve the Parlour appointed for the Yeomanry Court House'.[86] The mazer bequeathed to the Company by Richard Choppyn in 1536[y] appears to have been sold, with other silver, in 1598.[87] The Yeomanry, as well as the Company, possessed a quantity of pewter, including 'pewter pots with covers to drink in like jugs,[88] pottle[z] wine and ale pots',[89] platters, dishes, trenchers and saucers, porringers and pie plates. Sometimes 'a whole garnish[aa] of pewter vessels' is mentioned.[90] We read also of a 'standish[bb] of pewter' in the Court House.[91] Some of these articles may have been retrieved by the labourers whom we know were employed to search in the ruins at the time of the Fire.[92]

In the rebuilding, while the relative positions of the Livery Hall, the Parlour and the Court Room remained much the same, the conception of a merchant's dwelling house with its group of buildings around a court yard gave place to that of an Oxford or

---

v   A cup formed from the shell of a cocoa-nut mounted in metal; also one made of other materials to resemble this. *O.E.D.*

w   The tree yielding a hard wood, properly maple, used as a material for drinking cups. *O.E.D.*

x   A vessel formed from the horn of a cow or other beast, or in later times shaped after this, for holding liquid; a drinking horn. *O.E.D.*

y   See p. 232, note z.

z   Pottle pot: a two quart pot or tankard. *O.E.D.*

aa   A set of vessels for table use, *esp.* of pewter. *O.E.D.*

bb   A stand containing ink, pens and other writing materials and accessories; an ink stand. *O.E.D.*

Cambridge college, a main feature of which is a quadrangle having a line of connected buildings on each side. The architect was, in all probability, the Company's Surveyor, Captain John Caines. Several 'plots' were submitted by others, including Edward Jarman,[93] one of the City surveyors (who died in 1668), but in January 1671[94] we read that Mr Jones, bricklayer, is willing 'to perform all the bricklayer's work upwards from the foundations *according to the model or design drawn by Captain Caines'*. It was agreed that Mr Adam Taylor should do the carpenter's work.[95] On 7th June[96] the Court resolved 'that the carcase of this Company's Public Hall with its necessary appendices thereunto shall be erected and carried up with as much expedition as conveniently may be'. Notice of this resolve was given to Taylor and Jones, who were desired forthwith to put the same in execution.[97] The work proceeded and Caines received substantial payments for his services from time to time.[98] The rebuilding of the four houses on the street had already taken place.[99] In December 1673[100] the Court was informed that Alderman Sir Joseph Sheldon (p. 183) had agreed that if the Company would 'wainscot their Common Hall' he would 'cause the Parlour to be wainscotted', for which 'spontaneous' action he received hearty thanks,[101] and the work on both rooms proceeded. John Symes, joiner, was responsible for the wainscotting of the Livery Hall,[102] and he may have been engaged by Sir Joseph Sheldon to wainscot the Parlour and to carry out its exceptionally fine ornamental wood carving.[cc] The interior decoration of the Court Room, including the simpler wainscotting, for which Symes was again employed, was completed in 1677.[103] William Leybourn, Surveyor, was commissioned to 'draw maps in Vellum of all the Company's houses and lands'.[104] His survey and *ground-plat* of the Hall (Plate V) has already been referred to. In a note accompanying this drawing[105] Leybourn gives particulars of the upper floors, including the information that

---

[cc]   Of the style of Grinling Gibbons (1648–1720), of which another example can be seen in the Court Room of the Vintners Company.

Over the Kitchen, Pantry, Lobbie and West side of the Piazzaes is the Companies Comon Hall—over which are Garrets.
Over the Beadle's Dwelling, and the North end of the Piazzaes is the Companies Parlor. Over that their Court Room; and Garrets over that.
Over the South side of the Piazzaes are two Rooms one over the other,

one of which may have been the Counting-House. He adds that there are 'cellars under all Piazzaes'. It is hardly surprising that no Yeomanry Court House should be mentioned in view of their impending dissolution. (See Appendix A.)

The first major alteration to the building was carried out over two hundred years later when, in 1868, due to rotting timbers, the present ornamental ceiling in the Livery Hall replaced the old hammer-beam roof. In 1882 the four houses on Dowgate Hill gave place to an office building. Other changes have inevitably taken place, but in the main the original features of the Company's seventeenth century Hall have been retained or, when lost for a time, they have been restored. The pictures in the Livery Hall (among which are companion portraits of William III and Mary by Sir Godfrey Kneller, presented by Roger Monk[dd]) add to its beauty. In 1905 the acquisition of a piece of land on the northern boundary provided additional accommodation and gave better access to Cloak Lane. Although the building was considerably damaged in the Second World War it mercifully escaped the disaster that overtook so many of the Livery Companies, whose halls were either totally destroyed or damaged beyond repair. The most serious effect of the bombing was the destruction of the south-east corner of the Livery Hall, together with the little used south wing of the Court Yard, which was rebuilt in such a way as to facilitate the service of food from the Great Kitchen.

Commentary

Note a.

In the Patent Rolls for the fourth year of the reign of Edward IV there is a transcript of a grant dated 15th December 1464 to one

---

[dd]   Master in 1826–7.

Thomas Mongomery (or Montgomery), lately raised by the King to the order of knighthood, of 'three parcels of land, including (secondly) a messuage (or dwelling house) with two tenements annexed, in the old parish of *St Peter-le-Poor*. This parcel of land is described as lying between certain tenements on the west, *the Common Hall and tenements and gardens pertaining to the Commonalty of the Art of Talugh Chaundelers, London* on the east and north, and the highway of Bradstrete (otherwise Bradestrete or Broad Street) *on the south'*. In the fifteenth century the name 'Bradestrete' was given to two separate thoroughfares, the one extending the whole length of what is now Threadneedle Street, and the other corresponding to a part at least of what is now Old Broad Street. (See the article by H. L. Hopkinson in *London Topographical Record*, Vol. XIII, 1923, p. 26, concerning the location of Merchant Taylors Hall.) For a short distance *only* at the junction with Throgmorton Street, where Austin Friars is situated, can the houses in Old Broad Street be said to face *south*. (See Ogilby and Morgan's map, 1676, or William Morgan's map, 1681–2, which is even clearer.) Here, then, was the site of the Company's first Hall.

Note c.

As in the grant by Henry Fraunkellyn, Citizen and Vintner of London to Reginald de Conduit, Citizen and Alderman, dated 27th March 1335. The name 'Douegate' is cited by *Harben* as usual (in early deeds), an alternative of which was Douuegate, in which Stow mistook the second 'u' for an 'n', giving Downegate.

Note g.

Stow tells us that 'in Horsebridge streete is the Cutlers Hall' (See *A Survey of London reprinted from the text of 1603*, Vol. I, p. 244), which *Harben* regards as sufficient evidence that Horseshoe Bridge Street occupied the site of the present Cloak Lane. Our title deeds make it clear that this is not so. The street evidently disappeared after the Great Fire.

Appendix E

APPRENTICES

One of the ways in which the Craft Guilds were able to turn their powers of self-government to economic account was by controlling the number of full freemen, which could be achieved by placing a limitation on the number of apprentices that any one member could take at any given time.[1] Our Ordinances of 1538 imposed a limit of three. Under Article 43 of our Ordinances of 1589 past and present officers of the Company and Assistants were permitted 'to have and keepe three apprentices a piece and not above', *householders* being freemen could have but two.[a]

The companies strove to keep their members' apprentices under strict control. In the Court House at the Tallow Chandlers Hall in 1549 and later there were disguising coats and hoods for use when unruly lads were wipped.[2] An entry in the accounts for 1561[3] records that

this Court day before the Master, Wardens and Assistants in the parlour one John Whale now apprentice with Mr Dowcett (page 41) is whipped by two of our Company disguised with Hoods for offences by him done to his Master and Mistress being aged folkes

By Article 15 of the Ordinances of 1538 no man of the fellowship might of his own accord 'receyue or take into hys seruyce any mans apprentys of the same crafte whiche for hys prowde mynde and frowarde disposicyon wolde not be obedyent to his maister nor do his seruyce accordynge as he ought to doo'. By Article

---

a   See Unwin's valuable analysis of the system of apprenticeship in London and of the regulations imposed by the civic authorities and by individual companies. *The Gilds and Companies of London, Fourth edition.*

52 of the Ordinances of 1589 when any apprentice belonging to any member of the Commonalty 'shall goe or runne awaie' his master or mistress is to bring his indenture to the Hall 'to the intente that the day of his departure may bee entered and registred' and on his return 'the cause of his departure' is to be examined 'and the offence punnished', so that 'no abuse bee had about his freedome thereafter'. In October 1695[4] the Court of Assistants 'having taken notice of the great disorders and confusions occasioned by the members' apprentices appearing at this Company's Hall on the Lord Mayor's Days at dinner time' ordered 'that thenceforth all such apprentices as shall appear . . . shall remain in the Court Room and there be entertained with hot provisions . . .'

Appendix F

SOAP AND OIL

Part I

'Proclamacio pur Blake Soope'

20th May 1510

FORASMOCHE THAT aswell by the disceitefulle makyng of
blake soope within this Citee made with vnholsome licour as
Trane hering seme grece and other lyke as also by disceitefulle
chaunging and alteryng of blake soope brought and conveyed
from beyonde the See in to this realme in to Englisshe barelles
and other vesselles assised and marked after the maner of Englisshe
vesselles not oonely the Kynges subiectes of long tyme haue
suffred and daily suffreth grete damage bothe in theire bodies and
losse of theire goodes/but also by reason of suche vnlaufulle soope
chaunging & altering grete disclaunder redundeth to this Citee
IT IS THEREFORE vpon due & substaunciall prove before the
said Maire and Aldermen of the said disceit made adiugged
ordeyned and decreed that fromhensforth no parsone of what
condicion he be of straunger or denyzen take vpon hym herafter
to chaunge alter or pak any blake soope made in parties beyonde
the see in to any other vessell then in the same wherin it was
brought and conveyed in to this said Reame vpon payne of
forfeature of alle suche blake sope so chaunged and altered And
that no parsone fromthensforth make nor cause to be made within
the said Citee or libertie of the same any blake soope with Trane
hering seme pompe oyle butter gres or other suche vnholsome
and fatte licour but onely oyle olyve or Rape oyle vpon payne of
forfeature of alle suche Trane hering seme pompe oyle butter

gres or any other suche vnholsome licour founde in the handes of any parsone vsing or occupying the feate of blake soope making within this Citee or libertie of the same And ouer that alle blake soope made and tempred within suche vnlaufull and forbeden licour vppon due serche and seasour therof made by suche parsones hauyng feate and knowledge of making of suche blake sope as by the Maire for the tyme beyng shalbe assigned shalbe brought to the Yeldhalle there to be ordred and disposed according to the ordenaunce thereof made.

Part II

An abstract of the Act of Common Council against the employment of tallow in soap-making and of the regulations for enforsement.

17th March 1575

The Act recites that 'the greate and inordinate spendinge of talloughe in boyling of soape hath bynne founde to be one greate cause of the dearth of candells in this Citty and that for the same cause the boylinge of tallough for makinge of soape hathe bynne by sondry Lordes Maiors and thaldermen of this Cytty wholy forbidden, and bonds taken of the sope boylers that they shuld not offend agaynst the said prohibicion, and nevertheless the said inconvenience hath not bynne therby remedyed but rather by the boldness of some to offend, thother that were dewtifull and obedyent have bynne putto great losse and hynderaunce, which boldnes risith chefly of this that the myxture of tallough in soope cannot in the soope newe boyled nor in a good tyme after, specially in somer tyme be dissernyd'.

For reformation whereof, it is ordained 'that frome hensfourth no sopeboyler shall within the liberties of this Citty boyle any tallough for makinge of sope uppon payn to forfait for every such offence beinge therof dewly convicted all the soope so boyled or the valewe therof and that no chaundler nor other personne shall from hensfourth within the said liberties sell', etc. 'anny sope boyled with tallough on payne to forfeite', etc. 'and that yerely there shalbe appoynted one or mo honeste personnes and skylfull in making of soope' with power 'to enter into the boylinge hous and other places of ewery sope boyler within the Citty', etc., 'after every boylinge of soope and before the sellinge out of the same and then and there shall of the same soope take out a competent quantyte about a pounde' etc. 'for an assay and put the same into one lyttell box for that purpose specially to be provyded and upon the same box shall cause to be written the name of that soope boyler & the day of such assay taken and what quantitie of soope at the least he or they esteme the same whole boyling to conteyne'.

The box to be 'safly locked upp in one great chest in the guildhall with towe locks', etc. 'to thentent that after a reasonable tyme when the sope will showe whether the same be myxtd with tallough or no', etc. 'the said officer' (or officers) 'shall have the saide soope taken for assay to his owne use'.

Power of search for soap suspected of being mixed with tallow.

Penalty for 'selling out' soap before the same has been assayed.

Authority for any person 'that shall fynde anny speckelyd sope utteryd to be sold to seise the same and further to do therewith as the said sworne officer might doo.'

Forfeitures 'to be imploied to the relief of the poore in thospitalls' and 'thother moyte (sic) to hym that shall present the same.

Enacted that if any officer 'shall for anny corruption rewarde or undewe respecte conceale anny such offence or not pursewe with effecte agaynst thoffenders to hym knowen he shall for every suche offence be sett on the pillory or otherwise punished', etc.

Part III

Provisions for enforcing the regulations to be imposed upon soap-boilers according to a report made to the Court of Aldermen.

5th October 1620

That two officers, men honest and skillfull, be appointed to oversee the soape-makers, and that they may take a boxe not exceeding a pounde of the second course soape [made of seed oile, nutt oile, fish oile, as whale oyle and the like *without mixture of any tallough or stuffe*] from each soapemaker of every boyle of course soap that he maketh and bringe it to the Guildhall and there to be kept safe as it hath been in tymes past to th' end that *if it shall speckle* then the Soapemaker to forfeit all the said boyle of soape or the vallue thereof to the Chamber to bee distributed to such charitable uses as this honorable Courte shall appointe. We also thincke fitt that if the best soape be made or compounded with worse oile then olive oile or with course soape then the same to be marked for course soape and the offender to forfeite for every barrell soe mixed xxs. as aforesaid.

And for the better distinguishinge of the said three severall sorts of soape, we thincke fitt that the three markes hereafter mencioned be sett upon the best, second and third sort of soape, besides the marke of him or them that shall make the same vizt. the best to be marked with the Crowne upon the head or side of each caske and to be burnt on with a hott iron, and the second sorte of soape to be marked with a greate C to bee burnt on with a hott iron, and the third sort of soape with a W to bee burnt on with a hott iron so that it may be plainely bee seene.

And if any soapemaker or other person or persons usinge to make soape to putt to sale shall sell or putt to sale any soape before it bee searched and marked aforesaid, hee shall forfeite for every barrell soe solde or putt to sale xxs. of lawful money of England and for every halfe barrell xs. and for every ferkin vs. and for every halfe ferkin ijs. vjd. soe putt to sale un-searched and un-marked as aforesaid the same forfeitures to bee to the use *ut supra*.

Wee also thinke fitt that the said officers doe guage by weight all the said severall sorts of soape made by the Soapeboylers and putt in barrelles or other vessell or vesselles for sale and sett the true contents and weight of every cask or vessell upon the side and every barrell ought to hould xxxij gallons of soape every halfe barrell sixteen gallons and every ferkin eight gallons and soe after the rate for every lesser caske. And for such soape as shalbe made in the Citty of London libertyes or suburbes thereof the said officers soe to bee appointed Surveyors doe sett the Cittyes armes upon the head of every barrell caske or other vessell of soape soe to be putt to sale that it may bee knowne the same to be made and searched in London.

(The Report continues by reciting that 'there are at this presente greate quantityes of soape made with traine oyle and tallowe and, by reason of the tallough in it, some is sold for the best soape, and in truth is not'. The Committee accordingly recommend 'that there bee six Soapemakers forthwith appointed . . . with an officer of the Lord Maior . . . to enter into every Soapemakers warehouses, shoppes and workehouses and there to search, etc.', and that an Ironmonger and a Salter (named) 'men esteemed both honest and skillfull in the makeing of soape' be appointed Surveyors. They conclude by proposing an Act of Common Council, the provisions of which were later considered (*Jor.* 31, fo. 290b), but the Act itself has not been found.

Appendix G

LINKS AND STAFF TORCHES

Crude torches known as 'Links', consisting of tow and pitch, were used for lighting people along the streets,[a] but the Wax Chandlers made a superior article of which two varieties, the yellow and the black, are mentioned in their ordinances of 1664.[1] Links, as well as staff torches, were in vogue in the Lord Mayor's processions, which in course of time replaced the pageant of the 'Midsummer Watch',[2] (p. 108). Staff 'torches' were tall thick candles used for ceremonial purposes,[b] and our Wardens purchased both torches and links, for the Company's use from time to time, as we see from the following entries in our accounts.

1584–5	For a dozen and a half of staff Torches when certain of the Company went to meet the Queen at St James. For the carriage of them to the Fields and home	12d.[3]
1587–9	For seven Staff Torches and seven Lincks.	9s. 4d.[4]
1617–8	For Links for the Master and Wardens	2s. 6d.[5]

The Wax Chandlers' new Charter of 1652 authorized searches to be made for 'bad or corrupt wax lights, tapers, *burning links, etc. or any other sort of work in wax*'.[6] Although links, as such, are not mentioned in their early Ordinances, their Wardens are seen from their accounts to have been engaged in condemning 'lynkes nastely made' as early as the 'thirties of the sixteenth century,[7] and

---

a   O.E.D.

b   Ibid.

in April 1554 they appeared before the Court of Aldermen when

yt was agryed that Mr Chamberlyn shall cause to be redelyvered as manye of all such lynks as of late were browghte into the Chamber by the wardeins of the Wexchaundelers for that they were unlawfull and deceytefully made as the seyd wardeyns then reportyd.

It was also agreed that 'for the reste of the said lynks *that have been occupyed aboute the affayres and busyness of the Cytie*' the Chamberlain should 'see the sayd wardeyns contented'.[8]

As is well known, many wax chandlers made tallow candles, and in doing so came under the jurisdiction of our Company. Tallow Chandlers rarely handled wax, but some of our men evidently made both links and staff torches. There is no reason to suppose that they were the culprits concerned in the offences just recorded, but the fact is that the first hint of trouble between our two companies had come three months earlier,[9] when the Wardens of the Wax Chandlers had been warned to attend

for thanswerynge of the Taloughechaundelers bill.

The examination and hearing of 'the matter in variance' was committed to three Aldermen.[10] We hear no more of the affair at that time, but on 9th October 1561[11] we learn that

after the reading of the supplicacion here exhybited this day by the wardens of the Wexchaundlers against John Stoddard *Talowchandeler* who hath caused of late *a greate number of lincks & also some staffe torches* to be very falsly & deceit-fully wroughte & made to the hinderance & great disceite of the Quenes Hignes subiects, which the said Stoddard being here present coulde not deny . . . & alsoe the contemptuous disobedience of the said Stoddard towards this Courte, he the said Stoddard was *committed to warde*.

He was to remain there 'att my lorde mayres discrecion' and it was agreed that the said Wardens should 'always from tyme to tyme have the ayde & assistance of this Courte in all thinges that they shall lawfully doo for & concernynge there science & the common weale of this City'.

To make matters worse Stoddard's servant, Nicholas Stoddard, was convicted a few days later[12] 'of the beatinge of Edward Williams one of the wexchaundelers & Roger Wilcoks one of the lorde maiore's officers' when the Wardens

came lawfully to searche & do their duetie & office for the viewe and tryinge of

suche links & other stuf concernynge their science & occupacion as the saide
John Stoddard had made to be put to sale.

Before the week was out the Court had agreed[13]

that if the Wexchaundelers do cause a reasonable bill to be drawen ageinst the
next commen counsell for the true making & marking of all such links & staf
torches as shalbe made *by eny other persons then their owne felowship* to be putto
sale they shall have the lawfull favour of this Courte for the ferthering therof

and a few days later[14] it was ordered that a test should be made of
two of the defective links lately seized and other links 'being
truely made & of good stuf' by burnynge them to 'tyre whether
they be good and lawfully made or nott'. The result of the test
is not reported, but

after the longe & deliberat dibaytment of the untruth that is used by some
persones makers of links & staf torches betwene the Courte here the wardens
of the Wexchaundelers and alsoo the wardens of the Talloughchaundelers it
was finally ordered by the said Courte that the saide wardens of ether of the
saide companyes shall take order that nether they or eny of the saide severall
companies doo from hencsfurth make or cause to be made eny manner of
links or stafe torches to be putto sale but suche as shalbe truly made & of good
stuf uppon pain of forfeiture

Offenders were to 'make such fyne for the same' as should seem
reasonable to the Court, the Wardens of the Waxchandlers were
directed to make good and diligent search and to see offenders
punished, and it was ordered that Stoddard's servant should be
punished according to order.

Stoddard himself, as a member of the Yeomanry, came before
our Court three years later on the complaint of the Wardens of
the Wax Chandlers 'for making of Links *and other things*' contrary
to the recorded order of the Court of Aldermen.[15] He was
required to seal an obligation binding himself to the Master and
Wardens of our Company in the sum of £100 not at any time
thereafter to

make any Links or other wrought wax contrary to the order taken by the said
two Companies

10d. was spent on the same day 'in bread and wine *at the coming
of the Wax-Chandlers for Stoddard's Links*', which seems to have
put an end to the matter.

Appendix H

TALLOW MELTING

From *Letter Book BB*, fo. 12 (*Jor. 25*, fo. 121)

5th December 1599

Meltinghouses &c.

FORASMUCH as meltinge of grease kitchen stuffe and tallough in great and populous Cities and townes to the annoyance of the Inhabitants thereof is expresslye against the lawes of this Realme and nothinge more daungerous either for perill of fyer or to bringe contagion or infeccion of the ayre and wheare divers good lawes constitucions and acts of Comen Councell have been heretofore established for reformacion of such enormities, yet hethertoe noe sufficient remedye is provided in that behalfe, Be it now therefore ordeyned enacted & established by the right honourable the Lord Maior, the Aldermen his brethren and the Comons in this Common Councell assembled and by aucthoritie of the same That all acts of Comon Councell orders and ordinaunces concerninge the same now in force and not repealed or altered shall stand in force and shall be put in due execucion and be largely & liberally expounded against the offenders. And for further reformacion of the same enormities and abuses, be it further enacted ordeyned and established by aucthoritie aforesaide that noe person or persons from and after the five and twentith daye of Marche next ensuinge shall presume to use or exercise any meltinge house for tallough grease or kitchen stuffe within this Citie or the liberties thereof and therein melt or cause to be melted any tallough grease or kitchen stuffe to the annoyance of the neighbours dwellinge thereabout, but only in places remote from habitacion and usuall recourse of people, uppon payne of forfeiture of the stuffe soe melted or the value thereof for the first offence, and for the second offence to loose and forfeit the some of twenty pounds, and soe for every severall offence after twenty pounds, the one moitie of all which peynes penalties and forfeitures shalbe to the benefitt of the Chamber of London, and the other moitie thereof to him or them that will sue for the same paines penalties and forfeitures in the name of the Chamberlein of the said Citie for the time beinge, in her Majesties Courte houlden before the Maior and Aldermen of the Citie of London in the Chamber of the Guildhall of the same Citie by accion of debt, bill, plaint or informacion, wherein noe essoigne wager of lawe or proteccion shalbe admitted or allowed for the defendant.

Appendix I

WINES PRESENTED BY THE VINTNERS AS DEFECTIVE

The Report of Thomas Parker and Thomas Lambert Tallough-chaundlers who the IXth daye of this instant December weare appoyneted to Vewe certayne wynes which weare lateley presented by Vynteners in theyre serche to be defectyve whether the same or any parte thereof weare fitt for sawce or not

the reporte towchinge defectyve wynes

We have vewed & tested one Butt of the sayd defectyve wyne lieinge at the Queenes head in water lane[a] being the wyne of John Bennys, and fynd the same meete to make sawce of. vz vinegar,

Demaundinge at St Magnus Corner[b] the vewe of one butt of Alexander de Coone his wynes he aunsweared that theare was non defectyve to his knowledge, nor any could we fynd theare marked by the vinteners

wynes for sauce

Arnold Vanhove in Puddynge Lane[c] 'sayd he had sold awaye two buttes of wynes, to make aquavite, found defectyve as aforesayd,
In Minsinge lane[d] at Mr Wattes we found a Rem-

---

a   Water Lane—south out of Great Tower Street to Lower Thames Street. *Harben.* There were several Inns in the City known as the 'Queen's Head', but none has been identified in Water Lane.

b   St Magnus the Martyr—on the south side of Lower Thames Street, east of London Bridge. It stood at the head of the old London Bridge. *Harben.*

c   See Appendix D, p. 278.

d   Mincing Lane. See p. 301, note *dd.*

nant of wynes fytt for sauce, in a butt marked by
the vintners and for thother butt we could not see

Michaell Lemon refused to shewe us fower buttes
at Mr Blowers in Fanchurchestreete found defectyve

Mr Alderman Radcliffe sayd he had sent two pipes
of Canarye wynes fownd defectyve as aforesayd to
the sayd Arnold Vanhoven (sic) of whom he sayd
be bought them/

M^res Prannell had sent three buttes fownde defectyve as aforesayd at London stoune^e at her celler
hoame to her howse as it was informed us/

e   See p. 299, note *g*.

Appendix J

'A LIST OF PUBLICK HALLS IN LONDON'[a] IN THE YEAR 1483

These bene ye hallis y^t longe to ye Cytee of London

ffyrst The Yelde Hall[b]

Blakwell Hall[c]   leden Hall[d]

Mersers Hall w^{t}in Seint Thomas of Acres[e]

Grocers Hall in Conyhope lane[f] in Seynt Mildredes Paryssh in ye Pultrye

---

[a]   The Ironmongers Company (the only one of the Great Twelve Companies without a Hall in 1483, according to this list) acquired a site in 1457 but their Hall does not appear to have been built until some 35 years later. (*Some Account of the Worshipful Company of Ironmongers*, compiled by John Nicholl, F.S.A., Second Edition, 1866).

[b]   The site is described 4 Ed. VI, as in the parish of St Michael Bassishaw, abutting east on Bassingshawstrete, west on 'le Yeldehall Chappell', south on Blackwell Hall, north upon 'les grocers landes'. *Harben*.

[c]   On the west side of Basinghall Street, with a passage west to the Guildhall and south to Cateaton Street (Gresham Street) . . . Earliest mention 'Bakkewellehalle', 1356 (Cal. *L. Bk. G*. p. 67). In 1396 a messuage called Bakwellehalle and a garden in the parishes of St Michael de Bassyngeshawe and St Laurence in the Jewry were conveyed with the royal licence by John Fressh, Wm. Parker and Stephen Speleman, mercers, to the Mayor and Commonalty. (*Hustling Roll* 125 (65)). It seems thenceforth to have been used as a market place for woollen-cloths, and foreigners were directed to bring their woollen cloth to Bakwellehalle (Cal. *L. Bk. H* p. 449) . . . Burnt in the Fire of 1666 and rebuilt in 1672. Removed to make way for the new Courts of Law at Guildhall. *Harben*.

[d]   On the south side of Leadenhall Street between Gracechurch Street and Lime Street . . . .After the acquisition of the Leadenhall estate (for some years in the possession of the Nevill family) by the City in 1411, and the erection of the Granary in 1446 (*Harben*), the Hall seems to have increased rapidly in importance. Besides being used for the weighing and sale of cloth and wool, it was ordained in 1488 that the assay of leather should be held there only (Cal. *L. Bk. L* p. 251), and the petition of the citizens (set out in stow) against the leasing of the Hall by the City shows the value they attached to its use for public purposes in the 16th century . . . *Harben*. See pp. 33 on the subject of its use by foreign butchers and p. 77 respecting the weighing of our tallow there.

[e]   St Thomas of Acon—a collegiate church and hospital on the north side of Cheapside on the site now occupied by Mercers Hall and Chapel. In Cheap Ward. A house of the military order of the Knights of St Thomas of Acre. *Harben*.

[f]   North out of the Poultry in the Parish of St Mildred, Poultry. The chapel of St Mary de Coneyhope was in the lane and also the Grocers' Hall. The site is now occupied by Grocers Hall Court. *Harben*.

Drapers Hall in Seynt Swythyns Paryssh by london stone[g]

ffysshmongers . iij. Hallis ./ Wherof one ys at Oldeffyschstret in Seint Nycholas Golde Abbey Paryssh[h] & a noyer of yem ys in Stokffysshmonger rew in temstrete[i] & in ye Paryssh of Seynt Myghell in Croked lane and ye thryd of yem is in bryggestrete[j] in Seynt Margerete Paryssh . & all yese. iij. Hallys longen to ye ffysshmongers

Goldesmytes Hall in Seynt John Zakary[k] his parysshe in ffassour lane[l]

Tayllours Hall in Seynt Martyns Paryssh next ye well w[t] ij. bokettes. ffast by Seynt Antonys[m]

Habyrdasshers Hall in Seint Mary Stanynges Paryssh ffast by Gutter lane./[n]

Dunstone Hall in ffeyter lane next fletestrete[o]

Gerrardes Hall in basyng lane[p]

---

g   A rounded block of stone set in a large stone case, in which is an oval opening through which it can be seen. Built (at one time) into the south wall of St Swithin's Church on the north side of Cannon Street . . . Many suggestions have been made as to its origin. *Harben.*

h   Old Fish Street—West from Queen Victoria Street to Knightrider Street, in Bread Street and Queenhithe Wards. Formerly extended east to Great Trinity Lane. The street extended into the parishes of St Nicholas Cole Abbey, St Nicholas Olave, St Augustine next Oldefysshstrete, St Gregory, St Mary Magdalen. *Harben.*

Stockfishmonger Row—The portion of Thames Street extending west from Fish Street Hill to Old Swan Lane was so called. *Harben.*

j   Bridge Street—South from Eastcheap to Old London Bridge. Now Fish Street Hill. *Harben.*

k   St John Zachary—on the north side of Maiden Lane at its junction with Noble Street, in Aldersgate Ward. *Harben.*

l   Foster Lane—North out of Cheapside. 'Fastour lane', 1393. *Harben.*

m   St Anthony, Hospital of—on the north side of Threadneedle Street, in Broad Street Ward. *Harben.* The site of Merchant Taylors Hall which was acquired by the Company in 1347, and has not since changed hands, is in fact on the *south* side of Threadneedle Street. (See p. 283).

n   Gutter Lane—North out of Cheapside to Gresham Street. *Harben.*

o   This 'Hall' may have been the meeting place of the 'Fraternity of St Mary and St Dunstan', which according to Strype (ed. 1720. I. iii 262) was established in the old church of St Dunstan (or Donston) in the west (on the north side of Fleet Street) in the reign of Henry VI. *Harben.*

p   Gerard's Hall Inn (or 'Gerrardes hall')—on the south side of Basing Lane, adjoining St Mildred, Bread Street, in Bread Street Ward (Elmes 'Topographical Directory, 1831). Removed for the western extension of Cannon Street, 1853–4. In Stow's time a common ostrey (hostrey). *Harben.* The house and great hall were destroyed in the Fire of 1666, but the crypt escaped, and the house was rebuilt over it as a tavern. *Wheatley.*

Vynteneres Hall in Seynt Martyns in ye Vyntre [at ye Anker lane./ *Struck out*].^{q}

Salters Hall in Bredstrete by all Hallowyn^r

Skynners Hall in Walbroke in Seynt John Paryssh^s

Chaundelers Hall fast by it^t

Cuttelers Hall in ye Paryssh of Seynt Myghell fast by the Ryall^u

ffullers Hall in Canwyk strete w^{t}in Seint Martyns lane^v

Carpenters Hall w^{t}in ye Paryssh of all Hallowyn in london wall^w

Bruers Hall in Aldyrman bury^x

Bakers Hall in Warwyk lane^y

Barbar Hall in ye Paryssh of Seynt Oluf in Syluerstrete^z

Bochers Hall in Mungell Strete by Crephyll gate^{aa}

Saddelers Hall in an Aley in fawsser lane^{bb}

Dyers Hall in Seynt Martens parysshe in ye Vyntry at Anker lane^{cc}

---

q St Martin Vintry—at the south west corner of College Hill in Vintry Ward; Ogilby and Morgan's Map of London 1677. (This site is not mentioned in Harben's account of Vintners' Hall). Anchor Alley (or Lane)—south out of Upper Thames Street, on the west side of Vintners' Hall. *Harben*.

r All Hallows, Bread Street—on the east side of Bread Street at the corner of Watling Street (Ordinance Survey map of 1875).

s See p. 270.

t Note that the street in which our Hall and that of the Skinners is said to be situated had not yet become known as Dowgate Hill and see Appendix D.

u The Ryall (la Riole)—a tenement and afterwards a street, identified with College Hill. *Harben*.

v Canwyk (or Candlewicke) Street, later Cannon Street. *Harben*. See Volume III, Appendix D for the ancient relationship of the Fullers with the Shearmen, resulting in their union, in 1528, as the Clothworkers Company. The site of Clothworkers Hall in Mincing Lane appears to have been acquired by the Fullers in 1455. *Harben*.

w All Hallows, London Wall—on the north side of London Wall.

x Aldermanbury—North out of Gresham Street.

y Warwick Lane—South out of Newgate Street.

z St Olave, Silver Street—on the south side of Silver Street at its junction with Noble Street and Falcon Square.

aa Monkwell Street—South from Hart Street, Cripplegate, to Silver Street.

bb Foster Lane (see note l).

cc Anchor Lane (see note q).

Schermans Hall in Mynchyn lane[dd]
Cordenoors (Cordwainers) Hall in Dystafe lane[ee]
Gyrdellers Hall in Bassyngsawe be yond ye bere[ff]
Tylers Hall at all Hallown in y[e] london wall[gg]
Coryers Hall at Seynt Mary nax by Pappey[hh]
The Armorers Hall in Collman strete fast by the Bell[ii]

From the Harleian Collection in the British Museum. Ms. No. 541, fos. 225[b]–226[b]. Peter's day [1st August] 1 Richard III [1483].

---

dd   Mincing Lane—North out of Great Tower Street to Fenchurch Street.

ee   Distaff Lane—South out of Cannon Street.

ff   Basinghall Street, properly Bassishaw Street (New Remarks of London. Collected by the Company of Parish Clerks, 1732). *Harben.*

gg   All Hallows, London Wall. (See note *w.*)

hh   St Mary Axe—In Lime Street Ward. The Papey—a fraternity or brotherhood of S. Charity and S. John the Evangelist, of the Priests of London, founded in 1442. The hospital was by London Wall, opposite the north end of St Mary Axe Street. *Harben.*

ii   Bell Inn, Coleman Street—messuage called 'The Bell' on the east side of the street 'called Colman Streete, in parish of St Stephen Colman Streete, between the Armourers' Hall north and tenement of Thos. Offley south,' and a 'yerde' part of the possession of the College of Acon. 34. H. VIII. 1542 (*Calendars of the Letters and Papers of the reign of Henry VIII, etc. Domestic Series,* in the Public Record Office). *Harben.*

Appendix K

THE BARGE AND BARGE HOUSE

For over four hundred years[1] the companies proceeded by river to Westminster on Lord Mayor's Oath Day,[a] those not possessing barges having to hire them for the occasion. The Wardens' accounts for 1557–8 record the payment of 2d. for 'a cord for the bargeman' and 20s. for 'hire of the Barge'.[2] Twenty years later the charges on Lord Mayor's Oath Day were '26s. 8d. for the hire of the barge, 2s. for the hire of the cloth to the barge, 3d. for rushes, and 12d. for landing'.[3] In the accounts for 1603–4 10s. is entered as having been paid 'to the Master of the barge that the Company was used to go to Westminster in'[4] and in July 1611[5] we read that order has been given by the Court of Assistants

that Walter Snellinge, Waterman, dwelling on the Bankside shall be steersman to this Company ... and he to provide a Barge yearly with a Broad Cloth to cover the same and Rushes and Boards convenient for the Livery of this Company and to have every Lord Mayor's Day for the same yearly forty and four shillings.

His successor, Nicholas Snelling, whose address is given as 'the Falcon',[b] made a hiring charge in October 1649 of £4 for the day, with '6d. a piece for ten men for their breakfasts'.[6] On 28th September 1666[7] we read that £2 2s. has been paid

to the Master of the Goldsmiths' Barge for one half of the charge of the said Barge for carrying the Goldsmiths Company and this Company to and from Westminster to attend the Sheriffs of London being their Oath Day.

---

a   The procession by water originated early in the fifteenth century. It appears to have been last held in 1856, but there had been earlier occasions in that century when it had been laid aside.

b   The Falcon Tavern, Bankside, Southwark: the site of which was a little to the east of Blackfriars Bridge, where was once a ferry across the Thames. *Wheatley.*

On 11th August 1668[8] the Court learnt from the Clerk that Alderman Sir Joseph Sheldon, then Sheriff of London, who had lately completed his year of office as Master

had out of his great affection to the Company freely provided a Barge for the Wardens and Livery of this Company ...

It was reported also 'that a house was wanting to put the said barge in', and that such a house had been found, for which Sir Joseph was willing to pay the first year's rent. The gift of the barge and his offer of rent were both received 'with the highest presentments of gratitude immaginable', and 'the thanks of the Court and the whole Livery' were 'returned to him for the same'.

The number of watermen required for this barge was sixteen.[9] On 5th October 1670[10] we read that

at this Court, order was given unto Nicholas Snelling (Barge Master) that he take care and also give a strict charge to his men that in their Rowing to and from Westminster they do not willingly run or lay the Barge aboard any other Company's Barge or offend any other Company by scuffling with their Oars or throwing Water into their Barge or otherwise.

He was also to see that the coats and caps delivered to him 'for his crew of watermen to wear that day' were safely returned 'to the Beadle of the Company to lay up and preserve', and, the Court being informed 'that they had but 15 coats for the use of their 16 watermen' another coat 'suitable to the rest' was ordered to be provided and paid for out of the House stock.

A piece of ground at Lambeth was first considered as a permanent home for the barge,[11] but in October 1674 a Committee was appointed to view 'the ground at Chelsea belonging to the Apothecaries Company',[12] of which Mr Charles Cheyne, or Squire Cheyne as he was known at that time, was the ground landlord.[c] In the following year a double barge house was erected for the joint use of the Weavers Company and ourselves, adjoining the Apothecaries barge house.[13] We paid £3 a year for the use of this land, of which we recovered half from the Weavers.

---

c   See the series of documents at Guildhall Library: G.L. Ms. 6180 Box 6 286–99. The terrace of houses by the river-side known as Cheyne Walk is so called after Charles Viscount Cheyne, Lord of the Manor of Chelsea (d. 1698). *Wheatley.*

In 1738 we were granted a fresh lease of our part of the barge house, the Weavers part, afterwards occupied by the Vintners, then being empty. (See Plate VI.)

In 1676 Walter Hunt, shipwright, was engaged to carry out 'trimmings' and periodical repairs.[14] In 1680 Henry Balten is named as our Barge Master,[15] to whom 4 nobles was paid two years later 'to buy him a decent handsome coat to be worn in the Company's service'.[16] In 1691 he was provided with 'cloth for a coat and breeches, as well as a pair of stockings'[17] and doubtless he wore on his arm a silver badge bearing the Company's Arms, of which a late example can be seen at Tallow Chandlers Hall.

By 1694 Sir Joseph Sheldon's barge was worn out,[18] and Mr John Loftus, shipwright, was commissioned to build another barge at a cost of £120.[19] In the same year[20] Mr Samuel Audrey, carver, was engaged 'to carve the shield of Arms of the Company and other ornaments'. The new barge was to be '70 feet in length (or little more)', the 'house' was to be, in length, 30 feet, in breadth $11\frac{1}{2}$ feet, and the height to be $6\frac{1}{2}$ ft. On completion the barge was found to be too high for the barge house, which accordingly had to be enlarged. In the following year the old barge was sold for £6.[21]

It became necessary in 1722 to obtain a licence from the Lords of the Admiralty to keep and use the barge, one of the conditions being that it should not be used 'in the clandestine running of un-customed goods'.[22] By 1748 this barge, like its predecessor, had become worn out,[23] and it was decided not to use it on Lord Mayor's Day for fear of endangering people's lives.[24] Six years later it was sold without its shields, carved work and six wainscot forms for five guineas, this being 'the most money that could be gotton for it'.[25] The Court then decided to purchase the Haberdashers' barge[26] which seems to have lasted nearly thirty-five years before requiring a new bottom.[27] In 1785, yet another barge was built for us,[28] which in turn was sold in 1799 by auction for £50.[29]

We know that the barge was used from time to time 'for excursions of pleasure',[30] and that, prior to 1755 sons, friends and servants had come aboard on Lord Mayor's Day, a privilege then denied them, as well as the smoking of tobacco on board by all and sundry, on penalty of paying 6s. 8d. for each person.[31]

The following is a copy of the Precept received by the Company in 1682.

To the Mr and Wardens
 of the Company of Tallow Chandlers

By the Maior

Theis are to give you notice that the right Honoble the Lord Maior and Court of Aldermen have appointed on Munday the thirtyeth of October instant (being the day appointed for sweareing the Lord Maior for the yeare ensueing at Westminster) to be in theire barge by Eight of the Clock in the morning and that you faile not at that time to be in your barge with your usuall Trophyes & Ornaments Soe that his Lordship and Court of Aldermen may returne from Westminster in convenient tyme, which in former yeares hath been very late and unseasonable and upon theire returne to land at Blackfryers staires and from thence to Fleetbridge by the side of ye Channell And that you cause your barge to goe and returne in order according to your precedency, and that such persons of your Company as walke in the streets land at Blackfryers stayres aforesaid and that you be early and regular in takeing and keeping your standing in the streete and hereof faile you not this 19th of October 1682

Wagstaffe

(Endorsed)   Tallow Chandlers.
                    Monck.

Appendix L

The figures in brackets indicate the Companies' order of precedence.
(A list of the earlier Chartered Companies was given in Volume III, Appendix D, with the exception of the Tylers and Bricklayers (37), whose incorporation in 1568 was inadvertently omitted).

I. INCORPORATED COMPANIES

		YEAR	OBSERVATIONS
Turners	(51)	1604	
Butchers	(24)	1605	16th September
Gardeners	(66)	1605	18th ,,
Fruiterers	(45)	1606	February ,,
Curriers	(29)	1606	April
Plumbers	(31)	1611	
Founders	(33)	1614	
Apothecaries	(58)	1617	
Scriveners	(44)	1618	
Bowyers	(38)	1621	
Upholders	(49)	1626	
Makers of Playing Cards	(75)	1628	
Spectacle Makers	(60)	1629	
Clockmakers	(61)	1631	
Glaziers	(53)	1637	
Horners	(54)	1638	January
Gunmakers	(73)	1638	March
Distillers	(69)	1638	August
Glovers	(62)	1639	
Framework Knitters	(64)	1663	The Company was newly incorporated by Charles II with wider powers than those conferred by Oliver Cromwell in 1657.
Needlemakers	(65)	1664	February
Glass Sellers	(71)	1664	July
Poulters	(34)	1665	
Feltmakers	(63)	1667	The early feltmakers were known as hatters, cappers or hurers. In 1501 they were united with the Haberdashers, a union which was severed in a Charter of 2nd August 1604. This Charter, constituting a separate Company of the Art or Mistery of Feltmakers of London, was not at first recognized by the City, but it received confirmation from Charles II in 1667.
Wheelwrights	(68)	1670	February
Pattenmakers	(70)	1670	August

		YEAR	OBSERVATIONS
Tin Plate Workers	(67)	1670	December
Farriers	(55)	1674	
Coachmakers	(72)	1677	May
Masons	(30)	1677	September
Gold and Silver Wyre Drawers	(74)	1693	
Fanmakers	(76)	1709	
Loriners	(57)	1711	
Master Mariners	(78)	1930	
Basketmakers	(52)	1937	
Carmen	(77)	1946	
Musicians	(50)	1950	The City Minstrels' Charter obtained from James I in 1604 was revoked in 1634 by the action of the 'King's Minstrels'. The City Company, nevertheless, continued to exercise control for some time under various Acts of Common Council. The present Charter replaced the one revoked by Charles I.

II. THE FOLLOWING LIVERY COMPANIES OF ANCIENT ORIGIN POSSESS NO CHARTERS OF INCORPORATION

Weavers	(42)	This Company has the distinction of possessing the longest pedigree, substantiated by records, of all the City guilds. Its first Charter of Henry II confirms to the guild all the liberties and customs granted to it in the reign of Henry I, but it has no actual Charter of Incorporation.
Fletchers	(39)	
Paviors	(56)	
Shipwrights	(59)	In 1685 the 'free shipwrights' of London were declared to be under the rules of government of a Chartered Company of 'foreign shipwrights', but this control has long since ceased.
Woolmen	(43)	

III. EACH OF THE FOLLOWING COMPANIES HAS RECEIVED A GRANT OF LIVERY IN THE PRESENT CENTURY, AND SOME OF THEM HAVE ROYAL CHARTERS

Solicitors	(79)
Farmers	(80)
Air Pilots and Air Navigators	(81)
Tobacco Pipe Makers	(82)
Furniture Makers	(83)
Scientific Instrument Makers	(84)
Chartered Surveyors	(85), May 1977
Chartered Accountants	(86), June 1977

Note: The writer is indebted for most of the information contained in this Appendix to the learned authors of the *Armorial Bearings of the Guilds of London*, 1960.

Appendix M

SEVENTEENTH CENTURY SEARCHES

After the grant of the Charter of 1677, there are, as before, numerous cases of offenders being prosecuted, but sometimes, for one reason or another, they were treated with considerable leniency. In April 1683[1]

complaint being made that, in the last search for the Company, much bad wares and commodities were found amongst the tallow chandlers and that some of them were broken, spoiled and defaced, and that Henry Evolt, John Golding and John Bridge, being defaulters, were summoned and did appear and acknowledged their offences and promised amendment for the future, and being examined whether they had served to the Trade did all of them produce their testimonials of their service therewith, whereupon . . . this Court did dismiss them without any further prosecution against them for the same.

In April 1687[2] it is recorded that, on the appearance of fifteen persons

nombered of this Company, being candlemakers by Trade who, upon the late search made by vertue of certain Deputations under the Common Seal of this Company, were found deceitful in making false and adulterate candles,

the Court caused

one of the said Deputations to be read to them with other branches and clauses of this Company's last Charter relating to the aforesaid offences To the end they might render the more readier obedience and conformaty thereto for the future.

These persons, 'having severally submitted themselves and promising amendment', the Court then (after a serious admonishing of a due and careful observance of their said promises) was pleased to dismiss 'without charge or trouble'. In November 1691[3] divers persons exercising the trade of a tallow chandler, who, upon a late search were found to make 'false and adulterate candles', on acknowledging their offences and promising amendment were 'fined but 3s. 4d.' Next month Katherine Caseby, on appearing before the Court 'acknowledged her offence in making false and adulterate candles and promised amendment for the future', wherefore the Court 'believing her poor', dismissed her without fine.[4] In the following February a plea was made that adulterate candles found in a retailer's shop in Shoreditch were not of his making and the case against him was dismissed.[5] In April (1692) we again read of a promise to make amends and of a fine of only 3s. 4d.,[6] and the same thing happens twice in the following year.[7]

On the other hand prosecutions and more serious fines were not infrequent. In April 1687 there appeared before the Court of Assistants[8] one Edmond Waker, a candle-maker and member of the Company, against whom a complaint was made

that upon a late search pursuant to the said Deputation at the shop of the said Mr Waker very false and adulterate candles were found there, some of which the searchers *did then and there breake and make unfit for sale*, after which the said Waker refused to suffer the searchers further execution of their office and behaved himself in a very abusive and provoking manner and threatened to assault them, and besides brought a writ against Captain Loughton, one of the searchers.

It was pointed out to him that (apart from the Company's powers in their Charter) 'his aforementioned disobedience and misbehaviour' were contrary to his oath, as a member (p. 174). Yet the said Waker 'neither submitting himself nor making any manner of acknowledgment of his transgressions', the Court (with one consent) ordered that he should be proceeded against 'to the utmost severity of the Law'. This decision—so different from that taken on the same day in the case of the fifteen subservient Members—resulted in an information being laid in the Crown Office at the cost of the Company.[9] In May 1690 it was ordered that 'the offenders found at the last search be summoned before the Lord Mayor'.[10]

Appendix N

THE TRIALS (AND TRIBULATIONS)
OF WILLIAM COLLETT

This man, being by trade a baker, had to face no less than six trials connected with the sale of candles, at the instance of the Tallow Chandlers Company, commencing in 1689.

Mr James Moody (referred to in the minutes as one of the Judges of the Sheriffs' Court) was our Counsel on the first 'indictment',[1] and there are entries recording payment for the indictment, the swearing of witnesses and other expenses.[2] In February 1693 further expenses were incurred in again preparing witnesses for trial,[3] and on 3rd May we learn that the Master and Wardens and two Assistants, with 'such others as they shall appoint' are to attend 'the cause or indictment' summoned to be tried on the 9th instant, and that 'very able councell' are to be engaged.[4] The trial duly took place at the Court of King's Bench, Westminster, before the Lord Chief Justice Holt,[5] when the defendant's counsel produced 'an indenture of apprenticeship dated in the year 1685' in which the accused was 'bound an apprentice to one Robert Collett, a tallow chandler and the defendant's brother, for seven years'. Two witnesses were called, who swore that they had seen the indenture sealed, but, on being pressed, they were unable to remember whether this had taken place 'within many or few years' or whether in the reign of William and Mary or that of the previous monarch. On this evidence the jury found the defendant guilty, and on 19th May[6] our Clerk, Gilbert Brandon, received a copy of the 'rule' ordering that 'judgment be entered for the Lord the King and the Lady the Queen against the Defendant'.

We learn[7] from our minutes that only two days later Collett
had been indicted *for the second time*, and that on 28th June,1694
he had again been tried at the Court of King's Bench,[8] the charge
this time being for

exercising the trade of a tallow chandler, not having served thereto as an
apprentice.

On this occasion his plea was

that he had been taught and instructed by his brother Robert Collett, in the
said trade for the space of at least seven years, which he endeavoured to prove
by several witnesses, some of whom alleged that he was as servant of the said
Robert—which was notoriously false—others that he was a partner, with many
other indiscreet and dishonest allegations.

On this evidence his counsel

most strenuously endeavoured to make out by Law that the Defendant had
served to the said Art within the meaning of the Statute of the 5th Elizabeth.

But the Company's 'councel' did learnedly set forth

and most plainly made appear to the Court and Jury that, whatever had been
alleged or proved on the behalf of the Defendant, was not, nor could be taken
as, any proof of his service to the said trade, but at most as a partner with the
said Robert.

The defendant, therefore, was not entitled, 'neither had any right
to follow, the said Trade, according to the true meaning of the
said Statute'. Then,

after the Lord Chief Justice had summed up the evidence on both sides the Jury
(after a short withdrawal) brought a verdict against the said William Collett
and returned him guilty upon the said Indictment, which was recorded
accordingly.

We learn from the Wardens' accounts that £4 7s. 5d. was expended for a dinner for the Master and Wardens 'and on many
witnesses' at this trial.[9]

A third indictment followed,[10] to which the defendant pleaded
not guilty,[11] but on 12th July[12] he came before our Court with a
petition in which he 'acknowledged his error'[13] and 'prayed for
some relief',[13] He begged 'that he might be suffered still to follow
and exercise the said trade', but the Court gave him for answer

'that it was not in their power to grant him that freedom'. He then asked for 'six months' time for selling his shop goods', and he would then 'lay it down', but this also was refused.

A new order to prosecute was made,[14] and on 6th October[15] it is recorded that

this day in the forenoon at a quarter sessions held for the Liberty of Westminster and County of Middlesex at *Westminster Hall*, Mr Munday, being Councell for this Company, was tryed the Indictment found there the last Quarter Sessions against Mr William Collett for three months from xxj[th] of December last for exercising the Trade of *a candlemaker* having no Right thereto And after a short pleading on both sides the Jury by their verdict returned the said Collett guilty for one months exercising the said Trade, which makes *the third conviction* for the said offence.

Five days later[16] we read that

this day in the evening at quarter sessions held at Hicks' Hall[a] for the County of Middlesex . . . was tryed the Indictment found there the last Quarter sessions against William Collett for three months from xxiiij[th] of March last for exercising the Trade of *a Tallowchandler* having no right thereto,

when the accused was found guilty 'for one month's exercising the said Trade',

which makes *the fourth Conviction* . . .

On 19th January 1695[17] Collett again 'appeared at the Quarter Sessions at Hicks' Hall'

and confessed the 'indictment found against him at the last quarter session *for two months*, for exercising the Trade of *a candle maker*, having no right thereto, and thereupon did pay downe *four pounds* so by him forfeited for the same.

On 11th March[18] it was ordered that 'at the costs of this Company, Mr William Collett shall from time to time be *further prosecuted* as occasion shall require for his obstinate exercising the candlemaking Trade, having no right thereto, and for which he hath already been convicted *five times*'.

The last indictment of this tiresome man was tried at *Westminster Hall* on 5th October (1695).[19] The charge was for exer-

---

a   See Volume III, p. 112, note *h*.

cising the trade of a *Tallow Chandler* (having no right thereto) for three months beginning the 13th September 1694 and ending the 14th December following. The defendant's counsel produced, first, a seven-year indenture of apprenticeship dated 8th October 1694

whereby the said William Collett, the Defendant, was bound as an apprentice unto one Littleton, a tallow chandler by trade and a member of *the Salters' Company,*

and, secondly, a deed dated in November 1694 (which was within the period of trading mentioned in the charge), whereby the defendant's lease was assigned to Littleton for valuable consideration. It was proved that Littleton had bought 'all the stock and shop-goods of the defendant, and that the latter was now his servant', and also that the purchaser 'was entered in the Parish Roll as an inhabitant'. A plea by our counsel that these were fraudulent practices used for the purpose of avoiding the Statute failed, and the jury brought in a verdict of not guilty— *which* (writes Brandon) makes the *sixth* trial against the said Collett 'and convicted upon all the same save *only this last trial*' !

Authorities

(FOR ABBREVIATIONS SEE PAGE 8)

EARLY SEARCHES
THE CURRIERS AND THE SOAPMAKERS
SAUCE, HERRING AND CHEESE

Page	Note	
9	1	*Letter Book N*, fos. 262b–263.
10	2	*Rep.* 6, fo. 103b.
10	3	*Rep.* 4, fos. 209b–210; also *Rep.* 7, fos. 15b–16.
11	4	*Rep.* 7, fos. 40, 40b.
11	5	Ibid., fo. 184b.
11	6	„ fo. 197b.
11	7	*Letter Book O*, fo. 40b; *Rep.* 7, fo. 199.
11	8	Ibid., fo. 77; Ibid., fo. 258b.
11	9	*Rep.* 7, fo. 261b.
11	10	*Rep.* 8, fo. 32b.
11	11	*Letter Book O*, fo. 172b; *Rep.* 8, fo. 68.
11	12	*Rep.* 8, fo. 69.
11	13	Ibid., fo. 36.
12	14	*Rep.* 9, fo. 205.
12	15	*Letter Book P*, fo. 117b; *Rep.* 9, fo. 247b.
12	16	*Rep.* 9, fo. 247.
12	17	*Letter Book O*, fo. 214; *Rep.* 8, fo. 109.
13	18	*Rep.* 10, fo. 53b.
13	19	*Rep.* 8, fo. 119b.
14	20	25th October 1543. Both wills were proved on 19th November 1543. *P.C.C.* 27, Spert.
15	21	See *The Wax Chandlers of London* by John Dummelow, p. 33.
15	22	Will 25th August, Probate 24th November 1544. *Com. London*, 136, Story.
15	23	*P.C.C.*, 9, Mellershe.
15	24	*Rep.* 8, fo. 171 (sewn on).
16	25	*Rep.* 9, fo. 227b.
16	26	*Letter Book P*, fo. 132b.
16	27	*Rep.* 2, fo. 67.
16	28	See *The Curriers and the City of London* by Edward Mayer, p. 1.

Page	Note	
16	29	*Rep.* 3, fo. 214b.
16	30	*Rep.* 5, fo. 82.
17	31	Ibid., fo. 96b.
17	32	*Rep.* 8, fo. 72.
17	33	Ibid., fos. 173–173b.
17	34	*Letter Book P*, fo. 139b; *Rep.* 10, fo. 19.
17	35	*Rep.* 11, fo. 320.
18	36	Ibid., fo. 329b.
18	37	„ fo. 339.
18	38	„ fo. 340.
18	39	T.C.C., *Y.A.B.*, G.L. *Ms.* 6155, Vol. 1, 27th July 1518.
18	40	Will 10th August, Probate, 10th September 1555. P.C.C. 31, More.
18	41	*Rep.* 12, No. 2, fo. 484.
19	42	*Rep.* 14, fo. 147b.
19	43	*Rep.* 15, fo. 241.
19	44	Ibid., fo. 364.
20	45	„ fo. 397.
20	46	*Rep.* 11, fo. 257.
20	47	*Rep.* 15, fo. 441b.
20	48	Ibid., fo. 462.
21	49	*Rep.* 9, fo. 99.
21	50	*Letter Book R*, fo. 179; *Rep.* 12, No. 2, fo. 473.
21	51	*Rep.* 15, fo. 63.
21	52	*Jor.* 18, fo. 29b.
21	53	*Rep.* 15, fo. 66.
21	54	*Rep.* 18, fo. 384.
22	55	*Rep.* 17, fo. 5b; Ibid., fos. 143, 149b, *passim.*
22	56	*Rep.* 12, No. 2, fo. 483b.
22	57	*Letter Book X*, fo. 269.
23	58	T.C.C. Document in English. G.L. *Ms.* 6180, Box 3. No. 113. Printed in *T.C.C.R.*, pp. 106–7.
23	59	*Letter Book M*, fos. 172b–174.
23	60	T.C.C., *Y.A.B.*, G.L. *Ms.* 6155, Vol. 1 (1538–9).
25	61	*Rep.* 8, fo. 116.
25	62	Ibid., fo. 172.
25	63	„ fos. 172–173b.
25	64	Will 6th March, Probate 11th April 1524. *Com. London,* 41 Tunstall.
26	65	Will 7th March, Probate 23rd April 1536. *P.C.C.* 31 Hogan.
26	66	The grant is recited in a Deed Poll dated 15th May 1556. *Infra.* Note 71.
26	67	Will 18th December 1543, Probate 11th January 1554. *P.C.C.* 1, Pynnyng.
26	68	T.C.C., *L.A.B.*, G.L. *Ms.* 6152, Vol. 1, 12th October 1557.

Page	Note	
26	69	Ibid., 25th January 1569.
26	70	„ 3rd May 1576.
27	71	T.C.C. Account of the Company's lands, gifts, etc. G.L. Ms. 6165. Vol. 1. See the abstract 'Landes without Bushopsgate' printed in *T.C.C.R.*, p. 293.
27	72	20th October 1619. *Letters Patent by James I*, framed and glazed in the Company's possession. The document has a fine impression of the King's Great Seal, showing the 'reverse' side.
27	73	See *T.C.C.R.*, p. 169.
27	74	T.C.C., *L.A.B.*, G.L. Ms. 6152, Vol. 2 (1617–18).
27	75	Will 21st August, Probate 22nd September 1533. *Com. London*, 217, Tunstall.
27	76	T.C.C., *C.B.*, G.L. Ms. 6153, Vol. 1, 4th June 1611.
27	77	*Rep.* 8, fo. 116.
28	78	Ibid., fo. 177.
28	79	„ fo. 213b.
28	80	„ fo. 234.
28	81	*Letter Book O*, fo. 263.
28	82	*Letter Book P*, fo. 20b.
28	83	3 Henry VIII, cap. 14. (Printed in Statutes of the Realm). An exemplification, framed and glazed, bearing date 15th October 1512 is in the Company's possession. The Statute was at one time mistakenly supposed to belong to the reign of Henry VI.
30	84	*Rep.* 8, fo. 239b.
30	85	*Rep.* 9, fo. 102.
31	86	T.C.C., *L.A.B.*, G.L. Ms. 6152, Vol. 1, 28th Nov. 1549.
31	87	Ibid., 1st September 1555.
31	88	„ (1559–61).
31	89	„ (1564–5).
31	90	*Rep.* 12, No. 1, fo. 232.
31	91	T.C.C., *L.A.B.*, G.L. Ms. 6152, Vol. 1, 10th October 1553.
31	92	Ibid., (1553–5).
32	93	*Rep.* 14, fo. 369b.
32	94	Ibid., fo. 395b.
32	95	„ fo. 417b.
32	96	*Letter Book T*, fo. 80b.
32	97	*Rep.* 15, fo. 375.
33	98	T.C.C., *L.A.B.*, G.L. Ms. 6152, Vol. 1 (1564–5).
33	99	*Rep.* 15, fo. 432b.
33	100	T.C.C., *L.A.B.*, G.L. Ms. 6152, Vol. 1 (1566–7).
33	101	*Rep.* 11, fo. 217b.
33	102	See the *Encyclopaedia Britannica*, edition of 1968, Vol. 20, p. 727.
33	103	*Rep.* 11, fo. 296.

Page	Note	
	Page	*Note*
34	104	Ibid., fo. 362.
34	105	„ fo. 373.
34	106	„ fo. 390.
34	107	„ fo. 390b.
34	108	„ fo. 471.
34	109	*Rep.* 12, No. 1, fo. 21.
34	110	*Rep.* 14, fo. 13b.
34	111	Ibid., fo. 147b.
34	112	*Rep.* 15, fo. 335.
34	113	Ibid., fo. 337b.
35	114	„ fo. 350b.
35	115	„ fo. 355b.
35	116	T.C.C., *L.A.B.*, G.L. *Ms.* 6152, Vol. 1 (1563–4).
35	117	*Rep.* 15, fo. 364.
35	118	*Rep.* 16, fo. 387b.
35	119	T.C.C., *L.A.B.*, G.L. *Ms.* 6152, Vol. 2 (1591–3).
36	120	*Rep.* 15, fo. 386.
36	121	Ibid., fo. 459b.
36	122	„ fo. 470b.
36	123	T.C.C., *L.A.B.*, G.L. *Ms.* 6152, Vol. 2 (1595–7).
36	124	*Husting Rolls* (256–332) 276. 13. 20 (1596).
36	125	Will 19th February, Probate 6th March 1596. *Com. London.* Reg. 1592–7. fo. 305.
37	126	*Rep.* 18, fo. 299.
37	127	Ibid., fo. 101.
37	128	*Jor.* 20, fo. 198.
37	129	*Rep.* 19, fo. 69.
38	130	Ibid., fo. 186.
38	131	See the Exemplification of *Letters Patent of Queen Elizabeth I*, 15th April 1577, G.L. *Ms.* 6180, Box 7, No. 357.
38	132	8th July 1598. Public Record Office file. ST CHA 5/T13/16.
38	133	*Letter Book*, etc., fo. 159b.
39	134	*Jor.* 31, fo. 231b.
41	135	*Jor.* 1, fo. 83b.
41	136	*Rep.* 11, fo. 10b.
41	137	Ibid., fo. 13b.
41	138	*Rep.* 12, No. 2, fo. 412.
41	139	*Rep.* 13, fo. 5.
41	140	Ibid., fo. 349.
41	141	Will 3rd December 1561, Probate 22nd January 1562. *P.C.C.* 3 Street.
41	142	T.C.C. *L.A.B.* G.L. *Ms.* 6152, Vol. 1, 1545. Mar. 3.
42	143	Will 6th February, Probate 2nd December 1558. *P.C.C.* 4 Welles.
42	144	Will 13th September 1548, Probate 20th October 1558. *P.C.C.* 59. Noodes.

Page	Note	
42	145	T.C.C., *L.A.B.*, G.L. *Ms.* 6152, Vol. 1, 23rd July 1554.
42	146	Ibid., 17th January 1566.
43	147	*Rep.* 13, fo. 350b.
43	148	Ibid., fo. 353.
43	149	„ fo. 458, seq.
43	150	Ibid.
43	151	*Rep.* 13, fo. 452.
44	152	Will 8th March, Probate 1st July 1560. P.C.C. 38 Mellershe.
44	153	*Rep.* 10, fo. 38.
44	154	*Husting Rolls* (176–255) 250 dors. 84. (1559).
44	155	T.C.C., *L.A.B.*, G.L. *Ms.* 6152, Vol. 1, 17th January 1566.
44	156	Will 31st October, Probate 5th November 1563. P.C.C. 38 Chayre.
44	157	T.C.C., *L.A.B.*, G.L. *Ms.* 6152, Vol. 1 (1538–9).
44	158	*Husting Rolls* (176–255) 244 dors. 93 (1546).
45	159	Ibid., 246 dors. 8 (1550); 246 dors. 9 (1550).
45	160	T.C.C., *L.A.B.*, G.L. *Ms.* 6152, Vol. 1, 20th July 1563.
45	161	Ibid., 28th March 1565.
45	162	Ibid.
45	163	„ 19th December 1570.
45	164	*Rep.* 13, fo. 579.
45	165	*Rep.* 14, fo. 190.
45	166	Ibid., fo. 193b.
46	167	„ fo. 286b.
46	168	*Rep.* 15, fo. 18.
46	169	Ibid., fo. 27.
46	170	Will 14th March, Probate 27th March 1560. P.C.C. 22 Mellershe.
46	171	*Rep.* 15, fo. 80b.
47	172	Ibid., fo. 398.
47	173	*Rep.* 16, fo. 427.
47	174	*Rep.* 17, fo. 421.
47	175	Will 27th July, Probate 29th July 1581. *Com. London* G.L. *Ms.* 9172, Box 10.
47	176	T.C.C., *Y.A.B.*, G.L. *Ms.* 6155, Vol. 2, 28th July, 1560.
47	177	Ibid., (1571–3).
47	178	„ (1567–9).
47	179	*Husting Rolls* (256–332) 265 dors. 7 (1581).
47	180	Will 10th September 1589, Probate 5th February 1590. P.C.C. 8 *Drury*.
48	181	*Rep.* 25, fo. 61b.
48	182	*Rep.* 12, No. 1, fo. 173.
48	183	*Rep.* 19, fo. 258b.
49	184	*Jor.* 3, fo. 6.
49	185	Ibid.

Page	Note	
49	186	*Rep.* 1, fo. 153.
49	187	*Rep.* 2, fo. 206.
49	188	*Rep.* 3, fos. 187, 187b.
49	189	*Rep.* 4, fo. 147.
49	190	Ibid., fo. 147b.
50	191	*Rep.* 9, fo. 91.
50	192	Ibid., fos. 90b, 91.
50	193	*Letter Book S,* fos. 153b–154.
51	194	*Rep.* 5, fos. 191b–192.
51	195	*L. Bk. H,* p. 64; Riley *Memorials,* pp. 405–7.
51	196	*Jor.* 19, fo. 325b.
52	197	See *Rep.* 12, No. 2, fo. 71b, *Rep.* 13, fo. 279.
52	198	*Rep.* 13, fos. 340, 341.
52	199	'An Acte for buying and sellinge Butter and Cheese'. *Statutes of the Realm.*
52	200	'An Acte concerning the Traders of Butter and Cheese'. Ibid.
52	201	'An Act to prevent abuses committed by Traders in Butter and Cheese'. Ibid.
52	202	T.C.C., *L.A.B.,* G.L. *Ms.* 6152, Vol. 1, 28th September 1559.
52	203	*Rep.* 18, fo. 212.
52	204	T.C.C., *Y.A.B.,* G.L. *Ms.* 6155, Vol. 2 (1586–7).
53	205	T.C.C., *L.A.B.,* G.L. *Ms.* 6152, Vol. 2 (1587–9).
53	206	Ibid., (1587–8), (1587–9).
53	207	,, (1587–8).
53	208	T.C.C., *L.A.B.,* G.L. *Ms.* 5162, Vol. 2 (1594–5).
53	209	Ibid., April 1595.
53	210	T.C.C., *Y.A.B.,* G.L. *Ms.* 6155, Vol. 2, 18th July 1588.
53	211	Will 18th April, Probate 22nd April 1615. P.C.C. 28 Rudd.
54	212	See the mortgage dated 27th July 1648. G.L. *Ms.* 6180, Box 2, No. 58. Printed in *T.C.C.R.* p. 247.
54	213	T.C.C., *Y.A.B.,* G.L. *Ms.* 6155, Vol. 2 (1603–3).
54	214	Ibid.
54	215	,, 13th January 1603.
54	216	,, 25th March 1606.
54	217	T.C.C., *L.A.B.,* G.L. *Ms.* 6152, Vol. 2 (1608–9).
54	218	*Jor.* 8, fo. 170b.
54	219	*Rep.* 15, fo. 194b.
54	220	Ibid., fo. 197b.
54	221	T.C.C., *L.A.B.,* G.L. *Ms.* 6152, Vol. 2 (1613–14), (1616–17), (1619–20), (1624–5); *Y.A.B. Ms.* 6155, Vol. 2 (1618–19), (1621–2), (1622–3), (1623–4).
54	222	See *Letter Book QQ,* fos. 87b, 182, 216b; *Letter Book WW,* fos. 150, 164.

Page	Note	
54	223	T.C.C., *Y.A.B.*, G.L. *Ms.* 6155, Vol. 2 (1622–3).
55	224	T.C.C., *L.A.B.*, G.L. *Ms.* 6152, Vol. 2 (1587–9).
55	225	See *The Wax Chandlers of London* by John Dummelow, notes on Chapter 1, p. 22 (note 26).
55	226	Ibid., p. 165.

TALLOW AND CANDLE

56	1	*Rep.* 9, fo. 57.
56	2	Ibid., fo. 247.
56	3	*Letter Book P*, fo. 117b; *Rep.* 9, fo. 247b.
56	4	*Rep.* 10, fo. 30b.
57	5	*Letter Book P*, fo. 151; *Rep.* 10, fo. 32.
57	6	*Rep.* 10. fos. 33–33b; *Letter Book P*, fos. 151–151b.
57	7	*Letter Book P*, fo. 152b.
57	8	*Rep.* 10, fo. 170b.
57	9	Ibid., fo. 179.
58	10	„ fo. 208b.
58	11	„ fo. 209.
58	12	„ fo. 324b.
58	13	Ibid., fo. 207b.
58	14	„ fo. 208b.
59	15	„ fo. 254.
59	16	*Letter Book Q.*, fo. 81b; *Rep.* 10, fo. 329.
60	17	*Rep.* 11, fo. 14b.
60	18	Ibid., fo. 16b.
60	19	„ fo. 11b.
61	20	„ fo. 13.
61	21	„ fo. 16b.
61	22	„ fo. 428.
61	23	*Rep.* 12. No. 1, fo. 78b.
61	24	*Rep.* 12, No. 2, fo. 407b.
61	25	Ibid., fo. 412.
61	26	*Rep.* 11, fo. 162.
61	27	T.C.C., *L.A.B.*, G.L. *Ms.* 6152 Vol. 1 (1545).
61	28	*Rep.* 10, fo. 38.
61	29	T.C.C., *L.A.B.*, G.L. *Ms.* 6152, Vol. 1 (1551–3).
62	30	Will 25th March, Administration, 10th September 1552. P.C.C. 24 Powell.
62	31	*Rep.* 11, fo. 367b.
62	32	Ibid., fo. 427b.
62	33	*Rep.* 12, No. 1, fo. 78b.
62	34	Ibid., fo. 223b.
62	35	*Rep.* 12, No. 2, fo. 455b.
62	36	Ibid., fo. 544.
63	37	*Rep.* 13, No. 2, fo. 437.

Page	Note	
63	38	Ibid., fo. 453.
63	39	*Rep.* 13, No. 1, fo. 37.
63	40	See *Rep.* 13, No. 1, fos. 37, 145, 288.
63	41	*Letter Book S*, fo. 75b.
63	42	*Rep.* 13, No. 2, fo. 416b.
63	43	Ibid., fo. 421b.
64	44	T.C.C., *L.A.B.*, G.L. *Ms.* 6152, Vol. 1, 13th August 1556.
64	45	Ibid., Inventory (1556–7).
64	46	*Rep.* 13, No. 2, fo. 448b.
64	47	Ibid., fo. 449b.
64	48	T.C.C., *L.A.B.*, G.L. *Ms.* 6152, Vol. 1 (1557–9).
65	49	*Letter Book S*, fos. 75b, 153b; *Rep.* 13, No. 2, fo. 421b; *Rep.* 14, fos. 22, 75b, 142, 325, 472.
66	50	See *Rep.* 15, 227b, 330, 438; *Letter Book V*, fos. 96b, 173, 207b, 233b, 286b, 288b; *Rep.* 16, fos. 362b, 427b, 467, *Rep.* 17, fos. 3, 5b, 78b; *Letter Book X*, fos. 4b, 42, *Rep.* 17, fos. 143b, 153b, 306; *Rep.* 18, fos, 6b, 206b; *Letter Book X*, fos. 303b, 355, *Rep.* 18, fos. 308, 376b; *Letter Book X*, fo. 378; *Jor.* 20, No. 1, fo. 251b.
67	51	Rep. 14, fo. 142.
67	52	Ibid., fo. 75b.
67	53	„ fo. 147b.
68	54	*Rep.* 14, fo. 325.
68	55	Ibid., fo. 472.
68	56	*The Price Revolution in Sixteenth Century England*, edited by Peter H. Ramsey (1971), p. 4.
68	57	*Rep.* 15, fo. 63.
68	58	Ibid., fo. 227b.
68	59	See *Rep.* 15, fos. 330, 438, *Letter Book V*, fos. 96b, 173, *Rep.* 16, fos. 362b, 467, *Rep.* 17, fos. 3, 143b, 306, *Letter Book X*, fo. 42, *Rep.* 18, fos. 6b, 206b.
68	60	*Rep.* 16, fo. 467.
68	61	*The History of the Butchers Company* (1929) by Arthur Pearce, p. 72.
69	62	See *The Price Revolution in Sixteenth Century England*, op. cit., p. 4, for the Editor's references to statistics at both periods.
69	63	*Rep.* 18, fo. 308.
69	64	See *Rep.* 18, fo. 376b; *Letter Book Y*, fos. 76b, 152; *Rep.* 19, fos. 200b, 317b, 451; *Rep.* 20, fo. 82b; *Letter Book Z*, fo. 220b; *Rep.* 21, fo. 65.
69	65	*Rep.* 19, fos. 317b, 451; *Rep.* 20 fos., 82b, 325b.
69	66	*Rep.* 21, fo. 516b.
69	67	Ibid., fo. 521.
70	68	„ fo. 550b.
70	69	*Letter Book AB*. fo. 108b.

Page	Note	
70	70	*Rep.* 24, fo. 130.
70	71	*Letter Book AB*, fo. 108b.
70	72	*The Price Revolution in Sixteenth Century England*, op. cit. p. 4.
70	73	*Rep.* 34, fo. 538.
70	74	*Letter Book GG*, fo. 294b.
71	75	*Rep.* 34, fo. 566b.
71	76	Ibid., fo. 572b.
71	77	*Rep.* 44, fo. 339.
72	78	Ibid., fo. 345.
72	79	„ fo. 366.
72	80	*Rep.* 11, fo. 255.
73	81	Ibid., fo. 226.
74	82	*Rep.* 7, fo. 44b.
74	83	Ibid., fo. 62.
74	84	*Rep.* 11, fo. 150.
74	85	Ibid., fo. 309b.
74	86	T.C.C., *L.A.B.*, G.L. *Ms.* 6152, Vol. 1 (1549–51).
74	87	Ibid.
75	88	„
75	89	„ Vol. 1 (1551–3).
75	90	Ibid.
75	91	*Rep.* 12, No. 2, fo. 354.
75	92	T.C.C., *L.A.B.*, G.L. *Ms.* 6152, Vol. 1 (1553–5).
75	93	*Rep.* 13, fo. 506.
76	94	*Rep.* 14, fo. 76.
76	95	Ibid., fo. 79.
76	96	„ fo. 79b.
77	97	T.C.C., *L.A.B.*, G.L. *Ms.* 6152. Vol. 1 (1561–2)
77	98	Ibid.
77	99	Ibid. 25th June 1562.
77	100	„ (1562–3).
77	101	*Rep.* 15, fos. 147b, 148.
78	102	T.C.C., *L.A.B.*, G.L. *Ms.* 6152, Vol. 1, 24th January 1570.
78	103	*Husting Rolls* (176–253) 250 Dors. 15 (1558).
78	104	Ibid., 250 Dors. 40 (1559).
78	105	T.C.C., *L.A.B.*, G.L. *Ms.* 6152, Vol. 1, 28th April 1574.
78	106	*Husting Rolls* (256–332) 260 Dors. 46 (1575).
78	107	T.C.C., *L.A.B.*, G.L. *Ms.* 6152, Vol. 1, 3rd May 1564.
78	108	Ibid. (1565–6).
78	109	„
78	110	„ and (1567–9).
78	111	T.C.C., *L.A.B.*, G.L. *Ms.* 6152, Vol. 1, 4th October 1569.
79	112	Ibid., (1574–5).
79	113	*Letter Book V*, fo. 258b.
79	114	*Rep.* 16, fo. 372.

Page	Note	
79	115	*Rep.* 18, fo. 70b.
79	116	*Husting Rolls* (256–332) 260 Dors. 75 (1575).
80	117	T.C.C., *L.A.B.*, G.L. *Ms.* 6152, Vol. 1 (1581–2).
80	118	Ibid.
80	119	*Rep.* 18, fo. 101.
80	120	Ibid., fo. 107b.
80	121	,, fo. 101b.
80	122	,, fo. 298b.
80	123	,, fo. 70b.
81	124	See *Husting Rolls* (256–332) 264-22-36. (1580. Bell, Richard, deceased.)
81	125	Will 31st January, Probate, last day of February 1578. P.C.C. 7 Langley.
81	126	T.C.C., *L.A.B.*, G.L. *Ms.* 6152, Vol. 1 (1563–4).
81	127	*Husting Rolls* (256–332) 260. 23. 64 (1575).
81	128	Ibid., (176–255) 260 Dors. 15 (1558).
81	129	Will 30th April 1594, Probate 24th May 1595. P.C.C. 37 Scott.
81	130	*Husting Rolls* (256–332) 260. 25. 74 (1575).
82	131	*Rep.* 16, fo. 427b.
82	132	*Letter Book V*, fo. 214b; *Jor.* 19, fo. 143.
82	133	*Rep.* 18, fo. 378.
83	134	Ibid., fo. 438; *Letter Book Y*, fo. 21b.
83	135	*Jor.* 20, No. 1, fo. 251b.
83	136	*Rep.* 5, fo. 196b.
84	137	*Rep.* 7, fo. 31b.
84	138	*Letter Book N*, fo. 315; *Rep.* 7, fo. 94b.
84	139	Ibid., fo. 315b; Ibid., fo. 95.
84	140	Wills, 8th October (goods), 18th October (lands), Probate 25th November 1551. *Com. London* 100 Clyffe.
84	141	*Husting Rolls* (176–255) 246. 22. 105 (1552).
84	142	Ibid.
84	143	*Letter Book N*, fo. 315b; *Rep.* 7, fo. 97.
84	144	*Letter Book O*, fo. 64b; *Rep.* 5, fo. 127.
84	145	Ibid., fo. 1; *Rep.* 7, fo. 111.
85	146	*Rep.* 13, fo. 95.
85	147	*Letter Book V*, fo. 250b.
85	148	T.C.C., *L.A.B.*, G.L. *Ms.* 6152, Vol. 1, 15th January/ 3rd February 1551.
85	149	T.C.C., *Y.A.B.*, G.L. *Ms.* 6155, Vol. 2 (1561–2).
86	150	*Rep.* 24, fo. 268.
86	151	Ibid., fo. 481.
86	152	*Analytical Index to the series of records known as the Remembrancia. AD 1579–1664,* pp. 60–61.
86	153	*Letter Book BB*, fo. 4.
87	154	*Rep.* 28, fo. 169.

Page	Note	
87	155	*Rep.* 32, fo. 64b.
87	156	Ibid., fo. 314.
87	157	*Rep.* 34, fo. 83b.
87	158	T.C.C., *L.A.B.*, G.L. *Ms.* 6152, Vol. 2 (1619–20).
87	159	Ibid. (1620–21).
87	160	,, 2nd July 1636.
87	161	,, (1636–7).
87	162	*Rep.* 51, fo. 17.
87	163	Ibid., fo. 32.
88	164	*Rep.* 6, fo. 27b.
88	165	*Letter Book O*, fo. 19; *Rep.* 7, fo. 144b.
89	166	*Rep.* 8, fo. 72.
89	167	Ibid., fo. 96b.
89	168	,, fo. 103b.
89	169	,, fo. 172.
89	170	Will 18th December 1543, Probate 11th January 1544. P.C.C. 1 Pynnyng.
89	171	*Rep.* 11, fo. 225b.
89	172	Ibid., fo. 228b.
89	173	*Rep.* 12, No. 1, fos. 78b, 80.
89	174	Ibid., fo. 96.
90	175	T.C.C., *L.A.B.*, G.L. *Ms.* 6152, Vol. 1, 19th May 1545.
90	176	Ibid., (1549–50).
90	177	Will 18th November, Probate 27th November 1554. P.C.C. 12 More.
90	178	*Rep.* 12, No. 2, fo. 409.
90	179	Will 1st September, Probate 5th October 1558. P.C.C. 50 Noods.
91	180	*Rep.* 12, No. 2, fo. 358b.
91	181	Ibid., fo. 364.
91	182	T.C.C., *L.A.B.*, G.L., *Ms.* 6152, Vol. 1 (1551–3).
91	183	Ibid., (1553–5).
91	184	,, (1551–3)
92	185	,, (1549–51).
92	186	,, (1553–5).
92	187	Ibid.
92	188	,,
92	189	,, 17th February 1562.
92	190	,, (1561–2).
92	191	,, 25th January 1565.
92	192	*Rep.* 11, fo. 339.
93	193	*Rep.* 13, No. 2, fo. 500.
93	194	*Rep.* 14, fo. 14b.
93	195	*Rep.* 13, No. 2, fo. 553.
93	196	*Rep.* 15, fo. 469b.
93	197	*Rep.* 14, fo. 299b.

Page	Note	
93	198	Ibid.
93	199	*Rep.* 13, fo. 171b.
93	200	*Rep.* 13, No. 2, fo. 454.
93	201	*Rep.* 14, fo. 67b.
93	202	Ibid., fo. 65.
93	203	,, fo. 67b.
93	204	*Rep.* 16, fo. 207.
93	205	*Jor.* 19, fo. 143.
94	206	*Rep.* 16, fo. 358b.
94	207	Ibid., fo. 369.
94	208	,, fo. 423.
94	209	,, fo. 428b.
94	210	,, fo. 429.
94	211	,, fo. 443.
95	212	*Rep.* 18, fo. 70b.
95	213	T.C.C., *L.A.B.*, G.L. *Ms.* 6152, Vol. 1 (1557–9).
95	214	Ibid., 24th January 1558.
95	215	,, (1557–9).
95	216	,, (1555–7).
95	217	*Rep.* 16, fo. 450.
95	218	Ibid., fo. 471b.
96	219	*Rep.* 17, fo. 80b.
96	220	Ibid., fo. 162b.
96	221	,, fo. 165.
96	222	T.C.C., *L.A.B.*, G.L. *Ms.* 6152, Vol. 1, 5th October 1569.
96	223	*Husting Rolls* (256–332) 276 (20) 1596.
96	224	*Rep.* 18, fo. 48.
96	225	Ibid., fo. 70b.
96	226	T.C.C., *L.A.B.*, G.L. *Ms.* 6152, Vol. 1, 10th July 1567.
97	227	Will 16th July, Probate 15th September 1578. *Archd.*, *London.* Reg. 4–146.
97	228	*Rep.* 18, fo. 78b.
97	229	Ibid.
97	230	*Letter Book X*, fo. 269.
97	231	*Rep.* 18, fos. 213, 213b.
97	232	Will 20th October, Probate 18th December 1595. *Com. London.* Reg. 1592–7, fo. 283.
98	233	T.C.C., *L.A.B.*, G.L. *Ms.* 6152, Vol. 1 (1563–4).
98	234	Ibid., (1567–9).
98	235	,, 10th April 1565.
98	236	*Rep.* 18, fo. 221.
98	237	*Jor.* 20, No. 1, fo. 151.
98	238	*Rep.* 18, fo. 314.
99	239	*Letter Book X*, fo. 355.
99	240	Rep. 18, fo. 320.
99	241	,, fos. 43b, 44, 70b, 71, 71b; *Letter Book X*, fo. 231.

Page	Note	
99	242	*Rep.* 18, fos. 320, 321.
99	243	Ibid., fo. 320b.
99	244	„ fo. 321b.
99	245	„ fo. 322.
99	246	„ fo. 322b.
100	247	*Husting Rolls* (256–332) 276 (20) 1596.
100	248	Will 27th February, Probate 10th March 1602. *Com. London.* Reg. 1597–1603 fo. 267.
100	249	T.C.C., *L.A.B.*, G.L. *Ms.* 6152, Vol. 2 (1605–7).
100	250	Ibid., Vol. 1 (1578–80).
100	251	T.C.C., *Y.A.B.*, G.L. *Ms.* 6155, Vol. 2, 27th April 1578.
100	252	See the model recognyzance by which John Mynts was bound. (*Rep.* 18, fo. 320b).
100	253	*Rep.* 18, fos. 324, 334.
100	254	Ibid., fo. 334.
100	255	T.C.C., *L.A.B.*, G.L. *Ms.* 6152, Vol. 2 (1603), (1615–16).
101	256	Ibid., Vol. 1, 18th September 1567.
101	257	*Rep.* 18, fo. 324.
101	258	Ibid., fo. 334.
101	259	*Rep.* 19, fos. 38, 39.
101	260	Ibid., fo. 42.
101	261	Ibid.
101	262	„ fos. 45, 48b.
101	263	T.C.C., *L.A.B.*, G. L. *Ms.* 6152, Vol. 1 (1563–4).

CRESSET LIGHT

Page	Note	
102	1	See Riley *Memorials.* p. 433 (From *Letter Book H*, fo. cxi).
102	2	T.C.C., *L.A.B.*, G.L. *Ms.* 6152, Vol. 1 (1566–7).
102	3	Ibid., (1576).
102	4	„ Vol. 2, 9th July 1599.
102	5	13 Edward I (*Statutes of the Realm*, p. 96).
102	6	*Letter Book K*, fo. 168 (Calendar p. 215).
103	7	See *References respecting the mode of watching the City of London, abstracted from the Records.* Guildhall, Records, Pam. 376.
103	8	*Letter Book P*, fo. 131b.
103	9	*References respecting the mode of watching*, op. cit.
104	10	*Letter Book P*, fo. 176.
104	11	*Letter Book X*, fo. 2b.
104	12	*Rep.* 12, No. 1, fo. 112.
104	13	*Letter Book X*, fo. 94.
104	14	*Jor.* 12, fo. 334b.
105	15	*Rep.* 7, fo. 265b.

Page	Note	
	Page	*Note*
105	16	T.C.C., *L.A.B.*, G.L. *Ms.* 6152, Vol. 1 (1567–8).
106	17	Ibid., (1570–71).
106	18	*Rep.* 10, fo. 42.
106	19	*Letter Book P*, fo. 166.
107	20	Ibid., fo. 217.
107	21	*Jor.* 14, fo. 208.
107	22	*Rep.* 10, fo. 160b.
107	23	Ibid., fo. 210.
107	24	*Rep.* 15, fo. 351b.
107	25	*Rep.* 16, fo. 221b.
108	26	*Calendar of State Papers and Manuscripts relating to English Affairs existing in the archives and collections of Venice and in other libraries of northern Italy.* Setting of the Midsummer Watch. Vol. III, 1520–26. s. 224, pp. 136–7.
109	27	See *The Gilds and Companies of London* by George Unwin. (1963), p. 372.
109	28	*A Survey of London* by John Stow, reprinted from the text of 1603, with Introduction and Notes by G. L. Kingsford (1908, re-issued 1971), Vol. 1, pp. 101–3.
109	29	Ibid., p. 103.
109	30	*Jor.* 14, fo. 208.
110	31	*Jor.* 18, fo. 319b.
111	32	*Rep.* 15, fo. 447.
111	33	*Letter Book V*, fo. 106.
111	34	T.C.C., *L.A.B.*, G.L. *Ms.* 6152, Vol. 1 (1566–7).
112	35	Ibid., fo. 176.
112	36	T.C.C., *L.A.B.*, G.L. *Ms.* 6152, Vol. 1 (1567–8).
112	37	*Letter Book V*, fo. 118.
113	38	*Rep.* 16, fo. 225b.
113	39	Ibid., fo. 266.
114	40	*A Survey of the Cities of London and Westminster* by John Stow, reprinted, etc. and enlarged, by John Stype. 1720, Book 1, p. 257.
115	41	*Letter Book V*, fo. 241b.
115	42	Ibid., fo. 298b.
115	43	,,
115	44	T.C.C., *L.A.B.*, G.L. *Ms.* 6152, Vol. 1 (1570–71).
115	45	*Rep.* 17, fo. 160.
116	46	*Jor.* 20, No. 1, fo. 136b.
116	47	Ibid., fo. 222b.
116	48	*Jor.* 20, No. 2, fo. 412; *Jor.* 21, fos. 215, Ibid., fo. 296, 375b.
116	49	*A Survey of London* by John Stow. op. cit., Vol. 1, p. 103.
117	50	*Jor.* 21, fo. 441, seq.
117	51	*Jor.* 22, fo. 331.
117	52	See *Jor.* 22, fos. 107, 188b, 301b, 394b.

Page   *Note*

THE ORDINANCES OF 1538 AND AFTER
QUARTERAGE
AND THE CONFLICT WITH THE SALTERS

119	1	*E.M.C.R.*, p. 67.
119	2	*A History of the Salters Company*, by J. Steven Watson, p. 41.
119	3	*Letter Book I*, fo. ccxxxivb (Calendar, pp. 222–3).
119	4	*Letter Book K*, fo. 47b. (Calendar, p. 62).
120	5	*L. Bk.* pp. 321–2.
120	6	*Statutes of the Realm*, 1816, Vol. ii, pp. 298–9.
120	7	*L. Bk. K*, Introduction p. xli.
121	8	Ibid., pp. 223–4 and *History of the Worshipful Company of Pewterers* by Charles Welch, pp. 8, 9.
121	9	*L. Bk. L*, p. 128.
121	10	Ibid., p. 246.
121	11	*Jor.* 9, fo. 163
122	12	*L. Bk. L*, pp. 273–4.
122	13	*Rep.* 10, fo. 50.
122	14	Ibid., fo. 54b, seq.
122	15	Ibid., and see *Letter Book P*, fos. 153b–159.
123	16	An *Account of the Mistery of Mercers* by Sir John Watney, p. 32.
124	17	*The Tripple Crowns, a narrative history of the Drapers' Company*, by Tom Girtin, p. 48.
124	18	*History of the Worshipful Company of Pewterers*, by Charles Welch, p. 10.
124	19	*L. Bk. K*, p. 234.
124	20	Ibid., p. 333. Printed in *The Annals of the Barber Surgeons*, by Sidney Young, pp. 44–7.
124	21	*L. Bk. L*, p. 64. Set out in the return made by the Painters' Company to *the Livery Companies Commission of 1884.* (iii. 613–14).
124	22	*L. Bk. L*, pp. 143–4.
124	23	Ibid., p. 169.
124	24	Ibid., pp. 183–4.
124	25	„ pp. 184–5.
125	26	„ pp. 199–203.
125	27	„ p. 203.
125	28	„ p. 256.
125	29	„ pp. 258–9.
126	30	„ pp. 263–4.
126	31	„ p. 265.
126	32	„ p. 272.
126	33	„ pp. 293–4.
126	34	„ pp. 284–5.

Page	Note	
126	35	Ibid., pp. 310–13.
126	36	T.C.C., *Y.A.B.*, G.L. *Ms.* 6155, Vol. 1, fo. 2 (fo. 5).
126	37	Ibid., fo. 48.
127	38	„ fo. 59b.
127	39	„ fo. 61.
127	40	„ fo. 105.
127	41	„ fos. 105b–107.
127	42	„ fo. 112, seq.
127	43	„ fos. 118b, 119, seq.
127	44	„ (1523–4), (1524–5).
127	45	„ (1523–4), (1531–2).
127	46	„ (1533–4).
127	47	„ (1535–6).
127	48	„ (1536–7).
128	49	„ (1528–9).
128	50	„ (1530–1).
128	51	„ (1536–7).
128	52	„ fo. 155b.
128	53	Ibid.
129	54	„ (1539–40).
129	55	T.C.C., *L.A.B.*, G.L. *Ms.* 6152, Vol. 1 (1549–51).
129	56	Ibid., (1551–3).
129	57	Letters Patent of Henry VI, 24th February 1439. See *the Charters of the Merchant Taylors Company* by Sir Frederick Morris Fry and R. T. D. Sayles, pp. 19–25.
129	58	Letters Patent of Henry VI, 19th August 1444. See *History and Antiquities of the Worshipful Company of Leathersellers* by William Henry Black, pp. 26–9.
130	59	Ibid., pp. 30–31.
130	60	*L. Bk. K.* pp. 334–5.
130	61	*Rep.* 16, fo. 455b. Transcribed in *the Wax Chandlers' Charter and Ordinance Book of 1622.* G.L. *Ms.* 9496, fo. 17.
130	62	See Article 8 of the Ordinances printed on pp. 135–40 of the *Wax Chandlers of London,* op. cit.
134	63	*Rep.* 10, fo. 102.
134	64	Ibid., fo. 103.
135	65	„ fo. 145b.
135	66	See the list of Mayors and Sheriffs of London commencing on p. 276 of *L. Bk. F.*
135	67	*Rep.* 10, fos, 33, 33b; *Letter Book P,* fos. 151, 151b.
136	68	*Rep.* 11, fo. 13.
136	69	*Letter Book R,* fo. 8.
137	70	Ibid., fo. 51.
137	71	*Rep.* 14, fo. 428.
138	72	T.C.C., *L.A.B.*, G.L. *Ms.* 6152, Vol. 1 (1565–6).
138	73	Ibid., (1567–9).

Page	Note	
138	74	Ibid., 22nd March 1565.
138	75	,,
138	76	,, 3rd November 1575.
138	77	Ratification (illuminated) of Ordinances of this date framed and glazed, in the Company's possession. Authenticated copy. G.L. *Ms.* 6174, Vol. 1.
138	78	T.C.C., *L.A.B.*, G.L. *Ms.* 6152, Vol. 1, 20th February 1588.
138	79	Ibid., 20th April 1588.
140	80	,, 1st November 1589.
141	81	Authenticated copy. G.L. *Ms.* 6174, Vol. 2.
141	82	Letters Patent dated 29th July 1677. G.L. *Ms.* 6182. (Charter Box), *Ms.* 6173, Office copy.

LETTERS PATENT OF ELIZABETH I
(TYLER'S PATENT)
SOAP, VINEGAR, BARRELLED BUTTER, OIL AND HOPS

Page	Note	
142	1	Exemplification, at the request of Roger Price. G.L. *Ms.* 6180, Box 7, 357. The like, 28th April 1618, ditto. 358.
142	2	*A Survey of the Cities of London and Westminster*, op. cit. Book V, p. 210.
143	3	*Rep.* 19, fo. 207.
144	4	T.C.C., *L.A.B.*, G.L. *Ms.* 6152, Vol. 1, (1576–7).
144	5	Ibid.
144	6	*Rep.* 19, fo. 210b.
146	7	*Jor.* 16, fo. 202b.
146	8	*Letter Book V*, fo. 236b.
146	9	Ibid., fo. 292.
147	10	*Jor.* 18, fo. 183.
148	11	T.C.C., *L.A.B.*, G.L. *Ms.* 6152, Vol. 1, 20th July 1577.
148	12	Ibid., 12th July 1577.
148	13	Will 18th September, Probate 6th November 1578. *P.C.C.* 39 Langley.
148	14	*Rep.* 19, fo. 243b.
149	15	Ibid., fo. 247.
149	16	,, fo. 263b.
149	17	T.C.C., *L.A.B.*, G.L. *Ms.* 6152, Vol. 1 (1580–81).
150	18	Ibid.
150	19	,,
150	20	,,
150	21	See the *recital* in the Indenture of Assignment dated 25th June 1589. G.L. *Ms.* 6180, Box 7, 359.
150	22	T.C.C., *L.A.B.*, G.L. *Ms.* 6152, Vol. 1 (1580–81).
150	23	Ibid.

Page	Note	
150	24	Ibid.
150	25	„ (1581–2).
150	26	„
150	27	„
150	28	„
150	29	„
150	30	„
151	31	*Rep.* 21, fo. 28b.
151	32	T.C.C., *L.A.B.*, G.L. *Ms.* 6152, Vol. 1, 5th November 1582.
151	33	Ibid., (1582–3).
151	34	„ 11th November 1582.
151	35	„ 8th November 1582.
151	36	„
151	37	„ (1582–3).
151	38	„
151	39	*Rep.* 21, fo. 48.
151	40	*Rep.* 23, fo. 201b.
151	41	T.C.C., *L.A.B.*, G.L. *Ms.* 6152, Vol. 1 (1582–3).
151	42	Ibid.
151	43	„
151	44	„
151	45	„
151	46	„
151	47	„
152	48	„
153	49	*Analytical Index to the series of Records known as the Remembrancia*, op. cit., pp. 213–4.
153	50	T.C.C., *L.A.B.*, G.L. *Ms.* 6152, Vol. 1 (1582–3).
154	51	Note 21.
154	52	*Rep.* 20, fo. 461b.
154	53	T.C.C., *L.A.B.*, G.L. *Ms.* 6152, Vol. 1 (1583–5).
154	54	*Rep.* 21, fo. 232b.
154	55	Ibid., fo. 238.
154	56	„ fo. 504.
154	57	*Rep.* 22, fo. 2b.
155	58	*Rep.* 21, fo. 531.
155	59	G.L. *Ms.* 6180, Box 7, 359.
155	60	Ibid., 360.
155	61	„ 362.
155	62	„ 363.
155	63	„ 364.
155	64	T.C.C., *L.A.B.*, G.L. *Ms.* 6152, Vol. 2, 5th November 1589.
155	65	*Letter Book, etc.* fo. 313.
156	66	*Rep.* 22, fo. 125.
156	67	Ibid., fo. 130.

Page	Note	
156	68	Ibid., fo. 141.
156	69	„ fo. 32b.
156	70	„ fo. 35.
156	71	„ fo. 299.
157	72	*Husting Rolls* (256–332) 276. 13. 20 (1596).
157	73	T.C.C., *L.A.B.*, G.L. *Ms.* 6152, Vol. 2, 5th August 1596.
157	74	Will 25th February, Probate 29th March 1614. *P.C.C.* 22 Lawe.
157	75	T.C.C., *L.A.B.*, G.L. *Ms.* 6152, Vol. 2, 30th July 1591.
158	76	*Rep.* 22, fo. 316b.
158	77	Ibid., fo. 387b.
158	78	*Rep.* 23, fo. 47.
158	79	Ibid., fo. 185.
158	80	„ fo. 14.
158	81	„ fo. 15; *Letter Book AB*, fo. 151.
158	82	T.C.C., *L.A.B.*, G.L. *Ms.* 6152, Vol. 2, 3rd December 1595.
159	83	*Rep.* 23, fo. 544b.
159	84	*Rep.* 24, fo. 48.
159	85	See *Rep.* 24, fos. 83b, 87b, 109b.
159	86	*Jor.* 24, fo. 226.
159	87	T.C.C., *L.A.B.*, G.L. *Ms.* 6152, Vol. 2, 27th December 1597.
159	88	*Rep.* 24, fo. 205b.
160	89	Ibid., fo. 353.
160	90	„ fo. 414b.
160	91	*Jor.* 25, fo. 76b.
160	92	Ibid., fo. 98.
160	93	„ fo. 102b.
161	94	„ fo. 138b.
161	95	„ fos. 103, 138b.
161	96	*Rep.* 25, fo. 24b.
161	97	Ibid., fo. 39.
161	98	*Letter Book BB*, fo. 32.
161	99	*Rep.* 25, fo. 62.
162	100	„ fo. 85b.
162	101	*Jor.* 25, fo. 155.
162	102	*Letter Book BB*, fo. 34.
162	103	*Rep.* 25, fo. 95.
163	104	Ibid., fo. 96.
163	105	„ fo. 114.
163	106	„ fo. 208.
163	107	„ fo. 275.
163	108	*Rep.* 26, fo. 24.
163	109	Ibid., fo. 45b.
163	110	„ fo. 48.
163	111	„ fo. 49.

Page	Note	
164	112	T.C.C., *L.A.B.*, G.L. *Ms.* 6152, Vol. 2 (1603–4).
164	113	*Rep.* 26, fo. 95b.
164	114	Ibid., fo. 219b.
164	115	„ fo. 223b.
164	116	„ fo. 228.
164	117	„ fo. 232b.
164	118	*The Reign of Elizabeth, 1558–1603* by J. B. Black, second edition, pp. 232–4.
164	119	*Rep.* 26, fo. 265b.
165	120	*Rep.* 27, fo. 245.
165	121	T.C.C., *L.A.B.*, G.L. *Ms.* 6152, Vol. 2, 6th October 1606.
165	122	Ibid., 29th October 1606.
165	123	„ (1605–7).
165	124	„
165	125	„
165	126	„
165	127	„ (1606–7).
165	128	*Rep.* 28, fo. 109b.
165	129	T.C.C., *C.B.9*, G.L. *Ms.* 6153, Vol. 1, 26th November 1607.
166	130	Ibid., 10th December 1607.
166	131	T.C.C., *C.B.9*, G.L. *Ms.* 6153, Vol. 1, 1st March 1608.
166	132	Ibid.
166	133	Ibid., (1607–8).
166	134	*Rep.* 28, fo. 171b.
166	135	T.C.C., *C.B.9*, G.L. *Ms.* 6153, Vol. 1, 1st March 1608.
166	136	T.C.C., *C.B.9*, G.L. *Ms.* 6153, Vol. 1, 6th July 1615.
167	137	G.L. *Ms.* 6180, Box 7, 365.
167	138	T.C.C., *C.B.9*, G.L. *Ms.* 6153, Vol. 1, 19th March 1618.
167	139	Ibid., 6th May 1618.
167	140	*Rep.* 36, fo. 230.
167	141	*Rep.* 40, fo. 20b.
167	142	T.C.C., *L.A.B.*, G.L. *Ms.* 6152, Vol. 2, (1623–4).
167	143	Ibid., (1624–5).

THE STUART CHARTERS
THE CANDLEMAKERS
AND THE END OF SEARCHES

168	1	Inspeximus Charter of Edward VI, 18th February 1548, framed and glazed, in the Company's possession.
168	2	Framed and glazed, in the Company's possession.
169	3	T.C.C., *L.A.B.*, G.L. *Ms.* 6152, Vol. 2 (1605–7).
170	4	See *T.C.C.R.*, p. 156.
171	5	Ibid., p. 168.

Page	Note	
172	6	T.C.C., *L.A.B.*, G.L. *Ms.* 6152, Vol. 2 (1615–16).
172	7	Ibid. (1617–18).
172	8	Ibid.
172	9	Ibid. (1618–19).
172	10	Ibid.
173	11	Ibid. (1619–20).
173	12	Framed and glazed in the Company's possession. For a copy, see *T.C.C.R.*, pp. 176–8.
173	13	*London and the Kingdom*, by Reginald R. Sharpe, D.C.L., Vol. II, pp. 87–9.
173	14	T.C.C., *L.A.B.*, G.L. *Ms.* 6152, Vol. 2 (1634–5).
173	15	T.C.C., *C.B.9*, G.L. *Ms.* 6153, Vol. 1, 5th December 1639.
174	16	T.C.C., *L.A.B.*, G.L. *Ms.* 6152, Vol. 2 (1639–40)
174	17	T.C.C., *C.B.9*, G.L. *Ms.* 6153, Vol. 1, 22nd January 1640.
174	18	Ibid., 23rd January 1640.
174	19	Ibid., 28th November 1645.
174	20	T.C.C., *L.A.B.*, G.L. *Ms.* 6152, Vol. 3 (1653–4).
174	21	Ibid.
174	22	T.C.C., *C.B.11*, G.L. *Ms.* 6153, Vol. 3, 20th April 1664.
175	23	T.C.C., *L.A.B.*, G.L. *Ms.* 6152, Vol. 3 (1664–5).
175	24	T.C.C., *C.B.11*, G.L. *Ms.* 6153, Vol. 3, 20th April 1665.
175	25	T.C.C., *L.A.B.*, G.L. *Ms.* 6152, Vol. 3 (1667–8).
175	26	T.C.C., *C.B.12*, G.L. *Ms.* 6153, Vol. 4, 13th June 1669; 5th October 1670; 30th January 1673; T.C.C., *L.A.B.*, G.L. *Ms.* 6152, Vol. 3 (1668–9).
175	27	T.C.C., *C.B.10*, G.L. *Ms.* 6153, Vol. 2, 9th July 1650.
175	28	Ibid., 1st August 1650.
175	29	„ 15th July 1651.
176	30	„ 24th July 1651; 11th August 1651.
176	31	T.C.C., *C.B.11*, G.L. *Ms.* 6153, Vol. 3, 23rd July 1663.
176	32	T.C.C., *C.B.12*, G.L. *Ms.* 6153, Vol. 4, 20th April 1669.
176	33	G.L. *Ms.* 6180, Box 4, 149.
176	34	T.C.C., *C.B.12*, G.L. *Ms.* 6153, Vol. 4, 18th May 1671.
177	35	T.C.C., *L.A.B*, G L. *Ms.* 6152, Vol. 3 (1671–2).
177	36	T.C.C., *C.B.12*, G.L. *Ms.* 6153, Vol. 4, 20th December 1669.
177	37	Ibid., 19th January 1671.
177	38	G.L. *Ms.* 6180, Box 4, 146.
177	39	Ibid., Box 4, 145.
177	40	T.C.C., *C.B.12*, G.L. *Ms.* 6153, Vol. 4, 30th January 1673.
177	41	Ibid., 20th December 1673.
178	42	„ 17th November 1674.
178	43	G.L. *Ms.* 6180, Box 4, 162.
178	44	T.C.C., *C.B.12*, G.L. *Ms.* 6153, Vol. 4, 18th March 1675.
179	45	T.C.C., *C.B.9*, G.L. *Ms.* 6153, Vol. 1, 28th March 1615; 16th July 1616; 10th July 1623.

Page	Note	
179	46	T.C.C., *C.B.12*, G.L. *Ms.* 6153, Vol. 4, 18th March 1675.
179	47	Ibid., 5th May 1675.
180	48	G.L. *Ms.* 6180, Box 4, 163.
180	49	T.C.C., *C.B.12*, G.L. *Ms.* 6153, Vol. 4, 20th July 1675.
180	50	Ibid., 11th August 1675.
180	51	T.C.C., *L.A.B.*, G.L. *Ms.* 6152, Vol. 3 (1675–6).
180	52	G.L. *Ms.* 6180, Box 4, 164.
180	53	T.C.C., *C.B.13*, G.L. *Ms.* 6153, Vol. 5, 16th February 1676, 22nd February 1676; 1st March 1676; 20th April 1676.
180	54	See the addition to the paper headed 'Severall privileges agreed to be granted to the candle makers, March 1675–6' considered by Mr Steele. G.L. *Ms.* 6180, Box 4, 165 and 167.
181	55	T.C.C., *C.B.13*, G.L. *Ms.* 6153, Vol. 5, 20th April 1676.
181	56	See the paper without heading or endorsement commencing 'The first institucion of Corporacions . . .'. G.L. *Ms.* 6180, Box 4, 166.
181	57	T.C.C., *C.B.13*, G.L. *Ms.* 6153, Vol. 5, 2nd June 1676; 8th June 1676.
181	58	Ibid., 8th June 1676.
181	59	G.L. *Ms.* 6182. Original on Vellum, 3 skins, illuminated initial, great seal on silk cord.
181	60	*Rep.* 82, fos. 74, 74b.
181	61	T.C.C., *L.A.B.*, G.L. *Ms.* 6152, Vol. 3 (1676–7).
183	62	*Rep.* 82, fo. 74.
183	63	Ibid., fo. 85b, seq. G.L. *Ms.* 6180, Box 4, 171.
184	64	T.C.C., *L.A.B.*, G.L. *Ms.* 6152, Vol. 3 (1678–9).
184	65	Ibid.
185	66	T.C.C., *C.B.13*, G.L. *Ms.* 6153, Vol. 5, 19th February 1677; 5th March 1677.
185	67	Ibid., 13th March 1677.
185	68	Ibid.
185	69	„ 5th March 1677.
185	70	„ 19th March 1677; 2nd April 1677; 7th May 1677; 2nd July 1677; 18th July 1677; 1st August 1677.
185	71	T.C.C., *C.B.13*, G.L. *Ms.* 6153, Vol. 5, 1st August 1677.
185	72	Ibid., 11th July 1678.
186	73	„ 18th October 1678.
186	74	„ 6th November 1678.
186	75	Ibid.
186	76	Ibid., 16th January 1679.
187	77	*London and the Kingdom*, op. cit., Vol. II, p. 477 and footnote.
187	78	Ibid., p. 494.
187	79	„ p. 497.
187	80	„ pp. 498–500.
187	81	„ p. 504.

Page	Note	
187	82	Ibid., p. 505.
188	83	T.C.C., *C.B.13*, G.L. *Ms.* 6153, Vol. 5, 9th May 1684.
188	84	Ibid.
188	85	T.C.C., *C.B.13*, G.L. *Ms.* 6153, Vol. 5, 4th June 1684.
188	86	Ibid., 9th June 1684.
188	87	Ibid.
188	88	*London and the Kingdom*, op. cit., Vol. II, p. 506; *Jor.* 50, fo. 128.
189	89	T.C.C., *C.B.14*, G.L. *Ms.* 6153, Vol. 6, 9th June 1684.
189	90	T.C.C., *C.B.13*, Ibid., Vol. 5, 16th April 1684.
189	91	G.L. *Ms.* 6183, Vellum, 4 skins. Illuminated initial. Great seal on original cord.
189	92	T.C.C., *C.B.14*, G.L. *Ms.* 6153, Vol. 6, 2nd July 1685; 6th July 1685.
189	93	Ibid., 15th January 1685.
189	94	„ 14th July 1685.
190	95	„ 22nd October 1685.
190	96	*Rep.* 90, fos. 130, 144.
190	97	T.C.C., *C.B.14*, G.L. *Ms.* 6153, Vol. 6, 6th October 1685.
190	98	T.C.C., *L.A.B.*, G.L. *Ms.* 6152, Vol. 3 (1685–6).
190	99	*The Tripple Crowns* by Tom Girtin, op. cit., p. 271.
190	100	*The History of the Butchers Company* by Arthur Pearce, p. 105.
190	101	T.C.C., *C.B.14*, G.L. *Ms.* 6153, Vol. 6, 17th February 1688.
190	102	G.L. *Ms.* 6180, Box 4, 197.
190	103	T.C.C., *C.B.14*, G.L. *Ms.* 6153, Vol. 6, 27th February 1688.
190	104	Ibid., 19th July 1688.
190	105	„ 6th September 1688.
191	106	G.L. *Ms.* 6180, Box 4, 198.
191	107	*The Tripple Crowns*, op. cit. p. 272.
191	108	T.C.C., *C.B.14*, G.L. *Ms.* 6153, Vol. 6, 21st November 1688.
191	109	Original framed and glazed in the Company's possession.
191	110	T.C.C., *C.B.14*, G.L. *Ms.* 6153, Vol. 6, 29th November 1688.
192	111	*Statutes of the Realm*.
192	112	T.C.C., *C.B.13*, G.L. *Ms.* 6153, Vol. 5, 21st June 1677.
193	113	See a specimen framed and glazed at Tallow Chandlers Hall.
193	114	T.C.C., *C.B.13*, G.L. *Ms.* 6153, Vol. 5, 21st June 1677.
193	115	Ibid., 12th July 1678.
193	116	T.C.C., *L.A.B.*, G.L. *Ms.* 6152, Vol. 3 (1678–9).
193	117	T.C.C., *C.B.13*, G.L. *Ms.* 6153, Vol. 5, 29th June 1681.
193	118	Ibid., 21st February 1682.
193	119	T.C.C., *C.B.14*, G.L. *Ms.* 6153, Vol. 6, 13th June 1686.
193	120	Ibid., 17th June 1686.

Page	Note	
Page	*Note*	
194	121	Ibid., 16th June 1687; 14th June 1688; 13th June 1689; 26th June 1690.
194	122	T.C.C., *C.B.14*, G.L. *Ms.* 6153, Vol. 6, 4th February 1691.
194	123	G.L. *Ms.* 6177, 1 to 22.
194	124	T.C.C., *L.A.B.*, G.L. *Ms.* 6152, Vol. 3 (1691–2).
194	125	G.L. *Ms.* 6177.
194	126	T.C.C., *C.B.14*, G.L. *Ms.* 6153, Vol. 6, 29th February 1692.
194	127	Ibid., 6th April 1692.
195	128	„ 18th April 1692.
195	129	„ 6th June 1692.
195	130	„ „
195	131	„ 9th June 1692.
195	132	„ 20th June 1692.
195	133	T.C.C., *L.A.B.*, G.L. *Ms.* 6152, 7th January 1697.
196	134	T.C.C., *C.B.14*, G.L. *Ms.* 6153, Vol. 6, 29th February 1692.
196	135	T.C.C., *C.B.15*, G.L. *Ms.* 6153, Vol. 7, 13th March 1701.
196	136	Ibid., 5th September 1709.
196	137	„
196	138	Ibid., 22nd December 1709.
196	139	„ 24th December 1709.
196	140	„ 5th January 1710.
196	141	„ 3rd February 1710.
197	142	„ 6th February 1710.
197	143	„ 7th February 1710; 8th February 1710.
197	144	„ 9th February 1710.
197	145	T.C.C., *L.A.B.*, G.L. *Ms.* 6152, Vol. 4, 13th September 1709; 30th September 1709; 20th October 1709; 10th November 1709; 11th November 1709.
197	146	T.C.C., *C.B.15*, G.L. *Ms.* 6153, Vol. 7, 10th May 1709.
197	147	Ibid., 5th July 1709.
197	148	G.L. *Ms.* 6177. The last of 33 skins.
197	149	T.C.C., *C.B.15*, G.L. *Ms.* 6153, Vol. 7, 28th June 1710.

WIND OF CHANGE

Page	Note	
198	1	Waltham & Austin's case. See *The Economic History Review*, second series, Vol. X, No. 3 (April 1958). *The Breakdown of Gild and Corporation control over the Handicraft and Retail Trade in London*. By J. R. Killett, p. 383, note 9.
198	2	See the *Development of London Livery Companies*, 1960, by William F. Kahl, p. 26.
198	3	*Early History of the Guild of Merchant Taylors*, 1888, by C. M. Clode, Vol. 1, p. 205.
198	4	*The Development of London Livery Companies*, op. cit., p. 27.
199	5	Strype's *Survey of the Cities of London and Westminster*, op. cit., Book IV, Chap. II, pp. 33–6.

Page	Note	
199	6	*The Breakdown of Gild and Corporation Control over the Handicraft and Retail Trade in London*, op. cit., pp. 381–2.
199	7	Ibid., p. 384.
199	8	Ibid.
199	9	See *The Gilds and Companies of London* by George Unwin, Fourth edition, pp. 247–9.
199	10	*Jor.* 23, fo. 111b., 2nd June 1592.
199	11	*Rep.* 22, fo. 355b.
200	12	*Jor.* 29, fo. 350.
200	13	*Jor.* 32, fo. 148.
200	14	See *The Report of London Livery Companies Commission*, 1884, Part I, fo. 14.
200	15	*Rep.* 14, fo. 307.
200	16	*Rep.* 25, fo. 276.
201	17	*Rep.* 1 fos. 27b and 118.
201	18	Ibid.
201	19	*Rep.* 1, fo. 116b.
201	20	*Rep.* 9, fo. 266.
201	21	*Rep.* 12, No. 1, fo. 24b.
201	22	See, for example, *Rep.* 15, fo. 237b.
201	23	*Rep.* 22, fo. 7b.
201	24	A printed copy of this Act can be seen at Guildhall Library.
202	25	*Privilegia Londini* (1702), by W. Bohun, pp. 105–6.
202	26	*Rep.* 8, fo. 73b.
202	27	*Rep.* 12, No. 2, fo. 340.
202	28	Ibid., fo. 375b.
202	29	*Rep.* 30, fo. 197b.
202	30	*Rep.* 43, fo. 5b.
203	31	*Jor.* 40, fo. 189b.
203	32	*Rep.* 100, fo. 174.
203	33	*Privilegia Londoni*, op. cit., p. 99.
203	34	T.C.C., *L.A.B.*, G.L. *Ms.* 6152, Vol. 1 (1563–4).
204	35	T.C.C., *Y.A.B.*, G.L. *Ms.* 6155, Vol. 2, 31st August 1602.
204	36	See the recital in the Petition of 1661 (note 37).
204	37	*Jor.* 45, fos. 159b, 215b, 311.
204	38	*Rep.* 2, fo. 84.
204	39	*Rep.* 12, No. 1, fo. 63.
204	40	*Rep.* 15, fo. 320b.
204	41	Ibid., fo. 479.
204	42	*Rep.* 3, fo. 205.
204	43	*Rep.* 4, fo. 218b.
205	44	*Rep.* 8, fo. 95b.
205	45	Ibid., fo. 187b.
205	46	*Rep.* 13, fo. 112.
205	47	Ibid., fo. 113b.
205	48	*Rep.* 14, fo. 192; *Rep.* 15, fos. 110, 114, 439b.

Page	Note	
205	49	*Rep.* 17, fo. 197b.
205	50	*Rep.* 43, fo. 335.
205	51	*Rep.* 70, fo. 45b.
205	52	An Acte towching dyvers orders for Artificers, Laborers, Servants of Husbandrye and Apprentices, 5 Elizabeth I, C. 4, 1563. *Statutes of the Realm.*
206	53	*Privilegia Londini*, op. cit., pp. 115–16 (Allen v Tolley). See also *The Breakdown of Gild and Corporation Control in London*, op. cit., p. 384.
206	54	*Rep.* 48, fo. 66.
206	55	The King against Bagshaw, *Croke's Reports* (Cro. Car.) Vol. 4, 1633, p. 347 and 1634, p. 263.
206	56	Appleton *against* Stoughton, Croke's Reports op. cit., 1638, pp. 516–17.
207	57	T.C.C., *C.B.11*, G.L. *Ms.* 6153, Vol. 3, 5th November 1658.
208	58	Ibid., 9th August 1660.
208	59	*Rep.* 31, fo. 90.
208	60	Ibid., fo. 78b.
209	61	Ibid.
209	62	Ibid., fo. 79.
209	63	T.C.C., *C.B.11*, G.L. *Ms.* 6153, Vol. 3, 13th September 1664.
210	64	Ibid., 15th September 1664.
211	65	*Rep.* 93, fo. 28b, 6th December 1687.
211	66	*Rep.* 96, fo. 328.
211	67	T.C.C., *C.B.14*, fo. 340, G.L. *Ms.* 6153, Vol. 6.
211	68	Ibid., fo. 346. Ibid.
211	69	Ibid., fo. 354.
211	70	„ fo. 356.
211	71	„ fo. 359.
212	72	„ fo. 361.
212	73	*Rep.* 77, fo. 208b, 16th July 1672.
212	74	*Rep.* 83, fo. 149.
212	75	T.C.C., *C.B.14*, fo. 358, G.L. *Ms.* 6153, Vol. 6, 16th July 1693.
213	76	Ibid., fo. 372. Ibid.
213	77	*An Act of Common Council for regulating the Company of Masons*, London, 11th September 1694; *An Act of Common Council for regulating the Company of Plaisterers*, London, 19th October, 1694.
214	78	T.C.C., *C.B.* 15, fo. 126, G.L. *Ms.* 6153, Vol. 7, 8th August 1698.
214	79	*Rep.* 105, fos. 26–8.
215	80	T.C.C., *C.B.15*, fo. 177, G.L. *Ms.* 6153, Vol. 7, 23rd November 1700.

Page	Note	
215	81	T.C.C., *C.B.13*, fo. 49, G.L. *Ms.* 6153, Vol. 5, 2nd August 1682.
215	82	Ibid., fo. 51b. Ibid., 6th June 1683.
215	83	Ibid., fo. 52.
215	84	T.C.C., *C.B.14*, fo. 109, G.L. *Ms.* 6153, Vol. 6, 15th April 1687.
216	85	Ibid., fo. 190. Ibid., 21st March 1689.
216	86	Ibid., fo. 269. Ibid., 30th October 1691.
216	87	Ibid., fo. 293. Ibid., 4th April 1692.
216	88	Ibid., fo. 294. Ibid., 6th April 1692.
216	89	Ibid., fo. 335, Ibid., 26th November 1692.
216	90	Ibid., fo. 336. Ibid., 28th November 1692.
217	91	Ibid., fos. 336, 342.
217	92	Ibid., fo. 342. Ibid., 20th January 1693.
217	93	Ibid., fo. 354. Ibid., 18th May 1693.
217	94	Ibid., fo. 190. Ibid., 21st March 1689.
218	95	T.C.C., *C.B.14*, fo. 293, G.L. *Ms.* 6153, Vol. 6, 4th April 1692.
218	96	T.C.C., *C.B.14*, fo. 405, G.L. *Ms.* 6153, Vol. 6, 10th September 1694.
218	97	T.C.C., *C.B.18*, fo. 91, G.L. *Ms.* 6153, Vol. 10, 14th August 1723.
218	98	G. L. *Ms.* 6179 1, Opinion, 25th October 1732.
219	99	T.C.C., *C.B.15*, fo. 242, G.L. *Ms.* 6153, Vol. 7, 16th September 1703.
219	100	T.C.C., *C.B.20*, fo. 49, G.L. *Ms.* 6153, Vol. 12, 5th December 1775.
220	101	Ibid., fo. 54. Ibid., 2nd January 1776.
220	102	Ibid., fo. 55. Ibid.
220	103	Ibid., fo. 61. Ibid., 2nd April 1776.
220	104	Ibid., fo. 63. Ibid., 10th April 1776.
220	105	Ibid., fos. 64, 65. Ibid.
220	106	„ fo. 66.
220	107	„ fos. 63, 66, 92, 129. Ibid.
220	108	Ibid., fo. 67. Ibid., 28th May 1776.
220	109	Ibid., fo. 71. Ibid.
220	110	Ibid., fo. 176. Ibid., 23rd December 1780.
221	111	Ibid., fo. 187.
221	112	„ fo. 196.
221	113	*Rep.* 78, fo. 155b.
221	114	*Rep.* 80, fo. 257b.
222	115	Ibid., fo. 283.
222	116	„ fo. 313.
222	117	*Rep.* 83, fo. 12.
222	118	*Rep.* 84, fo. 99.
222	119	*Rep.* 85, fo. 201.

Page	Note	
Page	*Note*	
222	120	*Rep.* 86, fo. 197.
222	121	*Rep.* 87, fo. 23b.
222	122	*Rep.* 91, fo. 106.
222	123	*Rep.* 92, fo. 112.
222	124	Ibid., fo. 323.
223	125	*Rep.* 93, fo. 178.
223	126	Ibid., fo. 58.
223	127	*Rep.* 94, fo. 115.
223	128	*Rep.* 95, fo. 25b.
223	129	Ibid., fos. 91, 93, 123, 133, 263b, 269b, 272, 274.
223	130	*Rep.* 97, fo. 297, *passim.*
223	131	*Rep.* 100, fo. 174.
223	132	*Rep.* 101, fo. 152.
223	133	A printed copy of this Act can be seen at Guildhall Library. See also *the Breakdown of Gild and Corporation Control over the Handicraft and Retail Trade in London*, op. cit., pp. 385, 386.
224	134	Ibid., p. 385.
224	135	„ pp. 388, 389.
224	136	„ p. 389.
224	137	See the print at Guildhall Library.
226	138	*The Breakdown of Gild and Corporation Control*, etc., op. cit., p.p. 387–389.
226	139	See the manuscript copy of the Act at Guildhall Records.
228	140	T.C.C., *L.A.B.*, G.L. *Ms.* 1562, Vol. 5, 10th January 1788, 10th April 1788.
228	141	*Reports of Common Council*, 1827–8. (Guildhall Records); *The Breakdown of Gild and Corporation Control*, etc., op. cit., p. 393.
228	142	T.C.C., *C.B.20*, G.L. *Ms.* 6153, Vol. 12, 12th January 1792.
228	143	*The Breakdown of Gild and Corporation Control*, etc., op. cit., p. 393.
228	144	Ibid., p. 394.
228	145	Ibid.
228	146	See the printed copy of the Report, dated 29th November 1827 at Guildhall Records.
228	147	*Reports of Common Council*, 1854, (Guildhall Records); *The Breakdown of Gild and Corporation Control*, etc., op. cit., p. 394.
228	148	Ibid.
229	149	*The Breakdown of Gild and Corporation Control*, etc., op. cit., p. 387.

Commentary

Page	Note	
230	I *b*	[1] *Rep.* 4, fo. 50b; *Rep.* 5, fo. 37.
		[2] *Rep.* 6, fo. 40b.
230	*n*	[3] T.C.C., *Y.A.B.*, G.L. *Ms.* 6155, Vol. 1 (1530–31).
		T.C.C., *L.A.B.*, G.L. *Ms.* 6152, Vol. 1 (1549–51).
231	II *b*	[4] *Rep.* 3, fo. 212.
231	*g*	[5] T.C.C., *Y.A.B.*, G.L. *Ms.* 6155, Vol. 2 (1555–6).
231	*h*	[6] T.C.C., *L.A.B.*, G.L. *Ms.* 6152, Vol. 1 (1551–3).
231	*i*	[7] *Rep.* 15, fo. 330.
232	*l*	[8] *Jor.* 20, No. 1, fo. 52.
232	*u*	[9] *A Survey of London by John Stow*, reprinted from the text of 1603 with Introduction and Notes by Charles Lethbridge Kingsford, Vol. 1, p. 251.
232	*z*	[10] T.C.C., *L.A.B.*, G.L. *Ms.* 6152, Vol. 1, 24th September 1536.
232	*cc*	[11] Will 9th August, Probate 2nd September 1587. *P.C.C.* 55 Spencer.
232	*ff*	[12] G.L. *Ms.* 6180, Box 6, 275. Counterpart indenture, Latin, an abstract of which in English is printed in *T.C.C.R.*, pp. 62–71.
233	*qq*	[13] *Survey of the Cities of London and Westminster*, by John Stow, reprinted, etc., and enlarged by John Strype, 1720, Vol. II, Book V, p. 210.
233	*uu*	[14] T.C.C., *L.A.B.*, G.L. *Ms.* 6152, Vol. 1, 12th December 1566.
		[15] See *Jor.* 19, fo. 31.
		[16] *Rep.* 18, fo. 323.
234	III *d*	[17] T.C.C., *L.A.B.*, G.L. *Ms.* 1652, Vol. 1 (1549–51).
234	*h*	[18] See, for example, *Rep.* 13, fo. 351.
234		[19] T.C.C., *L.A.B.*, G.L. *Ms.* 1652, Vol. 1 (1551–3).
234	*i*	[20] Will 6th May, Probate 23rd May 1515. *P.C.C.* 7 Holder.
234	*m*	[21] *The Gilds and Companies of London*, by George Unwin, pp. 235–6.
234	*o*	[22] T.C.C., *L.A.B.*, G.L. *Ms.* 6152, Vol. 1, 3rd March 1545.
234	*p*	[23] Ibid. (1563–4).
		[24] Ibid.
235	*q*	[25] „ (1559–61).
235	*x*	[26] See *Rep.* 5, fo. 75, 218.
235	*cc*	[27] T.C.C., *L.A.B.*, G.L. *Ms.* 6152, Vol. 2 (1652–3).
235	I *d*	[28] *Rep.* 10, fo. 34b.
		[29] Ibid., fo. 35b.

Page	Note	
235	*k*	[30] *Jor.* 8, fo. 9b.
		[31] *Rep.* 1, fo. 14.
235	*l*	[32] *Rep.* 12, No. 2, fo. 289.
236	*q*	[33] T.C.C., *L.A.B.*, G.L. *Ms.* 6152, 3rd May 1567.
		[34] *Rep.* 16, fo. 358b.
		[35] T.C.C., *L.A.B.*, G.L. *Ms.* 6152 (1569–70).
		[36] Ibid. (1573–4).
		[37] *Rep.* 18, fo. 78b.
236	*r*	[38] *Rep.* 15, fo. 63.
		[39] Ibid., fo. 138b.
		[40] „ fo. 148.
236	*s*	[41] T.C.C., *Y.A.B.*, G.L. *Ms.* 6155, Vol. 2, 23rd January 1563.
237	*t*	[42] *The Wax Chandlers of London* (1973) by John Dumelow, pp. 39–40.
237	II *a*	[43] T.C.C., *Y.A.B.*, G.L. *Ms.* 6155, Vol. 1 (1549–51).
		[44] Ibid.; T.C.C., *L.A.B.*, G.L. *Ms.* 6152, Vol. 1, 22nd October 1560; 30th December 1561.
237	*d*	[45] *The Price Revolution in Sixteenth Century England*, op. cit., p. 4.
		[46] *Letter Book S*, fos. 153b–154.
237	*h*	[47] 9 Henry VI, c. 7–9. *Statutes of the Realm.*
238	III *e*	[48] *The Gilds and Companies of London*, op. cit., p. 123.
238	*f*	[49] *Rep.* 7, fo. 197.
238	*h*	[50] T.C.C., *L.A.B.*, G.L. *Ms.* 6152, Vol. 1 (1557–8).
		[51] Ibid.
238	*n*	[52] T.C.C., *L.A.B.*, G.L. *Ms.* 6152, Vol. 1 (1561–2).
238	*t*	[53] Ibid., 28th September 1563.
		[54] T.C.C., *L.A.B.*, G.L. *Ms.* 6152, Vol. 2, 9th July 1599.
	v	[55] Ibid., Vol. 1, 20th July 1563.
239		[56] „ 13th April 1557.
		[57] „ (1563–4).
	IV *n*	[58] *Rep.* 11, fo. 401.
		[59] *Rep.* 12, No. 1, fo. 227.
239	V *b*	[60] See *Rep.* 4, fos. 147b–148; *Rep.* 5, fos. 28–28b.
249	*k*	[61] T.C.C., *L.A.B.*, G.L. *Ms.* 6152, Vol. 2, 9th December 1595.
240	*o*	[62] *Rep.* 16, fo. 428b.
240	*p*	[63] T.C.C., *L.A.B.*, G.L. *Ms.* 6152, Vol. 1, 13th January 1558, (1555–7).
240	*r*	[64] *Rep.* 18, fo. 323b.
240	I *b*	[65] *The Social History of Lighting* (1958) by William T. O'Dea, p. 35.
		[66] See the *Plays of William Shakespeare, Volume the Eleventh*

Page	Note	
		& Second Variorum (1813), of the 5th edition of the Johnson-Stevens text of 1773, edited by Isaac Reed, p. 317.
240	*d*	[67] T.C.C., *L.A.B.*, G.L. *Ms.* 6152, Vol. 1, 1553–5.
240	*k*	[68] *Letter Book P*, fo. 176.
241		[69] *Letter Book V*, fo. 177b.
	m	[70] T.C.C., *L.A.B.*, G.L. *Ms.* 6152, Vol. 1 (1567–8).
241	II *a*	[71] Riley *Memorials*, p. 420.
241	*c*	[72] *Letter Book P*, fo. 194.
243	I *n*	[73] *Letter Book L*, fo. 8 (calender p. 16).
243	*o*	[74] *Jor.* 9, fo. 162.
244	II *p*	[75] *Wardens' Accounts of the Worshipful Company of Founders of the City of London, 1497–1681* by Guy Parsloe, pp. xxxvi-xxxvii.
244	*v*	[76] See these Ordinances in the Company's return to the inquiry instituted by the *City of London Livery Companies Commission* in 1884, p. 613–14.
247	I *k*	[77] See the *Gilds and Companies of London*, op. cit., Chapter XVII, on this subject.
		[78] Ibid., pp. 299–300.
		[79] Ibid., p. 295.
248	II *f*	[80] T.C.C., *L.A.B.*, G.L. *Ms.* 6152, Vol. 1.
		[81] Ibid., 1582–3.
248	*j*	[82] *Letter Book BB*, fo. 34, 24th April 1600.
249	*n*	[83] T.C.C., *L.A.B.*, G.L. *Ms.* 6152, Vol. 2, 9th December 1589.
249	III *b*	[84] *Rep.* 23, fo. 43b.
250	*g*	[85] *Letter Book BB*, fo. 34.
250	*k*	[86] *Rep.* 25, fo. 63.
250	IV *f*	[87] G.L. *Ms.* 6180, Box 7, 358.
251	I *b*	[88] Original framed and glazed. See *T.C.C.R.*, p. 42.
		[89] *London and the Kingdom*, Vol. 1, p. 343.
		[90] Inspeximus of Edward VI, 18th February 1548; Inspeximus of Philip and Mary 7th June 1558; Inspeximus of Elizabeth I, 3rd March 1561. All framed and glazed. See *T.C.C.R.*, p. 42–5.
252	II *d*	[91] *Rep.* 79, fo. 293b.
252	*h*	[92] See the *Armorial Bearings of the Guilds of London*, by John Bromley and Heather Child, p. 69.
253	III *a*	[93] London and the Kingdom, Vol. II, p. 394.
253	*b*	[94] See *The Triple Crowns*, op. cit., p. 266.
253	*c*	[95] T.C.C., *C.B.13*, G.L. *Ms.* 6153, Vol. 5, 4th June 1684.
253	*d*	[96] *The Triple Crowns*, op. cit., p. 268.
253	*h*	[97] G.L. *Ms.* 6180, Box 4, 199.

Page	Note	
254	I *a*	[98] J. F. Fraser's ed. 1826
254	*b*	[99] *The Development of London Livery Companies* by William F. Kahl, pp. 27, 28.
255	*i*	[100] For a recital of this Statute see the *Letters Patent* next referred to as set out in *L. Bk. F*, p. 14.

[101] *Letters Patent of Edward III*, 26th March 1337. *L. Bk. F*, pp. 14, 15.

[102] *See footnotes L. Bk. F*, p. 15, *L. Bk. I*, pp. 54, 69, and *Privilegia Londini*, 1702, p. 15.

255	*l*	[103] T.C.C., *Y.A.B.*, G.L. *Ms.* 6155, Vol. 2, 31st August 1602.
255	*p*	[104] A print of the Act can be seen at Guildhall Library.
255	*q*	[105] T.C.C., *C.B.11*, fo. 86b, *Ms.* 6153, Vol. 3, 31st August 1664.
255	*u*	[106] T.C.C., *C.B.15*, fo. 38, *8s.* 6153, Vol. 7, 22nd June 1708.
256	*x*	[107] A Print of the Mason's Act can be seen at Guildhall Library.

[108] The Plaisterers' ditto.

[109] The Summonses are contained in *C.B.14*, fo. 394, G.L. *Ms.* 6153, Vol. 6.

256	*z*	[110] *Rep.* 12, No. 2, fo. 284.
257	II *f*	[111] T.C.C., *C.B.20*, fo. 66, G.L. *Ms.* 1653, Vol. 12.
257	III *a*	[112] *The Breakdown of Gild and Corporation Control over the Handicraft and Retail Trade in London*, op. cit., p. 390, note 4.

Appendices

Appendix	Note	
A	1	See the *Wardens' Accounts of the Founders Company 1497–1681*, edited by Guy Parsloe, p. xxxviii.
	2	*L. Bk. I*, pp. 136–7.
	3	T.C.C., *Y.A.B.*, fos. 1 to 2b, G.L. *Ms.* 6155, Vol. 1.
	4	Ibid., Vol. 2 (1598–9).
	5	T.C.C., *Yeomanry.C.B.*, G.L. *Ms.* 6156, 21st June 1660.
	6	T.C.C., *C.B.15*, G.L. *Ms.* 6153, Vol. 7, 12th March 1696.
	7	Ibid., 2nd July 1693.
	8	T.C.C., *C.B.16*, G.L. *Ms.* 6153, Vol. 8, 12th July 1711.
B	1	*The Gilds and Companies of London* by George Unwin (1963), p. 190.
	2	*Stow's Survey of London*, reprinted from the Text of 1630, op. cit., Vol. II, p. 195.
	3	T.C.C., *L.A.B.*, G.L. *Ms.* 6152, Vol. 1, 8th May 1565.

Appendix Note

	4	Ibid., 10th March 1575.
	5	*Memorials of the Goldsmiths' Company* by Sir Walter Sherburne Prideaux, Vol. 1, p. 26.
	6	T.C.C., *L.A.B.*, G.L. *Ms.* 6152, Vol. 1, 28th May 1545.
	7	Ibid., 10th April 1555.
	8	T.C.C., *C.B.9*, G.L. *Ms.* 6153, Vol. 1, 10th February 1620.
	9	T.C.C., *C.B.14*, G.L. *Ms.* 6153, Vol. 6, 5th October 1686.
	10	T.C.C., *L.A.B.*, G.L. *Ms.* 6152, Vol. 3 (1691–2).
	11	T.C.C., *C.B.20*, G.L. *Ms.* 6153, Vol. 12, 14th July 1785.
	12	T.C.C., *C.B.9*, G.L. *Ms.* 6153, Vol. 1, 18th March 1618.
	13	T.C.C., *L.A.B.*, G.L. *Ms.* 6152, Vol. 2 (1588–9).
	14	Ibid. (1628–9).
	15	T.C.C., *L.A.B.*, G.L. *Ms.* 6152, Vol. 1, 1st September 1555.
	16	T.C.C., *C.B.10*, G.L. *Ms.* 6153, Vol. 2, 9th September 1652.
	17	See, for example, T.C.C., *C.B.13*, fos. 72b, 73, 73b, 74, G.L. *Ms.* 6153, Vol. 5.
	18	T.C.C., *C.B.19*, fo. 362, *passim*, G.L. *Ms.* 6153, Vol. 11.
C	1	*The Gilds and Companies of London*, op. cit., p. 29.
	2	*Acts of Court of the Mercers Company*, 1453–1527.
	3	T.C.C., *Y.A.B.*, G.L. *Ms.* 6152, Vol. 1, 6th December 1544.
	4	T.C.C., *C.B.14*, G.L. *Ms.* 6153, Vol. 6, 5th October 1686.
	5	*The Gilds and Companies of London*, op. cit., pp. 188–9.
	6	T.C.C., *C.B.9*, G.L. *Ms.* 6153, Vol. 1, 10th December 1607.
	7	Ibid., 9th July 1615.
	8	„ 11th June 1635.
	9	T.C.C., *L.A.B.*, G.L. *Ms.* 1652, Vol. 1, 1st March 1575.
	10	Ibid., 24th July 1571.
	11	T.C.C., *L.A.B.*, G.L. *Ms.* 6152, Vol. 2 (1618–19).
	12	T.C.C., *C.B.9*, G.L. *Ms.* 6153, Vol. 1, 8th November 1619.
	13	Ibid., 1st June 1620.
	14	T.C.C., *L.A.B.*, G.L. *Ms.* 6152, Vol. 2 (1617–18).
	15	*The Compleat Cook*, op. cit., page [6].
	16	T.C.C., *C.B.9*, G.L. *Ms.* 6153, Vol. 1, 11th June 1635.
	17	T.C.C., *C.B.12*, G.L. *Ms.* 6153, Vol. 4, 3rd February 1669.
	18	T.C.C., *C.B.13*, G.L. *Ms.* 6153, Vol. 5, 7th August 1676.
	19	Ibid.
D	1	G.L. *Ms.* 6180, Box 5, 246. Printed in *T.C.C.R.* Appendix A, pp. 198–200.
	2	Ibid., 248. Ibid., pp. 200–1
	3	„ 226. Ibid., p. 188.
	4	„ 231. Ibid., pp. 189–91.
	5	*Archaeologia*, Vol. 74 (1924), pp. 137–58 (*GL L*. 63. 12).

Appendix Note

6   T.C.C., *L.A.B.*, G.L. *Ms.* 6152, Vol. 1.

7   *A Survey of London,* by John Stow, op. cit., Vol. 1, p. 305.

8   Ibid., p. 283.

9   Indenture dated 6th August 1506 (see Volume III, p. 40, note *k*) but observe that the author's suggestion that Cloak Lane roughly corresponds to 'Horseshoebridge Lane' was erroneous.

10   T.C.C., *L.A.B.*, G.L. *Ms.* 6152, Vol. 1, 24th June. 1555,

11   Ibid., 8th July 1578.

12   „   Vol. 2, 5th December 1639.

13   „   G.L. *Ms.* 6152, Vol. 1.

14   T.C.C., *Y.A.B.*, G.L. *Ms.* 6155, Vol. 1.

15   T.C.C., *L.A.B.*, G.L. *Ms.* 6152, Vol. 1. 13th August 1545.

16   Ibid. (1561–2).

17   Ibid., 22nd October 1569.

18   T.C.C., *L.A.B.*, G.L. *Ms.* 6152, Vol. 1, 28th September 1570.

19   Ibid. (1569–71).

20   Ibid.

21   Ibid., 1st April 1572.

22   T.C.C., *L.A.B.*, G.L. *Ms.* 6152, Vol. 2 (1620–21).

23   T.C.C., *Y.A.B.*, G.L. *Ms.* 6155, Vol. 2 (1571–3).

24   T.C.C., *L.A.B.*, G.L. *Ms.* 6152, Vol. 2, 9th July 1599.

25   T.C.C., *L.A.B.*, G.L. *Ms.* 6152, Vol. 2 (1602–3), Vol. 3 (1656–7).

26   T.C.C., *L.A.B.*, G.L. *Ms.* 6152, Vol. 1, 2 (1563–4), (1569–71), (1627–8), (1637–8), (1653–4).

27   T.C.C., *L.A.B.*, G.L. *Ms.* 6152, August 1562.

28   T.C.C., *L.A.B.*, G.L. *Ms.* 6152, Vol. 1 (1556–7).

29   Ibid., Vol. 3 (1656–7).

30   T.C.C., *L.A.B.*, G.L. *Ms.* 6152, Vol. 1, 23rd November 1549; 1st September 1555.

31   T.C.C., *L.A.B.*, G.L., *Ms.* 6152, Vol. 3, 23rd July 1662.

32   Ibid. (1662–3).

33   T.C.C., *L.A.B.*, G.L. *Ms.* 6152, Vol. 1, 2 (1570–71), (1597), (1613–14).

34   Ibid., Vol. 1 (1585–6).

35   „   Vol. 1 (1576–7).

36   „   Vol. 1, 1576 Vol. 3 (1657–8).

37   „   Vol. 1 (1569–71).

38   „   Vol. 1 (1569–71), Vol. 2 (1585–7).

39   „   Vol. 1 (1583–5).

40   Ibid.

41   „   Vol. 1, 2 (1584–5), (1605–07).

42   „   (1584–6).

43   T.C.C., *C.B.11*, G.L. *Ms.* 6153, Vol. 3, 4th October 1666.

Appendix Note

44   T.C.C., *L.A.B.*, G.L. *Ms.* 6152, Vol. 1, 2 (1566–7), (1605–
6), T.C.C., *C.B.9*, G.L. *Ms.* 6153, Vol. 1, 6th May 1618.

45   T.C.C., *C.B.11*, G.L. *Ms.* 6153, Vol. 3, 4th October 1666.

46   T.C.C., *C.B.9*, G.L. *Ms.* 6153, Vol. 1, 18th October 1618.

47   Ibid., 8th Nov. 1619

48   Ibid.

49   T.C.C., *L.A.B.*, G.L. *Ms.* 6152, Vol. 1, 28th November
1549.

50   Ibid., 10th August 1551.

51   „   Vol. 2, 9th July 1599.

52   „   (1645–6).

53   „   Vol. 1, 1st September 1551.

54   T.C.C., *Y.A.B.*, G.L. *Ms.* 6155, Vol. 2 (1660–1).

55   T.C.C., *L.A.B.*, G.L. *Ms.* 6152 Vol. 1, 28th September 1563.

56   T.C.C., *L.A.B.*, G.L. *Ms.* 6152, Vol. 1 (1569–71).

57   T.C.C., *L.A.B.*, G.L. *Ms.* 6152, Vol. 2, 28th September
1599.

58   Ibid. (1597–8).

59   T.C.C., *C.B.9*, G.L. *Ms.* 6153, Vol. 1, 6th December 1631.

60   T.C.C., *L.A.B.*, G.L. *Ms.* 6152, Vol. 3 (1662–3).

61   T.C.C., *L.A.B.*, G.L., *Ms.* 6152, Vol. 2 (1597–8).

62   T.C.C., *L.A.B.*, G.L. *Ms.* 6152, Vol. 1 (1567–8).

63   Ibid., Vol. 2 (1601–2).

64   „   Vol. 2, June 1603.

65   T.C.C., *L.A.B.*, G.L. *Ms.* 6152, Vol. 2, 15th March 1604.

66   T.C.C., *L A.B.*, G.L. *Ms.* 6152, Vol. 2 (1603–4).

67   Ibid. (1651–2).

68   T.C.C., *Y.A.B.*, G.L. *Ms.* 1655, Vol. 1, (1519–20).

69   T.C.C., *Y.A.B.*, G.L. *Ms.* 1655, Vol. 2, 26th July 1596.

70   Ibid. (1563–4).

71   T.C.C., *L.A.B.*, G.L., *Ms.* 6152, Vol. 1 (1551–3).

72   Ibid., 1st September 1555.

73   „   Vol. 2, 9th July 1599.

74   T.C.C., *L.A.B.*, G.L. *Ms.* 6152, Vol. 1, 1576.

75   T.C.C., *C.B.11*, G.L. *Ms.* 6153, Vol. 3, 13th September
1666.

76   Ibid., 4th October 1666.

77   „   18th October 1666.

78   T.C.C., *C.B.9*, G.L. *Ms.* 6153, Vol. 1, 14th July 1636.

79   Ibid., 8th October 1640.

80   Ibid., 8th June 1643.

81   T.C.C., *C.B.11*, G.L. *Ms.* 6153, Vol. 3, 13th September
1666. T.C.C., *L.A.B.*, G.L. *Ms.* 6152, Vol. 3 (1666–7).

82   T.C.C., *L.A.B.*, G.L. *Ms.* 6152, Vol. 3 (1666–7).

83   T.C.C., *L.A.B.*, G.L. *Ms.* 6152, Vol. 3 (1656–7), (1662–3).
T.C.C., *C.B.11*, G.L. *Ms.* 6153, Vol. 3, 28th September 1662.

Appendix Note

84 T.C.C., *L.A.B.*, G.L. *Ms.* 6152, Vol. 1, 28th November 1549; 1st September 1555.

85 Ibid. (1562–3).

86 T.C.C., *Y.A.B.*, G.L. *Ms.* 6155, Vol. 2, 15th November 1573.

87 T.C.C., *L.A.B.*, G.L. *Ms.* 6152, Vol. 2, 21st September 1598.

88 T.C.C., *L.A.B.*, G.L. *Ms.* 6152, Vol. 1, 1st September 1555.

89 T.C.C., *Y.A.B.*, G.L. *Ms.* 6155, Vol. 2, 1st September 1555, (1556–7), (1575–6), 18th August 1617.

90 T.C.C., *L.A.B.*, G.L. *Ms.* 6152, Vol. 1, 28th November 1549.

91 T.C.C., *L.A.B.*, G.L. *Ms.* 6152, Vol. 1, (1580–1.)

92 T.C.C., *C.B.11*, G.L. *Ms.* 6153, Vol. 3, 13th September 1666.

93 Ibid., Vol. 3, 28th November 1666.

94 T.C.C., *C.B.12*, G.L. *Ms.* 6153, Vol. 4, 19th Jan. 1671.

95 T.C.C., *L.A.B.*, G.L. *Ms.* 6152, Vol. 3 (1670–1), (1671–2), (1673–4). T.C.C., *C.B.12*, G.L. *Ms.* 6153, Vol. 4, 7th October 1674.

96 T.C.C., *C.B.12*, G.L. *Ms.* 6153, Vol. 4, 7th June 1671.

97 Ibid.

98 T.C.C., *L.A.B.*, G.L. *Ms.* 6152, Vol. 3 (1668–9). T.C.C., *C.B.12*, G.L. *Ms.* 6153, Vol. 4, 3rd February 1669.

99 9th October 1672; 9th July 1674 (1669–70), (1670–2), (1672–3).

100 T.C.C., *C.B.12*, G.L. *Ms.* 6153, Vol. 4, 10th December 1673.

101 Ibid.

102 „   9th July 1674.

103 T.C.C., *C.B.13*, G.L. *Ms.* 6153, Vol. 5, 19th March 1677,

104 Ibid., 6th February 1678.

105 The book containing this and other drawings by Leybourn of properties 'surveyed and platted, anno dom. 1678' is in the Company's possession.

E   1 The Gilds and Companies of London, op. cit., pp. 264–5.

2 T.C.C., *L.A.B.*, G.L. *Ms.* 6152, Vol. 1, 28th November 1549.

3 Ibid., 18th April 1561.

4 T.C.C., *C.B.15*, G.L. *Ms.* 6153, Vol. 7, 10th October 1695.

G   1 See article 20 as summarized in *The Wax Chandlers of London* by John Dummelow, 1973, p. 77.

2 *The Wax Chandlers of London*, op. cit., p. 70.

Appendix Note

3   T.C.C., *L.A.B.*, G.L. *Ms.* 1652, Vol. 1 (1584–5).

4   Ibid., Vol. 2 (1587–9).

5   T.C.C., *Y.A.B.*, G.L. *Ms.* 1655, Vol. 2 (1617–8).

6   See the abridgement of the relevant passage on pp. 73–4 of *The Wax Chandlers of London.*

7   *The Wax Chandlers of London*, p. 145.

8   *Rep.* 13, No. 1, fo. 149.

9   Ibid., fo. 109.

10   „ fo. 113b.

11   *Rep.* 14, fo. 540b.

12   Ibid., fo. 543.

13   „ fo. 546.

14   *Rep.* 15, fo. 18b.

15   T.C.C., *L.A.B.*, G.L. *Ms.* 6152, Vol. 1, 5th October 1564.

K   1   See *English Pageantry*, Vol II, by Robert Withington.

2   T.C.C., *L.A.B.*, G.L. *Ms.* 6152, Vol. 1 (1557–8).

3   Ibid. (1579–80).

4   T.C.C., *L.A.B.*, G.L. *Ms.* 6152, Vol. 2 (1603–04).

5   T.C.C., *C.B.9*, G.L. *Ms.* 6153, Vol. 1, 4th July 1611.

6   T.C.C., *C.B.10*, G.L. *Ms.* 6153, Vol. 2, 22nd October 1649.

7   T.C.C., *C.B.11*, G.L. *Ms.* 6153, Vol. 3, 1st–28th September 1666.

8   Ibid., 11th August 1668.

9   „ 26th August 1668.

10   T.C.C., *C.B.12*, G.L. 6153, Vol. 4, 5th October 1670.

11   Ibid., 4th October 1671, 3rd June 1675.

12   „ 7th October 1674.

13   „ 3rd June 1675.

14   „ 2nd October 1676.

15   T.C.C., *C.B.13*, G.L. *Ms.* 6153, Vol. 5, 6th October 1680.

16   Ibid., 4th October 1682.

17   T.C.C., *C.B.14*, G.L. *Ms.* 6153, Vol. 6, 31st August 1691.

18   Ibid., 3rd May 1694.

19   „ 10th May 1694.

20   „ 28th August 1694; 27th September 1694.

21   T.C.C., *L.A.B.*, G.L. *Ms.* 6152, Vol. 3 (1694–5).

22   T.C.C., *C.B.17*, G.L. *Ms.* 6153, Vol. 9, 19th March 1722; 22nd March 1722.

23   T.C.C., *C.B.19*, G.L. *Ms.* 6153, Vol. 11, 11th July 1748.

24   Ibid.

25   „ 11th July 1754.

26   „ 19th September 1755.

27   T.C.C., *C.B.20*, G.L. *Ms.* 6153, Vol. 12, 14th October 1783.

Appendix Note

	28	Ibid., 9th November 1784.
	29	T.C.C., *C.B.21*, G.L. *Ms.* 6153, Vol. 13, 11th July 1799.
	30	T.C.C., *C.B.14*, G.L. *Ms.* 6153, Vol. 6, 4th July 1695.
	31	T.C.C., *C.B.19*, G.L. *Ms.* 6153, Vol. 11, 19th September 1755.

M 1   T.C.C., *C.B.13*, G.L. *Ms.* 6153, Vol. 5, 4th April 1683.

2   T.C.C., *C.B.14*, G.L. *Ms.* 6153, Vol. 6, 5th April 1687.

3   Ibid., 29th November 1691.

4   „   7th December 1691.

5   „   29th February 1692.

6   „   4th April 1692.

7   „   28th March 1693 and 22 August 1693.

8   „   5th April 1687.

9   Ibid.

10   „   6th May 1690.

N 1   T.C.C., *C.B.14*, fo. 293, G.L. *Ms.* 6153, Vol. 6, 4th April 1692.

2   T.C.C., *L.A.B.*, G.L. *Ms.* 6152, Vol. 3 (1692–3).

3   Ibid., 5th February 1694.

4   T.C.C., *C.B.14*, fo. 382, G.L. *Ms.* 6153, Vol. 6, 3rd May 1694.

5   Ibid., fo. 384. Ibid., 9th May 1694.

6   Ibid., fo. 389. Ibid., 19th May 1694.

7   „   fo. 390. Ibid., 15th June 1694.

8   „   fo. 392. Ibid., 28th June 1694.

9   T.C.C., *L.A.B.*, G.L. *Ms.* 6152, Vol. 3, 28th June 1694.

10   T.C.C., *C.B.14*, fo. 393, G.L. *Ms.* 6153, Vol. 6, 6th July 1694.

11   Ibid., 7th July 1694.

12   „   fo. 394. Ibid., 11th July 1694.

13   „   fo. 395. Ibid., 12th July 1694.

14   „   fo. 406. Ibid., 10th September 1694.

15   „   fo. 411. Ibid., 6th October 1694.

16   „   fo. 413. Ibid., 11th October 1694.

17   „   fos. 424–5. Ibid., 19th January 1695.

18   „   fo. 428. Ibid., 11th March 1695.

19   T.C.C., *C.B.15*, fo. 9, G.L. *Ms.* 6153, Vol. 7, 5th October 1695.

Index

Synopsis of earlier volumes

VOLUME I
The mystery in the making

Prologue
Chandlers and Sausers in the service of the Crown
Candle-making as an industry
The Company's origin as a craft guild

VOLUME II
The Crown, the City and the Crafts

London at the turn of the thirteenth century
The growing power of the crafts
The dawn of a new era
The City under mistery rule
The aftermath

VOLUME III
The Guild Catholic